The Watts History of Science Library

THE ORIGINS OF CHEMISTRY

THE ORIGINS OF CHEMISTRY

ROBERT P. MULTHAUF

Franklin Watts, Inc.
575 Lexington Avenue, New York, N.Y. 10022

Contents

Plates

Appearing between pages 192 and 193

TO THE MEMORY OF
MY PARENTS

Introduction

HISTORICALLY considered, the science of matter is an incongruous edifice, a structure erected by independent schools of architecture – philosophers, occultists, and chemists – each working largely independent of the others. Modern historians have excavated the complex structure even more independently than their ancestors built it, with the result that the philosopher finds his predecessors laying the foundations of the science of being (ontology), while the occultist marvels at the spectacle of alchemy, a labyrinth of wisdom the penetration of which has frustrated the generations of moderns, and the chemist sees a kind of technological sub-basement from which his illustrious ancestor, Antoine Lavoisier, was finally to emerge. The product is a series of histories of natural philosophy, alchemy, and chemistry, overlapping, but scarcely interlocking. Yet few would deny that the science of matter is a single subject, or that the integrated history which must some day be written will take all of its aspects into account. The book which follows is but an attempt to move in that direction by approaching one aspect, the history of chemistry, with greater attention to the full range of its complex ancestry.

Prior to the reorganization of chemistry by Lavoisier and his contemporaries in the latter part of the eighteenth century, the would-be chemist sought a foundation for the science in the writings of a multitude of alchemists, 'Paracelsians', 'iatrochemists', 'Peripatetics', and other eccentrics who seemed to constitute almost the entire population of his progenitors. The 'chemical revolution' changed all this. It was then possible to see the 'true' history of chemistry as the story of the gradual emergence from a wilderness

9

of fantasy, of the ideas and 'facts' which led up to that revolution. Such a history is regrettably skeletal, but from that time the future obviously presented a more exciting prospect than the past, and the majority of chemists have understandably tended to find in Lavoisier a sufficient founding father. A minority, however, not only kept alive the history of 'early chemistry', but built up what is perhaps the largest literature of any special branch of science excepting medicine.

The bizarre aspects of the early history of chemistry have proven peculiarly attractive to a succession of amateur historians (in the best sense of the term), who were professionally, with few exceptions, chemists of high standing. Such chemist-historians of the nineteenth century as Hermann Kopp[1] found the weird and often nonsensical literature which once represented nearly the whole written record of chemistry increasingly fascinating, as they were increasingly removed from it, and were drawn to it at the expense of the history of the brilliant century through which they themselves had lived. Kopp finally turned his full attention to the history of alchemy. This trend has continued and accelerated to the degree that some of the best historians after Kopp, such as Marcelin Berthelot and E. O. von Lippmann, ignored modern chemistry almost altogether. Their work, and that of successors leading up to the present day, has contributed much to the definition of the problem of early chemistry, but has largely left for the future the resolution of that problem.

The advent of the history of science as a professional discipline has brought questions of this kind under the scrutiny of scholars differently oriented, towards science in general as a phenomenon of intellectual history. Whereas it had long been conventional to see 'modern' science as the product of a revolt against antiquity and the Middle Ages – in particular against Aristotle and his 'Peripatetic' and 'Scholastic' followers – it required only the more comprehensive viewpoint which the professional historian cultivates to discover that such sciences as astronomy, physics and biology did in fact exist in these unenlightened times, for the Greeks had discussed them, and usually at great length. If misunderstood and misdirected, they still had objectives and much of their terminology in common with the

---

[1] For the works I have used by this and other authors see the bibliography.

modern sciences endowed with the same names. Here chemistry differs most strikingly, however, for it has before the eighteenth century little in common in either its objectives or its terminology with anything known to modern science. It does not fit the pattern which the historian has constructed for science at large, and he has tended to set it aside as a kind of perturbation in his system.

Aristotle or his predecessors named most of the branches of science as we know them. Aristotle defined them, sufficiently if not precisely, but he lacked even a name for the science of matter. In recognition of this basic difficulty modern historians have found that the Greeks had a word, χημεία (chemia), but they have only been able to connect it tenuously with the science of matter. It seems to have been used by none of the Greek and Roman writers to whom we are indebted for most of the recognizably chemical information we have from antiquity, and contributes an additional element of mystery to the history of chemistry, rather than the key to its elucidation.

This state of affairs has forced a peculiar orientation on the historian of science who concerns himself with chemistry. Whereas in the twentieth century the leading problem of the history of science has been the establishment of lines of communication between 'modern' and 'ancient' science, through the benighted Middle Ages, the historian of chemistry, finding almost nothing to connect to, has had to look for origins *in* the Middle Ages. There he has encountered a disreputable ancestor, but one not easy to deny, the alchemist, and the search for the origins of chemistry has been in very considerable part an inquiry into the significance of alchemy. Historians of early chemistry have become either historians of alchemy or gleaners seeking something they call 'practical chemistry' in a rather barren field of early technology.

Most comparable to what is attempted here is *The story of early chemistry*, published by John M. Stillman in 1924. Another history is perhaps sufficiently justified by the lapse of over four decades during which the chemical technology of pre-literate antiquity has been revealed in general outline, the study of ancient philosophy has produced at last particular studies of *natural* philosophy, and the crowd of Arabic and Latin writers have been to some degree sorted out and put into chronological order. Stillman's work, however, essentially predated the professionalization of the history of science.

It is still an important book, but his attempt to deal with the subject 'in a connected and systematic way' was only partially successful. More systematic than connected, it treated philosophy, alchemy, and 'practical' chemistry in essential independence, allocating praise and blame from the viewpoint of the modern chemist after a manner which has recently been characterized as 'inductive history'.[2]

I have tried to advance the degree of integration of these several aspects of the history of matter, and to give greater continuity to those aspects of the history which pertain to chemistry. A tentative assumption has been made that some degree of continuity does extend back to antiquity in the 'chemical' science of matter. While my criteria inevitably derive from the modern science of chemistry, I have not merely filtered out ideas which foreshadow those of modern chemistry, or 'facts' which are correct from its point of view. The test of relevance has been whether or not a particular idea – or a particular substance – seemed to have antecedents and consequences in the context of a science of matter concerned with terrestrial materials. Thus I have abandoned philosophy and alchemy when they seem to turn conclusively to ontology or esoteric alchemy.

Perhaps I differ most with Stillman and other earlier historians in the attention here given to the history of medicine. While no one has ever denied the closeness of the relationship between chemistry and medicine, it seems never to have been explored as thoroughly as has the connection between chemistry and philosophy, alchemy, and technology. I have become convinced in the course of this work that the continuous interaction of medical and chemical thought is a sort of missing link in the history of chemistry, and I have tried to rectify this deficiency.

I suspect that the failure of historians to do justice to the interconnections of medicine and chemistry is due in large part to their preoccupation with inorganic chemistry. My concern is also primarily with inorganic chemistry, for scientific chemistry did finally emerge from the concentrated investigation of a small number of identifiable substances, which were almost exclusively mineral; while

---

[2] Agassi, 1963 (it may be noted here that the method of citation depends upon reference to the bibliography, where it will be found that 'Agassi, 1963' refers to Joseph Agassi, 1963. 'Towards an historiography of science.' *History and Theory*, Beiheft 2).

the realm of organic substances remained almost as unknown as they had been two thousand years earlier. But the fact that chemists, having after a fashion mastered the inorganic kingdom at the end of the eighteenth century, proceeded to master the organic in the next century, does not justify an assumption that organic chemistry did not 'exist' before. On the contrary, one could say without much exaggeration that all chemistry was 'organic' up to the seventeenth century. Evidences from medicine were predominant in the armoury of the chemical theorist and his practice was largely governed by the supposed requirements of medicine. Thus it is not only possible, but in my judgment necessary, for the historian of early chemistry to seek for evidences of the sciences of the inorganic kingdom in the most 'organic' of all sciences, medicine.

Although a few manuscripts have been consulted, this study is primarily based on printed sources, and in selecting for emphasis those works which are most important to the development of the subject I am indebted to the existing literature of the history of chemistry. My objective, like Stillman's, is to deal with the subject in a connected and systematic way; that is, to produce a narrative as 'true' as the evidence allows, and readable by those having only a general interest in the subject. The subject, however, is littered with uncertainties and unsettled questions. These are noted in the footnotes which, it is hoped, will be useful to those inclined to the further pursuit of those questions.

Where I have cited a 'primary source', reference may be to an early edition or to a modern translation, or, where feasible, to both. The use of translations and 'uncritical' editions is often and rightly deplored, but it must be said that the day when the early history of chemistry can be written from sources of unimpeachable authority is very distant indeed.[3] It is my judgment that a greater weakness in this discipline than the use of imperfect sources is the use of a single edition of a long-lived book of many editions, as though it represented the considered thought of the author. This defect, however, is scarcely within the control of most scholars, since one would have to roam the world to encounter all of the editions of some of these

[3] The Berthelot–Rouelle edition of the Greek alchemical corpus (Berthelot and Rouelle, 1887–88) has been belaboured by generations of critics, all of whom nevertheless continue to depend upon it, as I have. It has recently been reprinted.

13

books.[4] As a substitute for the solution to both the problems of quality and quantity of editions I have given particular care to the identification of the works which I have used.

It is sufficiently evident that certain problems stand out as crucial to the further elucidation of this subject, of which the following are certainly among the most important:

1. The theoretical basis of primitive practical chemistry
2. The significance to chemistry of Greek natural philosophy
3. The genesis of Greek alchemy
4. The genesis of Arabic alchemy
5. The genesis of Latin alchemy
6. The evolution of Latin alchemy
7. The genesis of medical chemistry
8. The sources of inspiration of the Latin chemists of the seventeenth century

Comprehensive and well-founded analyses of these topics would virtually define the early history of chemistry. The most that can be claimed for the present study is that it may clarify some of them. In part such clarification should derive from the summary here of recent studies of special topics, in part from the simultaneous consideration of all aspects of the problem of early chemistry, and in part from the exploration of certain correlative questions which have emerged in the course of the study.

This may be illustrated by some remarks on the first question listed. The practical chemist has been tacitly defined as the craftsman who carried on the chemical arts imperfectly described by such Greco-Roman writers as Theophrastus and Pliny. It has been supposed, and archaeology has confirmed it, that this craftsman knew better than the philosophical authors who report his work how such things were done. Two further assumptions seem to have been made, however, which have not been confirmed. It has been supposed that the practical chemist was familiar with a wider range of substances than are mentioned in the literary sources. Neither archaeology nor the related literature of medicine and alchemy have

---

[4] The new four-volume *History of Chemistry* of J. R. Partington reveals for the first time the full scope of the literature of chemistry from the sixteenth century. This massive work began to appear in 1961, and vols. 2 and 3, covering the sixteenth, seventeenth, and eighteenth centuries, have been my principal guide to bibliographical data for this period.

14

as yet lent substantial support to this. It has also been assumed that theory, to the practical chemist, was either nonexistent or insignificant, and that this lacuna, in view of the character of the theories of philosophers and alchemists, is to be numbered among his assets. Here Eliade's recent work, which indicates that primitive metallurgy had as a theoretical basis the same thought which inspired the cosmogonic myths of early natural philosophy, has at least brought evidence to bear in an area where free speculation had reigned heretofore. The failure of recent research to support these assumptions about the 'practical' chemist thus tends to reduce the importance of that worthy as the key individual in the construction of a science of chemistry.

The attempt which is made here to press further the study of the genesis of Greek, Arabic, and Latin alchemy brings to the centre of the stage three important persons who, while not unknown, have certainly been neglected: Agathodaimon (third century B.C.?), Balīnūs (sixth century A.D.?), and Ibn Juljul (tenth century A.D.). As will be seen, the first two, at least, have been given some prominence in the writings of Stapleton, Ruska, and Kraus. They emerge here as key figures in the transition of alchemy between cultures. The evidence for this has been presented as fully as possible, but remains admittedly tenuous. It could hardly be otherwise, for their writings are barely known, and none has been subjected to special study. Each of them seems to deserve the special attention lavished by scholars of the last generation on al-Rāzī and Jābir ibn Haiyān.

The history of the science of matter in India, China, and elsewhere in the Far East has largely been left out of this account. This is primarily due to the rarity of special studies of the history of chemistry in those cultures, but it must also be said that such studies as have appeared have tended to indicate that the continuity from which the science of chemistry was to emerge was a phenomenon peculiar to the West. Natural philosophy, practical chemistry, and alchemy were all pursued in the Far East from a very early time, and with a high degree of independence. But it was surely the West which saw the origins of our science of chemistry.

I am indebted in this undertaking to more persons than it is practical to name, especially to previous students of the history of chemistry, whose names appear in my bibliography. Among the many libraries whose hospitality I have enjoyed are two of those most important to the history of chemistry, the Smith Memorial Library of the University of Pennsylvania, and the Library of Stanford University, which was used by Stillman. In the main, however, the work was done in the Library of Congress, the Folger Library, Dumbarton Oaks, and the National Library of Medicine, all of Washington, D.C. They entitle this city to the first rank as a centre of research in the history of science. To my colleagues at the Smithsonian Institution, and especially our librarian, Jack Goodwin, to Kay Chroniger and Deborah Mills, I owe the fact that the project did not founder along the way. Above all I am indebted to those who encouraged me to work in the history of science, Professors Edward Strong and John B. de C. M. Saunders of the University of California, the late Professor Ludwig Edelstein of the Rockefeller Institute, Dr. Eduard Farber of Washington, and Professors Richard M. Shryock and Owsei Temkin of the Institute of the History of Medicine of Johns Hopkins University.

Robert P. Multhauf
Washington, D.C.
February 10, 1965

Chapter One

Practical chemistry in antiquity

IT does not appear that the differentiation of any distinct chemical material is essential to the intellectual existence of the most primitive man. Some distinguishable materials, such as charcoal and common salt, undoubtedly came within his ken at a very early stage of civilization,[1] but they may have been preceded by certain pigments – the natural oxides of iron and manganese – used by the artists of the palaeolithic cave paintings at Altamira, Lascaux, and elsewhere (12,000–8000 B.C.).[2]

A salt called natron seems to have preceded common salt as an economically important entity in the Nile region, and samples have been dated as early as the fifth millennium B.C. Obtained from dry lakes, natron is primarily sodium carbonate (soda), adulterated with the chloride and sulphate. It was used, together with common salt and gypsum, in embalming, cleansing and food preservation.[3]

---

[1] Salt is not essential to the diet of a hunting society, but it is to that of the settled agricultural societies which had appeared by the sixth millennium B.C. (Childe, 1952: 33, 105). Charcoal does not generally appear among the artifacts of primitive societies, and we infer that its deliberate fabrication was concurrent with the development of metallurgy. It is mentioned in an Egyptian contract of about 2000 (Kees, 1933: 249). The oldest extant charcoal seems to be found in the 'solar boat' of Tutankhamen (c.1350 B.C.). On references to salt by Homer and other classical writers see Blümner in PW, 2nd Ser., Vol. 1: Cols. 2075–99.

[2] Windels, 1949: 95–6. Breuil and Obermaier, 1935: 11. Natural deposits of black manganese dioxide are found in these caves.

[3] According to Lucas, evidence of the use of natron has been found as early as the Tasian period (5000–4400 B.C.), the earliest era of Egyptian civilization (1948: 303). Natron appears

Although man was in possession of fire before the last ice age in Europe (*c.* 30,000 B.C.),[4] only from a far later period does archaeological evidence enable us to infer the development of thermochemical processes, specifically, from a little earlier than 4000 B.C. In recent years archaeologists have claimed to find evidences of metallurgy, fired pottery, and artifacts of glass-like composition which can be regarded as slightly prior to that date.[5] That the techniques involved were fairly widely practised in Egypt and Babylonia (and probably elsewhere) by 2500 is generally accepted. Fired (but unglazed) pottery and brick began to replace sun-dried clay in their respective spheres before 3000.[6] The addition to the natural mortars, clay and bitumen, of artificial mortars, burned gypsum (plaster of Paris) and burned limestone (quicklime) may have occurred at the same time.[7]

True glass has not been found earlier than about 2500. It was the end point of a more complex development which began before 4000 B.C. There is an obvious order of increasing complexity in the glass-like substances, the simplest being glazed stones (usually quartz or steatite [a coarse talc rock]), in which the stone is painted with soda and/or lime water and heated. Somewhat more complex is faience, a moulded product resulting from the heating of powdered quartz held together by soda or lime water. True glass, the earliest examples of which are about 1,500 years later than the earliest glazed stones, is a fusion of silica (usually sand) with 2–10 per cent of lime and 15–20 per cent of soda (or natron). Archaeological

in hieroglyphic writing as early as 3500, at which time *ntr* (pronounced neter) signified two materials of economic and religious significance, the inorganic salt referred to here, and a fragrant organic material, perhaps frankincense (Steuer, 1937. Lippmann, 1937: 592).

[4] Pietsch, 1940: 16.

[5] Hearths for the firing of pottery in an unenclosed fire, in a process resembling that long used for charcoal burning, have been found in neolithic European remains dated 8000–6000 B.C., but it is not clear that the product would have been in a full sense 'fired' pottery. Fragmentary remains of more conventional pottery kilns found in Mesopotamia have been generally dated 4000–3000, but Kathleen Kenyon has recently claimed to advance the date, for certain kilns in Palestine, to 4500 (1957: 85–6, 90). The origins of metallurgy and glass technology will be discussed below.

[6] Kiln-baked bricks have been found from about 3000 B.C. (Partington, 1935: 265. Scott, 1954: 391–4. Lloyd, 1954: 391–4, 461–2).

[7] According to Forbes, burned gypsum was used in Egyptian plaster in pre-dynastic times (before 3400), and lime was made before 2500 in Babylonia, where a kiln at Chafadje is given that date (1955: 235). R. C. Thompson dated Babylonian lime-burning from about 1600

investigation tends to support the sequence of increasing complexity as the order of discovery.[8]

This was not the end of the development of ancient technology in this area, however. Glazed pottery, which involves the difficult process of applying a glass-like surface to a porous fired clay, only appeared about 1,000 years after glass.[9] Previous to this the soda-lime-sand fusion product appeared in another form, as frit. Ground frit was in use as a (blue) pigment in Egypt about 2500, and it has been shown to have a definite composition, $CaO—CuO—4SiO_2$. It would seem to have been the oldest synthetic pigment.[10] The only other synthetic pigment of comparable complexity known in antiquity was the yellow lead antimoniate glaze found in Assyria from about 800. This pigment, which, as 'Naples yellow', is still made (by a different process), is thought to have been formed by heating together lead oxide or carbonate (litharge or white lead) and antimony oxide, all of which were themselves in a sense artificial, since they were products of the oxidation of minerals.[11] By the seventh century before Christ we encounter evidence of the use of antimony (sulphide) for the deliberate decolourizing of glass.[12]

(1936: 151). On the difficulty of differentiating the terms for these materials, see Levey, 1959: 167–8.

[8] Blue glazed stone beads from both Egypt and Mesopotamia have been dated before 4000. Faience, which depends primarily on Egyptian evidence, is held to be a bit later (Beck, 1934–35. Forbes, 1957: 110ff). Glass from Mesopotamia has been dated about 2500 (Beck, 1934, Frankfort, 1934: 56–8. Forbes, 1957: 110ff), at a time when glass was already 'a recognized product' of Egypt, according to another authority (Harden, 1956: 318–19).

[9] Franchet, relying on Egyptian evidence, dated colourless pottery glaze from about 1500 and blue glaze two centuries later (1911: 91–4). It is sometimes held that glaze preceded glass (e.g., Forbes, 1957: 113), but this seems to refer to the glazed stones rather than to pottery glaze.

[10] Plenderleith, 1950: 247. Blue frit is among the pigments found in the tomb of Perneb (2650 B.C.) (Toch, 1918: 118).

[11] Layard unearthed brick and tile glazed with lead antimoniate, tin oxide, and copper oxide, from Babylon (time of Nebuchadnezzar, 604–561 B.C.) and Assyria (time of Sargon II, 722–705 B.C.) (1853: 166 note). This was the beginning of the brick and tile glazing practices for which the Near East was famous through the Arabic period (see also Partington, 1935: 282–5). There is, however, a lack of agreement as to how lead antimoniate was made. Two different processes were current in the nineteenth century (S. F. Gray, 1831: 572) and yet a third predominates today (Gregory, 1942: art. lead antimoniate). On the production of Naples yellow see also Fougeroux de Bondaroy, 1766–2, Jacobi, 1941, and Rabate, 1947.

[12] Sayre, 1963.

Researches in the history of glass-like substances illustrate the present tendency to replace Egypt with Babylonia as the earliest site of technological innovation. Egypt was once the source of almost all of our earliest evidence, and is still the source of most of it. Yet the few reports now available on Babylonian technology have already led most authorities to surmise that priority belongs there.[13] At the same time another region, Persia, has begun to emerge as a possible rival to Babylonia.[14]

But the chemical inventions which were sufficiently interrelated to create an awareness of the transformation of matter as a particular art were in the field of metallurgy. The introduction of the major artificially produced metals – that is, those (with the exception of aluminium) which are still today the basic metals of commerce – may have begun as early as 4300 B.C., and was completed with the introduction of brass about 4,000 years later. Simply stated, it involved a chemical transformation accomplished through the heating of certain minerals in a reducing atmosphere, usually obtained by contact with the fuel. In practice, the details vary greatly from metal to metal; in some cases (e.g. lead) the successive steps of oxidation of the ore and reduction of the oxide proceed automatically, as though in a single step; in others (iron) the product, even after careful completion of the reduction process, requires further complex treatment before it answers the requirements of a useful metal; and in yet others (bronze) the initial step requires a physical combination of different ores or metals.

The minerals from which metals were first obtained, the hydrated carbonates of copper (azurite and malachite), the oxides of iron and tin (ochre [haematite] and cassiterite) and the sulphides of silver and lead (galena, which contains both), seem, with the apparent exception of tin oxide,[15] to have been in use as pigments prior to their

[13] Cf. Beck, 1934: 8. Harden, 1956: 319. Forbes, 1957: 130–31.

[14] This is most marked in recent scholarship on the history of metallurgy, on which see below. The situation can be illustrated by Beck's investigation of all samples of 'glass' known to him purporting to date before 1500 B.C. Of 28 samples, 20 were from Egypt, 6 from Babylonia, 1 from Persian Baluchistan, and 1 from France. Those appearing to be the earliest included some of those from Babylonia and the one from Persian Baluchistan (1934).

[15] Tin oxide found among cakes of pigment in the palace of Sargon II (722–705 B.C.) at Khorsabad (Partington, 1935: 292) represents the earliest archaeological evidence of tin as a pigment. But Forbes holds it to have been used to make opaque glass before 1500 B.C. (1957: 116).

exploitation as metallic ores. It has been noticed that the oxides of iron were used as pigments in prehistoric cave paintings. Lucas finds malachite and galena among Egyptian pigments *circa* 4000 B.C.[16] Also found among early pigments are the ores of some metals which were not clearly defined for millennia, the sulphides of arsenic (AsS, realgar, and As_2S_3, sandarach or orpiment) and antimony (Sb_2S_3, stibnite). Chemically prepared pigments, on the other hand, such as the oxides of lead (PbO, litharge, Pb_3O_4, minium) do not appear to have preceded the introduction of the metals.[17]

The antiquity of the metals

The question of the antiquity of artificially produced metals – that is, of metals smelted from ores – remains fraught with uncertainty, not only because of the great antiquity of metallurgy and the difficulty of differentiating native from artificially produced metals, but because archaeological investigation has been tending to the conclusion that the original home of metallurgy is outside of the centres of civilization which have been extensively excavated. The discovery of artifacts by Near Eastern archaeology indicates that gold, electrum (a naturally occurring alloy of gold and silver) and copper were in extensive use as metals, rather than as precious stones, before 4000 B.C. By 3000 B.C. the same condition existed with regard to lead, silver, and bronze (copper-tin alloy). During the next two millennia iron and tin joined the metals of commerce, and finally, about the time of Christ, the copper-zinc alloy, brass. Whatever precision is added to these dates by further research, it seems unlikely

[16] That is, in the Badarian period (Lucas, 1962: 210). The less common azurite was also used as a pigment. See also Partington, 1935: 58.

[17] Partington reports lead carbonate among pigments from about 3000 found at Ur (1935: 292–3), and R. C. Thompson holds that both natural lead carbonate (cerussite) and synthetic carbonate (white lead) are mentioned in the cuneiform tablets from the library of Assurbanipal (1936: 135–40). There is less evidence for the oxides. Forbes says that red lead was known in 'ancient Mesopotamia' (1955: 208), but I have found no early reference to it. He also holds litharge to have been used in Egyptian pigments before 3000 (1955: 219), but mentions only an example of about 400 B.C. Lucas (1962: 244, 348, 350, 362) assigns a late date to all examples of lead oxide found in Egypt.

that this order for the introduction of the metals into commerce will be significantly changed.[18]

Nearly all of these metals exist in the native state.[19] Unless native metals existed in greater quantity in the ancient Near East than is generally believed, however, only gold and electrum could have been derived from the native metals in the quantities indicated by extant remains from the dates indicated. It would follow that copper was the first metal artificially produced, and this is generally believed to have been the case.

As the most extensively excavated and dated civilization, Egypt has until recently furnished the major part of our evidence for consideration of this question. In the twentieth century, however, Mesopotamian archaeology has come to the fore, and most recently Iran has emerged as possibly the most important ancient civilization from the point of view of metallurgy.[20] The principal Egyptian copper ore (malachite) deposit, at Sinai, shows evidence of working as early as the Badarian period[21] (an era of three centuries beginning between 4200 and 3800 B.C.), but a few artifacts of copper and lead have been found in northern Mesopotamia from the corresponding era[22] (Halaf), and fabricated copper has been found in Iran from the

[18] Probable conclusions on the basis of present evidence are drawn by Aitchison (1960) as follows:

METAL	DATE OF INTRODUCTION	PLACE OF INTRODUCTION	PAGE REF.
gold	before 5000 B.C.	Armenia-Anatolia	11
electrum	3800	—	45
native copper	before 5000	Asia	19–20
smelted copper	4300	Armenia-Anatolia	36
bronze	4300	Armenia-Anatolia	61–2
lead	3500	—	43–5
silver (gold free)	2500	Asia Minor?	56–7
tin	1800–1600	NW Persia	78–9
iron	1400	Anatolia	100–01

[19] Native antimony and arsenic have also been found. Of the earliest metals known only the two copper alloys, bronze and brass, have not been found native, although native copper may contain tin as an impurity up to 2 per cent.

[20] Cf. Hrozny, 1953. Aitchison, 1960. Wertime, 1964. The fullest statement of this view known to me is in the unpublished dissertation of Hillen, 1955.

[21] Lucas, 1948: 242. This is modified in a later edition (Lucas, 1962: 202), which refers only to mining settlements from the old kingdom, the beginning of which is dated 2778 B.C.

[22] Hillen, 1955: 27.

preceding age[23] (Sialk). It is western Iran from which the Sumerian inhabitants of Mesopotamia are supposed to have emigrated,[24] and it is therefore suggested that they brought metallurgy with them – a theory which gains support from the richness of Iran in ores compared to the poverty of Egypt and the utter barrenness of Mesopotamia.

Much effort has been expended to reconstruct the accident which is supposed to have resulted in the reduction of malachite or (less probably) azurite to copper. Not only was it necessary to heat the ore, but to heat it to a temperature normally attainable only with an air blast, and in a reducing atmosphere. Copper smelters designed to operate with a natural draught have been found from late antiquity,[25] but attempts to show that copper ore could be smelted in an open fire without a blast have not been successful, and theories that copper smelting originated in a neolithic cooking fire or in fire-setting in a quarry have been generally rejected.[26] The most popular present theory of the origin of copper metallurgy holds it to have stemmed from the pottery kiln, and this has been supported by recent excavations of pottery kilns from the middle fifth millennium.[27] The transformation of an operation in which copper was merely melted into one where its ore was smelted in a reducing atmosphere is held by Hillen to have taken place between 4500 and 3500, probably first in Iran, but independently in several widely separated localities. But this evolution required a crucial 'accident' which would have placed copper ore in the furnace,[28] and this remains a mystery.

[23] Hillen, 1955: 29.

[24] Aitchison, 1960: 22. Hrozny, 1953: 30, 55–6.

[25] A smelter at Ezion–Geber (Palestine) seems to have been deliberately located so as to take advantage of a strong wind as draught, at a site otherwise entirely disadvantageous (Gulick, 1938: 3ff). The Incas also smelted with a natural draught 'wind furnace', which appears to have been capable of smelting even the more difficult sulphide ores (Caley and Easby, 1959).

[26] Coghlan, 1940. He succeeded, however, in smelting malachite in a 'furnace' made of a pottery dish covered by a porous pot.

[27] The archaeology of fifth-millennial Iran (Sialk) has indicated a correlation between the improvement of pottery kilns and the discovery of the fusibility of copper (see Coghlan, 1942: 31–2, and Hillen, 1955: 22). See also note 5 above.

[28] Hillen, 1955: 211–12. Aitchison estimates 4300 B.C. as the date of the discovery of copper smelting, and assigns the discovery to Armenia-Anatolia or trans-Caspian Persia (Iran) (1960, Vol. 1: 19–21, 28–9, 62). Both Hillen and Aitchison speak of the discovery as 'accidental'.

It could have been accomplished through its use in pottery glaze, but glazed pottery was apparently still unknown.

The supposed priority of copper over lead, hinges primarily on the evidence of excavations, and has been particularly supported by those made in Egypt, where indications of large-scale working of galena deposits does not appear much before 2000 B.C., about two millennia later than the corresponding evidences for copper ores. But a few artifacts of lead have been found in Mesopotamian excavations of about 4000 – too few to reverse the traditional order of discovery, but enough to justify our noting that galena could have been smelted in the proverbial neolithic cooking fire,[29] through simple heating at a low temperature, and without a reducing agent, for partially roasted galena acts in such a way that a portion reacts on the remainder to yield a metal without further addition. Against these indications that 'artificial' lead may have preceded copper must, however, be brought the evidence that silver, for which galena was also the principal ore, seems to have been decidedly rare until well after 3000.[30]

The second smelted 'metal' appears rather to have been the copper-tin alloy, bronze, but here again we are involved in mystery, for cassiterite is the only ore of one of the major metals which does not appear to have seen prior use as a pigment, nor is it found at all in Egypt or Babylonia. Complex ores containing both copper and tin do exist, but they are rare and have moreover failed to produce bronze in modern experiments. Cassiterite occurs as an unusually heavy stream pebble, and it seems likely that it was noticed in panning for gold[31] and then somehow found its way into the copper smeltery. This series of 'accidents' occurred before 3000 B.C., and probably came from the same Iranian region where we have located the discovery of copper metallurgy.

Tin itself can be smelted at a low temperature, but unlike galena its ore requires the addition of a reducing agent. This is also true of the rarer metals, antimony and bismuth, but where they are not

[29] For an experimental demonstration of this see Tylecote, 1962: 76.

[30] Cf. Aitchison, 1960; Vol. 1: 46–7. Levey, 1959: 179–80. The appearance of very pure silver after about 2500 may indicate the discovery of the cupellation process, in which the silver content of galena is concentrated and the oxidized lead absorbed by a material such as bone ash.

[31] Coghlan, 1951: 25ff. Aitchison, 1960: 62. Tylecote, 1962: 63.

lost through the tendency of their oxides to sublimate they are easily confused with lead, and they were so confused throughout antiquity. Iron was understandably the last of the classical metals to enter commerce in its smelted form, for not only does it require equally rigorous conditions to those of copper smelting, but it is even then scarcely 'metallic' without a further complex treatment. Until the improvement of iron working shortly before 1400, traditionally by the Hittites of Anatolia, iron was a rare metal and consequently precious.

Literary evidence for the early use of minerals

Although European travellers had been bringing home specimens of Egyptian handiwork since the seventeenth century, a group of French scientists who accompanied Napoleon on his Egyptian venture of 1798 made up what deserves to be called the first systematic archaeological expedition. The famous Rosetta stone was found on this occasion, and a quarter of a century later Champollion had begun the decipherment of Egyptian writing which was to make the numerous papyri and stone inscriptions useful. Large expeditions were sponsored by France and Tuscany in 1827 and by Prussia in 1843–5, after which the systematic archaeological exploration of Egypt became more or less continuous. Not only did the museums of Europe and America amass great quantities of the literature as well as the artifacts of the ancient Egyptians, but in Egypt itself the government established a museum in 1858 which now maintains the largest and most important collection of Egyptian antiquities.

In western Asia the transition from unsystematic collection to systematic excavation began with the work of Botta and Layard (1842–5), in an area subsequently identified as the site of ancient Assyria. The key to the decipherment of the cuneiform writing on clay tablets, on which this culture was documented, was found by 1846, but here, too, scientific archaeology was hardly practised before the 1880s.

Only in recent years have metals, pigments, cosmetics, etc., from early Near Eastern excavations been both dated and analysed, and the analyses are still not very numerous. In the case of written

25

records, however, the case is worse. From western Asia we have a medical tablet from Nippur, dated *c.* 2100 B.C., and a tablet of the seventeenth century B.C. relating to glass colouration. Considerable information on practical chemistry also occurs in the remains of the 'Library of Assurbanipal' (Assyria), which was found by Layard and dated in the eighth and ninth centuries B.C.[32] From Egypt there are a number of papyri relating to medicine,[33] one of which, the papyrus Ebers (*c.* 1550 B.C.), mentions a considerable number of drugs. But the oldest non-medical papyrus relating to chemistry appears to be a set of jeweller's recipes in the Leyden and Stockholm papyri from the third century A.D.![34] All of these date from nineteenth-century excavations with the exception of the tablet on glass colouration, which is not derived from any expedition. It was purchased from a dealer in antiquities, and is the product, apparently, of one of the 'private' excavations which were common in the nineteenth century and are still not unknown.[35] It is not likely that this exhausts the chemical data in documents already excavated, however. As Forbes has remarked, documents considered vaguely 'economic' are often stored away, and those which are published are indexed by kings and gods, not by oils, fats, and waxes.[36]

The Babylonian glass text of the seventeenth century B.C. mentions, according to Gadd and Thompson, lead, copper, lime, vinegar (and copper acetate), and saltpetre.[37] Saltpetre, which does not appear to have been known either to Arabic or European chemists prior to the thirteenth century A.D., is also found by Levey in the Nippur medical tablet of about 2100 B.C.[38] In his study of the Library of Assurbanipal (ninth–eighth century B.C.), Thompson adds a number of other materials for which we lack other evidence for many centuries: sal ammoniac, cinnabar, brass, and even fuming sulphuric

[32] The Nippur tablet, University of Pennsylvania CS 14221, is described in Levey, 1959: 148–9. The tablet on glass colouration, British Museum 120960, is described in Gadd and Thompson, 1936. Materials from the Library of Assurbanipal are described in R. C. Thompson, 1936.

[33] Eight, between 1900 and 1200 B.C., are mentioned by Leake, 1952: 7.

[34] On which see below, pp. 96–99.

[35] Gadd and Thompson, 1936.

[36] Introduction to Levey, 1959.

[37] 1936: 87.

[38] 1959: 149.

acid![39] If these identifications are correct it would appear that some materials known in remote antiquity were later lost, an event which seems without parallel in more historic times. The corresponding Egyptian document, the medical papyrus Ebers of the sixteenth century B.C., does not mention these materials, although it does seem to list much of the repertoire of practical chemistry as we know it from archaeology.[40]

The appearance of such materials as glaze (or glass), gypsum, asphalt, and charcoal in medical texts was commonplace during the next three millennia, and leads to the impression that lists of drugs are consistently the most reliable guides to the total number of inorganic materials known at any particular time, and this despite the fact that minerals were not especially prominent as drugs. Physicians prior to the European Renaissance were not inclined to experimentation with mineral drugs; but they did include in their lists any material whatever which was known – that is, any material which had some practical use or (as gemstones) some spectacular property. It was not without justification that the brief list of minerals in the pharmacopoeia of the Greek, Dioscorides, was long regarded by alchemists as the authoritative compilation of important substances.

Practical chemistry appears to have changed very little during the twelve centuries between the papyrus Ebers and the oldest extant Greek treatise on practical chemistry. To refer to this period in the history of chemistry as static, however, is to underrate the importance of its first steps. The lateness of the development of our science of chemistry is a measure of the difficulty encountered in making those steps. I have tried to deduce from Babylonian-Egyptian sources what some of them were: the development of thermo-chemical processes, one of which, metallurgy, appeared to have some generality; the production of artificial minerals, especially pigments, of more-or-less constant composition, by complex thermal treatment (blue frit, lead antimoniate); and the development of a process for obtaining a substance, gold, in a pure state. A few other such landmarks occurred in Greco-Roman antiquity.

[39] R. C. Thompson, 1936: 12–14, 29, 76, 101–4.

[40] Cf. Ebbell, 1937. About 20 per cent of the 78 drugs listed appear to be minerals. The index of drug names includes realgar or orpiment, limestone, malachite, magnetite, gypsum, naphtha, pumice, bitumen (?), red ochre, calamine, copper scale, sory (alum?), yellow ochre, and lye (?).

During the millennial domination of Greek literature – from about 500 B.C. – our topic, like many another subject, was given a new foundation. This foundation was in the attempt of the Greek natural philosophers to establish a general science of matter, and will be the subject of the next several chapters. As regards practical chemistry, their contribution was only relatively less important, for they advanced beyond description to lay the groundwork for the classification of substances.

Some evidence of an awareness of practical chemistry appears in Greek literature as early as Homer, and the early natural philosophers reveal a significant familiarity with materials;[41] but the earliest surviving Greek treatise dealing with the subject in a straightforward way is the short work, On stones,[42] written about 300 B.C. by Theophrastus, Aristotle's pupil and successor as head of the Lyceum at Athens. Aristotle himself had written extensively on natural philosophy, and had begun the tradition of 'natural history' with his encyclopaedic description of the animal kingdom. Theophrastus wrote – much more briefly – on the plant and mineral kingdoms, and the latter work deserves to be called the first treatise on practical chemistry.

Theophrastus seems to have been inspired in his description of 'stones' by a scientific purpose rather than by metallurgy, medicine, or colouring, but the only minerals he knows are those which were used in one of these arts. He divides 'the substances found in the Earth' into metals 'such as gold and silver', stones (λίθος), and earths, using the same term (γῆ) for 'earth' and for 'the Earth'. He is primarily concerned with precious stones and building stones, and

[41] The following Presocratic references to materials may be noted:

MATERIAL	AUTHOR	REF. TO DK
nitron (natron)	Anaximander	II 27, 5
	Democritus	II 108, 13
ios (copper acetate)	Empedocles	I 290, 2
psimmuthion (white lead)	Xenophanes	I 118, 978a, 10ff
	Dialexeis	II 408, 2
molubdos (lead)	Democritus	II 117, 24
kadmia (zinc carbonate ?)	Empedocles	II 290, 2
spodos (tin oxide)	pseudo-Pythagoras	I 466, 35
stypteria (alum)	Democritus	II 108, 18

[42] I have used Theophrastus, 1956.

refers to his 'earths' as 'immature stones'. His differentiation is on the basis of commonplace properties, mostly physical, such as colour, hardness, frangibility, inflammability, and power of attraction (amber, magnet). 'Earths', a sort of residual category, have, he says, fewer but more peculiar 'special qualities and powers'. The peculiarity of these qualities and powers is, in fact, that they are chemical. His earths include, with the exception of tin oxide, the pigments which have been mentioned as the first ores of the common metals. They also include gypsum, bitumen, cinnabar, the two arsenic sulphides (orpiment and realgar), and several varieties of clay. Finally, he includes among them white lead and copper acetate, neither of which occurs in nature. They were prepared through the corrosion of those metals by vinegar.

The penchant for encyclopaedic description of the arts and sciences was no less pronounced among the Romans, and Greco-Roman literature provides for the first time a basis for comparisons. Most comparable to Theophrastus' *On stones* are the *Natural history* of the elder Pliny[43] and the *Materia medica* of Dioscorides,[44] both from the first century A.D. Although their several purposes were not identical, the similarity of the practical chemistry which emerges from these three is remarkable – another indication of the limited scope of ancient practical chemistry.

It is apparent that the long history of mining and metallurgy had led, by the time of Theophrastus, Dioscorides, and Pliny, to the introduction of a few new mineral materials. Shaft had replaced open-pit mining, and new ores were being exploited. Pliny's principal silver ore was not galena, but an independent silver sulphide ore (argentite); his copper ore is the iron-copper pyrite, chalcopyrite, which is normally found below surface deposits of malachite or azurite. It is also apparent that other minerals had been turned up in the vicinity of metal mines. Most of Theophrastus' 'earths' are found, he tells us, in the vicinity of metal mines, and Pliny seems more interested in the 'other things' found with metallic ores than in the ores themselves. In this account of silver mining the other things are cinnabar and antimony sulphide (stibnite); the principal other thing found in copper mines is 'cadmia' (zinc silicate or

---

[43] I have used principally Pliny the Elder, 1929–32.
[44] I have used Dioscorides, 1950.

carbonate). And, finally, the practice of metallurgy produced by-products, such as the oxides of metals which do not occur naturally in this form.

This increase in the chemist's repertoire was not accompanied by a corresponding improvement in the differentiation of substances. The same mineral continued to pass under several names, usually associated with the geographical distribution of its production. Where one or more oxides of such a metal as lead were added to already-known compounds of natural occurrence the confusion was usually increased. This can be illustrated from the case of the oxides of lead.

The yellow and red oxides of lead (PbO, litharge; Pb_3O_4, minium, red lead) were known to Pliny and Dioscorides in a purely empirical way, and they associated them not with lead, but with silver, which appears to have been the principal objective of the manipulation of galena. Dioscorides describes two yellow substances, molybdana and lithargium, which appear in the course of smelting gold and silver, and which he regards as similar. He says that lithargium is also obtained from a lead sand. We infer from the source and colour that both were our litharge. Pliny gives us a clearer account of the same substance in his description of the 'scum of silver' which turns up in the course of smelting that metal. He also describes molybdana, in essentially the same language as Dioscorides, but confuses it with the sulphide (galena). The red oxide, minium, was equally well known, but there is no indication that it was obtained (as today) by the further oxidation of litharge or that the two were even considered to be related. Again Dioscorides describes two substances, ammion and sandarach, and again we infer from his description that both were minium. The former is obtained by heating 'a stone' which occurs with silver ore, the latter by heating white lead (the product of the prolonged action of vinegar on lead). Pliny similarly describes two substances, minium and sandarach. His description of the former is essentially identical to Dioscorides' description of ammion, but Pliny's sandarach is simply 'found in gold and silver mines'. He goes on to note that a 'false' sandarach is made by heating white lead.[45]

[45] See Dioscorides *Materia medica*, Bk 5; 100–3, 109. Pliny, *Natural history*, Bk 33; 106, 119. Bk 34; 173, 177.

Despite this confusion, however, and their probable lack of first-hand knowledge of the processes involved, Pliny and Dioscorides can be said to have known the oxides of lead in an empirical way. The same can be said of the oxides of copper. They knew more oxides, but had a poorer conception of what an oxide is than had Plato, who held such substances to be the result of the weathering of 'an earthy part' of a metal.[46] With the exception of zinc oxide, those which sublimate or decompose on strong heating (such as the oxides of arsenic, antimony, and mercury) do not appear in the works of the ancient technical writers. Zinc oxide appeared in large quantities in the flues of brass furnaces, and it is likely that the others were overlooked or confused with something else. Archaeologists have inferred a knowledge of the oxides of antimony on the part of the Assyrian pigment makers who produced 'Naples yellow'.

Chlorides, sulphides, and (with the exception of the vitriol-alum group) sulphates were not known unless they occurred naturally. It is doubtful that any were made artificially, except incidentally. Silver chloride, for example, appears as a by-product of the salt cupellation of gold. Pliny advocates this residue (in medicine) as a sort of wasted gold. Dioscorides' recipe for 'burned copper' (Bk 5; 87) recommends heating it alone (in air) or with salt, sulphur, or vinegar, which might have yielded the chloride, sulphide, and acetate, but he has nothing to say of what to expect. Such recipes suggest, if anything, a lack of discrimination.

There was less opportunity for confusion of the acetates, of which those of copper and lead were made very early. Lead acetate, however, was not clearly differentiated from the popular pigment, white lead (in the production of which it was an intermediate), and copper acetate (verdigris) is the only product of vinegar dissolution which was clearly discriminated.

Although vitriols and alums are now known as classes of substances differing in their metallic constituents, iron vitriol (ferrous sulphate) and potassium alum (potassium aluminium sulphate) were long the most commonplace materials passing under the names of vitriol and alum. Their metallic elements are among the most common in the earth's crust. Their combination with sulphur is less common, but occurs in regions of one-time volcanic activity, and the rarity of

46 *Timaeus*, 59C.

vitriols and alums in nature is principally attributable to their solubility. Where rain is infrequent they may be observed as efflorescences on rocks and under certain conditions they will form spectacular crystals. These crystals, and the peculiarly astringent taste of 'this kind of salty earth', as Pliny called them both, must surely account for the fact that they were noticed so early.

Alum has been traced in two of its principal uses, as an astringent medicine and for fixing dyestuffs, nearly to the beginning of the second millennium B.C., and evidence of its production has been claimed for a thousand years before that.[47] Iron vitriol is usually present as an impurity, and is altogether more common. Moreover it has the astringent taste. It was long suspected that the 'alum' of antiquity was really vitriol, but the dye fixing property does not belong to vitriol, and it is now accepted that alum was known in antiquity.

The 'salty earth' of Pliny, which he calls 'alumen' (Bk 35; 183), comes, he tells us, in several colours and is widely produced, from Armenia to Spain. 'Every kind' comes from a water which exudes from the earth, but it can also be formed by cooking the stone 'chalcitis'. Astringency – hence its Greek name, stypteria – is its most remarkable property, but in liquid form it is also indurative (susceptible to crystallization) and corrosive. It is used in dyeing as a mordant, in medicine, for purifying gold, and for blackening leather. The first use clearly refers to alum, the last two to iron vitriol, and the name 'chalcitis' to copper vitriol. That this less common (blue) vitriol should enter the picture is presumably due to the fact that it occurs in the drainage of copper mines, in which the Romans were particularly interested, and it has indeed been claimed that the Romans thought copper the essential constituent of all alums and vitriols. Nonetheless they were apparently differentiated by those who used them, and we have contemporary evidence from Herodotus and Galen that they were produced in large quantities.[48]

[47] Levey, 1959: 109, 158ff. Partington, 1935: 148. The earliest written reference to a substance which can be identified as alum is in the papyrus Ebers, but an Egyptian dyed leather piece of about 2000 B.C. in the Cairo museum seems to have been mordanted with alum (Singer, 1948: 3).

[48] Herodotus, *Histories* (2, 180), reports a contribution of 1,000 talents of 'stypteria' from Egypt. Galen, 1821–33, Vol. 12: 238–41 (*On medical simples*, Bk 9), has left a report of a visit to a calcanthum factory on Cyprus. See also Singer, 1948.

It is not surprising to find that the relatively subtle differences between the common soluble colourless (white) salts, sea salt, the alkali carbonates, sulphates and nitrates, were only vaguely recognized. 'Salt', meaning sea salt, is said by Pliny (Bk 31; 73) to be of two kinds, each of several varieties. The two kinds are 'natural' and 'prepared', and his rather confused account certainly includes some varieties which are identical with his 'natron'. But natron, as our late antique authors reveal, had accrued some new varieties of its own. Both Theophrastus (Bk 3; 7, 6) and Pliny (Bk 31; 107) mention a variety which was obtained by leaching plant ashes. This would have been potash (potassium carbonate), from ordinary land plants, or soda (sodium carbonate), from plants near the sea. In the course of the Middle Ages these sources of alkali became the most familiar to the European, and, as the product was purer and more homogeneous than Egyptian natron, the unique properties of the alkali carbonates became gradually known.

More completely obscured within the confusion of colourless salts were the nitrogen-containing salts, sal ammoniac and saltpetre. These might be called the salts of civilization, since they were long obtained principally from the refuse of domestic animals. For all practical purposes they were not known to the writers considered here, although they may be some of the more unusual salts briefly mentioned.[49] Each of these two salts had a revolutionary effect on chemistry when it entered the repertoire of the practical chemist in the ninth century (sal ammoniac) and the thirteenth century (saltpetre). Since the conditions for their formation existed in the more heavily populated regions of the ancient world we can assume that they were observed. But they were not, in any meaningful sense of the term, known.

Pliny does record (Bk 31; 114), in his discussion of the colourless salts, an event ultimately of the greatest importance, the formation of sodium hydroxide (caustic soda, lye) by treating natron with quicklime. This was the first substance known which was capable of intense and spontaneous chemical activity. But we are here

[49] Certain references by the Greeks and Romans to natron from caverns are supposed to refer to saltpetre; other references to a salt which sublimes may refer to sal ammoniac. References to natrons of a peculiar texture may refer to crystalline forms of saltpetre and sal ammoniac (see Ruska, 1923–1. Gibbs, 1938). According to Levey, saltpetre was known to the Assyrians (1959: 128, 152).

recording an event which was important to the later history of chemistry, not to Pliny nor to the best chemists for many centuries after him. Caustic soda had but one use, the manufacture of soap. It is not clear that Pliny knew true soap, but it was known to Galen (third century A.D.) and was common in Europe by A.D. 800. It seems to have been a discovery of the Gauls,[50] who were far from the mainstream of chemistry. Pliny does not consider its properties particularly remarkable. Its most conspicuous property, causticity, was that already known in quicklime, from the sixteenth century B.C. Pliny regarded the causticization of natron by quicklime as simply an intensification of that property.

More significant for the immediate future were two metallurgical innovations reported by the Greco-Roman writers, the introduction of mercury (quicksilver) and brass. Isolated samples of most of the metals have been found belonging to unaccountably early periods, and such is the case with mercury and brass. But it does not appear that mercury was effectively known much before the date, about 400 B.C., which Theophrastus gives for the invention of a process for its production by rubbing cinnabar in vinegar.[51] It appears thenceforth in virtually all chemical treatises, most of which describe the more common method of making it, by simply heating cinnabar.[52] The importance of mercury in late antique and medieval chemistry requires no emphasis.

The earliest known example of brass again considerably predates its regular appearance in excavations, and while it is held by some that brass was made in Persia from about 700 B.C., we are on firmer ground in regarding the Romans as its first deliberate fabricators.[53] Pliny probably included brass among his 'coppers', improved by smelting with a substance which was found in silver

[50] Gibbs, 1939.

[51] *On stones*, 58. It is also mentioned in Bk iv (385b) of Aristotle's *Meteorology*. If mercury was known before, it was probably from natural occurrence. For a summary of the early history of mercury, see Caley, 1928.

[52] Ebert, 1924–32, Vol. 14: 538, mentions cinnabar among neolithic European pigments, but evidences of it before Theophrastus are rare. It has recently been found as a pigment on fifth-century B.C. pottery in Athenian agora (Caley, 1946: 314–16).

[53] Partington says that brass containing 24.3 per cent zinc was known in Palestine 1400–1000 B.C. (1935: 475). The earliest known Roman brass coins date from about 45 B.C., twenty years before brass coinage became common (Caley, 1955). Brass also first appeared in Britain (at least as an intentional product) in the Roman period (Tylecote, 1962: 53).

mines (calamine or smithsonite) and/or which appeared as a sublimate (zinc oxide) in the flues of 'copper' furnaces. (Bk 34;100) Both were usually called tutia. Brass was not recognized as an alloy, but was rather regarded as another type of copper, and hence was to complicate further the problem of differentiating copper and its alloys. Like caustic soda, it was regarded as an improvement of a substance already known, and had little chemical significance. Zinc remained unknown until the sixteenth century A.D.

Theory

The surviving papyri and cuneiform tablets give scarcely a hint of the theoretical basis of practical chemistry, and the existence of any chemical theory before the Greeks has been questioned. It is more likely, however, that the theory has simply been lost. Eliade has made an impressive attempt at its reconstruction by combining evidences from the practices of modern primitive tribes with inferences drawn from alchemy. The animistic metallurgy he pictures seems more plausible than the extraordinary spectacle of a primitive chemistry utterly devoid of theory.

In primitive societies minerals participate in the sacred character of the earth. Like animals and vegetables, minerals have life; after an embryonic growth in the earth, they reach, in maturity, the state in which we know them as metals. The miner and metallurgist intervene and accelerate their normal maturation. They sometimes view the ore-reducing process as a kind of marriage ceremony, and in doing so they attain a magico-religious relationship with nature. This relationship corresponds to that of the agriculturist, who similarly speeds the growth of plants. But the work of the metallurgist is both more spectacular and more mysterious, and he occupies in primitive societies a special position as 'master of fire', and member of an occult religious society, the secrets of which are transmitted by rites of initiation.[54]

These ideas are reminiscent of those primitive theories of the universe which preceded the rise of scientific astronomy. They seem to demonstrate the indispensability of theory, but they are not

[54] Eliade, 1956: 8–9, 45–67, 75–88, 94.

easily connected with the theory which emerges in the early historical period. They are exclusively concerned with the cosmogonic question of the generation of the metals, whereas theory in historic times is also concerned with their definition and their relationship to other materials. Primitive theory casts little light on the evolution of the idea that there is a group of substances, limited in number, which possess the distinctive properties we recognize as metallic. This, as is the case with so many scientific questions, first emerges through the implementation of the evidences of archaeology and early technical writing with the literature of Greek natural philosophy, which exhibits for the first time rational curiosity as to the working of nature.

Among the Greeks, the term metal ($\mu\acute{\epsilon}\tau\alpha\lambda\lambda o\nu$) first denoted a valuable mineral site, then (in Herodotus, c. 450 B.C.) a mine, and finally the produce of a mine. In the writing of Lucretius (first century A.D.), we find it used in the modern sense. But among the Hebrews, Greeks, and Romans generally a metal was simply a valuable mineral, and the value of 'metals' was listed in an order which remained, quite consistently, gold, electrum, silver, lapis lazuli, malachite, copper, iron, and lead.[55]

Another scientifically irrelevant criterion of classification was the association of the metals with the planets, but the development of this association gives us some clue as to the differentiation of the metals as distinct substances. The association of gold and silver with the sun and moon is of pre-historic antiquity. In addition, from late antiquity five planets were differentiated as peculiar astronomical objects and five metals were associated with them. Copper, iron, and lead were consistently associated with Venus, Mars and Saturn; Mercury and Jupiter were for some reason the planets for which the other metals 'competed'. In a list compiled by Lippmann from nine writers spanning the first millennium after Christ we find tin, bronze, electrum and quicksilver (which was widely known after about 300 B.C.) alternating as the metals to be associated with Mercury and Jupiter[56]. This uncertainty reflects: (1) the imprecise differentiation of the principal alloys, electrum, bronze and (from

---

[55] On the etymology of the word 'metal' see Lippmann, 1919: 519, Schraeder, 1909, and Partington, 1935: 23.

[56] Lippmann, 1919: 216–17.

Roman times) brass, from the metals on which they were based, (2) the imprecise differentiation of tin (and other metals, such as antimony and bismuth) from lead, and (3) the unique character of quicksilver.

These lists do seem to indicate, however, that the definition of the metals as a particular class of mineral substances was relatively complete by the second century of the Christian era. But the copper alloys persisted on these lists, and the differentiation of the members within the class of metals was not completed to an equal degree until the end of the eighteenth century A.D., being much delayed by the persistence of the contradictory ideas (1) that there is a fixed number of different metals (which, for reasons already given, came to be seven), and (2) that the metals differ by imperceptible degrees of perfection from the basest (lead) to the most perfect (gold). Inasmuch as the prevailing theory of the nature of matter which came into prominence after Plato and Aristotle held it to be more or less indiscriminately transmutable, testing for purity was largely a matter of convenience. We presume that it was undertaken seriously in the case of the coinage metals, but have little evidence even for this. Nevertheless, the discovery of a method of 'parting' gold from metals alloyed with it marked a milestone in the history of chemistry. This process, as described by Agatharchides (second century B.C.), consisted of a manipulation in which the adulterated gold was heated with salt, straw, and other materials.[57] Partington believes the time of this discovery to be fixed by the disappearance of electrum from the Egyptian lists of metals after the seventh century B.C.,[58] but, as has been noted above, electrum long survived on lists elsewhere. Considered as a test for gold, Agatharchides' process was not a useful model for any general system of testing, for it depended upon the resistance of gold to all chemical treatment, which altered all adulterants.

Of the other metals, only silver and iron were clearly defined by

[57] The work of Agatharchides is not extant. He is quoted by Diodorus Siculus (Bk 3; 14), in a passage which is published in translation in Hoover, 1912: 279 note 8.

[58] Partington, 1935: 41. This agrees with the date assigned to the earliest authentic currency, by Gyges of Lydia, who is thought to have known how to separate gold and silver. Aitchison believes the process to have been known as early as 1500 B.C., and states that the complementary process, the deliberate alloying of gold and silver, was practised a thousand years earlier (1960: 61, 173).

writers through the European Middle Ages, both having very characteristic properties and no important alloys (excepting electrum, in the case of silver). Through the same period copper, bronze and brass were generally confused and lead seems to have been considered the chief member of a subclass, which included tin, antimony and, possibly, bismuth. One receives the impression from writers on metallurgy that it was not a lack of technique which inhibited the differentiation of these metals and alloys, but the lack, despite the contrary experience of the coiners, of an awareness that the metals differed distinctly and not by infinitesimal gradation. The differentiation of the seven metals seems to have owed more to astrology than to chemistry.

Chapter Two

From cosmogony to cosmology

The rise of Greek philosophy

THEOPHRASTUS, Pliny and Dioscorides were preoccupied in the treatises just discussed almost solely with the description of 'practical chemistry'. In view of the confusion of all but a few of the most familiar substances, it is not surprising that they undertook to make no extensive generalizations regarding chemical processes. But it does not follow that they had nothing whatever to say of theory. They did, in fact, take note of certain theories of the nature of matter and its changes, and not as new and provisional, but as matters of general acceptance. Theophrastus, for example, begins *On stones* by stating that some of the substances 'formed in the Earth' are made of water and some of earth. These theories had been formulated during the three centuries before Theophrastus by the Greek natural philosophers, a group with no evident involvement in practical chemistry, but with a great curiosity as to the world and its workings. Whereas the Babylonians and Egyptians have left us speculations (and these chiefly mythical) only on cosmogony, the origin of the world, the Greeks, from the sixth century, advanced to the question of cosmology, the explanation of the day-to-day changes visible in the world.

The philosophy of nature, our natural science, found in the sixth century B.C. the first expositors whose work left traces which can still

39

be detected. These traces are little enough: of Thales, reputed the first natural philosopher among the Greeks, we have two or three more-or-less contemporary fragments and a larger number of accounts written generations later, when he had become a legendary figure. It seems clear that he did reject from his explanation of nature arguments derived from the supernatural, and this is his chief claim to fame. But no less important was the astonishing circumstance that in Thales we encounter a thinker whose thought had consequences, who was not isolated, forgotten, or repudiated by later generations. Instead, in his own time he passed on some of his views to others capable of appreciating, extending, and correcting them, and they, in turn, captured the interest of their own successors. This chain has never been broken to the present day and, in fact, represents the essential beginning of the intellectual history of western civilization.

The image of Thales as the prototype of the Greek philosopher is suspiciously like that which is typically constructed for a 'founding father', yet it seems to have a considerable degree of probability. He was, we are told, a statesman who advised in the government of his city. He was an engineer, having channelled the Halys river to enable Croesus' army to cross. He travelled widely, and profited from the learning of older nations. Thus he picked up among the Babylonians the ability to predict eclipses, which he demonstrated in 585 B.C., to the astonishment of his countrymen. Among the Egyptians he learned how to measure the height of a pyramid from its shadow, and among the Babylonians the fact of the regularity of certain celestial phenomena which made eclipse prediction possible. He fabricated from these scattered bits of useful knowledge something no less interesting, if less immediately useful, the first purely rational description of the world. His innovation, therefore, was the application of knowledge to the description of nature for the sole reason of a curiosity as to its workings.

Perhaps the principal argument for the accuracy of this picture of Thales is the undoubted fact that from his time similar, and more well-attested, thinkers appeared among the Greeks in increasing numbers. For about a thousand years they brought the same rationalism to bear on every facet of human life, with the end result a complex and many-sided literature on almost every subject which has interested men up to the present day. So impressive was it that modern learning dares not even yet leave it out of account. So sophisticated was it that its full meaning is still hotly debated.

Of all of the subjects on which the Greeks were to philosophize, natural philosophy, or science, seems to have been the first. It was the favourite subject of Thales and of the majority of his successors for about two hundred years, at least of those whose remains permit us to reconstruct their opinions. If there were important moral or political philosophers in these days they were isolated figures. Natural philosophy was at the forefront of intellectual life, as it is today. The end of this period of five or six generations came with the rise to prominence of political and moral philosophy. The most important figure in this movement was Socrates (d. 399 B.C.) whose influence was so great that his predecessors have been known ever since as 'Presocratics'.

The emergence of Greek civilization was directly connected with the evolution of a new politico-economic idea, colonization. This occurred before Thales' time, indeed he was a product of it, as a citizen of a colony, Miletus, in Asia Minor. The Greek city-states and their colonies seem to have been in every sort of competition, economic, political, and intellectual. They pursued their rivalry with an abandon which ultimately became a factor in the decline of Greek power and influence, but it was certainly a causal factor in the spectacular development of natural philosophy, for the decline of philosophy in one colony saw its rise in another, usually through the emigration of dissenting philosophers. Thales bequeathed his philosophy to two successors at Miletus, Anaximander and Anaximenes. Because of their common location, approach, and near identity of subject matter we call them a 'school' (the Milesian), although it is doubtful that any formal instruction existed among them. They flourished from about 590 to about 546 B.C. By the time the Milesian school fell into decline, others were rising in other colonies. Of the two principal philosophers of the next generation, one, Heraclitus, philosophized alone at Ephesus in Ionia; the other, Pythagoras, left Ionia for Sicily, where he was to found one of the most durable of the schools.

Pythagoras spent his early life on the Aegean island of Samos, during the later years of Anaximenes, the last of the Milesian school.

Being neither inclined towards a strictly Milesian view of nature, nor to the politics of his native city, he emigrated to Croton, in Sicily. Religion and mathematics were his particular interests, and although his school ultimately exhibited the occultism which characteristically results from the amalgamation of these two, Pythagoras and his earliest followers adhered closely enough to natural philosophy, as outlined by the Milesians, to maintain the essential continuity of Greek philosophy. Unlike the Milesian, the Pythagorean school cannot be said to have declined, although in time it rather fragmented, and bits of Pythagorean doctrine turned up in almost all subsequent schools of philosophy. Plato, for example, was thoroughly imbued with Pythagorean ideology.

The fragmentation of Pythagoreanism was partly the consequence of the rise of a rival school in the Italian colonies, the Eleatic (named for Elea, in southern Italy), founded by Parmenides, who flourished about a generation after Pythagoras and Heraclitus. As Pythagoras was a dissident Milesian, so Parmenides was a dissident Pythagorean. Between 470 and 440 his school (his principal followers were Zeno and Melissus) applied the critical technique of *reductio ad absurdum* to earlier natural philosophies, and particularly to Pythagoreanism. Their contribution was not the construction of a new or improved natural philosophy; it was rather a clearing of the ground for more sophisticated doctrines. It may also be noted that they seem to have been the first to bring Athens into the circle of philosophical research, for the young Socrates is said to have heard Parmenides and Zeno lecture there.

During the generation between Parmenides and the beginning of the domination of natural philosophy by Plato and Aristotle three systems were propounded, each an attempt to rebuild natural philosophy in a form resistant to the Eleatic criticism. There seem no longer to have been favoured locations for philosophy, although the Athenian hegemony was approaching. Empedocles was from Acragas and philosophized at Thurii (both were in southern Italy), where he is said to have been prominent both as a physician and as a politician. Anaxagoras was from Clazomenae (southern Italy) and became prominent as a philosopher at Athens in the time of Pericles, whom he is supposed to have served as an adviser. He is said to have been prosecuted for impiety – for declaring the sun to be a mass of red-hot metal – and exiled to Lampsacus. Leucippus, the founder of atomism, has not been definitely associated with any particular place, and we have even less direct information on him than we have on the first philosopher, Thales. He was only a few years older than his famous protégé, Democritus, who, like Empedocles and Anaxagoras, was a contemporary of Socrates. Democritus was evidently a prolific writer; a list of his works compiled about A.D. 10 mentions writings on the planets (perhaps the first Greek work on this subject), theology, tactics, medicine, painting, and other subjects, from all of which only fragments survive. Like many another sage he is supposed to have acquired much of his learning in the course of his travels in the East, and it is perhaps to this aspect of his career that Democritus owes his appeal to the alchemists. He was the first prominent philosopher to be honoured, as was later the common custom, by the spurious authorship of alchemical works.

Matter and its changes

We will consider the views of the Presocratics on those basic problems, the nature of matter, the cause or causes of its manifest changes, and the mechanism through which these changes come about. That we can put to them these modern questions of cosmogony and cosmology is a measure of their distance from their contemporaries in Egypt and Babylonia, who remained, with the exception of the germinating Babylonian idea of astro-biological correspondences, content with a happy confusion of creation mythology.[1] That exception was to lead to a resurgence of Babylonian influence, but that was an event of the later history of science in Greece. In the hands of the Presocratics nature study was stripped of its theological content, and appears a very different topic.

A crucial role in the formulation of the Presocratic view of nature was played by observation of chemical, biological, and meteorological phenomena. Of these the former played the smallest and the latter the greatest role, a circumstance which gives the Presocratic cogitations on matter a peculiar aspect when seen from the point of view of modern chemistry. Presocratic discussions of matter are also characterized by the peculiarity that they regarded all phenomena,

[1] Cf. Frankfort et al, 1946: 39ff, 137ff.

even perception and thought, as material, in consequence of which the matter which suffered change and the causes of that change could never be satisfactorily disentangled. This remained the great defect which vitiated all of the series of increasingly ingenious world-pictures propounded by the Presocratics. The two great turning points in the history of their natural philosophy were the Eleatic demonstration of the untenability of a natural philosophy based on this universal materialism, and the subsequent invention of the conception that something could be real and yet immaterial, which allowed first the atomists and then (from a different point of view) Plato and Aristotle to begin the process of separating the question of the nature of matter from that of the causes of its changes.

The first question, of the nature of matter, does not seem to have been susceptible to anything resembling scientific delimitation by the cosmogonist. But in adding a concern with the question of change the cosmologist restricted in a beneficial way his freedom of choice in answering the first question. In the Milesians we see a mixture of cosmogonic and cosmological thinking. They assumed a single 'primal material' from which all else is made. Later philosophers gave the primal material a more remote status, and spoke of primary and secondary matter, or concerned themselves with one or more intermediate 'elements' ($\sigma\tau o\iota\chi\bar{\epsilon}\iota a$) which could be more directly conceived of as the building blocks of the sensible world.[2] This compromise between idealization and observation (which is also at the basis of the modern theory of chemical elements) made it possible to attempt more realistically the derivation of the primary constituents of bodies from observation. It also made it possible, since these 'elementary' constituents lacked the real primacy of the primal material, for confusion to arise as to the relationship between the

---

[2] Since the 'fragments' of the Presocratics are actually statements about or attributed to them by later writers, we lack certain knowledge of the real Presocratic terminology. Aristotle does not refer Thales' 'water' to 'primal material' ($\pi\rho\omega\tau\eta\ \ddot{\upsilon}\lambda\eta$) or to 'primal substance' ($o\dot{\upsilon}\sigma\dot{\iota}a\ \pi\rho\dot{\omega}\tau\eta$ or $\pi\rho\hat{\omega}\tau o\nu\ \dot{\upsilon}\pi o\kappa\epsilon\dot{\iota}\mu\epsilon\nu o\nu$) which seems to have been preferred in classical Greek, but to 'that which is in matter' ($\tau\grave{a}s\ \dot{\epsilon}\nu\ \ddot{\upsilon}\lambda\eta s$) 'element' ($\sigma\tau o\iota\chi\epsilon\hat{\iota}a$), and 'source' ($\dot{a}\rho\chi\dot{\eta}$), all of which he mentions synonymously (*Metaphysics* 983b). Diogenes Laertius refers Anaximander's 'indefinite' to 'source and element' (Bk II, 1), but Simplicius, quoting Theophrastus on Anaximander, refers to 'material source' ($\dot{\upsilon}\lambda\dot{\iota}\kappa as\ \dot{a}\rho\chi\dot{a}s$) (DK59A41). Simplicius also uses 'nature' ($\phi\dot{\upsilon}\sigma\iota s$) for matter, to contrast it with mind, and this term, the meaning of which has been successively modified until it has become our 'physics', is the most probable Presocratic term for primal material (Burnet, 1930: 10–12 and App. I).

same 'body', as, for example, water, considered as an element and as a 'thing', that is, as an object in the world to be explained. One philosopher, in discussing 'things', is likely to mention the 'elements' of another. Melissus, in his denial of the reality of things, mentions as examples earth, water, air, fire, iron, gold and stone.[3] Empedocles, who believed earth, water, air and fire to be elements, exemplified things by men, animals and gods.[4] In time the elements, too, tended to be relegated to the limbo of remote matter already occupied by the primal material, in favour of yet another 'principle' more conveniently associated with terrestrial phenomena. Such were Plato's geometric solids, the vitalistic 'pneuma' of the Stoics and the 'mercury' and 'sulphur' of the alchemists.

Thales, Anaximander, and Anaximenes disagreed as to the primal material, holding it to be, respectively, water, 'the indefinite', and air ($\H{v}\delta\omega\varrho$, $\tau\H{o}$ $\H{a}\pi\varepsilon\iota\varrho\sigma\nu$, $\H{a}\H{\eta}\varrho$). Too little remains of Thales' writing to enable us to be certain, but it seems more likely that he drew his conclusion from meteorological and biological observations than from earlier Near Eastern cosmogonic myths of the earth's origin in water.[5] Anaximander held that a variety of sensible things cannot arise out of any one of them, and substituted the plural, but otherwise incomprehensible, 'indefinite' as the primal material.[6] Anaximenes found an answer to this and reverted to a single substance which he called air. His answer was to regard the apparent differences in things as really quantitative variations in density, resulting from the continuous action of rarefaction and condensation in the world. That is to say, he explained the differences in things as differences in the physical state of a single primal material. He seems to have believed air ($\H{a}\H{\eta}\varrho$) and breath ($\pi\nu\varepsilon\H{v}\mu\alpha$) to be similar if not identical manifestations of it.[7] This concern to propound a primal material

[3] DK 30 A2.

[4] Simplicius, *Phys.* 159, 21 (quoted by Kirk and Raven, 1957: 328).

[5] Aristotle supposed him to have observed 'that the nutriment of all things is moist' (*Metaphysics*, 983b), and Theophrastus attributed to him the observation 'that corpses dry up' (DK 11A13). An indifference to myths is one of Thales' most notable characteristics.

[6] By $\tau\H{o}$ $\H{a}\pi\varepsilon\iota\varrho\sigma\nu$ he probably meant both the spatially indefinite and unlike any sensible thing. Cf. Kirk and Raven, 1957: 113: Burnet, 1930: 53.

[7] Anaximenes' $\H{a}\H{\eta}\varrho$ probably represented the adaptation of Thales' primal material to the principle of rarefaction and condensation, and corresponded to our atmosphere, while having at the same time vitalistic associations with breath and soul. Cf. Kirk and Raven, 1957: 146-7, 158.

45

from which things can plausibly be supposed to emerge, and into which they can decay, led the last great Ionian philosopher, Heraclitus, to propound yet another fire.

In these cogitations on processes which are cyclic or reversible we see the beginning of an abandonment of concern with the cosmogonist's material from which the world is made in favour of the cosmologist's material from which the things in the world are continuously generated and into which they decay. Meteorological and biological considerations predominated in Greek thought not only on matter but on the cause of change and the mechanism through which it comes about. We do not know what Thales thought about the cause of change, but his successor, Anaximander, held that the action of contending opposites, heat and cold, wet and dry, effected change,[8] and this idea was to remain a permanent feature of Greek natural philosophy, recurring in varying forms in nearly all of his successors. The idea that these causes somehow manifest their interaction through a vortex, a mechanism which brings heavy bodies to the centre of the world and light bodies to the periphery, may also have originated with Anaximander.[9] Anaximenes' theory of rarefaction and condensation was better suited to a world of cyclic change, and Heraclitus' idea of an upward and downward movement as the mechanism of change was still better because of its association with the action of a supposed fire in the sun on the earth and sea.[10] It represented an application of the theory of rarefaction and condensation which proved to have great appeal to his successors, and manifests itself in Aristotle's doctrine of the formation of metals and subsequently in alchemical theories, where it was embroidered with an astrological theory of celestial emanations.

The Greek philosophies originating in south Italy nearly a century after Thales differed markedly from those of the Ionians. It is difficult to determine to what extent this is the result of a different original motivation and how far it represents an advance to a more sophisticated level of thought. It seems likely that Pythagoreanism was originally a religious and not a natural philosophy, which was brought by Pythagoras' own scientific discoveries into the necessity

[8] Kirk and Raven, 1957: 129–33.
[9] Burnet, 1930: 61–2, and, less confidently, Kirk and Raven, 1957: 128, 132.
[10] Ibid, 148–9. Kirk and Raven, 1957: 199–201.

of establishing some relationship with the prevailing Ionian natural philosophy. This conjunction was occasioned by his discovery that the chief musical intervals are expressible in simple numerical ratios between the first four integers.[11]

Having discovered a correlation between mathematics and physics, the Pythagoreans attempted a thoroughgoing application of the former to natural philosophy. Confronted with the traditional questions of matter and change, they came to regard numbers themselves as material, and as the substance of all things.[12] The role of cause of change seems to have been somehow ascribed to mathematical contraries, such as even and odd.[13] Although Pythagorean numerology, as Parmenides was to point out, was not well suited to the explication of change, this venture into what we might call physical chemistry may be regarded as the pioneer attempt at the mathematization of chemistry, the first of a series of essays which were to include those of the later Pythagoreans to effect a picture of bodies as geometric shapes formed by a juxtaposition of their material numbers,[14] Plato's charmingly aesthetic theory of chemical change, the numerological scheme for analysis and synthesis set forth by one of the writers of the circle of the Arabic Jābir ibn Haiyān, and other schemes of more modern times. But its more immediate consequence was somewhat disastrous. In picturing the elements as geometric solids formed of material numbers, somewhat like the crystal lattice of modern chemistry, the Pythagoreans had to assume the existence of empty space in the interstices. By the third quarter of the fifth century the imaginative structures of natural philosophy were increasingly vulnerable to criticism, but it was the question of the existence of the void which particularly inspired the attack of Parmenides.

From Thales through Heraclitus natural philosophy became increasingly sophisticated, and increasingly sought to refine and extend its explanation. In consequence, and especially after its Pythagorean permutation, it generated 'loose-ends' which were susceptible to criticism. Such criticism was initiated by the onetime Pythagorean,

[11] Kirk and Raven, 1957: 229.
[12] Aristotle, *Metaphysics*, 985b–986a (cf. Kirk and Raven, 1957: 246–7).
[13] Ibid, 1092b.
[14] Kirk and Raven, 1957: 315–17

Parmenides, and extended by his pupils into a critique with which all subsequent natural philosophers had to reckon.

Through an unprecedented exercise in logical deduction, a dialectic which reminds us of Descartes, Parmenides 'proved' the impossibility of empty space and of deriving the multitude of things from any single primal material. He held that the acceptance of one of a pair of opposites, such as hot and cold, logically involves the rejection of the other, and denied the 'opposites' which were conventionally accepted as causes of change. He and his followers, Zeno and Melissus, criticized attempts to distinguish space from the body that occupies it and denied motion in general and rarefaction and condensation in particular, on the ground that both imply the existence of empty space.[15]

Parmenides concluded that that which exists, which he called 'the One', is a single, indivisible and homogenous sphere, timeless, changeless and (since there is no void either inside it or outside) motionless. It has in fact no perceptible qualities whatever. Modern criticism has shown that his argument depended upon his confusion between a negative prediction and a negative existential judgment,[16] but this does not seem to have weakened the contemporary force of his argument.

Subsequent world-systems were to a considerable extent inspired by the necessity of meeting Parmenides' criticisms. The three principal of these were propounded by Empedocles, Anaxagoras and Leucippus. The first two postulated a finite world, filled with matter, and increased the variety of the elementary substance. The latter held that empty space does exist, and that there is only one elementary substance, but gave each particle in it (the 'atom') the characteristics of the Parmenidean 'One'.

These three systems, and all that followed them, owe much to their heritage from the pioneers of Greek natural philosophy. Empedocles filled Parmenides' sphere with four distinct elements, fire, air, water and earth, and from their continual 'mixing' he formed the bodies of the sensible world.[17] The cause of this mixing

[15] Burnet, 1930: 317, 327. Kirk and Raven, 1957: 275.

[16] Kirk and Raven, 1957: 270.

[17] Empedocles' elements were probably the embodiment of the four 'qualities', hot, cold, wet and dry, rather than the cumulative primal materials of earlier philosophers. Cf. Burnet, 1930: 228; Kirk and Raven, 1957: 329.

he saw as a conflict between two new 'opposites', 'love' and 'strife', which proceeds in a never ending cycle in which love and strife alternately triumph, bringing about first the complete mixture of the elements and then their complete separation, the completion of each cycle being the beginning of its repetition.[18]

Anaxagoras filled the Parmenidean sphere with an essentially organic material, infinitely divisible, but retaining in each part, however small, the characteristics of a compact body. The things of this world existed from the beginning, and each of the infinitesimal parts of the Anaxagorean matter contains a portion of everything, but not in equal amount; it is the domination of one thing or another in the parts which leads them to form the things we see in the world. He appropriately gives these parts the name 'seeds'. As the cause of the operation of the cosmos Anaxagoras adopts another entity from the philosophy of organic beings, mind (nous), and he adopts as a mechanism Anaximander's vortex, motion.[19]

The final major Presocratic attempt to answer the Eleatic objections to the cosmologies of the natural philosophers was made by Leucippus and his followers, the atomists. Whereas Empedocles and Anaxagoras had accepted the Parmenidean finite world, filled with matter, and explained change through a diversity of elements, Leucippus postulated an infinite world, partly empty, and containing a single primal material. But this primal material, the atom, existed in the form of a multitude of particles devoid of any qualities whatever, except shape. Except for this deviation each atom has the essential characteristics of the Parmenidean 'One'.[20] But in consequence of their differences in shape the atoms can join together in aggregates to form bodies, and this they do in the course of their perpetual motion in empty space. The cause of this motion is gravitation, and its perpetuation derives from their mutual collisions in essentially the same manner as has been postulated by the modern kinetic theory.

Although the systems of Empedocles and Anaxagoras escaped the dilemmas of Parmenides, both remained subject to the difficulties inherent in the universal materialism of the Presocratics. Empedocles' love and strife and Anaxagoras' mind lacked virtually

[18] Kirk and Raven, 1957: 326–8.

[19] Ibid, 376–8. The arguments adduced here are biological; there is hair and flesh in food and drink. etc.   [20] Ibid, 404–5.

all of the characteristics of matter except materiality itself. Leucippus' system was not subject to this defect. In propounding the real existence of empty space the atomists cut the Gordian knot of Presocratic materialism and brought to the solution of its problems the conception of an entity which was not itself composed of matter and hence not a part of the problem to be solved. But it had been just the Pythagorean implication of the existence of void which had been the focal point of the Eleatic criticism, and Postsocratic philosophy was not to waive this objection. It was found easier to escape the difficulties of universal materialism than those of the void, for a solution to the former difficulty was found in the work of Socrates himself.

When natural philosophy emerged after its temporary eclipse in the fourth century, the idea of a force which was not in itself material had been manufactured by Plato out of Socrates' conception of 'the Good'. Empedocles' natural philosophy was reconstructed to take this into account, and so modified it became the basis for the cosmologies of two millennia. Atomism, at the same time, became increasingly unpopular. How, it was asked, did the falling atoms begin their process of random collision? How can chance collisions account for the recurrence of the particular things we observe?[21] The Postsocratic atomists attempted to answer these queries, and it is not clear that they were less ingenious in shoring up weaknesses in their doctrine than were the proponents of rival philosophies.[22] But there was more disposition to criticize the atomists for defects in their conception of the motion of atoms than there was to ask how we are to conceive the motion of the particles in the universes of Empedocles and Anaxagoras.[23] The basic objection to atomism was

[21] Aristotle, On generation and corruption, 825a.

[22] Leucippus and Democritus seem to have assumed the random motion of atoms to be their original motion, and were criticized by Aristotle (On the heavens, 300b) for failing to state their 'natural' motion. Epicurus gave them a natural motion, straight downward, impelled by their weight, which obligated him to postulate a cause, the cosmic swerve (παρακλίνειν Epicurus; declinare, Lucretius) to explain their initial collisions (Lucretius, Bk II, 216ff; cf. C. Bailey, 1928; 316–17 and Ernout and Robin, 1925–28: Vol. I: 242–4 for other ancient references).

[23] Anaxagoras met Parmenides' objection to empty space by agreeing that matter is infinitely divisible and hence requires no space between its parts. From Anaxagoras to Descartes the idea of vortex motion was used by advocates of the 'continuum' to account for motion in a universe to which the void was not admitted.

in its application to theology, for whereas the universes of Empedocles and Anaxagoras proved susceptible to division into areas of
physics and metaphysics, atomism, in the hands of Epicurus, became
a philosophy of resistance to this modification. As such it was out
of harmony with the temper of the age.

Chapter Three

The Postsocratic philosophies

THE century and a half between the rise of the Milesian school and the appearance of the atomists saw the development of Greek civilization to its highest point in art, literature and material culture. Empedocles, Anaxagoras and Leucippus lived during the golden age of Periclean Athens. But the confidence and optimism of this period were to be succeeded by a more sober mood. As the war of 1914, some two thousand years later, was to convert the extravagant optimism of Europe into a mixture of pessimism and confusion, so the Peloponnesian war of 431–04 B.C. transmuted the spirit of the Greeks. In the environment of recrimination which succeeded the Peloponnesian war in Athens, irreligion and economic materialism were most frequently cited by critics as the principal vices of the Greeks, and the greatest of the philosophers of the next two generations were particularly concerned with these problems. Socrates, the next great figure in philosophy, served as a soldier in that war, and his influence marked the emergence of ethics as a principal concern of the leading minds of Greece.

Nature had been the dominant object of philosophic thought during the period which has been reviewed. But the subject matter of philosophy came only gradually to be defined, and the title of philosopher was freely bestowed on anyone engaged in intellectual pursuits. Among the other intellectual pursuits to become prominent in the fifth century B.C. were the antecedents of the movement we call humanism, a movement inspired by the spread of an awareness among the Greeks of the uniqueness of their institutions as compared with those of peoples beyond their borders, and by the need for popular education in a democratic society. Sophism, as this movement was called, contested with natural philosophy for the attention of the intellectually-inclined young Greek of the mid-fifth century. Socrates was one of these who found natural philosophy dissatisfying and turned his attention to ethical and political philosophy. But in his later years he became disillusioned with the Sophistic emphasis on utility as a guide to human behaviour, criticized the Sophists' neglect of idealism in favour of a practicality which verged on cynicism, and took the first steps towards the creation of the idealistic ethics which we find fully developed in Plato and Aristotle.

The eclipse of natural philosophy of which the ascendency of Socrates was symptomatic proved to be only temporary. Socrates' student, Plato, returned to it in what is usually considered a somewhat light-hearted vein, but Plato's pupil, Aristotle, was no less important as a natural philosopher than in his thought on ethics and politics. He was probably the most influential writer on science that the world has yet seen.

After the deaths of Plato (347) and Aristotle (322), their teaching was continued at the Academy and the Lyceum, respectively, which became schools more nearly in the modern sense, with a succession of more-or-less notable masters extending over many centuries. Aristotle's immediate successor was Theophrastus, who has been noted as the author of the oldest extant treatise dealing with practical chemistry. In 308, Zeno of Citium, a Cyprian merchant resident in Athens, culminated an avocational pursuit of philosophy by founding the Stoic school, the name, like those of its predecessors, being taken from its meeting place. And two years later the fourth great school of this period was founded by Epicurus.

The climate of philosophy was no longer the same in fourth-century Greece. The development of ethical philosophy which Socrates had begun was accelerated as the political situation deteriorated, and especially after the death of Alexander the Great (323), when not only Athens, but Greece itself became a subordinate political region. The decline of belief in the traditional religion further accelerated the domination of ethics in philosophy, as did the trend towards specialization in natural science, which tended to remove it from the domain of philosophy.

Aristotle was probably the first scientific specialist, and it is a measure of his greatness that he accomplished this without ceasing to be a philosopher of the traditional sort. Shortly after him, we encounter the prototype of the modern scientist, for the typical Greek scientist after about 300 B.C. had little to do with ethical philosophy or with cosmological questions. But when we are concerned with the science of matter, we must remain with the philosophers, for the scientific experts of Hellenistic Greece were astronomers, mathematicians, anatomists and physiologists. And, curiously enough, one finds in the ethically-oriented Postsocratic schools of philosophy a deeper penetration into the question of the nature of matter than existed, so far as we know, among their cosmologically-oriented predecessors. Specifically, we find a series of attempts to explain the nature and interaction of the smallest parts of substances.

The Stoics and Epicurians, like Plato and Aristotle, both manifested a decided interest in physical questions, although the main tendencies of their physics were determined by their ethical point of view. Stoicism was materialistic in consequence of its ethical doctrine that virtue, the only 'good', is based on knowledge, and that knowledge consists in an agreement between mental conceptions and reality.[1] Hence rational study of nature was at the basis of Stoic ethics. Epicurianism, on the other hand, although the inheritor of atomism, was interested in nature in a way which was less conducive to its investigation. It employed itself with physics for the negative purpose of setting aside religious ideas upsetting to the quietude of man.[2] To this, atomistic physics was well suited, as it was to the Epicurian ethical view that man himself is, or should be, as independent of the world as the atom is of its fellows. This negative approach to nature further undermined the position of atomism, and in antiquity Epicurian atomism was regarded rather as the eccentric adjunct of a popular theory of morals than as a scientific explanation of the world.[3]

[1] Zeller, 1931: 229, 238.
[2] Cf. Windelband, 1901, Vol. I: 182. Zeller, 1931: 253.   [3] Bailey, 1928: 531-34.

Although we find these four philosophies existing as schools after 300 B.C., only one of them, the Stoic, shows significant further development. Atomism became the idiosyncrasy of an increasingly unpopular sect, and the Academics became worshippers at the shrine of Plato. Aristotle had as yet no such apotheosis among the Peripatetics, but the further development of his thought seems to have passed into the hands of the Stoics, whose most celebrated theorist, Chrysippus (c. 277–04 B.C.), flourished almost a century after the death of Zeno, the founder of Stoicism. It is ironic that we have less information on the natural philosophy of the Stoics than on that of Plato, for they were more interested in the subject and wrote more voluminously on it. Whereas all of Plato's works are preserved, only fragments of theirs remain. The Stoic natural philosophy which scholarship has reconstructed from fragments is principally that of Chrysippus, in whose time Athens was transformed into a cosmopolitan university town in which Plato and Aristotle were already established as the authorities to be reckoned with.

The new natural philosophy

While it may seem surprising, from the point of view of modern philosophy, to find the great ethical philosophers of antiquity so concerned with nature, it will be recalled that cosmology had been the cornerstone of all philosophy. After Socrates we find Presocratic natural philosophy supplemented rather than rejected. It remains nevertheless remarkable that philosophers primarily interested in ethics were able to go substantially beyond the cosmologists in their investigation of the science of matter. Their ability to do so seems ultimately due to their liberation from the Presocratic universal materialism.

The Presocratics never freed themselves from the point of view which regarded everything, even thought itself, as material. Hence the causes of change themselves became part of the thing to be explained. The atomists recognized, in the void, a non-material entity, but pure 'non-being' proved of limited help in explaining the workings of the world. The atoms had to account even for the substance of the gods, and the atomists, far from escaping the shackles of universal materialism, came to be particularly associated with

55

materialism. Their cause of change, the chance motion of atoms in the void, proved equally out of tune with the ancient predilection for teleology. The atomists were outside the mainstream of ancient natural philosophy, and those within it found another key to the differentiation of matter and cause, from what seems a most improbable source, the Socratic conception of 'the Good'.

Socrates' concept of 'the Good' was not evolved for the benefit of natural philosophy, but rather to separate from the evanescent world of change certain ethical concepts of eternal verity. Since change was pre-eminently the characteristic of matter ($\H{v}\lambda\eta$), the Good was rigorously defined as non-material.[4] But Plato, although he originally held a similarly limited conception of the Good, extended it, joining to it other ideal concepts, identified as Forms ($\iota\delta\epsilon\alpha\iota$), and in his dialogue *Timaeus* he finally transformed the idea of the Good into a whole world. In something of an inversion of the universal materialism of the Presocratics he considered the whole of the sensible world illusory and gave reality to a non-material, changeless world of Forms of which the sensible world is an imitation. Every sensible body in turn he regarded as an imperfect copy of a corresponding Form, thus bringing the concept of a real but non-material world of Forms into relationship with the sensible but not really existent world of matter (*Timaeus*, 28-9).

The recognition of such an entity as 'mathematics' as outside of the realm of nature led Plato, and after him Aristotle, to redefine the subject matters of natural philosophy. The discussion of the existent and the non-existent, and of the changing and the unchanging, was to be the basis for a system of classification, by implication in Plato, and overtly in Aristotle. It can be inferred from Plato's *Timaeus* that

> The world of Forms is . . . existent and unchanging.
> The sensible world is . . . non-existent and changing.

He differentiated the changing from the unchanging on the basis of

[4] Socrates was inspired to counter the tendency of the Sophists to regard good and evil as relative concepts, which he saw as the root of the immorality of his time (cf. Windelband, 1901: Vol. 1: 69). Socrates left no writing. We know him from Xenophon and especially from the dialogues of Plato. Since much of the Platonic 'Socrates' seems to have originated with Plato, it remains uncertain how much originated with Socrates. That the idea of the Good, and the rudiments of the system of Forms, originated with him seems certain (A. E. Taylor, 1933: 163-70), although the roots of the dichotomy between the world of the Forms and that of the senses is traceable to Parmenides (cf. Kirk and Raven, 1957: 270-1).

those properties associated by earlier philosophers with 'matter',[5] but was less clear on the differentiation of the existent from the non-existent. The word existence proved, for Plato, to be a term of broader implication than mere physical existence, and his idea that the sensible world is non-existent was related to his evaluation of its importance relative to that of the world of Forms. It did not exist 'in a full sense'.[6]

Corresponding to the absolute world of Forms there is an absolute science, mathematics, and it is the burden of the *Timaeus* to explore the possibility of using this science, with the aid of 'probability' (sensory evidence), to construct a plausible explanation of the sensible world. The less imaginative Aristotle objected specifically to the world of Forms and, in general, to the entire Platonic scheme (*On the heavens*, 299–300). But he was a student of Plato, and we find him proposing, on the same basis of existence and change, an entirely different system of classification. According to Aristotle:

> Metaphysics is . . . existent and unchanging,
>
> mathematics is . . . non-existent and unchanging,
>
> physics is . . . existent and changing,
>
> and he rejects the possibility of an entity . . . non-existent and changing.[7]

And so the functions of Plato's world of Forms were subsumed in metaphysics (a term coined by Aristotle) and mathematics, and the dichotomy between the Ideal and the sensible worlds was given for the first time a fully significant physical meaning. Change remained the essential and peculiar characteristic of the sensible world.

These resolutions of the problem of 'matter' enabled Plato and Aristotle each to construct a cosmology which was to a degree free of the Presocratic dilemmas. In effect, they separated from cosmology, by making them peripheral problems, the questions of the primal material and of such elusive entities as light, electricity, and magnetism. But this is not to say that they made no attempt to elucidate those questions.

[5] Cf. Aristotle's criticism (*On the heavens*, 299a), and Cornford's remarks on the commentary of Proclus (1937: 183–4).

[6] *Timaeus*, 52 c. Cf. Cornford, 1937: 24, 193–4.

[7] *Metaphysics*, 1025b–1026a. He uses the term motion rather than change, but the two seem interchangeable (cf. *Physics*, 200b). The definition of mathematics applied to only 'some parts of mathematics'. There is also a 'more physical' part of mathematics (*Physics*, 194a).

Since the sensible world of Plato's *Timaeus* is illusory, it can have no real primal material. He accounts for the apparent materiality of things by supposing that his Maker somehow induces a manifestation of triangular forms in 'space' (χώρα), which forms coalesce, according to the rules of solid geometry, to form solid figures which we recognize as the four elements (*Timaeus*, 49–52). His denial of the reality of matter does not seem to have constituted a categorical denial of materiality.[8]

Plato's essay towards the mathematization of nature was really subject to the same objections as had been the earlier attempts of the Pythagoreans. Aristotle expresses those objections (*Metaphysics*, 990b–993a), and attempts to get rid of the primal material by showing that an understanding of·it is unessential to natural philosophy. He notes (*On gen.*, 329) that 'in a certain sense' the substratum of any kind of change is 'matter' insofar as that process is concerned. 'The so-called elements' are thus in a sense the matter of sensible things. Their own substratum has no 'separate' existence; properly speaking it has no properties but materiality. It manifests itself in the elements because it is always bound up with 'the contrarieties' (ποιότητες), as he calls the four qualities he holds to be prior to all others, namely hot, cold, wet and dry. The Presocratics had given these particular qualities importance beyond the others,[9] but no connotation of energy. Aristotle substituted them for Empedocles' love and strife

---

[8] To provide a place for the sensible world Plato postulates a 'receptacle' or 'nurse', which he finally identifies as 'space'. This space differs from that of Newtonian physics not only in being finite (it is merely a place for the world), but in being endowed with some of the properties of matter. Form and space do have real existences. Form is non-material, but space not certainly so. Within it 'that which resembles Form, but is sensible' is somehow 'brought into existence'. It is like a mirror image, 'clinging in some sort to existence on pain of being nothing at all'. From what was it made? Aristotle believed Plato to be saying that matter and space are the same (*Physics*, 209b). The modern authorities, Zeller, Rivaud, Taylor, and Cornford, are all agreed that it was made from Plato's space, which, indeed, was filled with qualities. This 'nurse of becoming' is the scene of every sort of diverse appearance to the sight, 'continuously moved and perpetually being separated just as things are separated by means of a winnowing basket'. Among the diverse appearances are vestiges of the nature of fire, air, water, and earth, and out of this confluence of qualities the god, when the ordering of the universe was taken in hand, gave distinct configuration to the elements 'by means of shapes and numbers' (*Timaeus*, 52–53 [Cornford's translation]). See also Zeller, 1922: 740. Cornford, 1937: 177–203; A. E. Taylor, 1956: 456–7. Rivaud (1925: 65–7) concludes that Plato, like Descartes, identified substance with extension.

[9] Kirk and Raven, 1957: 329.

as a kind of energetic agency of the Maker in inducing the manifestations of the elements.[10] Some of Aristotle's successors were to
attempt their mathematization, giving them something like the
significance of the triangles in Plato's cosmology, and others were
to substitute the qualities for the elements themselves. Perhaps their
most immediate function was in removing men's minds even further
from the vexing problem of the primal material.

If the primal material was a logically-essential concept which was
elusive to empirical definition, light, electricity and magnetism were
empirical facts which seemed to resist any general conceptual scheme.
Plato's differentiation of reason from 'probability' (observation) and
Aristotle's distinction between perception and sensation freed them
from the necessity of regarding such psychic phenomena as 'knowing' as natural phenomena, but light (which served as a prototype
for electricity and magnetism) remained somehow within that
necessity. Plato and Aristotle provided explanations outside of their
cosmologies. Plato postulated an uninflammable fire, emitted by the
eye, as the material of light (*Timaeus*, 45b). Aristotle denied this,
substituting for it 'the diaphanous' (διαφανές), a fluid of even more
uncertain composition, a substratum of visibility which only manifests itself in the presence of the fiery element.[11]

Light, however, had been not only a problem to be explained,
but a source of explanation in cosmology. Its setting aside was to
leave a vacancy in the armoury of the natural philosopher, but this
one was to be filled by substituting not merely another equally troublesome entity, but one which was to be generally accepted to fulfil
the functions, without suffering their defects, of those which had
been abolished. This species of being, a rarefied, intangible,
and essentially hypothetical fluid, is foreshadowed in Aristotle's
diaphanous, and in the ether[12] with which he filled the heavens.
These, however, were fluids of limited function. More versatile
varieties were postulated soon after Aristotle, the most important
being the pneuma of the Stoics. Such fluids, frequently under the

[10] *On generation and corruption*, 329-30. On the relativity of Aristotelian 'matter' see Ross,
1959: 76. G. Boas, 1959: 35, 59n. 12.

[11] *On the soul*, 418b; *On the senses*, 439a. See also Hoppe, 1926: 8.

[12] *On the heavens*, 270b. On the resemblance between the diaphanous and the ether, as
conceived by Aristotle, see Beare, 1906: 58.

generic title of 'emanations', were to perform yeoman service to science as recently as the 'Newtonian' ether of our own grandparents.

If they did not originate the practice of 'neglecting' unessential (and often unanswerable) questions, Plato and Aristotle here show their ability to make use of it. If their solutions to the problems of the primal material and light remained imperfect and precarious, it will be evident from a further examination of their thought on the constitution of things that they had put themselves into a position to pursue something very like the modern chemist's science of matter. That they and their successors were able to debate the 'fine structure' of things owed much to their differentiation of material from non-material phenomena, to their success in separating physics from other areas of nature study, and to their reduction of cosmology to a set of manageable necessary questions.

Postsocratic cosmologies

Plato sought to bridge the gap between his two worlds through mathematics, and found the key in the theorems of harmonic proportions and in those of the five regular solids. The former was particularly utilized in his astronomy, while the latter gave him the key to the science of matter. From the outset his exposition shows the ingenious way in which he combines reason and probability. He takes as the primary manifestations of the sensible world the four Empedoclean elements, and holds it to be obvious that they are bodies, have depth, and are therefore bounded by surfaces. He poses the question as to the most perfect bodies which can be constructed, four in number, unlike one another, but such that some can be 'generated out of one another by resolution'. He answers this question by assuming as the most perfect bodies four of the five regular solid figures, the tetrahedron (pyramid), octahedron, icosahedron and cube, and showing how the surfaces of which they are constructed can be made up of two basic triangles, the right-angled isosceles and the right-angled scalene.[13]

[13] *Timaeus*, 31–2, 53c–d. Plato uses the fifth figure, the dodecahedron, 'for the whole, adorning it with constellations' (55c, Taylor's translation). It could not be formed from either of the simple triangles. The cultivation of the five regular solids is 'Pythagorean', although their formulation may have actually occurred in Plato's own time (Rivaud, 1925: 24, 81–2. Mugler, 1960: 246).

The *Timaeus* is something of an anomaly in the body of Plato's work, and it has often been represented as not seriously intended. It is not likely, however, that a scheme so carefully worked out could have been meant merely as a joke. More sympathetic authorities have seen it as an essay on the construction of an ideal cosmos, as a counterpart to Plato's ideal state, and Mugler has recently pointed out that cosmology was actually a recurrent theme in Plato's writings.[14] Within the context of his view of the relativity of mundane knowledge – he calls his cosmology 'a probable account' (*Timaeus* 57D) – Plato surely intended the *Timaeus* to be taken seriously. That he was less of a dogmatist than Aristotle (or than Kepler, whose mathematical inspiration so strikingly resembles his own) should not be used to deprive him of the credit for a scientific endeavour.

Despite Plato's picture of his Maker 'winnowing' out of chaos first the elementary triangles, then the Empedoclean elements, and finally sensible things (*Timaeus*, 52–3) it is difficult to picture a geometrically-constructed universe as other than a kind of gigantic crystal. But he cannot have it so, for change is the pre-eminent characteristic of the sensible world, and he goes on to picture the four elements as continuously dissolving into their constituent triangles. The small size and sharp edges of the fire particles enable them to intrude themselves into masses of water and air, cutting, disrupting, and hence causing transmutation of their particles. On the other hand he concludes, less graphically, that a small minority of fire particles can be overwhelmed by the others and themselves transmuted (*Timaeus*, 56–7).

All of these motions take place in a universe in which there is no void, as did, indeed, the corresponding processes in the universes of Aristotle, the Stoics, and the overwhelming majority of all cosmologists who opted for the continuum against the atomists. The vortex mechanism, which was prominent in Presocratic thought and emerges with equal prominence in Descartes, is not stressed by Plato, but is probably to be assumed. Such non-atomic corpuscularianism was the rule among cosmologists who denied the void, and seems not even to have been a point of contention.

Nevertheless Plato's very success in correlating the structure of

[14] Mugler, 1960.

the two worlds through mathematics leaves little room in which to manoeuvre his imagination towards the explanation of the transitory condition of the sensible world. He infers an explanation, without actually providing one, in regarding the world as an organism, and hence endowed with 'soul'. And yet his world soul itself proves to be a mathematically derived entity, and seems to have as its chief function the explanation of the regularities of astronomy.[15] In the last analysis, there is little between the world and the Maker upon whose activity its functioning depends.[16] In his *Epinomis*, a later work than *Timaeus*, Plato resorts to the ether as a substantial connection to the Maker, and peoples it with 'spirits' or 'demons' (δαίμονες) who occupy themselves with the details of the work.[17] In a sense this was an admission of defeat in Plato's cosmological enterprise, but we must recognize that he was wrestling with some of the most difficult problems natural science has to face. In adducing for their solution his Maker, the world soul, and the celestial emanations, he was striking out in a direction which most of his successors have seen fit to follow.

Aristotle, who was neither inclined towards Pythagorean numerology nor satisfied with a mere 'probable account' of nature, abolished Plato's dichotomy between ideal and sensible worlds. Mathematics, which for Plato had formed the bridge between the two worlds, is put by Aristotle entirely outside of natural philosophy. He then establishes his own dichotomy by subdividing physics into portions which deal with the perishable (the earth) and the imperishable (the heavens), the latter being subject only to a special type of change, circular movement, and involving a special type of otherwise unchangeable matter, the ether (*On the heavens*, 269a–270b). Thus Aristotle delineates the province of the science of matter with relative precision as tangible, terrestrial phenomena.

For the analysis of the perishable earth, the limits of which he

[15] *Timaeus*, 34–6. The composition of the world soul out of three kinds of 'existence', in accordance with the theory of harmonic proportions, is the second detailed application of mathematics to nature in the *Timaeus*.

[16] Cf. Rivaud, 1925: 35. The forms are intermediate causes (see *Phaedo*, 100; Aristotle, *Metaphysics*, 991b), but in the static sense of 'formula', corresponding to Aristotle's formal cause.

[17] Plato, 1927: 450–61. Subordinate divinities are also more than hinted at in *Timaeus*, 69.

sets at the sphere of the moon, Aristotle accepted the Empedoclean elements and, like Plato, he held them to be both the building blocks of nature and mutually transmutable among themselves. As an immediate cause of their interactions he adopted the afore-mentioned contrarieties (hot, cold, wet and dry). In his book *On generation and corruption* he alludes twice to three 'originative sources' of terrestrial transmutations ('coming-to-be'). The first reference (329a) mentions matter, the contrarieties, and the contraries (the four elements). He emphasizes that the latter are 'less' originative, and when he returns later on (335a) to originative sources he omits the elements altogether, mentioning Form (which he equates to the contrarieties), matter, and a third which is truly revolutionary. 'Vaguely dreamed of by all of our predecessors, it is the sun's motion along the inclined circle [that is, its north–south seasonal change of position] . . . that causes coming-to-be and passing-away.' Through the mechanism of the concentric spheres of (Aristotle's) heaven this motion is carried back to its ultimate source, the Maker. Whereas Plato, at least until his *Epinomis*, found nothing more tangible than his world soul to act between the Maker and 'things', Aristotle, using the sun's motion as a fulcrum, provided a mechanism to fill the gap between the Maker and the changing sensible world. In his view the rotation of the heavens is transformed by the sun's more complex periodic movement into a motion recognizable in the immediate realm of sublunary nature, an upward and downward movement. He associates specific movements with specific elements, upward with fire and air and downward with water and earth. It is the fact of the seasonal approach and retreat of the sun which prevents any final condition of stability in the interaction of the elements (*On gen.*, 336a–337a).

The Stoic natural philosophy was put together over a longer period of time, and principally after Plato and Aristotle had joined the Presocratics as 'ancient' authors. There is some question, however, as to whether or not it was ever really 'formulated', for the Stoics often appear to have been less concerned with propounding a doctrine than with merely suggesting a fruitful line of thought. In general they aimed at the abolition of the Platonic–Aristotelian dualism between nature and the supernatural; they regarded the cosmos as a single whole, and considered matter not only to be really existent, but to be the fundamental manifestation of nature.[18] Influenced by these general considerations, and by some acute criticism of the details of Aristotelian theory, they proposed a variant cosmology, replete both with new ideas and new contradictions, which was not to be lost with the Stoic writings of antiquity, for much of it was to become a part of the 'Aristotelianism' of the Middle Ages, and of alchemy.

The Stoic view, as it has come down to us, seems to be chiefly that of Chrysippus, who lived at a time when Aristotelian ideas were current, but had not yet been organized into a body of doctrine. Starting with the Empedoclean–Aristotelian idea of the elements, he modified it in such a way as to equate it to the Heraclitan view of fire as the primordial element. He associated only one contrariety (against Aristotle's two) with each of the elements, but held that one of the elements, fire, was actually the primal material. Fire is the basis of the other three elements, which are formed from it by increasing degrees of condensation, fire, itself, being reformed through its own action on earth.[19] This fire, however, as befitted a primal material, was less clearly involved in the operation of the cosmos than was another material, pneuma.

Pneuma ($\pi\nu\varepsilon\tilde{\upsilon}\mu\alpha$) was a venerable term signifying, variously, air, breath, and soul. Anaximenes had elevated it to the status of an important manifestation of his primal material, 'air', and it played an important part in the biology of the later Peripatetics, if not of Aristotle himself. He had used the word to designate gases or 'rarefied' air. The Stoics made it a compound of their elementary fire and air and gave it a role which more or less combined those of Aristotle's ether and Plato's world soul, although Stoic philosophy appears designed to combat Aristotle, who, we may imagine, was in late antiquity a more formidable adversary in natural philosophy than was Plato. The Stoic pneuma was the most versatile of emanations, a dynamic medium used not only to fill empty space and to explain astrophysical phenomena, but to explain cohesion and change among bodies on earth.[20]

Stoicism was a casualty of the philosophical wars of the early

[18] Windelband, 1901, Vol. 1: 180. Zeller, 1931: 233.
[19] Plutarch, 1795–1830, Vol. 4: 536 (De placitis philosophorum). Cf. Brehier, 1951: 135–40
[20] Sambursky, 1959. Brehier, 1951: 120–2.

Christian era, and few Stoic writings survived the Middle Ages. In more recent times the popularity of atomism has caused the Stoics to become even more obscure. In antiquity, however, they had the good fortune not to be followed by critics as acute as themselves, and their ideas had an influence which is only now being discovered. We now see that the loss of Stoic thought in natural philosophy was not so great as had been supposed, for much of it was integrated with Aristotelian philosophy in the early Christian era and subsequently passed for part of Peripatetic doctrine. It blurred Aristotle's dualism of heaven and earth, and thus made his doctrine more palatable to Christian and Moslem philosophers whose interest in establishing physical connections between these two extremes was not less than had been that of the Stoics. Chrysippus was not the last Stoic, and his successors continued to develop his germinal ideas for connecting heaven and earth through the pneuma. In this the greatest landmark seems to have been posted by Posidonius (c. 135 B.C.–c. 51 B.C.), who adapted the pneuma to the celestial mechanism of astrology, and established a chain not only of being but of substance between things and the First Cause. This was to prove appealing both to the student of 'things' and to the theologian. The late Stoic predilection for fire as an immediate cause and for the planets as remote causes goes far to explain their influence on the alchemist.

Although atomism of all of the philosophies of late antiquity remained most faithful to its Presocratic origins, it was a passive and somewhat perfunctory allegiance. Epicurus, as we shall subsequently see, made modifications in detail which seem to represent an attempt to reconcile atomism with certain generally agreed upon aspects of cosmology, notably with the Empedoclean elements. But the natural philosophy of Epicurus was distinctly ancillary to his ethics, and his successors were progressively to relax the rigidity of atomic natural philosophy to the point where it became virtually indistinguishable from the philosophies it opposed.[21]

---

[21] This is exemplified by Themison (31 B.C.–A.D 14.) the founder of Methodism, an atomic school of medicine. In explaining biochemistry by means of atoms and pores he made his doctrine more dependent upon the latter than on the former. It resembled Empedocles as much as it did Democritus (Allbutt, 1921: 192–4).

Chapter Four

Microphysics in antiquity

THE works of Plato and Aristotle reveal philosophies of nature in which cosmological generalization is accompanied by a significant attempt at the analysis of the questions of detail upon which cosmology ultimately rests. Since theirs are the earliest philosophical writings to survive in large part, it may be that the extent of their innovation is exaggerated; and yet it seems likely that the redefinition and reclassification of the subject matters of philosophy, for which Plato and Aristotle are to be credited, was an essential precondition to the effective discussion of detail in those areas of natural science which come to us under such names as astronomy, biology, physics, and chemistry.

It is not possible to give here a full account of the differentiation of these special sciences, which was the work of many centuries. It seems clear that Aristotle first gave physics a restricted meaning approaching that which we attach to it. It is equally clear that he did not differentiate chemistry, but left it essentially embedded in physics. That is to say, he equated motion and change, and regarded the movement of large bodies and chemical change as two aspects of the same phenomenon. Their rejection of atomism was a rejection of the void, not of particles, and neither Plato, Aristotle, nor their successors ever lacked particles upon which to base an analysis of nature.[1] The term 'microphysics', which has been coined in the twentieth century to characterize the physics of 'the atomic and corpuscular state',[2] seems well suited to describe that part of the

---

[1] Cf. A. Maier, 1949: 159, 179ff.
[2] De Broglie, 1955: preface.

cosmologies of Plato and Aristotle which is concerned with what we now call chemistry.

In working out the details of his geometric universe, Plato initiated the serious consideration of the fine structure of matter. Having through triangles, elicited by his Maker from space, accounted for matter without accepting its existence, he proceeds to an analysis of the differences between bodies in the sensible world. The evidence upon which he bases this analysis comes from both worlds, through reasoning on the ideal world of Forms, and through observation of the sensible world. He refers to the latter as 'probability'. Although he is by no means as dogmatic as Aristotle (his being merely a probable account) his evidences rarely, if ever, come into conflict, perhaps because he gives primacy to the ideal world, and only introduces evidence from the sensible world to support it. This is exemplified in his analysis of the forms of the elements, where he adds 'probability' to 'genuine reason' and takes the 'sharp pointed' pyramid for fire and the 'stable' cube for earth (*Timaeus*, 56a–b). He shows that the cube can be made up of right-angled isosceles triangles, while the other three solids (tetrahedron, octahedron, icosahedron) can be formed of right-angled scalene triangles. This is too simple a system for our variegated world, however, and he goes on to evoke different kinds of particles of each element, differing in the size of the triangles involved. For each triangle he postulates three sizes, and declares that they can form solid figures through any combination; that different-sized triangles, for example, can form solid figures of several different kinds of fire. He here regards light and fire as exemplifying different kinds of fire, and water and molten metal as two different kinds of water (*Timaeus*, 57c–d, 58).

Although Plato's references to substances elsewhere indicate that he was familiar with most of the materials in the repertoire of the contemporary practical chemist,[3] only a few of the most common-place substances are referred to in the cosmological analysis of *Timaeus*. That a pioneer theorist should utilize few examples perhaps

[3] He professes to be familiar with the gold production process in *Statesman* (303d), and elsewhere mentions gold, silver, copper, iron, 'aurichalcum' (without defining it), copper rust, iron rust, gypsum, common salt, natron, white lead, sulphur, and a number of precious stones. See Lippmann, 1913: 37–40.

requires no special explanation, but it is worth noting that Plato's cosmological geometry is coincidentally limited in the direction of inorganic nature. From the mutual conflict of the elements through which he brings about change, the element earth stands aloof, its particles not being adapted to transmutation into the other elements because they are constructed of a different kind of triangle (isosceles). From the point of view of chemistry, Plato's 'probable account' is curiously weakened because of his neglect of 'earth'. Even allowing for his elimination of the metals (regarded as forms of water) from this category of body, the limited number of transmutations possible within the different-sized earth cubes seems hardly adequate to account for the numerous stones and earths familiar from practical chemistry.

Another obstacle to the further elucidation of chemistry was Plato's acceptance of the mutual transmutability of the Empedoclean elements, whereby he obligated himself to include the elements themselves among the 'things' to be analysed. In modern terminology we would say that he started with sub-atomic chemistry. His analysis of structure, moreover, leaves the difference between the structure of the elements and the structures of compounds largely to our imagination; nor has he anything to say of intermediate degrees of structural complexity between the simplest compounds and more complicated things, although he undoubtedly acknowledged, as had his predecessors, that such intermediate compounded states existed.[4] Aristotle, who faced the same obstacles, found an escape from them by approaching the whole subject from the point of view of change.

Beyond the simplest compounds a conception of compounded matter is inextricably bound up with the concurrent conception of chemical change. In regarding the elements as transmutable, while continuing to consider them somehow as elements, Plato and Aristotle in effect transferred the whole problem of chemistry to their discussions of change. But Plato never seriously addressed himself to this kind of change, and he left his analysis of structure where we find it in *Timaeus*. Aristotle, on the other hand, made

---

[4] Plato is criticized by Aristotle for failing to bring intermediate structures into his analysis (*On gen.*, 315a), but the existence of such structures was recognized even by the earliest Greek philosophers.

change a subject of particular interest, to a degree that he scarcely has any names for the end-products of change.[5] Nevertheless he was able, almost as a by-product, to penetrate more deeply into the problem of structure.

The role of Aristotle's classification of motions in misdirecting dynamics has often been discussed, and the attention given this macrophysical topic has tended to obscure the fact that he gave equal (if not more) attention to microphysical motions and changes. Here he was more successful in redirecting a discourse of conflicting terminologies into what was to prove a more fruitful direction. The crucial term in the ideology of change was γένεσις, which has usually been translated 'coming-to-be'.[6] The term was tied to cosmogony and ontology, and had been a principal target of the Eleatic criticism. Aristotle was to be much preoccupied with it. He is fond of pointing out the relativity of terms, and in his *Physics* (190) he remarks that coming-to-be may be understood in several different senses; by change of shape, as a statue; by addition (προσθέσει), as things which grow; by putting together (συνθέσει), as a house; and by alteration (ἀλλοίωσις), as things which 'turn' in respect to their material substance. Again, in *On generation and corruption*, his special work on coming-to-be, he makes a qualified denial of the Eleatic claim that coming-to-be necessarily signifies coming-to-be out of nothing. The term, he holds, may also be understood to signify a change in which one entity comes-to-be through the simultaneous passing-away of another entity, thus leaving the question of 'being' out of consideration (*On gen.*, 317).

Aristotle finds his predecessors, lacking this distinction, engaged in a confused effort directed at the redefinition of change in an attempt to escape the Eleatic criticism. He finds Anaxagoras talking about 'alteration' (ἀλλοίωσις), Empedocles speaking of 'mixture' (μίξις), and the atomists using the term 'association' (σύνκρασις) He denies the justification of equating any of these to coming-to-be, since the last two imply the persistence in the end of particles of the

---

[5] The term homoeomeries (ὁμοιομερῆ – 'things with like parts') is employed by Aristotle and attributed by him to Anaxagoras, but it is not much used in Aristotle's analysis, which is written in terms of changes, alteration, mixing, etc.

[6] Aristotle usually uses pairs of terms, coming-to-be and passing-away, association and disassociation, etc. For the sake of readability I have eliminated the coordinate term where the sense does not require it.

ingredients, while alteration involves only a change in qualities (*On gen.*, 314–5). In pressing his analysis further, however, Aristotle discovers a conception even more subtle. He has found in the complex periodic motion of the sun a connection between the rotation of the heavens and the linear motions characteristic of sublunary nature. Coming still closer to earth he finds another connection between the up and down motions of the elements and changes on the microphysical level. This is through 'contact', a necessary condition in a cosmology which does not admit empty space, but one which Aristotle finds to have further implications. Since 'all things which touch one another will have weight or lightness' he argues that their relationship may be regarded as one of 'acting' and 'suffering' (*On gen.*, 323a), and this leads him, after a further lengthy rationalization, to postulate another degree of change less complete than coming-to-be, which involves the destruction of the ingredients, and more complete than any change in which the ingredients persist unaltered. This kind of change, which he defines as 'a unification of the ingredients resulting from their alteration' (*On gen.*, 328b22)[7] is one in which the compound exists actually but the ingredients only potentially. As a name for this newly defined kind of change he adopts one of the older terms, mixis(μίξις), which he appears to see in a new context, not that of association and alteration, with which he has begun, but that of certain other terms which had more or less synonymously signified mixing, compounding or blending. From this time discussions of change on the level of chemistry were to be conducted on the basis of these terms. Unfortunately for science, if not for philosophy, there were at least six virtual synonyms for mixis.[8]

Aristotle's argument is studded with exemplifications, but, like

---

[7] 'Η δὲ μίξις τῶν μικτῶν ἀλλοιωθέντων ἔνωσις.

[8] krasis (κρᾶσις) mixing, compounding, blending
synkrasis (σύγκρασις) mixing together, blending, tempering
synkrisis (σύγκρισις) putting together, compounding
synchysis (σύγχυσις) mixing together, blending, confounding
synthesis (σύνθεσις) putting together, compounding
mixis (μίξις) mixing, mingling

The dictionary definitions in the right-hand column give little clue to the use of these terms in Greek natural philosophy. Much light is cast on the question by Wolfson (1956) and Solmsen (1960), but I am aware of no thorough-going philological analysis of the Greek terminology of 'mixing'.

Plato, he only occasionally makes use of what we would call chemical phenomena.[9] Mixis was to be the touchstone of those who later sought chemistry in Aristotelian philosophy, and their instinct was surely right. But of this still unformed and unnamed science he had only a dim awareness. The production of fire by piling logs onto an already burning fire is 'growth' (αὔξησις), but when the logs themselves are set on fire, that is coming-to-be (On gen., 322a). The fact that in an alloy of tin and 'bronze' (copper) 'The tin almost vanishes, behaving as if it were an immaterial property of the bronze' leads him to consider this an example of mixis, but an analogous example, in which a drop of wine is placed in 'ten thousand measures' of water is no mixis, 'for its form is dissolved and it changes so as to merge in the total volume of water' (On gen., 328).[10]

It would appear that Aristotle's conception of chemical change, when first arrived at, was still obscured by its involvement with his metaphysical theories of causation. Having started with his famous classification of causes, he had moved, in On generation and corruption, to a concentration on the 'efficient cause', and out of this arose his intermingled doctrines of privation, actuality and potentiality, and agent and patient. In a later work, Meteorology, he has clearly settled as far as changes in mundane nature are concerned on the contrarieties, hot, cold, wet and dry. To connect them with the doctrine of action and passivity he here emphasizes their alleged division into active (hot and cold) and passive (wet and dry), and exemplifies their interaction through changes from both animate and inanimate nature. His most systematic discussion is concerned with processes effected by the active qualities, hot and cold. He directs his attention to 'concoctions' (πέψις) differentiated along biological lines as ripening (πέπανσις), boiling (ἕψησις) and broiling (ὄπτησις), and

9 Aristotle's familiarity with materials was probably equal to that of his student, Theophrastus. Cf. Lippmann, 1913: 100–13.

10 Wolfson (1956: 374–79) believes the union resulting when one ingredient is present in overwhelming proportion to be a third type (differing from σύνθεσις and μίξις), to which Aristotle gave no specific name. This type, which Wolfson calls 'union of predominance', was the only union which the Church Fathers found appropriate to describe the Incarnation. The Fathers gave it various names, notably συνάφεια (conjunction). It seems to me questionable, however, that Aristotle had discovered yet another category of change, as Wolfson believes. It is only certain that he was experiencing the usual difficulties of the theorist in fitting fact to experience. Aristotle does give names (αὔξησις or μίξις) to three of the four cases cited by Wolfson as examples of union of predominance. (On gen., 321–322a, 328).

with three opposites to these (*Meteor.*, 379b–381b). Medicine and cooking provide most of the examples of changes brought about by heat, although cupellation of gold is described as an example of boiling, and wine fermentation is described as a concoction without assigning it to any of the three types. Insofar as they are exemplified at all, the opposites to ripening, boiling and broiling, required by his conception of cold as an active quality, are illustrated from the bio-medical theory of humours.

Consideration of the passive qualities, dry and moist, leads Aristotle into an extended discussion of solidification and its opposite, which may be condensation, melting, or, occasionally, solution. This is principally devoted to speculations on the relative proportions of water and earth, the typically moist and typically dry elements, in various solid and liquid materials. Whether a substance is 'solidified' by heat (through evaporation) or cold (through freezing) carries much weight in this analysis. He is troubled by the fact that olive oil is thickened by both heat and cold, and finally explains it by an alleged accession of air (*Meteor.*, 383a–384b).

Some of these subjects, although barely touched upon by Aristotle, exemplify his astonishing influence, for they established doctrines which were to prevail for nearly two millennia. His classification of animal digestion as a process like unto cooking-by-boiling led to a near-fatal complexity in the hands of Galen, who, in controversy with those who held the view that animal tissues and organs were preformed in food, endeavoured to support the Aristotelian view by citing 'what the stomach contains, phlegm, bile, pneuma, heat', and the influence of 'the adjacent viscera, like a lot of burning hearths around a great cauldron'.[11] One of the most remarkable examples of the influence of Aristotle's least remarks is at the very end of Book 3 of his *Meteorology* where, after an extended discussion of phenomena occurring above the earth's surface, he takes brief note of sub-surface phenomena, the formation of metals and homogeneous minerals ('Fossiles'), such as sulphur and certain other stones. He remarks that they are formed, respectively, by 'vaporous' and 'smoky' exhalations, developed within the earth's interior, and brought by heat and dryness to their mineral condition (*Meteor.* 378a). This cursory notice, partly in contradiction to his general

[11] Galen, 1916: 251–5.

theories and partly irrelevant to them, had still to be reckoned with by mineralogists of the eighteenth century.

The consideration of microphysics was continued by the Stoics. Chrysippus held that there are two varieties of mixis, instead of the one propounded by Aristotle. These are that in which the substances are actually altered, which he called 'synchysis' (σύγχυσις), and that in which the substances interpenetrate while retaining their specific properties. The latter was called *krasis di holon* (κρᾶσις δι' ὅλον, total mixture) and exemplified by the case of the drop of wine. The drop of wine would not change to water, according to Chrysippus, in Aristotle's ten thousand measures of water, nor even in the whole ocean, but would merely expand to distribute itself throughout that volume.[12] Thus he would appear to have advanced the physico-chemical conception of 'solution'.

It is questionable, however, that Chrysippus' ideas derived from any profound interest in the science of matter. One cannot fail to note that his preoccupation with 'total' mixture is in sharp contrast to his indifference to chemical compound, which he seems to define in a negative way for the purpose of clarifying total mixture,[13] and that conception appears to be intended to exemplify in nature the manner in which the pneuma is supposed to be distributed through all things. Most of the attacks which were made on Chrysippus' doctrine of compounds and mixtures bear on a point which would hardly occur to a modern chemist. The doctrine of total mixture was believed to violate the principle that two bodies could not occupy the same place at the same time, for Chrysippus was reported to have held, and certainly did as far as the pneuma was concerned, that the interpenetration of one body by another in total mixture did not increase the volume of the body penetrated.[14]

A consideration of Stoic ideas of causation raises similar questions.

[12] Brehier, 1951: 125–6. Sambursky, 1959: 13.

[13] Chrysippus' doctrine is presented principally in terms of his definition of total mixture (*krasis di holon*), by Philo, 1932: 110–13; Plutarch, 1795–1830, Vol. 5: 398–402 (*Adversus Stoicos de communibus notitiis*); Alexander of Aphrodisias, 1549: 63v and Stobaeus, in SVF, Vol. 2: 153. There is general agreement that the phenomena given the name 'mixis' by Aristotle often involve the destruction of the ingredients, and should be called 'synchysis', in the sense of fusion or confusion. Philo's occasion for mentioning it is his desire to elucidate the 'confusion of tongues' by analogy with other kinds of confusion!

[14] Plutarch, loc. cit. Plotinus, 1924: 91–2 ('On total mixture', *Enneads*, Bk II, 7, 1). Alexander of Aphrodisias, 1549: 63v. This difficulty arises in the context of belief that the world

73

They reinterpreted Aristotle's doctrine of agent and patient in such a way that their agent and patient more resemble his form and matter, with form as well as matter being endowed with materiality. They thus come up with a duality which is not between the supernatural and the natural, but between two kinds of matter. One of these is the primal material; the other, their pneuma, is the form-giving agency, and, more specifically than in Plato and Aristotle, the *cause* of things.[15] Above all it is the cause of their coherence, of those intervals of stability when matter has the form of a particular thing. This function of pneuma is called 'tonos' ($\tau\acute{o}\nu o\varsigma$).[16] But the pneuma has other functions, and there are different kinds of pneuma (pneumata) corresponding to these different functions.[17] The sum of the activities of these pneumata is the physical state of a thing, for which they use the term hexis ($\H{\epsilon}\xi\iota\varsigma$, state). They seem to have balanced hexis against physis, applying the former to inorganic things and the latter to the organic.[18]

On the other hand, the Stoic exemplifications of mixis include Aristotle's few chemical phenomena, and a few more physico-chemical examples, the dispersal of incense in air, the dispersal of finely divided gold in drugs and other cases of drug compounding, and the distribution of heat in heated iron.[19] The inclusion of such examples surely belies any assertion that the science of matter was not involved. However secondary it may have been in his thought, Chrysippus was surely wrestling with questions which were first given a more satisfactory solution by the nineteenth-century molecular hypothesis. A typical nineteenth-century definition of the molecule is that which describes it as the smallest mass into which a substance can be divided without destroying its identity. The chemist arrived at this definition, according to Ostwald, in pondering the first questions to which he must address himself in considering

---

is a plenum and matter a continuum. That none of these critics points out that atomism was free of this difficulty is suggestive of the disregard for that theory in late antiquity.

[15] Plutarch, 1795–1830, Vol. 4: 550 (*De placitis philosophorum*). Cf. Brehier, 1951: 115–8.

[16] On 'tonos' see Brehier, 1951: 120; Sambursky, 1959: 5. The term originally signified bands, cords, or ties.

[17] The composition of various pneumata out of various combinations of fire and air would seem to indicate that the Stoic 'cause' was not only material, but had a sort of chemistry of its own, but of this we hear nothing.

[18] Sambursky, 1959: 7–11.

[19] Alexander of Aphrodisias: 1549. Stobaeus, SVF, Vol. 2: 152–3. Philo, 1932: 110–3.

a given material. Is it a homogeneous substance or a mixture? If the former, is it a pure substance or a solution? If it is a pure substance he then proceeds to the study of its smallest self-existent particle, called, by convention, the molecule.[20] The Greek natural philosophers evidently had no generally-agreed-upon term for this smallest self-existent particle, but with the exception of the Presocratic Anaxagoras, no one believed that a body could be repeatedly subdivided without eventually losing its identity, and the consequence was recognized, that there must be a point at which it 'passed away'. After Aristotle this passing-away was generally understood to be a transmutation which did not involve the question of the existence or non-existence of matter. He and the Stoics sought to define this critical point, and their conceptions of it were surely comparable to those of the modern chemist. They show considerable acuity in overcoming the intermediate steps outlined by Ostwald, Aristotle arriving at the conception of a homogeneous compound, and Chrysippus going beyond that to differentiate compounds from solutions.[21]

Both Aristotle and the Stoics recognized that their application of these concepts to the sensible world was limited by the limitations of the sole instrument they used, the naked eye (the balance was also available!).[22] But a no-less-remarkable limitation was in the sector of the sensible world to which they, like all of their predecessors, most frequently applied the naked eye, the organic kingdoms and the phenomena of meteorology! No factors were more important in the ultimate rise of chemistry as a science than the decision of chemists in the seventeenth century to turn their attention from the organic kingdoms to the inorganic, and the establishment of meteorology as a separate science. The interaction of 'the elements' in meteorological phenomena remains even today

[20] Ostwald, 1912: 194.

[21] Chrysippus' was a physical definition of solution. The alchemists were to use the term 'solutio' for any method of reducing a solid to a liquid, including melting. Arrhenius dates from about 1800 the attempt to decide whether solution is a physical or a chemical process (1912: 10).

[22] Although the use of the balance as an instrument for the precise measurement of specific gravity has a continuous history back to the third century B.C. (Archimedes) (cf. Bauerreiss, 1914), the significance of specific gravity to chemistry was long in becoming evident. The prevailing ancient conceptions of specific weight and volume actually mitigated against acceptance of Stoic theories of the nature of matter (cf. Sambursky, 1959: 14-5).

one of the most intractable areas of science. But we know its intractability by hindsight. If one regards change as the key to the science of matter, as did Aristotle and the Stoics, organic and meteorological phenomena would seem the logical places to begin its study.

Aristotle exempts Democritus from his charge that his predecessors failed to study things in detail. He finds merit in the atomist's theory that coming-to-be and passing-away result from the association and disassociation of atoms, while alteration results from their grouping and position (*On gen.*, 315). Thus it appears that the atomists, despite those limitations which have already been mentioned, made some attempt to explain the fine structure of things. Leucippus and Democritus have not generally been considered as susceptible to the influence of observation as Aristotle seems to suggest, but Epicurus, in his belief in the infallibility of sensation, held qualities to be real 'accompaniments' or 'accidents' of things. He accounted for them by some peculiar entanglements, of atoms in vibration, of others separated by a long distance while remaining somehow mutually involved, and of others shut in by other atoms interlaced around them.[23] Change was the touchstone of ancient atomism, even the 'close-locked shapes' of rock and iron being in unceasing vibration, leading to continual growth and decay through the loss and gain of atoms. Searching for the moment of stability which might be regarded as a line of demarcation between the free atoms and the things of the sensible world, their modern interpreter concludes that the ever-moving atoms of a compound can be regarded as forming a single body with one motion.[24]

These cogitations on fine structure seem to entitle the ancient atomists to a place in the history of microphysics and chemical change; but it is not the place modern chemistry might like to give them. As we will see, the 'corpuscularianism' of the seventeenth-century chemist took as its starting point not the ideas of the ancient atomists, but those of the despised Peripatetics. For atomism, as it got nearer to mundane nature, found it necessary to wrestle with problems identical to those which exercised the Peripatetics, and

[23] Epicurus, 1940: 5 (Letter to Herodotus).
[24] C. Bailey, 1928: 348. See also Lucretius' elegant synthesis of the world out of atoms, *De rerum natura*, Bk 5 (1940: 171ff).

tended to arrive at remarkably similar explanations. Epicurus, like Aristotle, concentrated on meteorological phenomena. He found clouds to consist of an entangling of atoms 'appropriate for producing this result', frost to be produced from dew particles, which 'undergo a definite kind of congelation owing to the neighbourhood of a cold atmosphere', and ice to result from 'the squeezing out from the water of particles of round formation and the driving together of the triangular and acute-angled particles which already exist in the water'.[25] Lucretius, too, found 'the sum of things' to be produced from 'the body of the earth and water and the light breath of air and burning heats'.[26] As has already been noticed, there was little to differentiate the atomist physicians of the Roman empire from their adversaries in their disputes concerning particles and pores.[27]

The Indian summer of ancient natural philosophy

In the early Christian era the ordered columns of contending philosophers dissolved into a confused melee in which it is difficult, from the distance of modern times, to differentiate friend from foe. One suspects that the difficulty was contemporaneous, for to the ranks of the Schools were added alien groups representing new viewpoints generally held to derive from imported 'Eastern' ideologies. These will be dealt with in the next chapter. But before leaving classical philosophy we must consider two philosophers who emerge in the second Christian century as lonely victors in a battle the objectives of which had been forgotten by everybody else. Galen of Pergamum (A.D. 129–99) and Alexander of Aphrodisias (fl. A.D. 193–217) were both ardent Peripatetics, and to them must be credited, in part, the fact that Aristotle had the last word.

The first centuries after the death of Aristotle had seen the diversion of the energies of the Peripatetics into debates with the other Schools on topics remote from Aristotle's scientific interests. This process is believed to have been reversed by the finding in the first century B.C. of a collection of Aristotelian works which became the basis for the Aristotelian corpus we know today.[28] The texts had been

[25] Epicurus, 1940: 22–5 (Letter to Pythocles). Bailey's translations.
[26] Lucretius, 1940: 167 (*De rerum natura*, Bk 5). Trans. H. A. Munro.
[27] See above, Ch. 3, note 21.   [28] Coutant, 1936: 19.

largely freed of interpolations by the time of Galen and Alexander, and they both combined a devotion to the 'true' Aristotle with a conviction that they understood him well enough to extend Peripateticism into regions yet unknown.

Galen's subject was medicine, and his voluminous works were to exercise an influence in that field comparable to that of Aristotle, himself, in natural philosophy. But Galen was more than a physician, for he held medicine to derive from physiology, physiology from physics, and the latter from philosophy. In philosophy he agreed with Aristotle in such subtleties as that the true element is beyond the reach of the senses and necessarily a product of reason, and in the impropriety of substituting (as was common in Galen's time) the contrarieties for the elements.[29] Altogether his writings exhibit a thorough familiarity with, and support of, the microphysical doctrines of Aristotle coupled with an unhesitating confidence in his own competence to fulfil those doctrines in the realm of organic nature.

Galen also regarded himself as a disciple of Hippocrates, but the two lived at opposite ends of the span of classical history, and Galen possessed virtually the whole corpus of Greek science, as well as the tradition of system-building. He was in a position to establish a comprehensive theoretical basis for biology and medicine, and he did not hesitate to do so. Anatomy and physiology had existed as independent sciences since the founding of the Museum of Alexandria, but their specialized character made them unsatisfactory to the Peripatetic Galen. He particularly objected to the tendency of the great physiologist Erasistratus (fl. 258 B.C.) to deal with the parts of the body independently, and to leave some parts altogether unexplained. Galen felt that physiology could only be elucidated by considering the body as a whole. He had personal experience in conventional anatomy and physiology, but was unable to find much connection between these sciences and medicine, and adopted for the latter purpose another physiology, derived from the Peripatetic and Hippocratic doctrines of elements, humours, and the contrarieties.[30]

The import of this physiology is the explication of disease, which

[29] Galen, 1821-33, Vol. 1: 413-4, 460 (De elementis).
[30] Ibid, 1916: 206-17.

Galen saw as a consequence of humoral imbalance, correctable either by the elimination of an excess humour or by the addition of the qualities characteristic of a deficient humour. The first is accomplished through medicines promoting evacuation or by bleeding; the second by the administration of drugs supposed to possess the requisite qualities. Medicines were consequently classified in terms of the contrarieties, and drugs were complexly compounded according to a procedure which came to be called 'polypharmacy'. Galen even held that diseases fall into the four basic classes of hot, cold, wet and dry, but he scarcely developed that notion.[31]

This system served as a framework from the shelter of which Galen dispatched his barbed criticisms of the ideas of others. As concerns the detailed exposition of his own ideas it was a very flexible framework, and one may surmise that its long life was partly due to the fact that his system combined formal comprehensiveness and symmetry with a toleration of deviation on almost any particular point. Galen's adversaries were usually persons long dead. He shuddered with indignation at the view of Erasistratus on the two biles, namely that they are useless substances ingested with the food. Galen held that the biles are formed in the body, and hence must have some function. But the best he can do is to suggest that they have something to do with the purification of the blood,[32] a rather unsatisfactory solution since the blood is also a humour. His real use for the biles is in their excess, which he sees as a cause of disease, and in this connection he betrays little interest in their supposed degrees of heat, cold, etc., and much in their bitterness and acridity, which he sees as a result of their formation in a 'fermentation' process ($ζύμωσις$).[33]

Galen reaches conclusions similarly significant to chemistry in his controversy over digestion, the adversary in this case being the atomist physician Asclepiades (c. 124–c. 40 B.C.), as well as Erasistratus. Asclepiades had held, according to Galen, that there is no such thing as real qualitative change, that food is merely broken up into its constituent particles and absorbed unaltered. Galen held that a qualitative change is evident in partially digested food obtained by

[31] Galen, 1916: 184–5.

[32] Ibid., esp. 190–1, 212–3.

[33] References to the biles cover eight columns in the index to Galen's collected works (1821–33, Vol. 20).

dissection or other means, and saw digestion as a several-stage process, beginning in the mouth and continuing in the stomach, liver, veins, and elsewhere. But the stomach is the source of contention, and on this point he combats both Asclepiades, who posited merely the rearrangement of atoms there, and Erasistratus, who denied the adequacy of bodily heat to the cooking process envisaged by Aristotle. Replying to the former, Galen pictures the viscera adjacent to the stomach 'like a lot of burning hearths around a great cauldron'. He contemptuously dismisses the latter, 'as if we were to suppose that it was necessary to put the fires of Etna under the stomach before it could manage to alter the food'. Aristotle, Galen concludes, has clearly stated in what way digestion can be said to be allied to boiling.[34]

Thus far Galen's ingenuity has been expended within the confines of the 'true' Aristotle, but the Peripatetic encyclopaedia was inadequate to the full range of physiological phenomena which had to be explained in Galen's time. The activity of the stomach is only the first stage of digestion (or nutrition) and is followed by a second, the formation of blood in the liver. This 'crude' blood is then carried to the heart, where it encounters air ingested from the lung (through the pulmonary vein) and again undergoes fermentation with the generation of a 'vital spirit' capable of the nutrition of the higher organs. When this in turn reaches the brain (via the arteries) yet another fermentation occurs, with the generation of 'animal spirits', pure and unmixed with blood. These are carried along the nerves to perform the highest nutritional functions.[35] Thus Galen adopts from the Stoics a series of pneumata to complete the Peripatetic system of physiology.

A similar attitude towards Aristotle characterizes Alexander of Aphrodisias, who was head of the Peripatetic school and the greatest, as well as one of the last, ancient commentator on the Aristotelian corpus. He is celebrated for his rigorous adherence to the 'true'

[34] Galen, 1916: esp. 254–61.

[35] Ibid, 1821–33, Vol. 3: esp. 491 (De usu partium) and elsewhere. Cf. Sprengel, 1815–20, Vol. 2: 112–61. Foster (1924: 12–3) and Charles Singer (1957: 58–61) seem to regard this pneumatology as the essential part of Galen's physiology. It seems to me that it may be considered an appendage to Galen's humoral doctrine much as the doctrine of the two terrestrial exhalations is auxiliary to Aristotle's meteorology. Humoralism and not pneumatology is at the basis of Galenic pathology.

Aristotle, and yet his writings seem to show an oscillation between conservative and liberal interpretation of the Master. His commentary on the *Meteorology* seems both more theoretical and more frankly dependent upon evidence from organic nature than had been Aristotle himself. Discussing the interaction of the contraries according to the doctrine of agent and patient relationship, Alexander virtually acknowledges its inapplicability to inorganic nature. Aristotle had mentioned the cupellation of gold as an example of boiling (ἔψησις); Alexander emphasizes the metaphorical sense of this, 'by an extension of meaning', because of the lack of a better name for the phenomena.[36] Equally conservative is his view of the celebrated vaporous and smoky exhalations from which the metals are formed, which he identifies more unequivocally than had Aristotle with the elements water and earth.[37] And yet Alexander is also credited with the authorship of a book on 'mixis', *De mixtione* (περὶ μίξεως), in which the involvement of celestial influences in mineral formation is finally admitted. When later he became to the Middle Ages a leading interpreter of the 'true' Aristotle, Alexander's authority would seem to have had much to do with the ease with which the Stagirite was reconciled to the emanation ideologies which abounded in that time.[38]

Thus Galen and Alexander reveal at once the vitality of Peripatetic thought in late antiquity on the mundane science of matter and the extent to which it had become permeated with elements of the Stoic doctrine which, among others, it was designed to combat. They were more-nearly enemies of the adversaries of Aristotle, himself, than of their own contemporaries. Most of the latter were scarcely parties to the controversy, but were delving into mysteries quite beyond the ken of Aristotle.

[36] Alexander of Aphrodisias, 1936: 49.

[37] Ibid, 34, 70.

[38] In addition to his *De mixtione* and his commentary on the *Meteorology*, Alexander wrote a commentary on *De generatione et corruptione*, which is lost. Like Aristotle himself, Alexander came to the Latins through the Arabs. See Cranz, 1960: 80.

Chapter Five
Prelude to alchemy

In 538 B.C. the ancient Babylonian empire fell before the Persians, who proceeded thirteen years later to the conquest of Egypt. This surge of Persian power finally overreached itself in an abortive attempt at the conquest of Greece at the beginning of the following century, and Persia's subsequent withdrawal saw the re-establishment of the kingdoms of Babylonia and Egypt. The next such comprehensive attempt at universal conquest was made a century and a half later by the Greeks under Alexander the Great. Independent Babylonian and Egyptian kingdoms did not survive this conquest, but it, too, left the seeds of its dissolution, in its failure to make a complete conquest of Persia. In the middle of the second century before Christ a resurgent Persia put an end to the Greco-Babylonian kingdom of Seleucius, and was only forestalled from further assaults on the West by the rise of the power of Rome in the last century B.C.

Nor did the appearance of Rome mark the end of military and political conflict. But it did provide several centuries of relative peace and a market-place for Greek scholarship, to which we owe most of our documentary evidence of the intellectual ferment which underlay five centuries of conflict between East and West. It is perhaps fortunate that the Romans combined intellectual tolerance with a lack of original religious and philosophical ideas, which made them receptive to and interested in the ideologies of the conquered peoples. The conquered peoples, Babylonians, Egyptians, Persians, Jews and Greeks, were in varying degrees endowed with original ideas; and the remains of a considerable number of writers from Roman times, and a few earlier examples, reveal that this period of half a millennium had witnessed continual competition and accommodation between the religious and philosophical ideas of five imaginative and articulate cultures. One of the products was almost certainly alchemy.

The history of this period, lying between antiquity and the Middle Ages, was long neglected. But this neglect is less to be blamed on the modern historian than on his ancient predecessors, who have conspired to leave a scanty documentary legacy, and that a confusion of extracts and commentaries. The violently polemical and sectarian philosophers of the time had little sympathy for the preservation of rival doctrines. By the handful of classicists who saw the works of Plato and Aristotle through the period, these contemporaries were uniformly abhorred. To the Christians and Moslems they were pagans, and decadent pagans at that.

Yet there were surely more philosophers than ever before. Names and doctrines abound; it is particular information about either that we lack. 'Selection' of those of significance has largely been made for the modern student by the erosion of time. The ingenuity of scholarship has been, and is, reconstructing an increasingly life-like image of the time; but the *dramatis personae* of the history of the science of matter remain dim figures, indeed, by comparison with those before and after them. Those which now seem most important, and upon whose reputed writings the analysis contained in the next two chapters is based, are the following:

Osthanes (or Ostanes), a Persian mystic who lived before 300 B.C., if he existed at all. He is often cited as a pioneer in magic and alchemy.[1]

Bolos of Mende, a Hellenized Egyptian who lived about 300 B.C. He was apparently a pioneer in the genre of writing which combined matter-of-fact information with folk-lore and superstition. He was reputed a student of Osthanes, and the author of *Physica et Mystica*, the sacred book of Greek alchemy.[2]

Maria 'the Jewess', an alchemist who seems to have been a little later than Bolos, although she is also reputed a student of Osthanes.

[1] On Osthanes (Ostanes), see K. Preisendanz in PW, Vol. 18, Pt 2, Col. 1610 ff. Lippmann, 1919: 66, 333, 362. Bidez and Cumont, 1938.

[2] On Bolos, see DK, Vol. 2, 210 ff. M. Wellmann in PW, Vol. 3, Cols. 676–7. Wellmann, 1928. Kroll, 1934. Festugiere, 1944: 224–7.

She is celebrated as the inventress of several types of apparatus for distillation and sublimation which revolutionized alchemy, if they did not precede it and make it possible.[3] We do not know whether Egypt or western Asia was the scene of the activities of Maria or of those of

Agathodaimon, an associate of Maria, whose name, being that of one or more ancient gods, raises the suspicion that he is pseudonymous.[4] One is tempted to think of him as a personified δαίμων out of Plato's *Epinomis*.

Hermes Trismegistus, 'the Thrice-great Hermes', a presumably legendary figure who ultimately came to be regarded as the 'father' of alchemy, but who was better known in antiquity as an astrologer, and that not earlier than about 150 B.C.[5]

Posidonius (*c*. 135–*c*. 51 B.C.), from Apamea in Syria. Head of the Stoic school in Athens. He was one of the most remarkable philosophers of antiquity, having been at once a scientist of the first rank and a leading figure in the adulteration of philosophy with magic and astrology.[6]

Apollonius of Tyana, an itinerant philosopher of the first century A.D., from Cappadocia. A sage of the Neopythagorean sect, his reputation was so great that he was put forward by the pagans, after his death, as a rival to Christ. According to the Arabs of an even later time, he was also an authority on the nature of matter, if not on alchemy.[7]

[3] On Maria see Lippmann, 1919: 46 ff. She is known only through numerous citations by Zosimos, for which see AAG, Vol. 3, 148–50, 170, 188, 194–6, 216, 228, etc.

[4] On Agathodaimon the alchemist see Jos. Fischer in PW, Supplementband 3, Col. 54. Lippmann, 1919: 60–3. Stapleton, 1953. He is frequently cited by Zosimos, for which see AAG, Vol. 3: 175–9, 197, 202, 205, 241, etc. Fischer (op. cit., cols. 37–59) and K. Wernicke (PW, Vol. 1, Cols. 746–7) speak mainly of Agathodaimon as a deity in Greek mythology and as a serpent deity in Greece and Egypt. He appears to have been the official deity of Alexandria! Nevertheless Agathodaimon became an honorific name and finally a proper name.

[5] On Hermes Trismegistus see W. Kroll, in PW, Vol. 8, Cols. 792–823. Lippmann, 1919: 54–60; 1938: 21–5. Especially Festugiere, 1944.

[6] On Posidonius see Reinhardt, 1921, and the long article by the same authority, published in 1953 in PW, Vol. 22, Pt 1, Cols. 558–826. Posidonius has been judged the veritable embodiment of the fusion of Greek philosophy with oriental mysticism (cf. Cumont, 1912), although we have little substantial evidence on him (cf. Edelstein, 1936).

[7] On Apollonius see J. Miller in PW, Vol. 2, cols. 146–7, Conybeare, 1927: Introduction, Kraus, 1942: 270–303. See also below, p. 125 ff.

Anonymous author of the *Leyden papyrus X*, an Egyptian writer of the third century A.D. who is believed to have been a practising goldsmith whose recipe book was interred with him. We know him only through this book.[8]

Zosimos, an alchemist, probably Egyptian, of about A.D. 300, the earliest writer known to us with certainty to have been an alchemist.[9]

Political and cultural leadership had slipped away from Athens before the time of Chrysippus. Philosophers became, if anything, even more numerous, but the majority moved away, intellectually as well as physically, from the traditional environment, while remaining 'Greek' in the important respect of language. Their principal preoccupation became the reconciliation of philosophy with the new oriental religions. As the leading Stoic philosophers consistently came from Syria, it is hardly surprising to find Stoicism taking the lead in the infusion of philosophy with oriental ideas. After Chrysippus the next three heads of the Stoa were deeply involved both in the elaboration of this mixed philosophy and in the dissemination of Stoicism among the Romans. The third of them, Posidonius, was a polymath who has been compared with Aristotle himself in the breadth of his interest and influence.

Although Posidonius' writings have almost altogether perished, the testimony of ancient writers who were influenced by him (e.g. Tacitus, Pliny) or who actually knew him (Cicero, Pompey) certifies his genius. His histories are supposed to have supplied Caesar and Tacitus with the ethnology of the Gauls and Romans. In his scientific work he attempted a measurement of the earth and demonstrated the relationship between the tides and the phases of the moon. He is even supposed to have written on practical chemistry. His most influential contribution to learning, however, was the philosophy underlying and correlated with these special studies. In his histories he contrasted the decadent East with vigorous Rome in a manner which seemed to picture Rome as a terrestrial manifestation of a divine order. In his natural philosophy he seems to have entertained the idea that the evident actions of the sun and

[8] On the Leyden papyrus X, see Berthelot, 1889: 3–70. Lippmann, 1919: 4–9.

[9] On Zosimos see Lippman, 1919: 75–93. Hammer–Jensen, 1921. Ruska, 1929.

moon on the earth were part of a general system of interaction between 'the stars' and terrestrial things. The principle underlying both ideas was that of sympathy between the macro- and micro-cosmos.[10]

Posidonius divided philosophy into three interrelated parts, physics, ethics and logic, and believed it necessary to begin philosophical inquiry with the first. Reason (meaning God) and an unqualified substance (matter) which contains it are his two principles, but he understands both in an original way. The first is no 'Unmoved Mover', but is within the world, a substance without form (in contrast to Plato's form without substance). The second exists only in thought, and is somehow replaced in the actual world by 'the elements'. So also is Reason replaced in the actual world by an intermediate 'power', soul, which appears to be the formative and moving element. It resembles the Stoic pneuma in its role as a cause of change.[11]

Posidonius has been supposed to have gone beyond these intermediaries, the elements and soul, and to have linked heaven and earth through man and a host of heroes and demons between which communication was possible through the medium of visions, divination and oracles.[12] This may accord him more than the evidence warrants, but as a symbol for the entrenchment in the West of the idea of a divine order modelled on that of the Chaldean astrologer he is probably more appropriate than any other known personage.

Posidonius seems to have drawn on Hellenistic empirical science for evidence in support of a philosophy which was basically an oriental pantheism. The opposite course was taken by the Platonists of late antiquity, who attempted to derive the sensible world from the supersensible. It will be evident from our discussion of medieval thought on the mundane science of matter that the differences between Stoicism and Neoplatonism were scarcely relevant on this level. Both agreed that one or more supermundane substances

[10] Cf. Reinhardt in PW, Vol. 22, 1, Cols. 631–2, 653–4. Duhem in SM, Vol. 2, 283. As regards chemistry, Strabo (Geography, 3, 4, 15) credits Posidonius with certain observations on the chemistry of copper.

[11] Cf. Edelstein, 1936.

[12] Cf. Cumont 1911, 1912.

existed, and that they played a comprehensive role in changes on earth. Perhaps the most conclusive influence in establishing such substances as factors in terrestrial change, however, was their final acceptance by Peripatetic philosophy.

The Peripatetic philosophy remained relatively free of the intrusion of theological considerations, and we find its defender, Alexander of Aphrodisias, in the third century A.D., still contending with the ancient enemies, Chrysippus and Epicurus. But he is obliged to give ground even on purely physical questions. Cosmologists were evidently troubled by the apparent contradiction between Aristotle's physics of concentric celestial spheres and the astronomy ('Ptolemaic') of eccentrics and epicycles. In the area of microphysics they were still troubled by the question of the sense in which the ingredients may be said to persist in a compound. In his special treatise on the latter question, Alexander, in a series of conjectures, seems to admit the influence of the stars in the formation of mineral compounds. A body may be said to have a 'proper nature' which manifests itself, when bodies unite to form compounds, in a tendency to animation. The immediate cause of this tendency to animation is weight or levity, the more remote cause the participation of a celestial emanation. The qualities of the elements may be controlled not only by the existence of such emanations but by the density and purity of the element and by its proximity to the heavens. The soul of a compound may not merely be the sum of these emanations in the ingredients, but it may also depend on a certain celestial conjunction at the time of the formation of the compound; perhaps all of these factors are involved.[13] Posidonius could hardly have done better.

Thus one or another doctrine of emanations had made a conquest of every school of ancient natural philosophy, long before Justinian's enforced termination of academic philosophy at Athens in A.D. 529. On the one hand the ground was laid for the philosophy which was to characterize alchemy. On the other hand, the doctrines of matter even of Plato and Aristotle had acquired an involvement of emanations from which they had still not been disentangled when the founders of modern science finally swept away the residues of classical natural philosophy.

[13] Alexander of Aphrodisias, 1549: 65.

Astrology and magic

Some time towards the beginning of the last millennium B.C., astrology appeared as an organized discipline in Babylonia, along with its Siamese twin, astronomy. We have seen that the latter influenced Thales, the founder of Greek natural philosophy. We shall now have to trace its development during the four centuries between Thales and the second decisive impact of Babylonian science on Greece.

Hellenistic writers make frequent reference to 'Chaldean astronomy'. The Chaldeans were the principal heirs of the Assyro-Babylonian civilization, although they had to contest that legacy with numerous other Semitic peoples. To them is credited the invention of that essential precondition to astronomy, an exact chronology. Thales testifies to their ability, before 600 B.C., to predict eclipses. A tablet dated 523 shows them able to calculate in advance the relative positions of the sun and moon, and by 200 B.C. they were able to determine in advance the principal phenomena of the planets. This science appears to have been conducted under the aegis of the priesthood, and we find evidence of an astral religion as early as the sixth century.[14] The patient observations of the Chaldean astronomers over many centuries were finally used by the Greek astronomers (some of whom came from Asia) to construct their well-known theories of the celestial motions. But before this time that other aspect of Chaldean astronomy, the astral religion, had made itself felt among the Greeks.

The argument of Plato's *Epinomis*, that mathematics is a gift of the gods and astronomy a divine science, scarcely differed from the general opinion of Greek philosophers, and although *Epinomis* has been called 'the first gospel preached to the Hellenes of the stellar religion of Asia',[15] the philosophy of Greece remained at this time essentially untainted by astrology. Some of the philosophers, such as Theophrastus, knew of astrology but did not believe in it.

[14] Cumont, 1912: 6–8, 16. See also Kugler, 1913: 130–5. H. Gundel, in PW, Vol. XX, 2, Cols. 2017–84, art. Planeten.
[15] Ibid, 30.

Perhaps the success of the Chaldean astronomers of Seleucid times in predicting the motions of the planets impressed the Greeks sufficiently to make the astral religion more credible to them, for it was very shortly after this that we first encounter those celebrated Greco-Egyptian writings, the astrological treatises of Nechepso-Petosiris and Hermes Trismegistus.[16] Or perhaps these writings reflect the immigration into Egypt of refugees from Babylon. At any rate, their appearance in Egypt marks the first flowering of astrology there, although it had been known since the Persian invasion of that country four hundred years earlier.

Chaldean astrology was not the product of primitive popular fancies, but rather an advanced scientific hypothesis,[17] and the doctrine of correspondences between events in heaven and on earth was a natural attempt to put it to use. After the observation, reported by Posidonius, that the course of the tides was related to the movement of the moon, scepticism seems to have become uncommon even among scientists. The celebrated astronomer Ptolemy stoutly defended astrology. Even ignorant men, he pointed out, are aware of the effects of the sun; and not only does the moon have similar effects, but also the stars and planets, as we see if we know their times and places well enough. He concludes that criticism of the science on the score of impossibility has been specious and undeserved.[18]

Astrology had become complicated by the time of Ptolemy. That of which he speaks was a relatively sober version which probably corresponds to that of the Chaldean astronomers, but a more widespread form in his time was that which was combined with magic.

Magic has to a degree been practised by all peoples in all times, just as we see traces of it in animistic metallurgy. But under the Persian religion of Zoroaster, which may go back to 1000 B.C., it appears as an organized body of doctrine which contrasts markedly with the relatively trivial magic of Babylonia, Egypt and Greece. Persian magic, like Babylonian astrology, has a basis in rudimentary observation. But it represents an attempt to establish a connection

---

[16] Cumont, 1912: 43. Lippmann, 1938: 22. Festugiere, 1944: 102–3.

[17] Jastrow, 1905–12, Vol. 2: 236. Neugebauer, 1952: 164.

[18] Ptolemy, 1906: 4–19 (*Tetrabiblos*, I, 2).

89

between phenomena which are really unrelated. Cumont has declared that, 'If astrology was a perverted astronomy, magic was physics gone astray.[19]

If Platonic and Aristotelian philosophies were forced to accommodate themselves to astrology during the Hellenistic period, they seem to have been free of the intrusion of magic. The same was not true of some other fragments of the philosophical community, which reorganized under the new names of Hermeticism, Gnosticism and Neopythagoreanism. These were conspicuously lacking in the logical rigour which characterized the older Greek natural philosophy, and, as such, were ideally suited to the imaginative speculations of the nascent alchemy. It has been difficult, however, to prove that they predate that science. It may be significant that their origins seem to coincide with it.

In their origins it is difficult to disentangle Hermeticism and Gnosticism. They seem to differ principally in that the first aimed predominantly at mundane knowledge, while the latter had a primarily religious objective. This is in accord with the view that Hermeticism represented an attempt to reconcile Egyptian traditions, which were relatively conservative, with Greek philosophy and Chaldean astrology.[20] The Egyptian god, Thoth, the father of all learning (and real author of all books!) was given the name Hermes, by the Greeks, as early as the time of Plato, and he was one of several deities whose names replaced earlier descriptive names for the planets among the Greeks of the fourth century.[21] But the first 'Hermetic' literature appeared in Egypt about 150 B.C. The earliest Hermetic books suggest that it was a blend of Platonic and Stoic philosophy, in which the Platonic dualism of a real world of being and an unreal world of matter is combined with the orientalized pantheism of the later Stoics. Among the alchemists, Hermes was later to be cited as one of the principal authorities, but this idea does not appear to have been primitive to either alchemy or Hermeticism.

Gnosticism was a syncretistic religious movement which originated in Babylonia.[22] It is older than Christianity, and particularly

[19] Cumont, 1911: 184.   [20] Ibid, 233 n.41.

[21] W. Gundel, in PW, art. Planeten, Vol. 20, 2, Col. 2029.

[22] On Gnosticism see Wilhelm Bousset, arts. Gnosis and Gnostiker, in PW, Vol. 7: Cols. 1502–33, 1534–47 and Jonas, 1963.

exhibits the synthesis of astrology and magic which is thought to have been accomplished in Babylon following the conquest in the sixth century B.C. But under the name Gnosticism the movement is scarcely heard of before the Christian era. Paradoxically, it is both more famous and less well-known than Hermeticism. This is a consequence of its involvement with Christianity in the first and second centuries. The Fathers of the Christian church, who tended to tolerate, if not favour, Hermeticism, saw Gnosticism as a rival religion, and consequently sought, with considerable success, the eradication of its literary manifestations. Nevertheless Gnosticism exercised a powerful influence for several centuries, and notably on alchemy, for it incorporated a large part of the occult and magical notions which were to be appropriated by the devotees of the metal-ennobling Art. It honoured a variety of deities, and the idea of a correspondence between the Babylonian planet-gods and the seven metals may have come to alchemy through Gnosticism. It was characterized by dualisms of light and darkness, good and evil, and an ideology of redemption rites, and may have been the source of the idea of practising a sort of redemption rite on the base metals.[23] The lugubrious environment within which alchemy was usually pursued was typically Gnostic, for Gnosticism represented an inversion of the Greek ideology of the planets as beneficent dieties, made possible by, if not a necessary consequence of, the depersonalization of the planet-gods by the Chaldean astrologers.[24]

The revived Pythagoreanism, which has been given the name Neopythagoreanism, appeared about 50 B.C. It, too, reveals an amalgamation of Greek and oriental ideas. It owed more to Posidonius, especially to his commentary on Plato's *Timaeus*, than to the older Pythagorean mysticism, but it was particularly characterized by a symbolism of numbers to which it attributed an active force and a mystic power.[25] This feature was to enjoy a brief flowering in the Arabic alchemical treatises associated with the celebrated name of Jābir ibn Haiyān, who attributed it to Apollonius

---

[23] Sheppard, 1957. There is an early Babylonian reference to the contents of the metal-lurgical furnace as an 'embryo', but this is also an idea found in primitive metallurgy (Cf. Eliade, 1956: 74).

[24] Jonas, 1963: 254-7.

[25] Cumont, 1912: 49-50. Festugiere, 1944: 14-18.

of Tyana, a wandering philosopher of the first century A.D. Apollonius was one of the most famous Neopythagoreans. He appears to have played no part at all in Greco-Egyptian alchemy, but in Arabic alchemy, where he will be considered at greater length, he enjoyed a great reputation.

Thus we see that a compound of astrology and magic, supposed to have been developed in Babylon from the sixth century B.C., can be traced in the West in Hermeticism (c. 150 B.C.), Stoic philosophy (Posidonius, d. c. 51 B.C.), Neopythagoreanism (c. 50 B.C.), and the obscurely dated Gnosticism. The aspect of schools, if not religions, which these ideologies later assumed, can hardly have existed during this formative period, when they were drawing from the same sources and from each other. This period, the last two centuries before Christ, was also that in which alchemy was formed.

'Physica et Mystica', the sacred text of Greek alchemy

Our extant sources compel us to begin the search for the origins of alchemy in the Greek kingdom of Egypt, and, specifically, in Alexandria. Established in 331 B.C., this was the most notable of numerous cities founded by Alexander for Greek settlement in the conquered lands. After his death in 331, the empire was divided among his lieutenants, and Alexandria became the capital of one of them, Ptolemy I. Through the first century of the Christian era, Alexandria remained the metropolis of the western world. Like some of its successors, it became the centre of activities of the most variegated kind. Here, about 300, Ptolemy established the most celebrated educational institution of the ancient world, the famous Museum, which was to be the scene of the greatest triumphs of Greek science. Here also assembled the motley group who were to prove by their literary legacy the existence of that supposed science of metallic transmutation which we call alchemy.

Aristotle, despite his multitudinous preoccupations, had found time to make a special science of biology. It is probably no coincidence that in the next generation the natural philosophers of the

Museum found it possible to pursue astronomy, mechanics, optics, anatomy and physiology also as special sciences, but it can only be called remarkable that chemistry too should appear, in the same place and time, in the guise of an exact science. The groundwork had been laid for the exact sciences as pursued at the Museum. But the science of matter had not even been subjected to concentrated scrutiny among the Greeks; it had been merely an incidental product of their philosophy. A partial answer to this riddle seems to lie in the fact that the alchemists were probably not Greek. They seem to have been 'natives', that is, indigenous inhabitants of the lands conquered by Alexander.

Zosimos, the earliest certain alchemist of whom we have literary remains, seems to regard a work called *Physica et Mystica* as the cornerstone of the science. It is attributed to 'Democritus', but it is entirely out of character with the atomist of that name, and is now believed to derive from Bolos of Mende (in the Nile delta), who flourished about 200 B.C. Later writers refer to him as a forger of writings under the name of Democritus.[26] He was probably a Hellenized Egyptian. He is known to have interested himself both in the practical arts and in folk-superstition, astrology and magic, and was mentioned as the author of works dealing with such various subjects as medicine, agriculture, miracles, and the art of the jeweller.

The *Physica et Mystica*[27] looks much like a work on the art of the jeweller. After three opening recipes for purple colouration, it is divided into two parts, called gold-making (chrysopoeia) and silver-making, or 'the fabrication of asem'. The processes are not readily convertible into modern terms, but comparison with similar recipes from later technological sources indicates that they are genuine goldsmith's recipes. As its title suggests, however, the *Physica et Mystica* is more than a recipe book. It is characterized by enthusiastic digressions which appear irrelevant to its recipes, but which are of interest because of their resemblance to the phraseology

[26] By Callimachus (d. *c.* A.D. 240). Columella (first century A.D.) refers the same works sometimes to Democritus, sometimes to Bolos. I shall customarily refer to him as (Bolos) Democritus. See M. Wellman in PW, Vol. 3, Cols. 676-7.

[27] I have used the edition of Berthelot and Rouelle, AAG, Text: 41-53. (French) trans.: 43-57.

93

which we find knitted into the fabric of subsequent alchemical theory.

Several of these digressions appear to express the Aristotelian theory of the contrarieties as causes of change. Another, which is appended as a closing sentence to nearly every recipe, is translated, 'One nature (φύσις) rejoices in another nature; one nature triumphs over another nature; one nature masters another nature'. Inasmuch as it had become conventional in late antiquity to refer to the contrarieties as 'natures', this might be taken as a dramatic statement of the activity of the contrarieties in bringing about changes in matter. But the same phrase appears, in part, in an Egyptian astrological treatise (Nechepso–Petosiris) contemporary with Bolos, and it appears to derive ultimately from the literature of astrology and magic.[28]

The *Physica et Mystica* exists because of its preservation by the Greek alchemists, who wrote commentaries on the *Physica et Mystica*, much as the Peripatetics wrote commentaries on Aristotle's works. Modern students of alchemy have generally agreed with them that (Bolos) Democritus is the earliest known alchemist, but they do not agree with the ancients that this provides the key to the origins of alchemy. The *Physica et Mystica* appears to be something of an anomaly in the literature either of alchemy or technology.

The 'Physica et Mystica' as a technological treatise

The hypothesis that the alchemist's avowed foundation work derived, at least in part, from a technological treatise on the art of the jeweller compels us to attempt a more detailed analysis of that art. Archaeology has provided ample evidence of the popularity of precious stones and metals among the royalty of the ancient Near

[28] Bidez and Cumont, 1938: 244, refer it to 'Stoic pantheism'. Festugiere, 1944: 231–2, refers it to 'the Magi'. Both agree that it is an expression of the medico-magical system of sympathies and antipathies, which is a concept combining Greek philosophy, astrology, and magic. But the alchemist, Zosimos, quotes Aristotle to the effect that the qualities triumph (?) over each other (αἱ ποιότητες οἱ ἀλλήλων παρέρχονται). (AAG, text: 150; trans.: 152) and Hammer-Jensen regards the phrase as a mystic statement of Aristotle's theory of mixis (1921: 91).

East, and of the skill with which they were worked. With the decline of the Near Eastern kingdoms in late antiquity the power to command such luxuries was transferred to the Greeks and then to the Romans. At the same time, because of the relatively greater economic democracy existing in those societies, the demand increased greatly. But Egypt and Mesopotamia[29] remained the principal sources of the jeweller's work. Pliny furnishes ample testimony for the importance of the Roman market in the first century of the Christian era.

Pliny does not approve of metallurgy. 'How innocent, how happy, nay more, how even luxurious would life be, if our desires did not go deeper than the surface of the earth, and were satisfied, in a word, by what is within our reach!' He regards the very fact of the use of gold in jewellery as an intensification of its misuse, and wishes that gold and silver could be 'driven utterly from our lives'.

Speaking of the evils following the introduction of metal coinage, he first indicates that its weight was reduced and remarks upon its adulteration. Denarius-testing had recently been established by law as a profession. 'It is curious that money-testing is the only profession in which one must make a study of what is false.' But his animus is particularly directed at the jeweller. 'The man who first set gold upon the fingers was the greatest evil doer in history'. In a discourse on the introduction of gold into Roman society he mentions gilding, which was even used on the ceilings of private houses. Fire-gilding was legal, but he notes a fraudulent adulteration of the quicksilver apparently designed to economize on gold. The emperor Caligula (A.D. 12–41) had financed a project for making gold from orpiment (arsenic trisulphide), 'and he certainly obtained some excellent gold, but in such small quantity that . . . the attempt has not been repeated.'[30]

Pliny assumes the craving for precious metals to have been less widespread in earlier times, and his remarks suggest that precious-metal imitation was something of a novelty to the Romans. A

[29] The recipes in the Library of Assurbanipal correspond closely to those in the papyri (cf. Johnson, 1939: 31).

[30] Pliny's remarks on this subject are contained in his *Natural history*, Bk 33. I have quoted from paras. 3, 8, 57, 64, 79, 100, and 132, in the edition of K. C Bailey: 1929–32.

counterfeit denarius, he says, 'is viewed with interest, the spurious coin being purchased at a cost of several genuine denarii', and he tells us that gilding was so popular that a gilded article was valued above one of solid gold.[31] But if this differed from earlier times it was probably principally in the size of the elite group which could afford to covet the precious metals. Seven hundred years earlier, Homer, in his two poems, had mentioned gold no less than 236 times, half as often as 'copper' (including bronze), twice as often as silver, and four times as often as iron. And his shield of Achilles seems to have been a marvel of the jeweller's art. It represents an effect of 'painting in metal, in which gold gave the colour yellow, white if alloyed with silver and redder if alloyed with copper. Silver was 'white' and copper, red. Black was obtained by mixing powdered sulphur with lead, copper, or silver, to form a compound later known as niello. Homer seems not to have actually known how this was done, and to have based his description on Mycenean work, of which examples have actually been found in shaft graves.[32] Although niello seems to have been most extensively used in Crete, it has been found in Egypt before 1750 B.C., as have most of the other techniques of which Pliny speaks.[33]

The older view that goldsmithing was secret work in which the Egyptian priests themselves were involved is not probable. The Egyptian temples did maintain craftsmen in jewellery making, and the Crown did attempt to control gold production to the point of monopoly, but it is doubtful that such monopolies were consistently maintained over long eras of Egyptian history. We know that votive offerings and amulets in the form of jewellery were sold in booths in the neighbourhood of temples. Amulets were considered magical, and it seems to have been the making of amulets, rather than jewellery-making per se, which was secret work in which the priests themselves may have been involved.[34]

An authentic Egyptian jeweller's recipe book has been known for

---

[31] *Natural history*, Bk 33, 49, and 132. His contemporary, Seneca, also remarks on the excessive lust for gold among the Romans, but notes with satisfaction that it was just as bad in earlier times (Seneca, 1910: 207).

[32] Gray, 1954: 1–4.

[33] Kees, 1933: 134–5.

[34] Partington, 1935: 16–18. The argument that the papyri represent the work of the priests themselves rests principally on the fact that they are deluxe copies (cf. Johnson, 1939: 52–3).

some time. It was part of a group of papyri purchased in Thebes in 1828, and placed in libraries in Stockholm and Leyden. The papyri are believed to date from the third century A.D. (although representative of a much older literature), and to have been looted from a tomb, perhaps that of the author. It was subsequently found that a jeweller's recipe book was divided between the two libraries, the smaller part, principally dealing with the imitation of precious stones, being in Stockholm, and the larger part, on the imitation and 'multiplication' (debasement) of precious metals, being in Leyden. The latter, which contains most of the material relevant to alchemy, is designated X in the Leyden collection.[35]

The Leyden papyrus X consists of 101 recipes, followed by a number of passages on the nature of the raw materials. It is interesting that the latter are from Dioscorides. About 34 of the recipes are concerned with gold, including 14 for writing in letters of that metal; about 30 involve 'asem', the Egyptian name for electrum. There are recipes for gilding, silvering, and colouring metals purple. Gilding, the prototype of these processes, is done by two methods, which later came to be called the fire and lead gilding processes. Pliny had only mentioned the former, but the lead gilding process was in all probability the older.[36] There are other processes for 'augmenting', and 'doubling' gold, by alloying it with lead, copper, zinc (introduced as the oxide), and asem, and others for gilding the base metals without the use of gold, as with an alloy of copper and asem, or with a paste of copper, iron, and arsenic compounds in vegetable gum. And there are, finally, a number of recipes for

[35] For the Leyden papyrus see Leemans, 1885: 209–49 (Greek text and Latin trans.); Berthelot, 1889: 28–50 (French trans.); Caley, 1926 (English trans.). For the Stockholm papyrus (more properly called the papyrus Holmiensis, since it has been in the Victoria Museum at Uppsala since 1906) see Lagercrantz, 1913: 3–42 (Greek text); Caley, 1927, (English trans.). On the literature on these documents see IHS, Vol. I; 339–40.

[36] Fire gilding is accomplished by painting the object in question with a gold amalgam. It is then heated to drive off the mercury and leave a thin layer of gold. Because of the toxic effect of mercury vapour the process is now illegal. Lead gilding involves the dipping of the object in a molten alloy of lead and gold, followed by corrosion which similarly removes the lead. Other metals than lead can be used, and this seems much the older process. The mercury process could hardly predate knowledge of mercury, whereas a process analogous to lead gilding seems to have been applied to an electrum spear head from Ur (c. 2700 B.C., Stapleton, 1953: 31). This process was also used in Precolumbian America, where mercury was not used (communication of Prof. William C. Root to Seminar on Technical Studies in Ancient Metal Artifacts, Freer Gallery of Art, Washington, D.C., June 13, 1961).

purifying, soldering, and testing the metals. The typical metallurgical process in this treatise is a simple melting in which two to five metals, and sometimes other minerals, are thrown successively into the melt. This is usually a recipe for 'asem', which seems in this text to signify almost any alloy. The most common ingredients of the asems are tin, silver, mercury, and lead. The author treats asem as he does gold and silver, 'doubling' it, colouring it, and using it to make an ink. He even has a test for it, for he states that false asem turns black when heated in brine.[37]

Berthelot saw the emphasis on asem in the Leyden papyrus X as indicative of the condition which, among the alchemists, made the belief in metallic transmutation possible. Egyptian asem was ordinarily our electrum, a naturally occurring metal which had been recognized to be a mixture of gold and silver as early as the seventh century B.C., and which was sometimes deliberately fabricated. But it is clear that the concept of an alloy was only vaguely understood long after that; hence in the time of this papyrus asem was a naturally occurring metal which could both be made from and transformed into other metals.[38] Since it was also a precious metal it was of special interest to the jeweller.

But the author of the Leyden papyrus X does not claim to have accomplished metallic transmutation. He occasionally appears to use the word 'gold' as we sometimes do today, when we intend merely to refer to the colour which is typified by this metal.[39] He sometimes indicates that only imitation is involved, and, on occasion, claims that the result will even fool the expert.[40] The remarkable thing about the papyrus is just in its emphasis on imitation.

It is true that less costly substitutes were used from the earliest times, as well as that the metals were modified to achieve unusual effects, as we see in Homer's account of the shield of Achilles. But in the Leyden papyrus X we find recipes for precious metal imitation which are clearly fraudulent in intent. Why did the Egyptian goldsmith turn to the fabrication of imitation jewellery? It is not unlikely that it was connected with his loss of the gold monopoly and to the general impoverishment of the temples at a time when the demand

[37] *Leyden papyrus X*, 1889: 42 (Recipe 64).   [38] Berthelot, 1889: 62ff.
[39] Ibid., 20.   [40] *Leyden papyrus X*, 1889: 30, 37–8 (Recipes 8, 38, 40).

for fine metal work was increasing among the Greeks and Romans. If we may judge from the religious currents of the time, the demand for jewellery in the form of the amulet must also have been decidedly brisk.

The subject matter of the *Physica et Mystica* has been found to be so similar to that of the Leyden papyrus as to leave little doubt of a common origin. The former has a total of only 27 recipes, as compared to 101 in the Leyden papyrus. The number of recipes referring to gold, however, is comparable, if we exclude the 14 in the papyrus which refer to gold writing, a subject not covered in the *Physica et Mystica*. Eliminating these, the papyri have 17 gold recipes (there are none in the Stockholm papyrus), and the *Physica et Mystica* has 13.

The recipes of the *Physica et Mystica*, however, are relatively much less precise than those in the Leyden papyrus X, to a degree which makes it uncertain that they are practical and not merely literary prescriptions. The author commonly gives the reader a choice of ingredients, many of which have resisted decipherment into the terms of modern chemistry. Hammer-Jensen has also pointed out that sulphur, which enters into only two of the recipes in the papyrus, is an ingredient of over half of those in the *Physica et Mystica*. She sees the emergence of 'sulphur' as an important ingredient in an otherwise largely unintelligible recipe as critical to the genesis of alchemy.[41]

The 'Physica et Mystica' as a theoretical treatise

The association of the literature of technology with that of magic has been elucidated by Wellmann, in a study of Hellenistic encyclopaedias which went under such names as 'Physica', or 'Physica dynameis', and contained treatises on such mundane subjects as agriculture, geography, and the crafts along with others on the lore of the magical powers of natural objects. Wellmann regarded these encyclopaedias as prototypes of subsequent composite works on 'Properties', 'Secrets', and 'the nature of things'. He saw Pliny's *Natural history* as an example of the latter and credited Bolos with

[41] Hammer-Jensen, 1921: 41.

the authorship of certain special treatises underlying Pliny's chapters on minerals and on the magical powers of plants.[42]

More recently one category of ancient technological treatise has been identified under the name 'Baphika' (colouring, or dyeing). Although no complete example exists, fragments have made possible the reconstruction of its principal feature which was a subdivision into four sections, dealing with colouration imitative of gold, silver, precious stones, and that most esteemed of all dyes, purple.[43] The *Physica et Mystica* deals with three of these, and seems originally to have covered precious stones as well.[44] The Leyden and Stockholm papyri, taken together, cover the same four topics, and thus appear to be another example of the Baphika literature.

The papyri are free of the occult, but not quite conclusively so, since another papyrus in the Leyden collection is devoted to magic, and is written in the same hand as the Leyden papyrus X.[45] This curious fact, added to Wellmann's observations on the Hellenistic encyclopaedic literature at large and to the undoubted mixture of technical recipes and occult theory in the *Physica et Mystica*, leave us with the impression that the practical chemist and the occultist of the Hellenistic period found a meeting place in the atelier of the goldsmith.

The nature and significance of this relationship remains largely a mystery. The relationship of its most complete surviving example, the *Physica et Mystica*, to the alchemical literature of the early Christian era, however, is susceptible to some degree of analysis. (Bolos) Democritus remarks that he was studying under Osthanes 'how to make a concordance of the natures', but that before the course was completed his master died, from having swallowed a poison designed (successfully, it would seem) to separate soul from body. Advised to invoke a 'demon' in search of certain books by Osthanes of which Bolos had been unaware, the disciple was directed to a temple where, in a column which was rent asunder, he saw inscribed the phrase immortalized in *Physica et Mystica*, 'One

[42] Wellmann, 1928. Wellmann held Anaxilaus of Larissa (first century B.C.) to be the intermediary between Bolos, the papyri, and Pliny. See also Bidez and Cumont, 1938: 117.

[43] Festugiere, 1944: 220.

[44] According to the fourth–fifth century A.D. alchemist Synesius (AAG, Vol. 2: 57).

[45] Berthelot, 1889: 8, 32. The papyri mention the names Phimenas, Africanus, Anaxilaus, and Democritus, which may refer to the alchemical literature (cf. Johnson, 1939: 54).

nature rejoices' . . . etc. He says that he marvelled that his master's writings could be condensed in so few words.[46] It was these words in particular which interested the alchemists of the Greek text. This mystic aphorism was the first of a series over which they were to labour as industriously as they ever did in the laboratory, and from which they were to construct much of the theoretical basis of alchemy.

[46] AAG, Vol. 3, 45. It may be noted that Festugiere (1944: 226) concludes that the *Physica et Mystica* as we have it is not earlier than the first century A.D., and that it is not Bolos' work.

Chapter Six
Alchemy

FROM beginning to end alchemical literature has been attributed to notable personages, nearly all of whom have been relieved of the burden by modern criticism. In the earliest extant alchemical manuscript these include such miscellaneous celebrities as Hermes, Cleopatra, Isis, and Moses. We have from these and other Greek-writing alchemists, numbering about forty, complete treatises or fragments totalling about eighty thousand words. They are collected in a Greek manuscript of which a number of late copies exist, the oldest having been written in the tenth or eleventh century A.D., perhaps copied from a lost Byzantine original about two centuries older.[1]

According to F. S. Taylor, who has made the most serious attempt to establish the chronology of this Greek text, Zosimos of Panopolis, although about sixteen other authors represented in the text are believed to predate him, is the earliest definite person from whom we have a substantial treatise manifestly dealing with transmutation. In fact we know little enough of Zosimos. We have from him a collection of fragments from a kind of alchemical encyclopaedia called *Cheirokmeta*, and believe him to have been a real person who flourished at Alexandria towards the end of the third century A.D. And although fragmentary, the remains of the *Cheirokmeta* are substantial and exhibit many of the classic features of alchemy; the use of secret words (including the root word, chemeia (χγμέα), of

---

[1] F. S. Taylor, 1930: 109, 112. Venice Marcianus MS 299 is tenth-eleventh C. Taylor postulates a seventh-eighth C. Byzantine original, from which are also derived Paris Greek MS 2325 (thirteen C) and Paris Greek MS 2327 (fifteenth C). See also Taylor, 1937. Mention of 'the Greek text' here refers to the edition by Berthelot and Rouelle, AAG.

the term chemistry);[2] the comparison of alchemy with sexual generation; the role of spirits in bringing about changes in matter, and the designation of sulphur, mercury, and arsenic as mineral spirits; and the ferment-like Xerion (which was to become Elixir), whose intervention was supposed to ensure the success of the under-taking.[3]

Taylor also gave 'definite personalities' to two of the sixteen authors in the Greek text whom he judged to be earlier than Zosimos, namely the aforementioned (Bolos) Democritus and a lady-al-chemist known as Maria, sometimes further identified as 'the Jewess'. The others are divided into four 'followers' of Democritus, four members of the 'school' of Maria, and others too fragmentary to be classified at all. (Bolos) Democritus is indeed a more well-defined figure than is Zosimos, and he has left in the *Physica et Mystica* a substantial treatise; but it is questionable, as we have already noted, that he was an alchemist. Maria, whose fame still survives in the French name, bainmarie, for the water bath, appears to have invented the apparatus which permitted the alchemist to adapt distillation and sublimation to metallurgical (or pseudo-metal-lurgical) processes. She certainly was an alchemist, but although she may have left some small fragments[4] we know her almost exclusively through references in later writers, and particularly through Zosimos, who esteemed her the equal of (Bolos) Democritus.

In seeking the origins of alchemy, therefore, we are dependent upon a small number of treatises spread in time over more than half a millennium and for the most part fragmentary or apocryphal. Since it is questionable that the most famous and well-preserved tract, the *Physica et Mystica*, is concerned with alchemy at all, the student of the origins of alchemy has recourse, of necessity, to the *Cheirokmeta*

---

[2] AAG, text; 213; trans.: 206. If Zosimos is correctly dated, this would be contemporary with the use of the word for the gold and silver makers against whom Diocietian's decree of A.D. 296 was issued. There are a number of possible sources of the word, chemistry. Hopkins, 1934: 94 7n, lists seven. On this knotty question see Lippmann, 1954: 50-1.

[3] Large fragments of the work have been put together by Berthelot from the Greek (AAG, text: 107-252; French trans.: 117-242) and from the Syriac (CMA, Vol. 2: 203-66 [French trans.]). These fragments may be in part from other works of Zosimos, and are certainly in some cases from later writers than Zosimos. Other writing attributed to Zosimos is extant in Arabic manuscript (Stapleton and Azo, 1910: 65).

[4] A short Arabic tract attributed to 'Mary the Copt' was published some years ago, but it is allegorical and without evident chemical significance (Maria, 1927).

of Zosimos, a work supposedly written over 500 years later. Here we find Egyptian metallurgy and the Egyptian priesthood specifically associated with 'the Art' (as Zosimos commonly calls alchemy), and we find (Bolos) Democritus referred to frequently and with great respect as 'the Philosopher'. But the *Cheirokmeta* also mentions other authorities and other subjects, including persons of stature apparently equal to that of (Bolos) Democritus, who appear not to be Egyptians, and a kind of metallurgy not found either in *Physica et Mystica* or in the craftsmen's papyri of Leyden and Stockholm.

The materials mentioned by Zosimos are virtually identical to those in the earlier Egyptian sources,[5] but the method of manipulating them is quite different. Zosimos tends to convert (Bolos) Democritus' cementation processes into distillatory processes, using apparatus associated with Maria, and although (Bolos) Democritus mentioned distillation briefly in *Physica et Mystica*, with a claim to have written on it more extensively elsewhere,[6] we not only lack any such work but find that where Zosimos refers to (Bolos) Democritus in connection with distillation he usually does so in an attempt to show him to be in agreement with Maria.[7] For the alchemy of repetitious distillatory processes supposed to lead through a series of colour changes to the elixir, in which Zosimos was the prototype of many generations of successors, he seems above all indebted to Maria.

While the presence of Maria 'the Jewess' in the alchemical pantheon suggests that it was not quite an exclusive club of Hellenized Egyptians, Maria has been generally relegated to a vague role as intermediary between (Bolos) Democritus and Zosimos. Stapleton, however, has recently suggested that a not insignificant number of the alchemists of the Greek text were of Seleucid, rather than Egyptian, origin. The basis of this suggestion was in the discovery in

[5] The difficulty of correlating ancient names with specific substances is particularly severe in alchemy because of the practice of secrecy. F. S. Taylor says (1930: 124) that over 500 substance names appear in the Greek manuscript, but Berthelot's survey of the materials of early chemistry (1889: 228–68) does not indicate that the Greek text mentions any substances not identified in our survey of practical chemistry (Ch. 1 above).

[6] The author of *Physica et Mystica* concludes with the words, 'there is nothing more to describe, except the rise of vapour (νεφέλης) and water; but I deliberately pass over these in silence, inasmuch as they figure largely in my other works.' (AAG, text: 53; trans.: 57).

[7] AAG, text: 146, 157, 182–3; trans.: 148, 157, 180.

Cairo of an alchemical tract attributed to another of the authorities of the Greek text, Agathodaimon.[8]

Agathodaimon was a member of Maria's 'school', and a figure of whom Zosimos speaks with respect, and not infrequently. Taylor had thought him to be Egyptian, but Stapleton thinks he may have lived in Harran, in Seleucid Syria, between the fourth and first centuries, B.C.[9] Stapleton tends to place Maria in the same environment and to transfer what is perhaps the most crucial phase in the genesis of alchemy from Ptolemaic Egypt to Seleucid Syria.

The reconciliation of theory and practice

Zosimos' alchemical *Cheirokmeta* is actually a series of letters to his 'sister', Theosobia. Their fragmentary character, and the intrusion of some passages from one or more later authors, preclude the reconstruction of a coherent Zosimian alchemy, and to this difficulty is added the obscurity of his mystical approach. The spirit of the work is fairly expressed by his own introduction, where he speaks of 'the composition of waters, movement, growth, embodying and disembodying, drawing the spirits from bodies and binding the spirits with bodies. . . '[10] Such imagery is given more attention in Zosimos than is the delineation of the operations themselves. But his objective seems clearly enough to be the reconciliation of (Bolos) Democritus and Maria.

In a 'detailed exposée of the work', he cites (Bolos) Democritus extensively, mentioning only the agreement of Agathodaimon on the importance of sulphur. He lists at some length the materials necessary 'for gold', 'for yellowing', 'for purple (iosis)', and so on. 'Theion hudor', which can be translated either divine water or sulphur water, often seems to play a critical role.[11] In an 'abridgement of the sacred art of the fabrication of gold and silver', he gives recipes from Maria and then points out that 'the Philosopher'

[8] Stapleton, 1953.
[9] Ibid.: 37.
[10] AAG, text: 107; trans.: 117.
[11] Ibid., 159–67; trans.: 158–66. Iosis had three meanings in classical Greek, arrow, poison, and rust or verdigris. Gold colouration, the last step in the alchemical synthesis, was only its most obvious alchemical signification. See Berthelot, 1889: 254–5, and note 15 below.

([Bolos]-Democritus) agrees with her.[12] The recipe with which the Philosopher agreed was for a process in which a sandwich of copper and gold is exposed to the fumes of 'sulphur water' and gum. Zosimos seems to support the claim of the author of *Physica et Mystica* to have written on such reflux processes, but Maria and Agathodaimon are obviously the authorities, and Maria is credited with the invention of the apparatus.

Among the materials used for metal colouration in the *Physica et Mystica*, mercury, sulphur and the arsenic sulphides (realgar and orpiment) are susceptible to distillation or sublimation. The essence of Maria's alchemical practice seems to have been in the treatment of the base metals with these 'spirits', or with the divine or sulphur water. This bizarre reagent represented a new avenue to the niello-making process, through hydrogen sulphide rather than sulphur. In its early history it seems to have been a solution of hydrogen sulphide, obtained from calcium polysulphide which was in turn prepared by heating together lime and sulphur.[13] An interpolated passage in the *Cheirokmeta* mentions a new method of preparing it, by the distillation of eggs.[14]

It is a hazardous but unavoidable duty of the student of the history of chemistry to attempt to reconcile such process descriptions with chemistry as we understand it. The most plausible attempt is probably that of Hopkins, who took as his guide the emphasis on colour changes occurring during the operation. According to Hopkins the critical colour sequence was black, white, yellow, and purple, a view he derives from Maria, as reported by Zosimos.[15] Hopkins explains this sequence by holding that the alchemist generally began with a black alloy of the imperfect metals (lead, tin, copper, and iron), known as the 'tetrasoma' (four-membered body). This alloy was then 'whitened' (on the surface) with mercury or arsenic. Following this, it was yellowed with gold or sulphur water, and, in a final step, it was purpled. In imagining how the last may

[12] AAG, text: 145–8; trans.: 148–50.

[13] Recipe 89 in the *Leyden papyrus X*, 1889: 46–7.

[14] AAG, text: 141–3; trans.: 143–5. Zosimos, himself, is cited in this chapter.

[15] Hopkins, 1934: 69, 92ff. There is some question as to whether the last step, iosis, is to produce purple or red. Lippmann calls it red (1919: 47). The passage in Zosimos is in AAG, text: 199; trans.: 194. It is of interest, and perhaps not insignificant, that Pliny names black, white, yellow, and red as the four basic colours of the Greek painter (*Natural history*, Bk. 35, 31).

have been accomplished, Hopkins points out the violet bronze colour of alloys containing a fraction of gold.[16]

The treatise of Agathodaimon recently publicized by Stapleton provides us with an opportunity to make a similar analysis of a comparable work. The principal key to the work, it declares,[17] has been called by Hermes (Agathodaimon's only authority) 'a stone which is not a stone', because it is a stone in appearance but not in its property of dissolving. It is made from a single material, which dissolves and becomes a clear water and pure spirit which is the essential nature of stones. Mixed with something (unnamed), pulverized by fire, and evaporated to paste it becomes a stone (like ?) copper burned in its own sulphur. If it is manipulated wisely it is leaf-like and many coloured, and upon further treatment with small quantities of liquid it becomes gold.

The secret of the Art is in the removal of grossness, the reduction of the material used to a state of subtleness. Fire is the enemy of the operation, and much attention must be given to the degrees of heat employed, but the stone itself is purified by fire. In the course of the operation colours appear, red, yellow, white, black and green. The final tincture is purple, of a sweet taste and fragrant odour, its origin in well-tempered earth and soft soil of weight exceeding all else in heaviness. Important, if vaguely defined, agents in the process are a 'gum' (kolla) and 'a fiery poison extracted by fire from the natures', apparently obtained through distillation.

Agathodaimon not only has a different colour sequence from that mentioned by Zosimos, but begins, it would appear, with copper as the metal to be transmuted. It is possible, however, to devise a similar sequence for his process if we assume that the 'single material' of his Stone was realgar (arsenic disulphide). Realgar can be made by fusion with natron (soda) or mercury to yield arsenious oxide, 'a stone which is not a stone', in the sense of Theophrastus' mineralogy as well as according to Hermes, and it is, indeed, 'a fiery poison'. It is also capable of forming 'a clear water' (solution) and 'a pure

[16] 1934: 100.

[17] What follows is based on Stapleton's summary of a Cairo Arabic manuscript. 1953: 40–3. Through the courtesy of the Library of the History of Science Museum, Oxford, and with the assistance of my colleague, Sami Hamarneh, this has been compared with the original text.

spirit' (white sublimate). If it be mixed with vegetable oil (Agatho-daimon's gum?) and heated, it yields another sublimate (elemental arsenic) which can be applied to copper in the kerotakis and will give it a silvery colour. But in the further conversion to gold our sequence breaks down. We may suspect that Agathodaimon's did as well.

An unusual variety of colour effects is possible in the chemical manipulation of arsenic compounds. Within the above context a sequence can be devised which would at least approach that indicated by Agathodaimon. If, as he advocates, the degrees of heat are care-fully controlled, the red realgar can be converted into the yellow sulphide, orpiment. This is accomplished through fusion with sulphur. Or we may take the red to refer to copper and the yellow to orpiment, as starting materials. In either case, if orpiment then be fused with mercury or natron we obtain the white sublimated oxide which we have imagined to be 'the Stone'. If this material be fused in turn with oil or gum, we obtain a black sublimate, the element itself. Elemental arsenic is a 'tincture' capable of giving a silvery colour to copper, an action of which the compounds of arsenic are not capable. Here again, like the typical alchemical disciple, we fail on the last steps, the production of the colours green and violet. Perhaps, however, we may find a clue in returning to the 'clear water', a solution of arsenious oxide. For if copper be digested therein the resulting solution will be coloured green, and if this be distilled the resulting distillate will be blue.[18]

There are other indications of the importance of the arsenic compounds in early alchemy. It will be recalled that realgar was the material in the gold-making (or extracting) project reported by Pliny. One of the gilding processes in the Leyden papyrus X uses arsenic and 'gum'.[19] Arsenic compounds are mentioned more frequently than either mercury or sulphur in the *Physica et Mystica*, being involved in 10 of the 24 recipes, in the form of realgar, orpiment, and 'white arsenic' (the oxide), and being used in the vaporous as well as the solid form.[20]

---

[18] This is only one of several colour sequences which can be accomplished by the chemical manipulation of the arsenic sulphides. For others, see K. C. Bailey, 1929–32, Vol. 2: 207.

[19] *Leyden papyrus X*, 1889: 40 (Recipe 50).

[20] The 'Sibylline oracles', an occult work from Roman times, contains a riddle which the later alchemists held to be a revelation of Hermes and Agathodaimon on the philosopher's

Hopkins's theory is an extension of that of Hammer-Jensen, who held alchemy to rest on the discovery of distillation and of the manifold chemical properties of sulphur, which were first revealed through its manipulation in distillatory processes.[21] In emphasizing the first of these Zosimos differs from the *Physica et Mystica*, and he differs in both from the Leyden papyrus X. It seems to me that in the treatise of Agathodaimon arsenic rather than sulphur may have been the key material. It is possible that arsenic was, in fact, the 'sulphur' on which Hammer-Jensen bases her theory of the genesis of alchemy. The arsenic sulphides were often regarded as varieties of sulphur; 'arsenic' and 'sulphur' were often confused by Zosimos, and this confusion remains in Hammer-Jensen's analysis.[22] The arsenic sulphides produce the variegated effects noted by the alchemists more readily than does sulphur or even the sulphur water. It seems, in short, that if we substitute arsenic for sulphur in the theories of Hammer–Jensen and Hopkins those theories not only explain the treatise of Agathodaimon, but explain more satisfactorily the work of Zosimos, on which they are based. But whether the early alchemist focused his attention on mercury and sulphur or on arsenic, it was clearly directed to materials which are not only reactive, but readily vapourized. The invention of the requisite apparatus was Maria's contribution.[23]

There is evidence that simple distillation was known to Aristotle (*Meteor.*, 358b), and even to the Babylonians of a much earlier time.[24] But where apparatus is indicated it was of the most primitive type. Dioscorides (Bk. 5: 70) describes the condensation of mercury from cinnabar in an inverted cup, compared to which Maria's variety of retorts are revolutionary indeed. Her most complex apparatus was the

---

stone. Interesting, if inconclusive, is the fact that European alchemists of the sixteenth century advanced the theory that arsenic was the key to this riddle (Lippmann, 1919: 63). Agathodaimon's interest in arsenic is mentioned by Zosimos (AAG, text: 150; trans.: 152).

[21] Hammer–Jensen, 1921: 41, 44.

[22] 'Dass die Mischung von Schwefel (oder Schwefelarsen oder einer anderen Schwefelverbindung) und Quecksilber im Destillationsapparate dasselbe ist wie die Mischung von Feuer und Wasser, kann kaum bezweifelt werden. . . . Kerotakis mit aufgehängtem Schwefel oder Arsenik zur Behandlung der Metalle mit Schwefel – oder Arsenikdampf' (Hammer–Jensen, 1921: 51, 57).

[23] These are illustrated in some of the manuscripts. See Berthelot, 1889: 127–73.

[24] Levey, 1959: 34–6.

tribukos, a three-beaked alembic for making the sulphur water, but the most important was the kerotakis, a sublimatory. The kerotakis was a closed vessel containing a sort of shelf as a diaphragm. On that shelf a solid material could be subjected to an atmosphere of distilled or sublimed vapour. It enabled the alchemists to convert cementation processes into distillatory processes.

The practical effectiveness of this apparatus is a matter of some doubt. The treatment of a metal in the kerotakis would be considerably less profound than would be the same process conducted as a cementation. In view of the incredible attenuation of alchemical operations it would not be safe to call the kerotakis processes superficial, but they could hardly have been economical metallurgy. And, of course, they were not supposed to be mere metallurgy. The real focal point of the alchemist's attention was not the manipulation of the base metal, but the preparation of the reactive material, or elixir.

Further doubt is cast on the effectiveness of the apparatus by the apparent failure of the Greek alchemists to discover alcohol or the mineral acids, substances which revolutionized alchemy when they became known to Latin elixir-hunters of the twelfth century A.D.[25] This is often attributed to the introduction of more efficient condensate cooling apparatus than the simple air-cooled tube which served as an outlet from Maria's alembic. It is not less likely, however, that it was due to the failure of the Greek alchemist to exploit the 'alums and salts' in which the mineral acids were finally discovered. The prominent role played by these substances in Arabic and Latin alchemy was occupied in that of Zosimos by sulphur (and /or the arsenic sulphides), and the divine or sulphur water he recovered from these operations intrigued the Greek alchemists much as the mineral acids were to fascinate the Latins.

Whatever the contributions of Maria's apparatus to chemistry, its principal contribution to alchemy was in facilitating the reconciliation to theory and practice. Such materials as mercury, sulphur, and the arsenic sulphides corresponded to the Aristotelian 'agent', and to the 'tincture' of the Baphika literature. As distillable materials they also became 'spirits' equivalent to the Stoic pneumata. This seems to be the essence of the alchemist's reconciliation of theory and

[25] See below, p. 204ff.

practice as we find it in Zosimos.[26] Zosimos' apparent references to the 'philosopher's stone' are probably later additions to the *Cheirokmeta*,[27] but he approaches the conception in his discussion of the divine or sulphur water. Its curious combination of divine and mundane attributes made it ideal for the role of a 'philosopher's stone', and already in Zosimos we see the beginning of its career as a favourite reagent of the esoteric alchemist who preferred its divine to its sulphurous attributes.[28]

Despite his esteem for it, the sulphur water is for Zosimos only one of a number of 'unique' tinctures, and tincturing is only one of several avenues of approach to the desired result. The analysis of colour sequences has indicated that iosis, the giving of a purple (or red) colour, was the critical tincturing process. A third avenue of approach was through the Xerion ($\xi\acute{\eta}\varrho\iota o\nu$), a substance which acted like a medicine or like a ferment ($\zeta\acute{v}\mu\eta$).[29] The term Xerion had been used for a medical powder (Aetius Medicus 6, 12, late second century A.D.), and was to be the parent of the Arabic word, al-iksir (elixir). Out of these several expressions of the idea which is embodied in the modern word, catalyst, emerged the elixir, appropriately an Arabic word, for it is only among the Arabic-writing alchemists that we find the concept fully developed.

The authors subsequent to Zosimos in the Greek manuscript appear to have been commentators, or, to put it more specifically, they appear not to have been chemists, but students of the ancient literature. They exhibit on the one hand the conviction that the key to alchemy is to be found in the writings of the ancients, and on the other the tendency to interest themselves in the perfection of the human soul rather than in the perfection of the base metals. This endeavour, which was finally to prevail in Greek alchemy, and

[26] Quoting Hermes, Maria, and Agathodaimon, Zosimos on one occasion speaks of the crucial role of the spirits ($\pi\nu\epsilon\acute{v}\mu\alpha\tau\alpha$) mercury, sulphur, and arsenic, and emphasizes their distinction from soul ($\psi\upsilon\chi\acute{\eta}$) (AAG, text: 150–2; trans.: 152–3). This is a virtual statement of the position they were to occupy in Arabic alchemy, but seems somewhat incidental in Zosimos.

[27] Zosimos in AAG, text: 198–204; trans.: 194–9, and Berthelot's note, trans.: 194.

[28] An interpolated passage in the *Cheirokmeta* states that the name sulphur water is given to all of the liquids used (AAG, text: 184; trans.: 181).

[29] AAG, text: 114, 127, 145, 167, 175. $\xi\eta\rho\acute{o}\varsigma$, 'dry' in classical Greek, was the root of the name $\xi\acute{\eta}\rho\iota o\nu$ for medical powders, and finally for that alchemical medicine, the philosopher's stone, or elixir.

which persists to the present day, has been called 'esoteric' alchemy. By contrast, that alchemy which remained concerned with the science of matter is called, despite its own preoccupations with the occult, 'exoteric' alchemy. The seed of esoteric alchemy is evident in Zosimos himself. From the century after him we have two alchemists, Synesius and Olympiodorus, both represented in the Greek manuscript by complete treatises, who are generally thought to be real persons.[30] Their commentaries on the *Physica et Mystica* (Synesius) and on 'Zosimos, Hermes, and the Philosophers' (Olympiodorus) add considerably to alchemical imagery, but nothing significant to the science of matter. By the time of Olympiodorus alchemy had been 'accommodated to a melancholy natural philosophy and to Christian mysticism',[31] and a century after him we find in a work by Stephanus, a philosopher at Byzantium in the time of Heraclius, a clear statement that alchemy is a mental process.[32]

The origins and fate of 'Greek' alchemy

Attempts to reconstruct the earliest alchemy have of necessity been based primarily on our only substantial relic of the subject in antiquity, the Greek text, and on the technologically-related Leyden papyrus X. These sources point to Egypt, for the authors of the Greek text, so far as they can be identified, seem to be Hellenized Egyptians. The most prominent of them, Bolos and Zosimos, were almost certainly Egyptian. The papyrus provides the technique, (Bolos) Democritus the ideology, and Hermes the philosophy which we find thoroughly mingled in the full-blown alchemy of Zosimos.

That this reconstruction had weaknesses has never been denied. The papyrus provides the technique for Bolos, but the technique of Zosimos seems rather to be that of Maria. Zosimos' repeated insis-

[30] But not the bishop Synesius (d. 415); nor the historian (c. 365–c. 425) or the sixth-century Neoplatonic philosopher, both of whom were called Olympiodorus. On Synesius see Lippmann, 1919: 96–8; 1954: 131, and AAG, text: 56–69; trans.: 60–74, for his writing. Olympiodorus' work is in AAG, text: 69–106; trans.: 75–115, and he is discussed in Lippmann, 1919: 98–102.

[31] Lippmann, 1931: 10.

[32] Stephanos, 1937, and Taylor's note 61 thereto.

tance that (Bolos) Democritus and Maria are in agreement suggests that he is trying to hoist his countryman aboard a bandwagon which came from foreign parts.[33] It may well be that Bolos provided the ideology – at least it would otherwise be difficult to account for the esteem in which he is uniformly held – but it does not appear that Hermes really provided the philosophy. This notion probably evolved later than the time of Zosimos. Although he was to become the patron saint of alchemy in Renaissance Europe, Hermes was primarily known in antiquity as an astrological writer.[34] The philosophy of Zosimos – as, indeed, that of Bolos – is essentially Greek.

Greek theories of matter would seem in themselves a sufficient justification for an attempt at metallic transmutation, and one receives the impression that these theories were more fundamental to (Bolos) Democritus and Zosimos than were their own excursions into the occult. And yet there is mysticism in (Bolos) Democritus and Zosimos which cannot be altogether explained away. We have no record of alchemy pursued purely on the basis of Greek philosophy.

Gnosticism was the most purely Asiatic of the new philosophies. Maria, 'the Jewess', may have been from Asia. Agathodaimon, the most prominent member of her 'school', probably was too. Students of the origins of Arabic alchemy have concluded that it derived principally from Asiatic rather than Greco–Egyptian sources.[35] These circumstances have long since led authorities on alchemy to surmise the existence of a more-or-less independent development of alchemy in Asia. But in the absence of recorded evidence, this remains more difficult to reconstruct than that structure we label as Greek alchemy.

Few periods in human history have equalled the Hellenistic in the

---

[33] Lippmann attributed alchemy to 'the fully Hellenized Egyptian priesthood' (whom he held to be familiar with metallurgy), but recognized the influence of 'the Orient' (1931: 9–10). Hopkins saw alchemy terminating in Egypt after Diocletian's decree of A.D. 292 against it, and thinks some of the alchemists fled to the East where they continued to work (1934: 8–9). F. S. Taylor consistently held alchemy to be Egyptian, but admits that the earliest alchemists may have been Jewish, and calls Maria, the Jewess, the originator of the major part of the Greek alchemical process (1930: 116. 1949-1: 29).

[34] Lippmann, 1938.

[35] See below, Ch. 7.

internationalization of all aspects of human culture. Under these circumstances a 'Greco–Egyptian' and an 'Asiatic' alchemy are equally improbable. Were we not in possession of the Greek manu-script and the Leyden papyrus X, it is likely that alchemy would be pictured as a peculiarly Asiatic science, for this is its aspect from Arabic sources. Were we possessed only of the evidences of the Latin Middle Ages it would appear to have been an Arabic science. Inasmuch, however, as early alchemy has been commonly presented in the guise of a Greco-Egyptian science, the immediate problem is the recovery, insofar as possible, of its Asiatic elements.

Both Maria and (Bolos) Democritus were reputed students of Osthanes, who has already crossed our path as the first writer on magic, according to Pliny. Pliny believed Osthanes to have been a companion of Xerxes, but he was also reputed to be a pupil of Zoroaster himself, which would put him several hundred years earlier. In any case he is clearly associated with Persia, and an appro-priate symbol for the combination of astrology with Zoroastrian magic, with its dualisms of light and darkness and good and evil. This union is thought to have been wrought at Babylon, after the Persian conquest. At first a learned theory taught by 'mathematicians', it came in time, as spread through the Empire by the Roman soldier devotees of the 'Mysteries of Mithra', to be a sacred doctrine revealed to the adepts of exotic cults, which have all assumed the form of mysteries.[36] At some midpoint in this history it seems to have come into fashion among the learned in Egypt, and to have been the source of, among other things, the mystic phrase, 'One nature rejoices . . . etc.'[37]

Gnosticism seems to have been the principal carrier of magico-astrological theories to the West, although we remain without substantial documentation of its existence there in the last two centuries before Christ. We know that it was widespread in the early Christian era, and that, with the fourth-century triumph of Christianity, the Gnostics were either assimilated into the Christian community or driven to remote parts of the Empire. One such outpost was the Syrian city of Harran, which seems to have retained a primitive form of Gnosticism – and in fact to have been 'the last

[36] Cumont, 1912: 52–3.
[37] Bidez and Cumont, 1938: Vol. I, 244–6. But see above, Ch. 5, n. 28.

outpost of Sumerian, Hittite, and Babylonian civilization'[38] until the tenth century A.D. It is said that the Harranians aroused the antipathy of the early Moslems, not because they practised another religion, but because they had no sacred book, and hence seemed to the Moslems to have no religion at all. The story goes on to say that the Harranians in response scrutinized the scriptures for a tribe to associate themselves with, and became, in consequence, Sabaeans.[39]

A late Arabic writer wrote of the Sabaeans that they had seven temples dedicated to the seven planets, which they considered as intermediaries employed in their relation to God. Each of these temples had a characteristic geometric shape, a characteristic colour, and an image made of one of the seven metals. They had two sects, star and idol worshippers, and the former held their doctrine to come from Hermus al-Huramisah, through the prophet Adimun, names which stand for Hermes Trismegistus and Agathodaimon.[40] According to other Syrian legends, the bodies of these two worthies are the real tenants of the great pyramids of Egypt.[41]

Stapleton has advanced the idea that the origin of alchemy itself is to be traced to Harran, and has placed Agathodaimon there about 200 B.C., thus making him, rather than Bolos, the critical figure in the origin of alchemy, and Asia, rather than Egypt, the immediate source of its theories. Such a picture of the origins of alchemy would dispose of a number of problems, most notably that of explaining the rise of Arabic from 'Greco-Egyptian' alchemy. But this theory is not yet sufficiently well established to be susceptible to criticism, and the evidence yet assembled can hardly be said to outweigh that which has given rise to the theory of a Greco-Egyptian origin of alchemy. The undeniable involvement of Asiatic ideology and technique might lead to an alternative theory of the invention of alchemy in Egypt, by Asiatic refugees from the Persian invasion of the second century B.C. An alchemy conducted in Egypt, by Semitic immigrants, using the Greek language, would not be strange in a world which saw Rome submitting to Stoic philosophers of Syrian origin, and which was to witness a contest between Syrians and Egyptians for the honour of having founded the Greek philosophies of Neopythagoreanism and Neoplatonism.

---

[38] Stapleton, 1953: 23. [39] O'Leary, 1949: 172. From the *Fihrist*.
[40] Stapleton, Azo and Husain, 1927: 398–403. [41] Ruska, 1926: 64.

In any case Greco-Egyptian alchemy did 'decline', and the decline was rapid by the temporal standards of ancient history. Zosimos was not only the first undisputably alchemical writer; he also seems to have been the last of those in the Greek text to maintain a balance between theory and practice. With his near contemporary, Synesius, theory began to overbalance practice. Although he commented on the *Physica et Mystica* it is questionable whether or not Synesius was familiar with laboratory operations.[42] Later writers were almost certainly not. They saw Democritus as a pioneer not in the science of matter, but in the mystic science of the human soul.

[42] Festugiere, 1944: 238-40.

Chapter Seven

The medieval East

IN the fifth, sixth, and seventh centuries after Christ the ancient world gradually dissolved into that of the Middle Ages. As the political stability which Rome had imposed over a vast area from India to Spain was eroded by internal decay and external abrasion, the variegated populations of the Empire began to reassemble into fragmentary principalities, and to barricade themselves against barbarian invasion from outside the Empire. The *coup de grâce* was administered to the ancient world, and a new order was established, through a most improbable agency, the nomadic Arab. Emerging from his desert fastness in the second quarter of the seventh century, he continually extended his political and religious hegemony for a century, during which he conquered more than the southern half of the former Roman Empire, from Persia to Spain. The Arab was to decline as a political factor in this vast realm, but his language and religion were to prevail. Henceforth this region was to be 'Arabic', in the same sense as much of it had earlier been 'Greek'.

Milestones in the formation of the medieval world were the transfer of the capital of the Empire to Byzantium (at the founding of Constantinople, 330), the decline of the Museum of Alexandria after about 400, the expulsion of the learned academicians of the Nestorian sect from Edessa (Syria) and the migration of their philosophers to the Persian medical school at Jundishapur (489), the forced closing of the philosophical schools at Athens (529), the founding of Islam and the Arab conquest of Syria, Persia and Egypt (622–43), the successful defence of Constantinople against the Arabs (717), and the defence of Western Europe against them in the battle of Tours (732). These dates enclose the formative period of the medieval world.

The pattern thus set for the Middle Ages saw three relatively-independent cultures, Arabic, Byzantine, and Western European, established in what had been the Greco-Roman world. The student of intellectual history is confronted not only by the problem of differentiating the three, but by that of distinguishing that which is original in their thought from that which is residual from the cultures from which they descended. All three tended to be theocratic, and to regard with disfavour the secular orientation of the 'pagan' learning of Greco-Roman antiquity. But this was more a matter of spirit than of fact. It led to such remarkable dislocations as the flight of academic philosophy from Athens to Persia, and the flight of Islamic philosophy from Bagdad to Persia and then to Spain – the ends of the Moslem world; and, finally, to the gathering of those loose ends in Western Europe, an event which foreshadowed the 'renaissance' of that region and the end of the Middle Ages.

These bizarre migrations are primarily reflected in our written, rather than in archaeological, sources. The latter bespeak a widespread practice of the chemical technology outlined in Chapter One, particularly of that part associated with the goldsmith; and not only in metropolitan Byzantium and Bagdad, but in the remotest parts of the medieval world.[1] Surviving artifacts indicate that no techniques of practical chemistry were lost, and few gained. They suggest that the technique of the craftsman continued to outdistance his science, and that he developed to the utmost the possibilities inherent in his materials while continuing to utilize only those materials known from high antiquity. The few new materials or chemical techniques introduced during the Middle Ages seem to have influenced the theorist greatly, but the technologist very little. But as always it must be said that the literary reticence of the technologist makes our conclusions about him somewhat suppositious.

The Eastern Roman, or Byzantine, Empire was the logical and avowed successor to the ancient Roman Empire. When, in 800, Charlemagne's foundation of a Western 'Roman Empire' was added to the accomplished alienation to Islam of Africa and most of Asia, Byzantium became a beleaguered fortress of the ancient culture.

[1] Maryon, 1956.

Among the most remarkable features of this fortress was its monumental disinterest in one of the particular features of the culture it defended, natural philosophy. As is suggested by the chronology just reviewed, the pursuit of natural philosophy and science had virtually ceased in the Roman Empire before its political disintegration. The internal history of Byzantium provides no reason to contradict this impression. The last author, or authors, of the Greek alchemical text – and, consequently, the compilation of that text – belonged to Byzantium. But it was Synesius, who is reliably associated with that kingdom, who defined alchemy as a mental operation, and who established its independence of the science of matter. So far as we know, alchemy was not pursued at Byzantium after him, even as an esoteric science.

The existence of the Greek text testifies to the importance of Byzantium as an archive of ancient records. It also seems to have preserved the recipe book of the goldsmith, in a form very like that of the Leyden and Stockholm papyri; for Byzantium, which among the Christians had a near monopoly through the sixth century on the decorative arts,[2] is in all probability the source of the first of the remarkable succession of tracts on the chemistry of the arts which are found in Europe from the eighth century. It is astonishing that no similar tracts have been turned up in Arabic, where we find, instead, a new type of writing on practical chemistry, which can only be called 'practical alchemy'.

Arabic natural philosophy

Mohammed died in 632, and was followed until 661 as titular head of Islam by four successors who took the title Caliph, each being elevated according to the circumstances existing at the time of the death of his predecessor. The time of these first Caliphs saw the conquest of Syria, Egypt, and Persia, and gave the Arabs a taste of power which led to 'the first civil war', and the establishment of a dynasty of Caliphs, the Omayyads. During this period the economic life of the Arabs continued to be based on the tent city of their nomadic past, and their intellectual life varied principally in the

[2] R. P. Johnson, 1939: 70–6.

emergence of a literature of commentary on the Koran. These circumstances continued to prevail for another century, until the overthrow of the Omayyad dynasty and the foundation of that of the Abbasids, with a 'permanent' capital at Bagdad. With this dynasty began the massive conquest of Greek philosophy and science which was to make Arabic the successor to Greek as the language of learning. A tradition of the study of Greek philosophy in Syriac translation had existed since the sixth century at nearby Jundishapur. Under the stimulus of royal support a massive programme of translation into Arabic was undertaken. Most of those who translated from Greek into Arabic were Christians, although the Sabaean community at Harran is prominently mentioned in connection with mathematical translations, and has, indeed, been called 'the source of Hellenism to the Abbasid age'.[3] By the middle ninth century an original, if Greek oriented, Arabic philosophy had come into existence. The period of about two centuries between the founding of Bagdad (763) and the death of the philosopher al-Fārābī (950-1) has been called the golden age of Arabic philosophy, a statement which must be understood to refer to the practice of philosophy by the Arabs themselves. An orthodox and anti-intellectual reaction gained momentum in Bagdad during the lifetime of al-Fārābī, and the great philosophers of Islam subsequently appeared elsewhere.

Islamic natural philosophy is dominated by three figures, al-Kindī, an Arab of the mid-ninth century, al-Fārābī, a Turk who died about 950, and Avicenna, a Persian who died in 1037. To these must be added the Persian physician al-Rāzī (c. 850-923-24) who, if less important to philosophy in general, had particular importance to natural philosophy. Three of these flourished in Bagdad, but Avicenna worked in Persia after the orthodox reaction in that city. They all represented a secular and quasi-Hellenic learning appropriately known as 'falasifa', and they tended to be even more encyclopaedic in their interests than had been their classical Greek models. This is indicated by the fortunate survival of a tenth-century Arabic book catalogue, the *Fihrist*. There al-Kindī is credited with no less than 36 works on technology and chemistry.[4] One of these which has recently been published, on the extraction of

---

[3] Afnan, 1958: 9, 14, 15. See also O'Leary, 1949.
[4] Flugel; 1857: 33-5.

perfumes, indicates that the often fantastic distillation apparatus of Maria had by the time of al-Kindī taken a more modern and utilitarian form.[5] All four philosophers mentioned alchemy. Al-Kindī and Avicenna disapproved of it, although it is not clear whether they denied the possibility of gold-making or merely the claims of alchemists.[6] Al-Fārābī seems to have believed in alchemy,[7] and al-Rāzī not only believed in it, but practised it. He was the only major Arabic philosopher to have been personally involved in alchemy.

These savants pursued with increasing zeal the objective of abolishing the Aristotelian dichotomy between heaven and earth, for among the Arabs, as among the Christians, the First Cause was the Deity, to whom the world was directly connected. Al-Kindī was celebrated as an astrologer as well as a natural philosopher, and he filled in the space between God and the world with emanations, which he called 'intelligence of incorporeal substance', residing between God on the one hand and the triad of soul, form and matter on the other.[8] Five 'eternal substances' were postulated as ingredients of all things by both al-Kindī, who mentioned matter, form, place, motion, and time,[9] and al-Rāzī, who spoke of God, soul, matter, space, and time.[10] Al-Fārābī, though reportedly denying astrology, organized the emanations even more specifically into a system of spheres,[11] and Avicenna gave a certain finality to the Stoic substitu-

[5] Garbers, 1948: 19, 20.

[6] Flugel (1857) mentions two works on alchemy by al-Kindī, 'Warnung, die auf die Trugkunste der Alchymisten aufmerksam macht', and 'Abhandlung über die Nichtigkeit der Anmassung derer, die sich des Besitzer der Kunst Gold und Silber zu machen rühmen, und über ihre Betrugereien'. I know of no detail on these works. Flugel says al-Kindī showed the worthlessness (Nichtigkeit) of alchemy (1857: 13), and Muhammad Jamāl al-Dīn ibn Nubatah (d. 1366) had declared that al-Kindī's work (apparently the second listed above) had said that 'men cannot do what only nature can' (al-Ahwani, 1960: 8; I owe this reference to Dr Sami Hamarneh). But there seems to be some question as to whether al-Kindī denied alchemy or only alchemists. Levey has merely stated that he 'displayed skepticism' (in Farber, 1961: 23), and Afnan says that he 'argued for it as a legitimate pursuit' (1958: 206). On Avicenna see below, note p. 131-2.

[7] In his On the origins of the sciences he lists as one of eight parts of physics, 'alchemy, which is the science of the conversion of things into other species' (al-Fārābī, 1916: 20–21).

[8] Al-Kindī, 1897: 30 (De quinque essentiis). Cf. Flugel, 1857: 10–2. Dieterici, 1892: 179–83.

[9] 1897: 30 (De quinque essentiis).

[10] Meyerhof, 1941: 55–6.

[11] 1892: 179–83 (Risāla fusūs al-hikam [Bezels of philosophy]).

tion of pneumata for the Peripatetic forms by regarding the forms themselves as emanations.

These cogitations represent an effort to adapt Peripatetic doctrines of metaphysics and the nature of the heavens to Moslem thought. But having established the desired connection between heaven and earth the Islamic philosophers went still further, and attempted to maintain a consistent doctrine on the level of microphysics. Aristotle, in accordance with his opinion as to the relativity of terminology, had not much concerned himself to maintain consistency between his metaphysics and his physics, and had largely abandoned his metaphysical doctrine of matter and form when discussing changes in terrestrial things, for which he had recourse to the elements and qualities (the contrarieties), privation, and action and passion. The Arabs declined to leave 'form' out of account, and gave it as important a role in chemistry as they did in metaphysics.

In his *Catalogue of the sciences* (Kitāb ihsa al-ulum), al-Fārābī makes a doctrinaire Peripatetic distinction between natural and artificial bodies, and between the simple and the compound. The simple body is not made of anything other than itself, whereas the composite body is made not only of 'the combinables' (as Aristotle had called them in *On generation and corruption*), but also of 'form'.[12] Aristotle had held 'the combinables' and form to be insufficient to explain changes in things (*On gen.*, 335b), but the Arabs had a new idea, which was to recomplicate the vexing question of the sense in which the ingredients persist in a compound. Avicenna, who codified the conception, if he did not originate it, held that mixis involves a weakening or 'remission' of the contrarieties, but added that at the moment of remission the new substance is endowed with a new 'substantial form'.[13] If this provided (as it did) a connection between the mundane science of matter and the 'eternal substances' of the Arabic philosophers, it also represented a remixing of physics and metaphysics which was of no benefit to the former, for it tended to restore questions of matter to the realm of ontology. The doctrine of substantial forms was to be argued over by Arabs and Latins

[12] 1953: 161.
[13] 1955–58, Vol. 2: 44–45. See also Maier, 1952: 23–24. Support for this can be found in Aristotle's logical work, *Categories* (10b), to the extent that he held qualities to admit of variation of degree.

until it became the 'Peripatetic' doctrine against which the natural philosophers of the seventeenth century were to rebel.

It was not only chemistry which was affected, for al-Kindī and al-Fārābī pressed forward with an attempt to explain the First Cause in terms of terrestrial physics, while at the same time defending the uniqueness of God.[14] They satisfied neither the theologians nor all of the falasifa. Al-Rāzī went so far as to deny the possibility of a reconciliation between philosophy and religion,[15] and his opinion was increasingly shared by Moslem theologians. Abbasid metaphysical toleration began to break down under the Caliph Mutawakkil (847–61) who backed the orthodox Sunnite sect against Moslem liberalism. Although this finally stifled the pursuit of philosophy at Bagdad, the objectives of the falasifa, in a transmuted form, continued to preoccupy certain secret societies which were the natural products of a period of oppression. The most important of these were the mystic societies of the Sūfī and the Ismā'īlī, the first anti-scientific and the second pro-scientific. These societies had political as well as philosophical objectives, and the Ismā'īlī were to stray into the extremes of both. In 930 they sacked Mecca, and stole the black stone of the Kaaba. A generation later they conquered Egypt where they set up an independent dynasty (the Fatamid). In philosophy they wandered into Neopythagorean number mysticism, theories of correspondence between macrocosm and microcosm, and alchemy.

Arabic philosophy was to become independent of Bagdad, however. The Abbasid Caliphate had never secured control over the whole territory of Islam, and as time went by the geographical extremities showed increasing independence. Here was refuge for the falasifa, after the orthodox reaction at Bagdad. In the eleventh century Persia provided both the refuge and, in Avicenna, the philosopher. One of the greatest of Islamic thinkers, he, like Alexander of Aphrodisias some eight centuries earlier, undertook the restoration of the 'true' Aristotle. As has already been related, the consequence for the mundane science of matter was decidedly regressive. Shortly after Avicenna's death the wave of orthodoxy

[14] Al-Kindī, 1897. Al-Fārābī, 1892: 179–83. 1900: 27–30. Cf. Duhem, SM, Vol. 4: 465, and Madkour, 1934: 94–5, 68–72.

[15] Kraus, art. 'al-Rāzī' in EI-1.

spread over Persia and Avicenna's mode of philosophizing disappeared. But it was to emerge again in Moslem Spain, where the following century was to produce another major figure, Averroës, and where philosophy was finally to be transmitted to the Christian West.

The Eastern alchemists

The aforementioned Arabic bibliography of the sciences, *Fihrist*, was completed by the Bagdad bookseller, al-Nadīm, in 987. In a section devoted to alchemy al-Nadīm reports that the first to have Arabic translations made in astronomy, medicine and alchemy was Khālid (d. *c.* 704), son of the second Omayyad Caliph, Yazīd.[16] Khālid was allegedly instructed by a Christian monk, Morienus, and there is a work extant in Latin which purports to recount this instruction. This work identifies itself as a translation made from the Arabic in 1144 by Robert of Chester, who was one of the most celebrated of the twelfth-century Latin translators. It has been widely regarded as the earliest extant Latin translation of an Arabic alchemical work,[17] but its connection with Khālid has been discredited by Ruska, whose study of the Khālid-Morienus question led him to consider the association of Khālid with alchemy to be without foundation.[18]

This far from exhausts al-Nadīm's *Fihrist*, however. There is a list of 45 books, representing nearly as many authors, which al-Nadīm believed to have been known to Khālid, and which should thus be pre-Arabic. Since these books are described in such general terms as 'the book of Democritus', they cannot be identified with certainty, and, in fact, can in only a few cases even be identified with any probability. Three of the works from the Greek text seem to be listed, those of (Bolos) Democritus, Zosimos and Pelagius.[19] Also

[16] This and subsequent citations of the *Fihrist* refer to the English translation of the tenth discourse, on alchemy, by Fück (1951).

[17] Printed in BCC, Vol. 1: 509–19, and translated into English by Holmyard (1925). It exists in Latin manuscripts as early as the thirteenth century (CLAM, No. 66), but has not been found in an Arabic version.

[18] Ruska, 1924–1: 50–52.

[19] 'The book of Democritus' (*Physica et Mystica*?), 'The book of Zosimos to all the scholars on the Art', and 'The epistles of Pelagios on the Art'. Pelagios is represented in the Greek text by a work called 'On the divine and sacred art', which is printed and translated in AAG, Text, 253–61; (French) trans., 243–50.

listed are Jāmāsp and Asfidūs, purported to be a Persian alchemist and his follower, and Stapleton has recently discovered works attributed to these authors.[20] Another tract listed, the *Book of Crates*, was published many years ago as an example of early or pre-Arabic alchemy.[21] It states that Khālid, himself, is the author or abbreviator, but this has been rejected along with other ascriptions to Khālid.

Al-Nadīm also gives a list of 'names of philosophers who have discussed the art', comprising 52 names, only a few of which are duplicated in the list of books known to Khālid. Khālid himself is thirty-fifth on the list, which is headed by the names of Hermes and Agathodaimon, followed by certain names which can be identified – Balīnūs (Apollonius of Tyana), Plato, Zosimos, Democritus, Osthanes and Mary – among a larger number of unknowns. These familiar names all appear among the first dozen on al-Nadīm's list. The attribution of alchemical writing to such famous Greeks as Apollonius and Plato was particularly characteristic of Arabic writers, and reached its culmination in the ninth- or tenth-century *Turba philosophorum*, a bizarre account of a supposed convention of ancient philosophers which has been dubbed 'a report of the hermetic association for the advancement of alchemy'.[22] The deciphering of this multitude of references will long remain a standing challenge to the student of alchemy.

The persistence with which Balīnūs is mentioned by Arabic writers requires that he be taken seriously. It is generally agreed that the name refers to the philosopher Apollonius (first century A.D.), of Tyana, a city in the same part of Syria (now part of Turkey) which produced most of the important Stoic philosophers.[23] Like them Apollonius became a prominent figure in the intellectual life

[20] Reference is to a manuscript treatise, 'Risalah of Jamas the sage, for Ardrashīr the king, on the hidden secret: and it is a wonderful treatise translated from Persian into Arabic' Copies in the Rampur and Hyderabad libraries are discussed in Stapleton, Lewis, and Taylor, 1949: 88, and in Stapleton, 1953: 28. The treatise by Asfidūs, in the Cairo library, is largely a paraphrase of Jāmāsp (Stapleton, 1953: 26).

[21] CMA Vol. 3: 44–75 (French trans. from Leyden Arabic MS 440). The origin of this work remains very uncertain. Ruska (1924–1: 16–24) considered it to be of Coptic origin and dated it after Olympiodorus (sixth century) and earlier than the eighth century; but he subsequently (1935–1: 51) held that there must be a Greek or Greco-Iranian prototype.

[22] Ferguson, 1906: Vol. 2, 478–9. Ferguson lists 100 proper names which appear in the *Turba*. For an analysis of the work and its date see Ruska, 1931.

[23] Kraus, 1942: 270 ff., includes an extensive bibliography on Balīnūs–Apollonius.

of Greece and Rome. He was equally cosmopolitan, although usually referred to as a Pythagorean, and is supposed to have visited 'the Magi in Babylon', and other wise men from India to Spain. He was reputed a wonder-worker, sometimes being listed as such with Zoroaster and Osthanes, and was even set up among the pagans of third-century Rome as a rival to Christ.[24]

Attention was called as early as 1799 to the existence of a work called *Book of the secret of creation* (Kitāb sirr al-haliqua) which was attributed to Balīnūs.[25] It is a summary astrological cosmology treating of the heavens, earth, and man. Although it contains nothing contradictory to alchemy, it is not concerned with gold-making, and its relevance to that art has only become evident since the studies of Ruska and Kraus in the two decades after 1925 first revealed the esteem in which Balīnūs was held by such notable Arabic alchemists as al-Rāzī and the Jābirian writers.

The *Secret of creation* has never been printed, but it exists in both Latin and Arabic manuscript versions.[26] These exhibit a remarkable number of the favourite notions of Arabic alchemy, and seem to carry them to a time prior to al-Rāzī and the Jābirian authors. It contains the theory that metals derive from a mixture of mercury and sulphur,[27] mentions sal ammoniac and borax, and in general refers to substances in a way which anticipates the systematic discussions of al-Rāzī.[28] It incorporates the 'Emerald tablet of Hermes

---

[24] Conybeare, 1927: Introduction.

[25] Silvestre de Sacy, 1799.

[26] On the manuscripts see Ruska, 1926: 124–8. Three have been described and printed or translated in part, namely from: (1) BN Arabic MS 959 (sixteenth century, purportedly copied from a tenth-century MS – see Silvestre de Sacy, 1799), (2) BN Latin MS 13951 (twelfth century – see Nau, 1907), and (3) Leipzig Arabic MS V. 832 (sixteenth century, purportedly copied from an eleventh-century MS – see Ruska, 1926: 124–63). There appears to be considerable variation between these three manuscripts, and while I have used BN Latin MS 13951 (in microfilm) I have not attempted a complete analysis of it. A critical edition is much to be desired.

[27] BN Latin MS 13951, fol. 12v. Also in the Leipzig Arabic MS, according to Ruska, 1926: 142.

[28] Ruska states that the *Secret of creation* anticipates al-Rāzī's classification of minerals (1926: 171), apparently on the basis of a reference to 'vitriol, salt, and borax' in Gotha Arabic MS 82, although Ruska in another place calls this passage an interpolation (ibid.; 152). 'Sale', 'alumine', 'atramento', and 'sal armoniaco' are mentioned in BN Latin MS 13591 (fols. 13r–15v), but not in a way which I would call classificatory. I have been unable to find borax in this text.

Trismegistus',[29] which was to be esteemed by the Latins of the later Middle Ages as one of the most profound of all alchemical writings. As though this were not enough, a Jābirian writer has been shown by Kraus to have assigned to Balīnūs another of the most celebrated 'Jābirian' theories, according to which substances can be synthesized by the mixture of elements and qualities according to a mathematical formula![30]

Despite general agreement that the name Balīnūs refers to Apollonius, it is doubted that Apollonius, who lived in the first century A.D., can have been the author of the *Secret of creation*. The *Fihrist* mentions Balīnūs as an 'early' author,[31] but al-Rāzī believed the *Secret of creation* to have been written in the time of the Caliph al-Ma'mūn (813–33),[32] In modern times we find Kraus in accord with al-Rāzī and Ruska siding with the *Fihrist*.

The crucial question at this stage is whether or not the *Secret of creation* is a pre-Arabic work, and here Ruska and Kraus were not very far apart. The aforementioned *Book of Crates*, which has been variously dated from the sixth to the eighth century, was regarded by Ruska as one of a whole family of treatises deriving from the *Secret of creation*, which he calls 'die Apollonischen Schriftenkreise', another member of which is the Syriac *Book of treasures* of Job of Edessa, who appears to have died in 835.[33] Kraus held the *Book of treasures* and the *Secret of creation* to be from a common source, which would appear to be the pre-Arabic version of the latter.[34] Thus Kraus' late dating of the *Secret of creation* seems to have been largely a reservation as to the primitive character of the extant versions.

The date of the *Secret of creation* has also been sought through the

---

[29] The *Emerald tablet* concludes the *Secret of creation* in BN Latin MS 13951 (fol. 31r). Ruska's discovery of the *Emerald tablet* in the Leipzig manuscript of the *Secret of creation* (Ruska, 1926: 163) was the source of his interest in Balīnūs. On early European writing on the *Emerald tablet* see Steele and Singer, 1928; Ruska, 1926: 180–6. It is a literature of commentary on its mystic phraseology which may have begun as early as the translator Plato of Tivoli (fl. 1134–45), but which does not seem to have been associated with Balīnūs.

[30] Kraus, 1942: 188, 196. This is apparently not in the *Secret of creation*, however.

[31] Fück, 1951: 92. Balīnūs is the fourth of 52 'names of philosophers who have discussed the art' listed in the *Fihrist*.

[32] According to Kraus, 1942: 275.

[33] Ruska, 1926: 123.

[34] 1942: 275–8.

name, Sadijous the priest (sometimes called Sagijus of Nablus), which appears as that of the editor (or translator) in Arabic versions. These efforts have been inconclusive, but lend further credence to the belief that the work is essentially pre-Arabic.[35] Ruska doubts that it is Syriac. He concludes his study of the parentage of the *Emerald tablet* with the suggestion that the *Secret of creation* was written between 600 and 750, and was a product of the mixed and essentially non-Christian culture of the Oxus-Jaxartes region of north-east Persia. He further suggests that its cosmology may have originated in the intellectual centre of that region, Balkh, and has been carried from there to Islam by Khālid ibn Barmak, founder of the dynasty of ruling government officials at Bagdad during the first flourishing years of the Abbasid Chaliphate after 750.[36] This Khālid (not to be confused with Khālid ibn Yazīd) presided over the Arabic 'conquest of Greek philosophy and science' which has been mentioned earlier. But he was a native of Balkh, the legendary home of Zoroaster and the Magi. Ruska conjectures that the Christianization of Syria in the fifth century may have driven the speculative natural philosophers into this land of the Magi. If we cannot connect Apollonius with the *Secret of creation*, we may imagine that, through Khālid ibn Barmak, the Magi endowed the West with something in return for Apollonius' visit long before, to 'the Magi in Babylon'.

The career of Balīnūs is the most recent of the enigmas of Arabic alchemy, and follows closely on that of Jābir ibn Haiyān, one of the strangest stories in the bizarre history of alchemy.[37] Under the name Geber he enjoyed among the Latins the reputation of the greatest of alchemists, and deservedly so, for a group of treatises which

---

[35] The name, 'Sadijous the priest', which appears in the version discussed by Silvestre de Sacy (1799), was tentatively identified by Nau (1907: 99) with the well known Syrian translator, Sergius of Reschaina (d. *c.* 536), but this identification has not been accepted by later authorities. Ruska held 'Sagijus of Nablus', as he appears in MS Leipzig Arabic V. 832, to have lived later than the eleventh century (1926: 111), but Kraus believed that he lived in Syria in pre-Islamic times (1942: 280).

This seems to leave the question open, as al-Rāzī mentions both Sergius and Balīnūs as alchemists, but does not speak of any connection between them (Stapleton and Azo, 1910: 72–3). The *Fihrist* mentions Balīnūs, Sergius (as author of three books), and 'Saqiyas'. Such are the peculiarities of Arabic orthography that the latter is held to be a misreading of Asfidus ! (Fück, 1951: 94, 120, 123).

[36] Ruska, 1926: 166–75. Cf. Plessner, 1927.

[37] For a summary of the Jābir–Geber literature, see Kraus, 1943. Ruska, 1937-I.

circulated under his name from about 1300 constituted the first comprehensive treatment in Latin of both theory and practice. Modern scholarship has laboured mightily to reconstruct Jābir's biography, with the following result: (1) the Latin writings attributed to Geber have not been found in an Arabic version, and probably originated in south Italy in the thirteenth century; (2) there is in Arabic a large body of alchemical writing attributed to Jābir, but little known to the Latins of the Middle Ages; and (3) Jābir, who also enjoyed a great reputation among the Arabs, was not the author of all of these works; indeed, he may never have existed at all. The major part of the Arabic Jābirian alchemy is part of the natural philosophy of the Ismā'īlī sect.[38]

Kraus, the leading authority on 'the Jābir question', believed that the tradition of Jābirian alchemy may have begun in the second half of the ninth century, with the appearance of an alchemical treatise reminiscent of those of the later Greeks, the *Book of mercy* (Kitāb al rahma or Kitāb al uss).[39] It was probably at the end of that century that Ismā'īlī alchemists now unknown borrowed the name of Jābir as the author of two large collections of works on practical alchemy, the *Hundred and twelve books* and the *Seventy books* (their Arabic names are consistent only as regards the number), the former a group of relatively independent treatises and the latter a more systematic work. A more comprehensive natural philosophy including a theory of alchemy, appeared in the celebrated *Book of the balances* (Kitāb al-Mawāzīn), at the beginning of the next century, and, towards 950, in the *Five hundred books*, fourth and last of the Jābirian collections. By the second half of the tenth century the entire Jābirian corpus had been constituted, and was generally, if not unanimously, admitted as the authentic work of Jābir.[40]

Jābir has been regarded as one of two outstanding alchemists produced by the Arabic world, the other being al-Rāzī. Al-Rāzī, who has already been mentioned as a philosopher, was one of the

---

[38] Kraus, 1942: xlv, speaks of Shi'ite alchemists. The Ismā'īlī were an extremist branch of the Shi'ite sect, who were among the Moslems principally interested in philosophy and the occult. Their rise paralleled that of Islamic alchemy.

[39] CMA, Vol. 3: 163–90 (French trans. from Leyden Arabic MS 1264). Darmstaedter, 1925 (Latin version from Florence MS Riccard. 933 [thirteenth century]). For a comparison of these with other MSS see Kraus, 1942: 5–9.

[40] Kraus, 1942: lxv.

most distinguished figures in Arabic science. He was born in 864, received his early education at the Persian town of Raiy, and moved to Bagdad after about 894. There he became a prominent physician and began the series of medical works which have given him the reputation as the greatest of Islamic medical writers. His medical works were influential in the later revival of European medicine, and were still used in Dutch medical schools, among the most advanced in Europe, in the seventeenth century! He died in 925.[41]

Al-Rāzī wrote on most of the sciences then recognized, and on mathematics and metaphysics, but most of this seems to be lost except for his work on medicine and alchemy. There were 19 alchemical works, according to the *Fihrist*, a unit of 12 books, variously titled, and 7 other works. Extant are two of the 12 books and two of the other works. The most important, which seems to summarize the alchemy of al-Rāzī, is the *Book of the secret of secrets* (Kitāb sirr al-asrār).[42]

Al-Rāzī's most notable characteristic is his rationality. He has been referred to as a tenth-century Boyle,[43] and (which certainly would not be said of Boyle) the author of the most caustic criticism of established religion of the Middle Ages.[44] This stress on mundane rationality constitutes the most conspicuous difference between al-Rāzī's alchemy and that of the Jābirian writings, which are in many respects very similar. Of the voluminous Jābirian writings only the *Book of mercy* is mentioned by al-Rāzī, and, as we have noted, this was the earliest work in the Jābirian corpus. There are resemblances which are sometimes startlingly close between some of al-Rāzī's writings and parts of the *Hundred and twelve* and the

---

[41] Heym, 1938. See also Kraus, art. al-Rāzī, in EI-I.

[42] Ruska, 1935–1. Another authority, al-Bīrūnī (d. 1048) said that al-Rāzī wrote 21 alchemical works (Ruska, 1923–2: 45). According to Ruska (1935–2: 286) both a *Book of secrets* (Kitāb al-asrār) and a *Book of the secret of secrets* (Kitāb sirr al-asrār) are extant from al-Rāzī. Ruska does not, however, describe their differences, nor does he go into this in his exposition of the *Book of the secret of secrets* (1935–1), where most of the Latin versions cited are called *Liber secretorum*. It seems questionable that there were actually two books. Heym believed that *Kitāb al-asrār* rather than *Kitāb sirr al-asrār* is 'the true title of al-Rāzī's book' (1938: 186.n 16). A comparison of Stapleton's exposition of the *Kitāb al-asrār* with Ruska's description of the *Kitāb sirr al-asrār* gives the impression that they are very similar, indeed, if not identical (cf. Stapleton, Azo, and Husain, 1927: 231–2; Ruska, 1935–1: 34).

[43] Stapleton, Azo, and Husain, 1927: 335.

[44] Kraus, art. al-Rāzī in EI.

Seventy books, but these seem to point to common dependence on some earlier source (Balīnūs?) rather than to borrowing between al-Rāzī and the Jābirian writers.[45] It is unlikely that the two later Jābirian collections, the *Book of the balances* and the *Five hundred books*, existed in the lifetime of al-Rāzī.

The illumination of alchemy by the Arabs was like a meteor which flashed across the tenth-century sky. There were Islamic alchemists before and after al-Rāzī and the Jābirian writers, but they exhibit little distinction, even within the context of alchemy. The meteor seems to have left a glow in the West, in Arabic Spain, from which European alchemy was to be ignited in the twelfth century, but this is a story reserved for a later chapter.

Alchemical theory

Theories of mineral formation are found in greater or lesser detail in the works of al-Fārābī,[46] the Faithful Brothers[47] (Ikhwān al-safā', a tenth-century secret society), and Avicenna, and they show an elaboration of their Aristotelian base both in the direction of a more perspicacious observation of geological phenomena and in that of an extended involvement of emanations, as exemplified by the 'mineralizing virtue' evoked by Avicenna as the agent of mineral formation.[48] The Arabic natural philosophers were acquainted with alchemy, but the influence this might be expected to exercise on their theories of matter is not evident. Despite their effort to unify the philosophies of heaven and earth their ideas remained in the end largely compartmentalized in the Peripatetic tradition. Alchemy, moreover, was an enterprise which the leading Arabic philosophers opposed. It is ironic that al-Rāzī, the only thoroughgoing alchemist among the leaders of Arabic thought, is characterized in his alchemy by a devotion to practice and an indifference to theory.

In the present state of Arabic studies the attitudes of leading Arabic philosophers towards alchemy will remain nebulous. It is only certain that several of them disapproved of it. Avicenna seems to have denied the possibility of alchemy on the ground that 'species' cannot

[45] Kraus, 1943: lxi–lxii.　　　　　　　　[46] Cf. al-Fārābī, 1892: 183.
[47] Dieterici, 1876 and 1879, include German translations of relevant passages.
[48] Avicenna, 1927: 33–42.

be changed, and on the basis of the less confidently expressed opinion that their specific differences derive from differences in the proportions of the elements which are both unknown and beyond the powers of the alchemist's techniques to determine. But these sturdy reservations are undermined by his attempt to reconcile the mineralizing virtue with the Aristotelian subterranean exhalations and by his admission of the involvement of the ubiquitous mercury and sulphur. It is not clear that Avicenna's denial of alchemy was equivalent to a denial of the possibility of metallic transmutation.[49] More important, it is not clear that Arabic alchemy was significantly influenced by Avicenna. By far the most influential philosopher among the Arabic alchemists seems to have been Balīnūs.

The astrological cosmology in Balīnūs' *Secret of creation* begins with chapters on the heavens, followed by others on the seven spheres of the planets, on meteorology, on the metals and their sympathy with the planets, on mercury and sulphur as parents of the metals, on minerals, vegetables, and animals, and, finally, on man.[50]

'The divine word was the cause of all creation', according to Balīnūs, and the first thing to appear was the light of the word of God. It gave birth to action, action to movement, and movement to heat. The agitation of heat gave rise to a division of matter, by reason of its volatility and lightness. In a second stage generation took place. Here heat acted as male, cold as female, and their union produced humidity and dryness. Cold and dryness then produced (the element) earth, and finally 'the creatures of the three realms' appeared, and *the* Earth was formed.[51]

The most original aspect of this cosmogony appears to be in the reference to 'creatures of the three realms', for this signifies the division of 'things' into the categories animal, vegetable and mineral.

[49] Avicenna, 1927. It is perhaps worth recalling the words of the late-fifteenth-century Latin encyclopaedist, Polydore Vergil, who asks whether alchemy is 'lawful'. He reports that lawyers have pondered this. It appears unlawful since it belongs to God alone to change one substance into another. Yet they considered that it is lawful, because all metals proceed out of sulphur and mercury, which 'if they receive air, water, and heat sufficiently, are turned into gold'. Therefore human art does not turn one substance into another, but heat and temperament – which the alchemists supply by their art (1868: 237).

[50] BN Latin MS 13951. Cf. Silvestre de Sacy, 1799. Nau, 1907. Ruska, 1926: 141–7. These three texts show considerable variation in detail.

[51] Silvestre de Sacy, 1799: 144. This passage is not mentioned by Nau but seems to be present in the manuscript studied by Ruska (1926: 149).

And despite his reference to minerals as 'creatures', Balīnūs seems to differentiate them quite clearly as inanimate, 'purely corporeal, devoid of movement and life'.[52] And yet having registered this clear distinction between the animate and the inanimate, he proceeds to introduce that peculiar animation of the mineral kingdom which was characteristic of alchemy. Along with other sub-lunary bodies, minerals owe their existence to the celestial bodies, and the seven metals (the seventh is mercury) are bodies each having a spirit in sympathetic correspondence with one of the spheres of the seven planets. The metals have sexual characteristics, gold, iron and lead being male, copper, tin and silver, female, and mercury being hermaphroditic. Mercury, finally, is the 'principle' of the other metals, being itself formed in mines by a repeated volatilization of water, and undergoing a kind of fermentation with sulphur in the formation of the other metals. Many other minerals are uncompleted metals, especially the fusible minerals, which can be divided into different degrees of perfection.[53]

The alchemist Zosimos had already applied to the mineral kingdom a science of 'the composition of waters, movement, growth, embodying and disembodying, drawing the spirits from bodies and binding the spirits with bodies . . .',[54] but within the context of metal ennoblement, not of cosmology. It is difficult not to suppose that such a cosmology as that of Balīnūs must underlie the ideas of Zosimos. As matters stand, we must wait several centuries after Zosimos' death for the first clear statement of the cosmology underlying alchemy. As might be inferred from Zosimos, himself, it exhibits two contradictory developments: on the one hand, a clear-cut distinction of the mineral kingdom as inanimate, which contrasts markedly with the vague and generalized vitalism of earlier natural philosophers; and on the other the establishment of a specific vitalism based on sex and fermentation, which was to persist in alchemy to the end of its history as a branch of science.

A precise placement of the *Secret of creation* in the history of science must await a critical edition. None of the several surveys of the work,

[52] Silvestre de Sacy, 1799: 150.

[53] Ibid., 1799: 149–53. Although not set forth in detail this ideology is also indicated in the remarks of Nau (1907) and Ruska (1926).

[54] See above, p. 105.

however, have produced evidence that Balīnūs was an alchemist, and this despite his apparent role as the author of the *Emerald tablet*, the sacred text of European alchemy, and the indebtedness to him of the leading Arabic alchemists, who seem to have paid little attention to the *Emerald tablet*, but owe to Balīnūs much of their theory on the rational practice of alchemy. Not only does the *Secret of creation* exhibit some of this theory, but Balīnūs is frequently acknowledged as a predecessor, especially by the Jābirian writers.

Perhaps most remarkable of all is the assignment to Balīnūs of the 'theory of the balance', by the Jābirian author of the *Seventy books*, for the *Secret of creation* does not seem to contain this. Oddly enough, the *Book of treasures* of Job of Edessa does suggest it. Job says that the metals differ in degrees of perfection, as in the tendency of all except gold and silver to rust and to have a disagreeable smell and taste, for the reason that they 'do not possess balance of parts'.[55] Job was neither an alchemist nor an astrologer, but aside from the astrology his view of the genesis of metals is very similar to that of Balīnūs. Kraus has remarked on the curious circumstance that Job's *Book of treasures* deals with almost the same topics as the *Secret of creation*, but in the reverse order, and believes them to have a common source.[56] The place of astrology in the *Secret of creation* is taken in the *Book of treasures* by the Aristotelian contrarieties, or 'simple elements' as Job calls them, and, indeed, the work is a virtual *tour de force* on the multifarious interactions of the hot, cold, wet, and dry.[57] One receives the impression that Job may be engaged in cleaning up a pagan tradition for Christian consumption.

The Jābirian *Seventy books* expounds the theory that the metals form in the earth through a proportionate mixture of mercury and sulphur under the influence of the planets. But emphasis is given to the idea that each metal is characterized by two qualities within and two without. This is developed in detail for each metal.[58] A similar but not identical theory appears in the *Book of the balances*, which presents a cosmology in which the Neoplatonic theory of emanations

[55] 1935: 173, 177.
[56] Kraus, 1942: 275–8. The common source would appear to be the lost pre-Arabic version of Balīnūs' *Secret of creation*.
[57] Job of Edessa, 1935: 25, 67, 124, 138, 179.
[58] Books 32–8 of the seventy Books. Kraus, 1942: 1.

is schematized in concentric circles, which are made rigidly physical.
The Jābirian authors here give a similar concrete reality to the primal
material and the contrarieties,[59] and are concerned with differentiating
the philosopher's prime mover from the religious God, but the
principal burden of the *Book of the balances* is to describe in more
detail the generation of the metals from the contrarieties. According
to this theory each body represents an equilibrium of the natures
(contrarieties) composing it, and that harmony is expressible numerically by the musical harmony which governs the heavens. The
qualitative differences and degrees of intensity of the natures are
analogous to the differences of tones in the musical scale. He supposes
each body to represent a balance between internal and external
qualities, each metal being characterized by two internal and two
external qualities. Thus each metal is an inversion of one of the others,
and transmutation is a simple changing of qualities, and can be
accomplished in the same way as a physician cures by counter-
balancing an excessive humour by one of contrary quality. The
elixirs are the alchemist's medicines.[60]

In addition to this invocation of the mathematical relationships of
the harmonic celestial spheres, the Jābirian writer derives a numerical
expression of the balance of natures according to the series $1:3:5:8$
equals 17, the latter number being an expression of complete
harmony. This attempt to apply mathematics to the science of matter
betrays the influence of Plato, Archimedes, the humoural physicians,
and the numerous ancient writers on magic squares and other
mathematical puzzles. But the Jābirian writer attributes the theory to
Balīnūs!

Most important, and perhaps original with the Jābirian author of
the *Seventy books*, was the link between theory and practice provided
by the idea that 'things' can be separated not only into their elements
but even into the contrary qualities by distillation. He takes the
inflammable and non-inflammable vapours which are usually evolved
when organic matter is subjected to destructive distillation for fire
and air, and the condensable liquid which follows for water. The
residue is 'earth'. With equal enthusiasm – although, we may suppose, with less success – he then attempts the division of these elements into the pair of qualities of which each was made. Whatever

[59] Kraus, 1942: 149–50, 163–4.   [60] Ibid., 2, 128–9, 309.

basis this has in practice derives from his observation of organic materials, but he claims it to be applicable to all of nature, and holds even the hardest stones to be distillable.[61]

This theory has a particular appeal as a rational – if misguided – attempt to reconcile theory and practice, and as an early attempt at the application of mathematics to the science of matter. It appears, one must note with regret, that its influence did not even extend to all of the authors of the Jābirian corpus, for the author of the *Seventy books* himself has final recourse to the elixir. The use of elixirs derived from the distillation of organic materials has been called a Jābirian innovation. It denotes the transition of Arabic alchemy from a technological to a medical orientation, a repetition of its evolution as we have observed it in the case of the Greek alchemists. It is in their extensive pursuit of the elixir that the Jābirian treatises resemble those of al-Rāzī, for that stern empiricist, too, is obliged to have recourse to it. Despite their efforts at originality the expectations of the Arabic alchemists really reside in that magic catalyst to which they gave the name 'elixir'. As Ruska has remarked,[62] the elixir is a mark of all alchemy.

Practice

It has been remarked that virtually all chemical materials known in antiquity are to be found in ancient drug lists, such being the pre-suppositions and uncertainties of ancient medicine. The alchemist seems to have been of similar mind, and the alchemically-useful substances mentioned by Arab writers seem again to include virtually all materials known. The result, of course, is that the inorganic materials listed by medical writers and by alchemists are virtually identical. It will be recalled that the author of the Leyden papyrus X used Dioscorides as an authority on materials. Similarly al-Rāzī's word for material, 'uggar', is from the Syriac term for the raw materials of pharmacy. It is not inappropriate that the term was translated by an early Latin translator simply as 'species'.[63]

The Arabic writers are distinguished by attempts to classify these substances. The metals, which alone among inorganic materials

[61] Kraus, 1942: 5, 10.   [62] Ruska, 1935–1: 75.   [63] Ibid., 36.

seem to have been previously distinguished as a class, are defined by a Jābirian writer as fusible, malleable, shiny, and sonorous. It would appear that the ancient alloys, electrum, bronze and brass, were identified as mixtures, for neither al-Rāzī nor the Jābirian writers include any of them among the metals. On the other hand, their seventh metal is not mercury, but 'Chinese iron' (kharsini), a metal which is thought to have been an imported alloy of complex composition.[64] To this class the Arabs add another which is logical enough in the context of the theory and practice of alchemy, 'spirits'. Spirits are substances which are entirely vaporized by fire, namely, sulphur, arsenic (the sulphides), mercury, and sal ammoniac, to which the Jābirian writers, not following a rigorous distinction of minerals from animal and vegetable materials, sometimes add camphor and oil.

The Jābirian writers mention a third class, 'mineral bodies', which is more than reminiscent of Theophrastus' 'earths', since it includes everything else. 'Mineral bodies' are *not* malleable and do not vaporize *entirely* in fire, a negative definition which is followed by an attempt to subdivide them into three groups on the basis of the amount of spirit they contain.[65]

Here al-Rāzī, possibly following Balīnūs, differs from them very markedly, for he classifies the remaining materials under four headings, vitriols, boraxes, salts, and stones. The rationale of these subdivisions seems to involve an attempt to distinguish soluble from insoluble minerals and to use taste as a guide to the differentiation of materials, as well as a recognition of the importance of certain materials (vitriol and borax) of common use, as indicated by such names as ink vitriol, cobbler's vitriol, and goldsmith's borax. The names of the six vitriols can be reconciled with the ancient names for varieties of vitriol and alum, but borax seems not to have been known in antiquity.[66] Although it is clear that our borax (sodium

---

[64] Chinese iron was reputed the best, among the Arabs (Carra de Vaux, 1921–6, Vol. 2: 361, quoting the fourteenth-century geographer, Abū-l Fidā), but kharsini is believed to have been something more, a mirror-surface alloy having as its principal ingredients copper, zinc, and nickel (Laufer, 1919: 556). Stapleton, Azo, and Husain have noted the inclusion of kharsini among the metals cultivated by the Harranians, whom Stapleton regards as the first alchemists, and believe it to derive from Harran's position on the ancient trade-route to China (1927: 340–42, 403).

[65] Kraus, 1942: 18–20. [66] Lippmann, 1954: 45.

tetraborate) is included here, the six varieties of al-Rāzī's borax seem to include some other salts. Borax occurs in central Asia as a saline deposit, like natron,[67] and Ruska believes that al-Rāzī's boraxes included natron and perhaps magnesium and calcium sulphates (Epsom and Glauber's salts).[68] The problem of differentiating soluble white salts seems to have been nearly as difficult for the early chemist as it is for the modern student of his works. Al-Rāzī probably knew something of these salts, as they are known to occur in regions with which he was familiar, but they remained essentially outside the cognizance of the chemist for another seven centuries.

Al-Rāzī's 'chemical cabinet' is only slightly expanded beyond that which would be expected in the workshop of a chemist a thousand years earlier, the only additions which seem both new and important being borax, sal ammoniac, and artificial cinnabar (which seems to have been mentioned earlier in European practical chemistry). Of these sal ammoniac was by far the most significant. Both in its volatility and its property of acting on the surface of metals sal ammoniac resembled those materials long most esteemed by alchemists, mercury, sulphur, and the arsenic sulphides. Ancient references to a salt which sublimes may refer to sal ammoniac, but its real entrance into the repertoire of the chemist dates from the ninth-century Arabs. They got it from the East from (volcanic?) deposits in the Tarim basin, although they also knew of its preparation through the distillation of hair.[69] Modern studies have shown that

[67] The names būrak and tinkal, used by al-Rāzī, are both Persian (cf. Laufer, 1919: 503). On borax see further, below.

[68] Ruska, 1935-1: 48.

[69] As a colourless ('white') salt which occurs in natural volcanic deposits, sal ammoniac is one of those which must have been encountered very early, but it is mentioned obscurely, if at all, in early texts, and long played no significant role in the repertoire of the chemist (cf. Partington, 1935: 147-8. Lippmann, 1954: 116-17). Its properties were sufficiently spectacular to ensure its prominence in alchemical experimentation once they were recognized, as they were by al-Rāzī. He speaks of sal ammoniac (Nusadir) as a mineral from Chorasan and Samarkand, and the geographer Mas'ūdī (d. c. 957) speaks of having visited, when a young man, mountains in central Asia (Sogdiana) 'beneath which' sal ammoniac was produced (1861-77: Vol. I, 347). It is remarkable that al-Rāzī also seems to be the first to speak of sal ammoniac from animal materials, which he calls 'hair sal ammoniac' and designates as the 'second kind' (Ruska, 1928). In later times Egypt became a principal source of sal ammoniac, sublimated from animal excrement, but we lack evidence that this predated Arabic times. China may have known sal ammoniac at the beginning of the Christian era (Wu and Davis, 1932: 257), but the Chinese also appear to have imported it later from the same source from

the sublimate, at ten degrees above the sublimation point, contains only 17 per cent of undecomposed ammonium chloride, the remaining 83 per cent consisting of a mixture of equal volumes of ammonia and hydrogen chloride.[70] This mixture recombines into ammonium chloride on condensation, but in the gaseous state, as in the process of the kerotakis, it would act much like hydrogen chloride, and have the effect of cleaning the oxidized surfaces of the metals. It is still used for this purpose in cleansing the surfaces of iron and copper for tinning. It may be that long-continued alchemical processes had a more profound action on metals. The early-eighteenth-century chemist G. E. Stahl declared that 'The attenuation which sal-ammoniac gives to metals' enables them to 'the easier assume a mercurical form, or change into a running mercury'. Stahl held it to have this action even on gold.[71] In the next generation Pierre Macquer reported that the chlorides of silver, copper, iron, tin, lead and mercury are formed through their distillation with sal ammoniac,[72] an eventuality which would require a very great prolongation of the process.

From the point of view of our science of chemistry, al-Rāzī's most important innovation was in his attempt to classify what had been vaguely known since Theophrastus as 'earthy' substances.[73] He accomplished not only the establishment of classes of salts and metallic ores (his 'stones'), but also the elimination from chemical consideration (with some exceptions) of such intractable materials as precious stones and building materials, and, finally, the introduction of a new class of 'artificially prepared substances', comprehending the two oxides of lead, the acetate of copper and carbonate of lead (white lead), plus some uncertainly-identifiable oxides and slags.

From the point of view of the alchemist this new picture of the

which the Arabs obtained it (Laufer, 1919: 503–8. Schafer, 1963: 218) which should hardly have been necessary if they knew its production from animal excrement. Stapleton (1905) regards the discovery of sal ammoniac from organic materials as a consequence of 'the re-establishment of a belief in the essential connection between animals, plants, and minerals and a consequent revival of faith in the efficacy of organic materials in alchemical research'. It seems more probable, however, that the discovery of sal ammoniac was a cause rather than a consequence of this development (cf. Ruska, 1923–7).

[70] Parkes, 1939: 398.   [71] Stahl, 1730: 105–6.
[72] Macquer, 1778: article 'ammoniac'.
[73] Cf. Stapleton, Azo and Husain, 1927: 321–4.

subject matter of chemistry long continued out of focus. He remained preoccupied with metal ennoblement, and saw as al-Rāzī's most important innovation the establishment of his favourite materials, mercury, sulphur, and the arsenic sulphides – together with sal ammoniac – as a class of substances known as spirits. It is probable that this idea derived from the Arabs' introduction of sal ammoniac into the repertoire of the alchemist, although Zosimos (quoting Hermes, Maria, and Agathodaimon) had long since referred to the first three as spirits (πνεύματα).[74]

A second 'contribution' of al-Rāzī to alchemy was his systematization of alchemical procedures, which can again be characterized as an orderly presentation of ideas already current. Al-Rāzī works out a sequence of laboratory operations, consisting of (1) purification, (2) separation into fine parts, (3) mixture and (4) removal of 'water' (meaning solidification), and proposes to conduct these operations under the guidance of those properties which are susceptible to laboratory manipulation, such as colour, texture, salinity and inflammability.[75] One of the methods for 'separation into fine parts' was solution, and it becomes clear that the invention of new solvents was a principal reason for the Arabs' interest in salts. The close resemblance between the practice of the Jābirian writers and al-Rāzī is most marked in their passages on such 'sharp waters'. These waters range from simple mixtures to distillates obtained from complex mixtures. They are not always fluid and some of the processes refer to melting rather than dissolution.[76] But among them we find the rudiments of processes which were finally to lead to the discovery of the mineral acids, sulphuric, hydrochloric and nitric.[77]

[74] AAG, text: 150–2; trans.: 152–3. Zosimos was not, however, addicted to classification.

[75] Stapleton, Azo and Husain, 1927: 327.

[76] This is exemplified by al-Rāzī's *Kitāb sirr al-asrār* and the Jābirian *Kitāb al-riyāḍ*, and by the works produced by each under the title *Book of properties* (Kitāb al-khawāss). Ruska and Kraus are in agreement in attributing the resemblances to a common dependence on an earlier source rather than to mutual copying (cf. Ruska and Garbers, 1938; Kraus, 1943: lxii).

[77] The mineral acids were to be revealed in processes involving the distillation of various mixtures of vitriol, alum, common salt, saltpetre, and sal ammoniac. All of these ingredients, except saltpetre, are used to prepare the Arabic sharp waters, but the mixture or conditions of reaction seem almost invariably such as not to yield an acid. A possible exception is a 'fast working water' prepared by grinding together and distilling black marcasite and sal ammoniac, if black marcasite can be supposed to have been iron vitriol or decomposed pyrite (cf. Ruska and Garbers, 1938: 34).

The mineral acids manifest themselves clearly only about three centuries after al-Rāzī, in the works of Europeans, some of whom were alchemists, but others of whom were concerned with the production of medical elixirs. Ultimately they all probably deserve to be called his disciples (although they seem to have regarded themselves as disciples of Jābir), since they are continuing procedures established by him. The medical alchemists – or medical chemists – will be discussed in a later chapter. Those alchemists more directly connected with al-Rāzī were concerned with the manipulation of mercury for the production of elixirs, and require us to consider in some detail his own cogitation on that topic, as contained in the *Secret of secrets.*

There are two sections, 'On the sublimation of quicksilver for whitening', and 'On the sublimation of quicksilver for reddening'.[78] Each consists of a series of recipes for a product which he scarcely describes, and which he merely recommends for 'whitening' copper or 'reddening' silver. The recipes for reddening, of which there are five, are generally too complicated for analysis, four being the fewest ingredients in any one of them. It is here that he describes the preparation of artificial cinnabar. It is an ingredient, its preparation being annexed to the recipe! Each recipe consists of a sequence of reactions, in the course of which new raw materials are added. There is much repetitious sublimation and mention of 'red waters', and the nature of the ultimate product is anything but clear.

The sublimations for whitening are simpler, although there is the additional difficulty that in four of the six recipes the mercury used is 'solidified', meaning alloyed. There would be a clear rationale in this series of processes were we to assume that al-Rāzī knew of the corrosive and poisonous white sublimate of mercury, mercuric chloride, and was attempting to produce analogous or related substances. Five of the six recipes include salt and/or sal ammoniac as an ingredient. Three of them contain vitriol. In three of the recipes mercuric chloride is a probable product, but in each case it seems to have been an intermediate, for he goes on to add ingredients which make the final product a matter of substantial doubt. In two of another series of recipes, 'on the sublimation of sal ammoniac', he distils together sal ammoniac and vitriol, in a process which could

[78] What follows is based on al-Rāzī, 1937: 103–10.

have produced the gas hydrogen chloride and might have led him to hydrochloric acid. But it clearly did not.[79] In both cases, al-Rāzī seems to have approached, but not reached, a discovery which was to have a profound effect on alchemy when it was finally unveiled.

Al-Rāzī's classification of alchemical procedures was to set the pattern of later European practice. The Jābirian theorists, although interestingly scientific in their theory of the separation of the elements and qualities by distillation, do not seem to have convinced even the authors of the Jābirian practical treatises, who were preoccupied with the idea of using distillation for the preparation of elixirs. It has been suggested that sal ammoniac was discovered in the course of studies of the supposed magical properties of hair, and that the Jābirian alchemists were induced by this discovery to make a general search for new 'elixirs' through the distillation of organic material.[80] It can only be called remarkable, and suggestive of the need for additional study, that sal ammoniac should appear simultaneously from two sources, and should simultaneously appeal to al-Rāzī and to the Jābirian alchemists from two different points of view. The Jābirian idea that the elixir should be sought through the distillation of organic materials seems to have been much less influential, although both al-Rāzī and various European alchemists found it necessary to express disapproval of it. Such 'spirits' as camphor and oil, which appear as products of the Jābirian experimentation, had no reactive power in the context of alchemy, and do not appear to have interested alchemists generally.

[79] Al-Rāzī, 1937: 110. He emphasizes the redness of the product, which suggests that he calcined the mixture to iron oxide, disregarding the vaporous products. Hydrogen chloride was undoubtedly prepared many times before it was discovered that a corrosive solvent, hydrochloric acid, resulted from its dissolution in water. We do not find this clearly recognized before the seventeenth century.

[80] Stapleton, 1905, thinks China the most probable source of this discovery.

Chapter Eight

The medieval West

THAT the political ascendency of Rome in the last centuries of the pre-Christian era represented no corresponding cultural ascendency hardly needs to be pointed out. The acclimatization of such learned Greeks as Galen to the environment of Rome testifies to a certain continuity there of the intellectual preoccupations of the Greeks, but Galen represented rather an end than a beginning. A consideration of other leading writers of the Empire indicates that natural philosophy had lost its vitality, and was becoming a perfunctory and superficial résumé of the philosophy of classical Greece. Plutarch (A.D. 51–124), another Greek resident in Rome, made frequent references in his *Moralia* to the 'opinions of the philosophers', which exemplify, when collected together, the detached and conservative attitude of the intellectual of imperial Rome. Some, he says, hold the cosmos to be composed of atoms and a void; others say that a formless primal material yielded the four elements through a 'massing and attenuation'. Of the latter, some maintain this massing to be a process whereby a very fine primal material called the ether was progressively thickened into fire, air, water, and earth, while others declare that the elements arose out of the combination of the four principles hot, cold, wet and dry, and that only these existed in the beginning. Plutarch calls such assertions very bold, and holds with Plato that we are unable to discover the ultimate essences of things. As to cause, he considers fire to be 'the first cause of all things', and equates it to motion.[1]

[1] These are Plutarch's opinions as extracted by Lippmann (1948: 3–4) from no less than ten different treatises in the group called *Moralia*. Plutarch, himself, did not summarize his views.

The Stoic Seneca (*c.* A.D. 3–65) had written a book, *On natural questions*, dealing principally with what we would call meteorology and astronomy. His remarks on the nature of matter are illustrative of the bold assertions referred to by Plutarch. The question of the elements comes up in a curious way in his discussion of the sources of rivers. A river, he says, is produced by a supply of water that is always constant. 'If you ask me, therefore, how the water is produced, I will ask in my turn how air is or earth is produced. If there are four elements in nature, you are not entitled to ask where water, one of them, comes from; it *is* the fourth part of nature.'[2] He does, however, admit an obligation to explain where 'things' come from, which he does by postulating transmutations of the elements with what can only be called reckless abandon in a Stoic who presumably believed the transmutation of the elements to occur in a rigorous sequence.

In the same spirit is the cosmology of Pliny's *Natural history*, which appeared about A.D. 77. He 'sees no reason to doubt' that there are four elements, the cohesion of which is maintained by a 'balance of forces' (*mutuus complexus*) under the control of the sun, which he calls 'the soul or spirit of the world and the principal regulator and divinity of nature' (Bk II, 4). This brief statement does not go so far as the cohesion of 'things', and makes no reference to those things from the mineral kingdom which he deals with elsewhere, and on which he has already been cited as a principal source.

In the age of imperial Rome the active pursuit of philosophy passed, as it had in the time of Socrates, into the hands of persons primarily interested in metaphysics and morals, such as the philosopher-emperor, Marcus Aurelius, and above all into those of the theologian of Christianity. Their familiarity with the literature of ancient philosophy is impressive, as is certified by the case of the first of the Fathers of the Western Church, Tertullian (*c.* 160–*c.* 240), whom we find using the terms of the Peripatetic-Stoic debate on physical union – including the examples from chemistry – in his consideration of the nature of the Incarnation.[3] But this was *using* the science of matter, rather than advancing it. The thought of the Fathers cannot be called superficial, but its profundities were oriented elsewhere than towards nature.

[2] Bk III, 13. Seneca, 1910: 124.   [3] Wolfson, 1956: 385–8.

Natural philosophy played a small part in the rationale of developing Christianity. Some reliance upon it was inevitable in the exposition of the *Book of Genesis*, and a more-or-less compatible philosophy was found in Plato's *Timaeus*. In the fifth century a sufficient explanation of nature for a philosophy which was essentially directed at the supernatural was formulated by St. Augustine (354–430). It was Platonic except for the abolition of his dichotomy between heaven and earth. Whereas Plato, who had given reality to a non-material 'model', declared the sensible world to be illusory, and denied the existence of matter, Augustine not only reinstated matter, but posited a spiritual as well as a terrestrial substance.[4] The mutability of the spiritual matter, of which the angels are made, was of greater moment to the early Christians than were the transmutations with which the chemist is concerned.

Although the bulk of ancient philosophical writing was actually lost in the West at this time, enough of Aristotelianism and Stoicism remained in the works of such as Pliny and Galen to feed any inclination for speculative natural philosophy. As it was, these residues coexisted with Augustinian Platonism in such medieval encyclopaedias as those of Isidore of Seville (d. 636) and Rhabanus Maurus (d. 856) through the end of the first Christian millennium. To this weakness of European natural philosophy we probably owe the fact that the ninth-century Islamic reaction of orthodoxy against philosophy had no counterpart in Christendom. It undoubtedly owed much to the intellectual qualities of such churchmen as Augustine and the contrasting weakness of secular philosophy in the West, but it also reflects the uncongeniality of the climate of semi-barbarous Western Europe to the sophisticated complexities of oriental thought. The celebrated case of Johannes Scotus Erigena (d. *c.* 878), profound but neglected exponent of Neoplatonism at the court of Charles the Bald of France, confirms this.[5] While Erigena remained an isolated figure, Augustine's shadow-picture of nature, as reaffirmed by

---

[4] (Augustine, 1912; Vol. 2: 335ff.) *Confessions*, Bk 12 and elsewhere. Cf. Gilson, 1955: 73 and 593n. 24.

[5] Although Erigena's *magnum opus*, *De divisione naturae*, devotes book 3 (of 5 books) to the nature of the created universe, he contributes little, if anything, to the mundane science of matter. His neglect of minerals is indicated by his habitual exemplification of 'things' solely by plants and animals (Johannes Scotus Erigena, 1870: Bk 3. See also Bett, 1925).

Boethius (d. 535),[6] continued through the first Christian millennium to satisfy the requirement of European philosophy.

The history of natural philosophy in Western Christendom really begins with the translation, during the period 1150–1250, of the works of Aristotle and his major Arabic commentators. By the latter date Aristotle's works had entered the curriculum at the University of Paris and the first of the great Christian naturalists, Albertus Magnus, was in a position to summarize, in his *Summa de creaturis*, the opinions of 'the Peripatetics'. Some, he reports, say that there is one and the same matter for all substances, both corporeal and incorporeal; it is 'with quantity' in corporeal substances, 'without quantity' in incorporeal substances. Others say that we should distinguish between generable things, in which there is a composition of matter and form, and non-generable things.[7] In any case, Albertus does not consider either of these points of view untenable, for he acknowledges that matter cannot be the same in incorruptible heavenly bodies and in generable and corruptible things. In fact he admits the possibility of two 'truths' on such questions. One can say that matter is everywhere the same when we are speaking an abstract logical language, but when we are dealing with concrete reality we must distinguish between the point of view of the theologian and that of the philosopher. To the theologian, following the *Book of Genesis*, matter is one. To the philosopher, matter is the subject of change (*est principium corporis mobilis*), and consequently different sorts of change require different sorts of matter.[8] Nevertheless he does find it necessary to condemn the view that goes so far as to postulate two or more different *kinds* of matter, not only because of its conflict with *Genesis*, but because of its tendency to reverse Aristotle's dictum that matter has no existence except in form.

The Peripatetics whom Albertus is reporting were a crowd of Greeks, Jews and Arabs of discordant opinions, but uniformly dedicated to the improvement of Aristotle with emanation ideologies. The view which Albertus condemns seems to be that differentiating matter into five kinds which we have found to be conventional

---

[6] Boethius, 1918: 79 (*A treatise against Eutyches and Nestorius*). See also Cooper, 1928.

[7] Albertus Magnus, 1890–9, Vol. 34: 333–4.

[8] Ibid. : 335.

among the Arabs.[9] But Albertus' lack of dogmatism on the question was sufficient to enable his successors to attribute to him a work called *Philosophia pauperum*, in which different kinds of varieties of matter are elaborately classified as follows:[10]

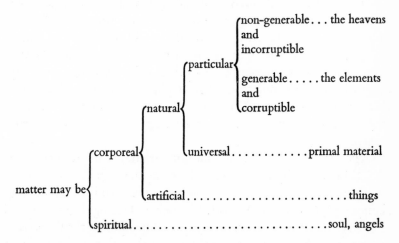

			non-generable... the heavens and incorruptible
		particular	
			generable..... the elements and corruptible
	natural		
corporeal		universal...........primal material	
matter may be			
	artificial.......................things		
spiritual.............................soul, angels			

That Albertus' contemporary and sometime rival, Roger Bacon, did not find the idea of different kinds of matter in contradiction to *Genesis* is evident from his commentary on Aristotle's *Physics*, where we find him declaring that:

spiritual matter is not subject to quantity, movement or change.
the celestial bodies are subject to quantity and movement, but not change.
sensible matter is subject to quantity, motion and change.[11]

[9] The 'five eternal substances' of al-Kindī and al-Rāzī have been mentioned above (p. 121). Although their names change, five kinds of matter are consistently differentiated by Arabic writers, as in the *Fons vitae* of the eleventh-century Spanish Arab Aviceberon (1895: 26). Roger Bacon (1928: 46) attributes the idea of different kinds of matter to the *Fons vitae*. Duhem (SM, Vol. 5: 465–7) thinks it came ultimately from Erigena, but this seems likely only insofar as Erigena shared a general Neoplatonic idea.

[10] I have constructed this outline from the narrative of *Philosophia pauperum, seu Işagoge in libros Aristotelis physicorum, de caelo et mundo, de generatione et corruptione, meteororum et de anima*, in Albertus Magnus, 1890–9, Vol. 5: 447–8. Hirsch (1950: 125) lists nine printed editions of the *Philosophia pauperum* before 1500. He follows Grabmann (1918) in ascribing the work to the obscure Alfred of Orlamünde.

[11] In his *Quaestiones supra libros quatuor physicorum Aristotelis*, Roger Bacon considers the questions of whether matter is in spiritual beings and whether the same matter is in celestial

This would seem to have been another appropriate point for Christian controversies analogous to those which led to the eclipse of the falasifa in Islam, but no such crisis seems to have arisen in Christendom. That it failed to appear is probably to be credited to Albertus' student, Thomas Aquinas (1225 or 1227–1274), who undertook with large success the elimination from theology of irrelevant subject matter, including the mundane science of matter. By ascribing new meaning to the principles of Aristotle, Thomas approached the question of the being of God from the viewpoint of theology, not from that of philosophy. From his time it became unnecessary for Christians to deny philosophical solutions to problems which are really indifferent as far as Faith is concerned.[12]

The philosophy of different kinds or varieties of matter was a part of Christian cosmology, derived from the totality of ancient doctrines of emanations, and completing a trend which had its beginnings in Plato and Aristotle themselves. During the long period of relative indifference to the science of matter among the Christians, this question, because of its pertinence to the relationship between God and the world, was the liveliest aspect of Christian cosmology; but with the recovery of Aristotelian natural philosophy it was seen to be somewhat peripheral. Albertus and his contemporaries seem to have been the last to give the question full attention.

In relation to the history of chemistry Albertus and Roger Bacon are perhaps the most interesting figures of the Middle Ages, for their works reveal both the culmination of the Christian natural philosophy of the first millennium and the beginnings of that of the second. They reveal not only contributions to the emanation-oriented Christian cosmology, but to the analysis of generation and corruption in terms of the newly-recovered Aristotelian literature, and, thirdly, to an enterprise in which their activity is almost unique, the philosophical consideration of alchemy. The latter episode, which virtually

---

(in the astronomical sense) beings. He concludes, 'ad hoc notandum quod sicut actor Fontis vite distinguit triplicem materiam, sic ad presens distinguimus: est enim materia spiritualis, sensibilis, et media; spiritualis est que (non) subjacet quantitati, motui, nec contrarietati; et hec est in spiritualibus et intellectivis et animabus; media quae subjacet quantitati, motui, sed non contrarietati, et est in celestibus; sensibilis est que subjacet omnibus istis, scilicet quantitati, motui, contrarietati, et hec in generabilibus et corruptibilibus' (1928: 46).

[12] Gilson, 1955: 364–5. Thorndike, HMES, Vol. 2: 600.

began and ended with Albertus and Roger Bacon, will be reserved for the next chapter.

For both Aristotle and alchemy the Latin West was indebted to Arabic Spain, which not only transmitted the ancient literature, but amended it along the way. Spain had been conquered by the Moslems in the early eighth century, had established its independence of Eastern Islam in the ninth century, and had enjoyed a period of intellectual prosperity as the restraints of orthodoxy had cut off the pursuit of falasifa in the East. The contributions of Arabic Spain to alchemy will be considered below (pp. 160–66). Its contributions to the elucidation of generation and corruption are associated with one who had nothing to do with alchemy and little to do with mundane nature. Averroës (1126–98) was nevertheless one of the most influential of all Aristotelian commentators, and his theoretical approach to generation and corruption did much to move the discussion into the realm of ontology.

In the course of his discussion of generation and corruption Aristotle had settled upon 'mixis' as a name for changes of the kind we call chemical. The Stoics had advanced still further into the subtleties of microphysical changes, but when the discussion re-emerges among the Arabs we find it concentrated upon mixis. Among the Arabs and Latins 'mixtion' seems to have the clear significance of compounding, and while the compounds are not always (or even usually) chemical, the arguments are relatively free of the diffuseness of ancient doctrine. They centre on mixtion, and when in the seventeenth century chemistry became a respectable topic for philosophical discussion no one seems to have had any doubt that mixtion was the proper term for chemical change.

Aristotle had regarded mixis as somehow intermediate between the ingredients, and had viewed the formation of a compound as the product of an action of the contrarieties. Avicenna had considered this inadequate to account for the full range of evident differences between a compound and its ingredients and had added a 'substantial form'. He saw the formation of a compound as the product of a change (a remission) in the contrarieties *plus* the simultaneous addition of an appropriate 'substantial' form.[13] This proposal to

[13] See above, p. 122.

involve 'form' in mixis, as it had not been involved by Aristotle and his contemporaries, made the question more interesting to practitioners of pure philosophy, and came to dominate the discussion through the end of Peripatetic philosophy. Averroës pointed out that contradictions emerge if we are to suppose that a compound contains its own form, plus those of its ingredients, plus the forms of the elements, and he attempted to avoid those contradictions by supposing that not only the contrarieties but also the substantial forms undergo remission. This led to difficulties of its own, such as the question whether the form of a compound is the remitted form of the elements or a separate form (*forma mixta superaddita*).[14]

This highly philosophical discussion of mixtion was resumed among the Latins, although not by Albertus and the author of *Philosophia pauperum*, who were generally closer to Aristotle himself than were their successors. They devote themselves to extended discussion of the full range of microphysical changes, generation, alteration, mixtion, confusion, and so on.[15] Both make a point of preferring *mutatus* or *transmutatus* to *motus* when speaking of chemical change, and neither pays much attention to 'form'. Albertus, who alludes to it several times in discussing generation and corruption, equates it to species. In all this they were closer to the spirit of the seventeenth century than to the Scholasticism which was to follow them.

It was perhaps natural that Aristotle himself be mastered before his commentators could be appreciated. As the Arabic commentators became more fully known the Latin's access to the 'true' Aristotle became clouded by a concurrent necessity of deciding on many points between Avicenna and Averroës. The Latins generally sided with Avicenna, for the idea of a remission of forms was too blatantly in contradiction with the Stagirite. Thomas Aquinas did not follow his teacher Albertus on mixtion, but opted for the improvement of Avicenna. He seems to have relied on Avicenna's remission of the contrarieties to adapt ingredients for a change which was then

[14] Maier, 1952: 28–9, citing Avicenna in his commentary on *De generatione* (in manuscript) and Averroës in his commentary on *De caelo* (from his *Opera*, Venice, 1550).

[15] See Albertus Magnus, 1890–9, Vol. 5: 477 (*Philosophia pauperum*) and Vol. 4: 371–5 (Albertus' commentary on generation and corruption).

completed by their endowment with a new form, and thus to have differed from Avicenna only in suppressing the idea of the multiplication of forms in the compound.[16]

The 'Thomist' version of Aristotelian philosophy was the starting point of most Scholastic discussions of the fourteenth and fifteenth centuries, and such discussions were numerous. By the latter half of the fourteenth century criticism of the Thomistic synthesis had evolved a philosophy so generally divergent as to acquire the appellation 'modern way', as against the 'old way' of Thomas. The modern way, associated with the 'nominalist' or 'terminist' philosophy of William of Ockham (c. 1300–c. 1350), was primarily concerned with logic and metaphysics rather than natural philosophy. Not very original was Ockham's conclusion that 'Reason and experience promote us to introduce matter and form as concurring to the constitution of composite things so that from the potentiality of matter the form is being brought forth to its act'.[17] But the approach to nature through logic, which Ockham represents (although he was not solely responsible for it), was to be of immense importance to science, for it led into yet another attempt at the mathematization of nature, and this one was to end not in frustration but in the 'scientific revolution' associated with Galileo and the seventeenth century.

As suggested by the above quotation from Ockham, the philosophers of the modern way accepted the involvement of form in a compound. But they approached the whole subject from a new point of view. They were concerned with such questions as the maximum and minimum sizes of the smallest particles which could be conceived of as endowed with form, with the temporal limits of the existence of a particular 'thing', and with the analysis of differences in qualitative intensities.[18] These explorations began in contexts which appear to have been remote from the science of matter, but in the fifteenth century they turned increasingly in the direction

[16] Thomas Aquinas, 1882–1930, Vol. 3: appendix, xx (*De generatio et corruptio*, Bk 1, Lectio 24). He says that the form of a simple body exists 'non actu sed virtute' in a mixture. Maier (1952: 35) describes this as a compromise ('tertio opinio') between Avicenna and Averroës.

[17] Tornay, 1938: 38 (citing Ockham's *Summulae in libros physicorum*, Venice, 1506).

[18] C. Wilson, 1956, traces these questions through writers of the fourteenth through sixteenth centuries.

of physics and to what Ockham had called 'numerical' distinction.[19] They generated a literature which came to centre on the question of whether or not the increase in the intensity of a quality involves a part-to-part addition. This approach was particularly associated with a group at Oxford, the most prominent of whom was Richard Swineshead, often called 'Calculator', who were to turn the discussion onto questions of time and motion and in the direction which led to Galileo.[20]

Qualitative intensities were also studied through the direct consideration of the qualities hot and cold. Galenic medicine had always featured a suppositious scale of degrees of heat and cold, but we find attempts, such as that of Giovanni Marliani (d. 1483),[21] to establish 'numerical' distinction in a context neither Galenic nor experimental, but purely philosophic. In that context the interaction of hot and cold must be that of an agent and a patient, but even the most theoretical Peripatetic could not overlook his everyday experience in mixing hot and cold water. Whichever is the patient in this case, it obviously exercises a reaction on the agent. The immediate consequence of these studies seems to have been a mere complication of the theory of agent-patient relationships. In the same environment of logico-mathematical discussion we find attempts to set a boundary to the range of a potency, as to 'the power of Socrates to lift a weight', and to fix other boundaries such as are implied in natural and temporal maxima and minima. With the loosening of a few Peripatetic bonds, studies of the intensities of qualities (hot and cold) became quantitative, and led, in the seventeenth century, to the invention of the thermometer. Studies of natural minima also proved fruitful at that time in that they were susceptible to reconciliation with the revived atomism of that century. On the whole, however, the preoccupations of the 'calculators' tended to separate the Aristotelian doctrines of motion and change into a sector dealing with macrophysics, which proved susceptible to mathematization, and another concerned with microphysics, which was at least problematical, and tended to be set aside. To the critical philosophers

[19] Ockham speaks of matter as 'numerically' distinct, and in general seems preoccupied with things which can be distinguished numerically. See Tornay, 1938: 35–51.

[20] On the medieval precursors of Galileo see Duhem, 1906, 1913–59; Maier, 1949; Clagett, 1950.   [21] See Clagett, 1941.

of the seventeenth century, Scholastic cogitations on natural minima and the remission of forms and qualities seemed conspicuous examples of the type of Peripatetic hair-splitting which the seventeenth century particularly wished to avoid.

The chemistry of the arts

The most important contribution of the Western Middle Ages to the science of matter lay outside of philosophy, in practical chemistry, where we encounter for the first time a continuous literature, a series of recipe collections on the chemistry of the decorative arts which has been traced in Europe from a late-eighth-century treatise called *Compositiones ad tinguenda*. This work, which has been described as 'based mainly on Italian knowledge and practice, greatly influenced by Graeco-Byzantine learning and skill',[22] resembles the ancient Baphika literature, both in its scope and contents; indeed, one of the recipes appears to be a translation of a recipe contained in the Leyden papyrus X.[23]

Of the four topics of Baphika treatises, gold and silver metallurgy, purple colouring, and artificial precious stones, the Leyden papyrus X deals with the first three and its companion, the Stockholm papyrus, deals with artificial gemstones. There are also a number of recipes for colouring in hues other than purple, and some descriptions of raw materials. In the *Compositiones* we find what has been regarded as these same topics, reinterpreted in a way which yields a conventional manual for the practitioner of the fine arts. It seems less likely that it descended from the Baphika treatises than that both derived from a genre of an ancient artist's recipe book of which no example is extant.

Many manuscript versions exist of the genre of work represented by the *Compositiones*, two of which have been defined under the names *Mappae clavicula* (Key to painting) and *De coloribus et artibus Romanorum* (On the colours and arts of the Romans).[24] Both of

[22] Johnson, 1939: 88.   [23] Ibid.: 56.

[24] My discussion is based on printed versions of (1) *Compositiones ad tingunda*, from Biblioteca Capitolare (Lucca) MS 490, dated *c.* 800 (see Muratori, 1774, Burnam, 1920, and Hedfors, 1932), (2) *Mappae clavicula*, from Phillipps MS 3715 in the library of Thos. Fitzroy Fenwick, Cheltenham, England (see Phillipps, 1847), and (3) *De coloribus et artibus Romanorum*, from a

these date from the tenth century, and exist in variant versions extending over several centuries. They are distinguishable from all preceding chemical writings by a limited and clearly conceived objective, and constitute a source of information on the chemical technology of medieval Europe which is without parallel in Byzantium or Islam. They mention almost no material not applicable in the decorative arts, but since the great majority of all mineral substances known to practical chemistry, alchemy or medicine were applicable to the decorative arts, this limitation scarcely diminishes their value as guides to the materials known in medieval Europe. The clarity of these writings places our knowledge of the subject on a much firmer footing. It reveals, however, that the substances known were precisely those known in antiquity, with scarcely any additions.

Johnson has shown the close similarity of most of the recipes in the Compositiones treatises to those known in the ancient world, in some cases to those described on the clay tablets in the Library of Assurbanipal.[25] The sole new material in the Compositiones, itself, is synthetic cinnabar (mercuric sulphide),[26] but the synthesis of this long-known natural material also appears in Islam in the slightly later works of al-Rāzī. The Compositiones does not appear to be influenced by Arabic sources, and it is unlikely that al-Rāzī was influenced by the Compositiones. It is difficult not to suppose that synthetic cinnabar had appeared in the course of the endless alchemical manipulation of mercury and sulphur,[27] and that

---

critical edition of eight manuscripts of varying length (see Ilg, 1873) and from Bibliothèque Nationale (Paris) Latin MS 6741 (see Merrifield, 1849, Vol. 1: 182–257). This is the earliest manuscript of (1), but (2) exists in a shorter unprinted version of the early ninth century. It seems to be agreed that (3), in both the versions of Ilg and Merrifield, represents a tenth-century work in the first two of its three books and a twelfth- or thirteenth-century work in the third book. On these matters see Johnson, 1939.

[25] Johnson, 1939: 31–2.

[26] Compositiones, 1774: col. 712. 1920: 131. 1932: 57. D. V. Thompson regards the discovery of this pigment, called 'vermillion', as revolutionary in medieval painting (1936: 106–7), although other authorities doubt that natural and synthetic cinnabar can be reliably distinguished either in a painting or in a prepared pigment. In any case, the most important authority on pigments in this time, Cennio Cennini, does not even mention natural cinnabar, but only 'cinabro . . . made by an alchemical process performed in an alembic' (1933: Ch. 38), and in this he seems typical of other Renaissance authorities on painting.

[27] Hammer-Jensen thinks that some of the recipes for the 'fixation' of mercury in the Greek alchemical manuscript signify the preparation of synthetic cinnabar (1921: 47, with

the *Compositiones'* author and al-Rāzī only pioneered in clearly describing it. Arabic influence is indicated, however, as early as the twelfth century, when borax appears in the European recipe books.[28]

There is a continued interest in gold-writing and gilding, and there are a few attempts to imitate gold, but the *Compositiones* and its successors are remarkable in lacking both alchemical gold-making and the fraudulent simulation which characterize the papyri.

In the absence of critical editions mutual comparisons of these collections can only be made with caution. Due allowance must be made for presumed variations of the accessible (printed) texts from the originals (although the unique importance of the 'original' version of a compilation is somewhat unclear), and for the uncertain character of a considerable number of the recipes. The total number of recipes can be specified only very approximately, for neither the early scribes nor modern students of this literature have been clear on where one recipe ends and another begins.[29] The longest collection (*Mappae clavicula*), finally, contains about $3\frac{1}{2}$ times as many recipes as the shortest (*De coloribus*). But if we remain undeterred by these difficulties, we find that such a comparison suggests certain conclusions so strongly that it seems doubtful that they will be overturned by the critical editions which are still awaited. We find, for example, that the proportion of recipes devoted to metal and colour production and application remains remarkably constant. It also remains consistent with the Leyden and Stockholm papyri, and may be summarized as follows:

---

reference to AAG, text: 224, 19ff., 234, 15ff.). The process is not quite simple, since the immediate product obtained by heating mercury and sulphur is a black isomer of mercuric sulphide. The red isomer is obtained when this is sublimed.

[28] Borax is mentioned in Bk 3 (12–13c.) of the *De coloribus* (1849: 242; 1873: 82–3) in the twelfth-century version of the *Mappae clavicula* (1847: 225 [recipe cxcv, 'atincar sive burrago'] and is probably the 'parahas' mentioned in the twelfth-century *Schedula diversarum artium* (Hawthorne and Smith, 1963: 105).

[29] For example, in the case of the *Compositiones*, we have three printed editions of the same manuscript, which is subdivided into 120 recipes by Muratori, 114 by Burnam, and 161 by Hedfors. Since the recipes run one into another they are really not susceptible to precise differentiation. In Table I I have based my analysis on Hedfors.

TABLE I

	METAL PREPARATION AND APPLICATION[30] %	COLOUR MAKING AND APPLICATION %	TOTAL %
The papyri	36	27	63
Compositiones	24	30	54
Mappae clavicula	43	40	83
De coloribus	24	37	61

The most striking apparent deviation is in the total figure for the *Mappae clavicula*, which is, as is indicated, the most nearly exclusively concerned with these two topics. The real deviation is in the other three, however, for each of them gives substantial attention to one other topic which differs in each case.

TABLE II

	METALS AND COLOURS %	MATERIALS AND FASTENINGS %	CERAMICS AND GLASS %	ARTIFICIAL GEMSTONES %	TOTAL %
The papyri	63	4		21	88
Compositiones	54	35	1		90
Mappae clavicula	83	12	4		99
De coloribus	61	4	29		94

The deviation of the papyri is in the inclusion of that Baphika topic which seems not to have interested the authors of the European collections, artificial gemstones. To some extent this seeming lack

[30] Detailed consideration of the metallurgical recipes indicates that the proportion devoted to gold-writing is approximately constant throughout the four works cited. The asem recipes in the Leyden papyrus X account almost precisely for the difference between the proportion of metallurgical recipes in the papyri (36 per cent) and that in the *Compositiones* and *De coloribus* (each 24 per cent). The large number of metallurgical recipes in the *Mappae clavicula* also merits comment. It is primarily due to a very large number of gold recipes, and many of them are quasi-alchemical. One receives the impression that the compiler (at least of the twelfth-century version I have used) had access to an ancient Baphika treatise (the *Physica et Mystica*?) whose content he simply superimposed on a Latin collection of the *Compositiones* type.

It is to be emphasized that no attempt is made here to achieve a precise differentiation between such subtly different processes (at least they are subtle in these collections) as metal colouration and alloying, glass colouring and ceramic glazing, etc.

of interest simply represents its transfer to glass and ceramics, and we see that the *De coloribus* is peculiar in the attention given this topic. The *Compositiones* gives the greatest attention to such routine matters of the painter's trade as raw materials and methods of fastening (solders and glues).

These deviations suggest that these works have significance other than their mere exemplification of the medieval craftsman's recipe collection. They also seem to be the ancestors of the specialist's handbooks of the Renaissance. In this role we may see the *Compositiones* as the ancestor of such celebrated painter's manuals as that of the early-fifteenth-century Cennino Cennini,[31] and the *De coloribus et artibus Romanorum* as a primitive version of the glass treatise of Antonio Neri.[32] Even the *Mappae clavicula* has a significant deviation, in its inclusion of a number of recipes for incendiary mixtures, which would seem to make it an ancestor of the late-thirteenth-century *Liber ignium* of Marcus Graecus.[33]

Curiously enough, none of these seems to be the prototype of the Renaissance metallurgical manual, for notwithstanding the attention they give to metals, and despite their elimination of alchemical recipes, their 'metallurgy' is almost exclusively that of the goldsmith, who is not involved in primary metallurgical production. The pioneer work in this field seems to have been a twelfth-century treatise called *Schedula diversarum artium*, which, while retaining some dependence on the Compositiones collections, is essentially a different kind of work. It is, in fact, the earliest example of the Renaissance

---

[31] Cf. Herringham, 1899: xxiiiff.

[32] Antonio Neri's *De arte vetraria* was published in 1612. Table II admittedly exaggerated the importance of the recipes relating to glass in the *De coloribus*. In absolute terms the work contains only about twice as many glass recipes as do the *Compositiones* or *Mappae clavicula*, and less than half as many as the twelfth-century *Schedula diversarum artium* of Theophilus, which is usually mentioned as the first important work on glass. The third part of the *De coloribus*, which contains a third of its glass recipes, is, moreover, probably later than Theophilus. But if we were to eliminate the third book from consideration the proportion of glass recipes in the *De coloribus* would rise to 33 per cent. Whatever may be said of the merits of the glass recipes in *De coloribus* (and this is for the specialist literature to reveal), it remains, so far as we know now, the first work of practical chemistry to devote more than cursory attention to this subject.

[33] *Mappae clavicula*, 1847: 236–40 (about 15 recipes, some for protection against incendiaries). Partington (1960: 88) speaks of this as 'of the earlier tradition' of Greek fire, referring presumably to the era prior to the utilization of saltpetre. Marcus's *Liber ignium* is printed in Hoefer, 1842–3, Vol. 1: 491–7, and elsewhere. The work is analysed in Partington, 1960.

specialist's handbook. It is not a collection, but the original work of one man, whose name, Theophilus, is mentioned in the text, and who is believed to have been identical to Roger of Helmarshausen, a Benedictine monk-craftsman of north Germany, some of whose work is still extant in Paderborn.[34] Although he actually gives a smaller number of metallurgical recipes than any of the collections, Theophilus has something to say on the basic processes for the production and refinement of metals, and includes, in addition to the recipes, an equal number of short sections on the tools of the trade. Add to this the elimination of much of the redundancy of the collections and it becomes apparent that Theophilus' work is quite another genre of metallurgical treatise. We know of no predecessor. It is the first of a long line, the forerunner of such printed books as the late-fifteenth-century German Kunstbüchlein and the *Pirotechnia* of Vannoccio Biringuccio. It is interesting to note that one of the extant manuscripts of *Schedula diversarum artium* is known to have once belonged to another writer in this series, George Agricola.[35]

With specialization some innovation becomes apparent. The metallurgy of copper and the production of brass, which we have had to infer from archaeological evidence and from vague indications by Pliny and other ancient authors, are described with relative clarity in the *Schedula*.[36] The same work describes clearly for the first time the analytical process of cupellation and the salt-cementation method of separating gold and silver, and adds a new method of 'parting' (separating gold and silver) of which we have no earlier record, the method of melting with sulphur.[37] To this the fifteenth-century *Probierbüchlein* adds two more methods of parting, by melting with antimony sulphide and by treatment with nitric acid.[38] The first may have been an innovation of the author of the *Probierbüchlein*, but nitric acid was familiar to alchemists long before this time. The fifteenth-century painter's manuals also show a few innovations, the celebrated blue pigment, ultramarine, a product of

[34] Dodwell, 1961: xxxiii–xliv. Hawthorne and Smith, 1963: xv–xvii.

[35] Ibid.: lii.

[36] See especially Bk 3, Chs. 63–9 (Theophilus, 1961: 120–8. 1963: 139–45). There are errors in Theophilus' copper metallurgy, especially in his confusion of the alloys. It may be doubted that he was personally familiar with the fundamental metal-winning processes.

[37] Ibid., Bk 3, Chs. 23, 33, 34, 69, 70.

[38] *Probierbüchlein*, 1949: 114, 128 (antimony) 124, 131 (acid).

the laborious physical manipulation of lapis lazuli, and the yellow pigment, 'mosaic gold', a useful (if chemically indescribable) product, for once, of random experimentation in melting together incongruous materials.[39]

This rate of innovation is remarkable enough in the context of the static chemical technology of the previous millennium. In fact, however, European alchemy and medical chemistry, the genesis of which took place some three centuries after the earliest extant Compositiones treatise, exhibit a rate of innovation by comparison to which the literature of practical chemistry appears relatively conservative. The appearance of nitric acid in the Probierbüchlein is no necessary indication of an influence of alchemy on the author, for it had already been applied in medicine and had appeared in a new genre of catch-all recipe book known as the 'book of secrets'. Such collections, which achieved enormous popularity in the sixteenth and seventeenth centuries, were made up with slight discrimination from many sources, medical, alchemical and practical. Perhaps the prototype was the thirteenth-century Liber sacerdotum, in which data on practical chemistry are mixed with miscellaneous recipes from other sources, some of which appear to be Arabic.[40]

[39] Cennini, Chs. 62 and 159 (1899: 47, 138; 1933: 36, 101). See also Le Begue, who calls it purpurinum (1849: 55). Both works date from the early fifteenth century. Ultramarine was produced by a laborious process of washing the blue colour out of lapis lazuli, for which Cennini used 'lye' (see D. V. Thompson, 1936: 145-8). The use, and presumably the invention, of ultramarine seems to have originated in Central Asia, near the ancient mine which was the only source of lapis lazuli (see Gettens, 1950). 'Mosaic gold', prepared by melting together mercury, tin, sal ammoniac and sulphur, was almost certainly prepared by thirteenth-century alchemists (Cf. Geber, 1922: 106), but first appears as a pigment in the fifteenth-century treatises of Cennini and Le Begue (Cf. D. V. Thompson, 1936: 181-4).

[40] Although nothing has been found in Arabic corresponding to the Latin treatises on the arts, there is a substantial Arabic literature on mineralogy which dwells on the medical and astrological matters which were characteristic of the books of secrets (see Ruska, 1913-4). Berthelot believed the Liber sacerdotum to be a translation from the Arabic (CMA, Vol. 1: 179). Ruska reached the somewhat contradictory conclusions that it is one) connected with the Mappae clavicula, and two) a translation of an abbreviated version of al-Rāzi's Book of secrets (Kitāb al-asrār) (1936: 124-5). The work was edited by both of these authorities, and Berthelot translated it into French (Berthelot, CMA, Vol. 1: 179-228. Ruska, 1936).

The 'book of secrets', which was anything but secret, was a popular, and probably profitable, publication designed to meet a popular demand for a general recipe book. It seems to me that the Liber sacerdotum was a private (or commercially unsuccessful) book of secrets. The same might be said of the interesting collection put together much later by Peder Manssen (c. 1462-1534) (see Johannsen, 1941).

The compilers of books of secrets cast a wider net than had those of the Compositiones collections, indeed, the latter were among the fish in that net, along with their counterparts in alchemy and medicine. Through the book of secrets, which seems to have been aimed at the literate layman, the craftsman's recipes became more respectable and the alchemist's secrets more commonplace. But both were on the way to being inundated by a flood of recipes relating to that subject which has always interested men more than any other, medicine.

Arabic alchemy in the West

The first European alchemy was Arabic in the fullest sense of the word. The Art seems to have come to Arabic Spain during the reign of Abd-al-Rahman III (912–61),[41] and it was in Spain, two centuries later, that the Latins got their first taste of it, through the inclusion of a few alchemical tracts among the prodigious output of the Latin translators of the period. Some of the most influential of these translations appear to be works which originated in western Islam, North Africa and Spain, from what the Latins called the 'Moorish' alchemists.

Two treatises which were particularly influential among the Latins of the thirteenth century have been assigned by modern scholarship to the Moorish alchemists, although they were attributed in thirteenth-century Europe to al-Rāzī and Avicenna. The *De aluminibus et salibus* is indeed much indebted to al-Rāzī, but from the point of view of chemistry it improves on him.[42] Since it contains numerous Spanish terms, and cites the Moorish pharmacist Ibn

[41] On alchemy in Arabic Spain see Ruska, 1933.

[42] Since it introduced the important artificial substance, corrosive sublimate (see below, p. 162–3).

A comparison of the *De aluminibus* (DA) with the *Secret of secrets* (SS) yields the following information; both begin with 'spirits', of which SS lists 4 and DA (which puts sal ammoniac among the salts) only 3. Then come metals, and the 7 listed by SS are reduced to 6 in DA by the elimination of 'Chinese iron'. Stones follow in both works and the 13 of SS are reduced to 3 in DA, talc, marcasite, and glass, the latter of which is not mentioned in SS.

SS has three more categories, comprising 6 'atraments' (vitriols and alums), 6 boraxes and 11 salts. DA has only one additional category, 'alums and salts', which mentions 5 'alums' (including vitriols) and 10 salts. Of the latter, 7 duplicate those in SS, the most important omission being 'salt of urine'. Borax and sal ammoniac are included among the salts. See also Ruska, 1935–1: esp. 85. 154.

quæ fuffecerit: cuius rei caufam poni-
mus, Spirituū effe naturam, vt ad fubli-
mia tendant, non ad inferiora: quare fa
ciliùs lateraliter, quàm in decliue, pro-
filiunt. His organis A. B. defignatis,

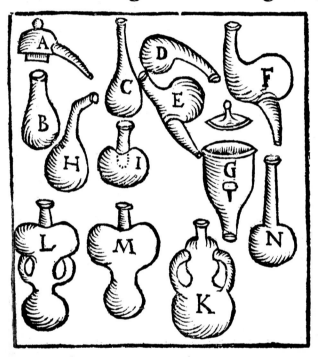

ea, quæ fucco magis abvndant, folent
deftillari: quia liberiùs afcendunt, &
eorū Mercurius faciliùs, quam Mars,
attollitur.

    Ad roftrum galeæ vas recipiens ap-
                    F ij   plica-

I VARIETIES OF CHEMICAL VESSELS
From Gerard Dorn, *Chymisticum artificium naturae*, Frankfurt, 1568

II DISTILLATION: AS SEEN IN EGYPT BY THE EXPEDITION OF NAPOLEON

From *Description de l'Egypte, Etat Moderne*, Paris, 1817. Planches, T. 2

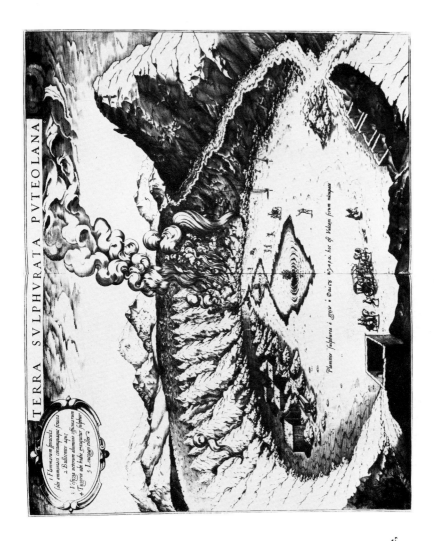

III THE ALUM AND SULPHUR
WORKS AT PUTEOLI
From M. Mercati, *Metallotheca*, Rome,
1719

IV VITRIOL PRODUCTION, A ROMANTIC VIEW
From M. Mercati, *Metallotheca*, Rome, 1719, p. 62

V DISTILLATION OF SULPHUR

From M. Mercati, *Metallotheca*, Rome, 1719, p. 78

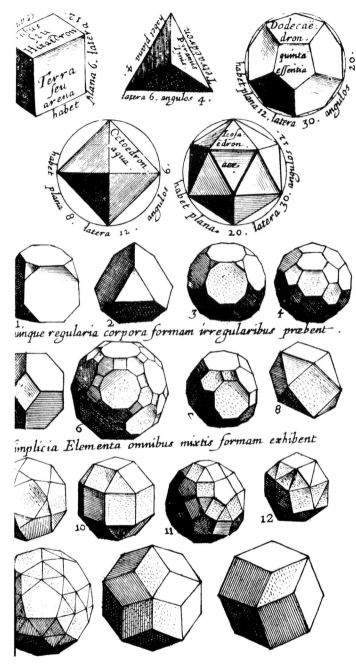

VI WM. DAVISSON'S SCHEME FOR ANALYZING SUBSTANCES IN TERMS
OF THE FIVE 'PERFECT' SOLID FIGURES
From his *Philosophia pyrotechnica*, Pt. III, Paris, 1642

des valées, s'affemblent en riuieres & defcendent enfin iufques à la mer.

LXV.
Pourquoy
l'eau de la
mer ne
croift point
de ce que
les riuieres
y entrent.

Or encore qu'il forte ainfi continuellement beaucoup d'eau des concauitez qui font fous les montagnes, d'où eftant éleuée elle coule par les riuieres jufques à la mer, toutesfois ces concauitez ne s'épuifent point, & la mer n'en deuient point plus grande: Dont la raifon eft, que la Terre exterieure n'a pû eftre formée en la façon que i'ay d'écritte par le débris du corps E , dont les pieces

font tombées inégalement fur la fuperficie du corps C, qu'il ne foit demeuré plufieurs grands paffages au deffous de ces pieces, par où il retourne autant des eaux de la mer vers le bas des montagnes,qu'il en fort par le haut qui va dans la mer. De façon que le cours de l'eau en cette Terre,imite celuy du fang dans le corps des animaux , où il fait vn cercle en coulant fans ceffe fort promptement de leurs veines en leurs arteres, & de leurs arteres en leurs veines.

VIII THE MERCURY EXTRACTION WORKS AT ALMADAN, SPAIN
From *ASP*, année, 1719, plate 23

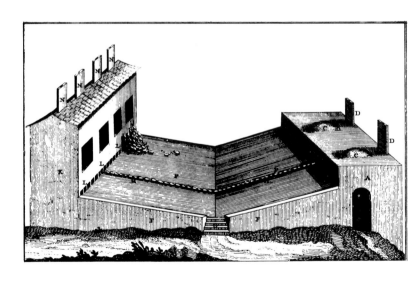

IX A MERCURY DISTILLATION FURNACE AT ALMADAN. AT THE RIGHT
THE STRUCTURE HOUSES TWO FURNACES, AND AT THE LEFT CONDEN-
SATION CHAMBERS. THE TWO CONNECT THROUGH A 'PIPE' MADE OF
GLOBULAR SECTIONS (ALUDEIS), WHICH ARE SHOWN IN PLACE IN THE
FRONT FURNACE AND DISASSEMBLED IN THE REAR FURNACE
From *ASP*, année, 1719, plate 24

ment existed. But he considers only al-Rāzī among the Arabs, and him in reference to the *luminus luminum*, which we believe to derive from the Moorish alchemists. Lacinius is more interested in proving that such Latin alchemists as Arnold and Raymond are not in disagreement, which he does (as also with al-Rāzī) mainly by claiming that they do not really mean what they say.[47] In general he is concerned to show that they abhor the idea of transmuting with organic materials and that they are concerned with relating the elixir to the traditional 'principles' of the metals, mercury and sulphur. He further finds them to be in agreement that the Stone is simple and not compound, and finally concludes that it is in mercury itself.

These views happen to be precisely those of 'Petrus Bonus', purported author of the *Pretiosa margarita novella* from which Lacinius takes the name of his collection. Bonus' problem, which also becomes that of Lacinius, is to decide what the Stone *is*, once he has convinced himself that it is *in* mercury. Because of the 'corrupting influence' of sulphur, he has declared that it consists 'of mercury exclusively, without any trace of external sulphur'. Here he finds a clue, in deciding that there must also be an 'internal sulphur', and this sulphur becomes the Stone sought by this school of alchemy.[48]

While all this may not be quite as clear as some modern admirers of Lacinius and Petrus Bonus have claimed,[49] it is clearer than the writings in which this point of view seems to have first appeared, those attributed to Arnold and Raymond. The most frequently cited authorities in the fourteenth and fifteenth centuries, Arnold and Raymond are each credited with the authorship of some 40 or 50 tracts.[50] Their reputations, nevertheless, hinge primarily on two works, a *Rosarius* (inc. *iste namque liber vocatur Rosarius . . .*), which is believed to be authentically Arnold's,[51]

---

[47] Cf. Lacinius, 1546: 165, 176v. 1894: 362, 383.

[48] Lacinius, 1546: 94v–99v. 1894: 225–33.

[49] In praising its clarity, Waite admits that the reader unacquainted with alchemy will probably not appreciate this (1894: viii).

[50] Thorndike lists 41 Lullian titles and 51 titles attributed to Arnold in continental manuscripts (HMES, Vol. 3: 52–84, 654–76 [esp. 655–6], Vol. 4: 3–64, 619–52 [esp. 624]). See also D. W. Singer, 1928–31, and Ferguson, 1906.

[51] Thorndike says that 'there seems to be no good reason for doubting' that Arnold wrote treatises on the transmutation of metals, and thinks the work beginning 'Iste namque liber vocatur Rosarius' (BCC, Vol. 1: 662–76) the most likely of several called *Rosarius* (HMES,

and a *Testamentum* regarded as the work of one of Raymond's disciples.[52]

Each of these long treatises is divided into a 'theoretical' and a 'practical' part, but the division is rather meaningless in any modern sense of these terms. Arnold's *Rosarius* gives, in its theoretical part, the theory which has already been described and which led to the idea of the Stone as a 'philosophical' sulphur. Its practical part, which seems not to be connected with the theoretical, includes a long account, reminiscent of the Arabic Jābirian alchemists, of the composition of elixirs by the 'separation of the elements' and their recombination in the correct proportion according to weight. Lacinius's 'recapitulation' does not clarify matters much by advising us to sublime together the fixed and volatile parts of the Stone, making 'the fixed volatile and the volatile fixed by alternate solution and sublimation'.[53]

Raymond's reputed *Testamentum* is similarly preoccupied with a philosophical sulphur, but the author wavers between deriving it from mercury itself, as he does when he is speaking more theoretically, and deriving it from 'middle minerals', and particularly from vitriol. He seems to feel that he has come upon the solution to the problem of the 'humidities' which had troubled earlier alchemists. The homogeneous union of the elements of metals, he says, prevents the separation of their humidities, 'but the humid minerals and middle minerals . . . atrament vitriola, et azoquea, marcasitae, alumina, sales, et baurax . . . do not have their humidity fixed in nature by dry material, but have it volatile and fugitive from fire'.[54] Such

---

Vol. 3: 54, 676–8). Lippmann agrees (1931: 45), and Ganzenmuller, who considers some Arnoldian alchemy authentic, says that the *Rosarius* 'was probably drawn up by students on the model of an authentic work'. ([1938]: 54). Neither he nor Lippmann identify clearly which *Rosarius* they refer to. The tendency to accept some of Arnold's alchemy as genuine, while rejecting Raymond's, is a reflection of the fact that Arnold's other works, unlike Raymond's, do not reveal passages specifically critical of alchemy.

[52] On the spurious authorship of Lullian alchemy see Thorndike, HMES, Vol. 2: 867–8, Vol. 4: 3–64. See also Ganzenmuller, (1938): 55, Lippmann, 1931: 135. There is general agreement that the *Testamentum* is the oldest Lullian alchemical work (Ganzenmuller) and keystone of the Lullian alchemical corpus (Thorndike). D. W. Singer, who gives the fullest description of the text, draws no conclusion as to its authenticity. She describes it as a 'chameleon-like text', and indicates that the 'most convincing' version is one which has not been printed (1928: 43–52). I have used the one printed in BCC, Vol. 1: 707–78, 790–822.

[53] Lacinius, 1546: 158v–159. 1894: 349.   [54] Ch. 57. BCC, Vol. 1: 742b.

middle dispositions are the causes of the conjunction of body and spirit which occurs in all natural generations. In the generation of the Stone the critical media are strong waters, particularly those derived from the green lion (*leo viridis*).[55]

It will be recognized that he is speaking of the acids (and corrosive sublimate) prepared by the distillation of iron vitriol with one or more additional materials. 'Green lion' (*leo viridis*) was long an alchemical secret name for the vitriol (ferrous sulphate) commonly used in the generation of all of the only gradually differentiated mineral acids. There is a tract called *De leone viride* in the *Sanioris medicinae* which opens with what appears to be a straightforward recipe (since nothing is added) for the generation of sulphuric acid.[56]

Notwithstanding his concern to avoid the corrupting influence of sulphur, and a disinclination for 'middle minerals', this also seems to be the burden of Lacinius' remarks. His consideration of Raymond does not derive from reading the *Testamentum*, but from Raymond's supposed summary in his 'Letter to King Rupert'.[57] Raymond must be aquitted, Lacinius feels, of the allegation that he advocated animal and vegetable Stones. Lacinius accomplishes this by transferring the virtues of *those* Stones from alchemy to medicine![58] He finally comes out for a mineral Stone, which we are presumably supposed to attribute to Raymond, the production of which begins with a 'water' from dry vitriol, cinnabar and saltpetre.[59]

Lacinius is similarly enigmatic in discussing the views of al-Rāzī and Albertus. The habit of speaking mysteriously of the use of the mineral acids in alchemy was characteristic of writers who can probably be placed in the first half of the fourteenth century, and who are mostly pseudonymous. The writings attributed to Arnold,

[55] Ch. 58–Ch. 60. BCC, Vol. 1: 773b.

[56] In Roger Bacon, 1603: 264–85. The author names himself as Raymond Gaufridus, and says that he is explaining a declaration of Roger Bacon. At the conclusion he says that he has obtained Roger Bacon's release from an incarceration occasioned by this very declaration. Gaufridus (1250–1311) was General of the Franciscan order in 1289.

[57] Lacinius 1546: 159v. 1894: 350.

[58] Ibid, 160v–164v. 1894: 351–8. The animal and vegetable Stones 'contain quintessences which are useful in medicine and in preserving the human body', among which is 'potable gold'. This is the ideology of medical chemistry, on which see below, Ch. 10.

[59] '*Facito aquam ex vitriolo siccato sale nitro atque cinabrio . . .*' Lacinius, 1546: 166. 1894: 363.

Raymond, Petrus Bonus, and others,[60] belong to this group. In Lacinius' own time, however, this style was anachronistic, for the key to the alchemical secret had long since been openly exposed, in a number of works dating after about 1350. A *Rosarius minor* informs us that 'the key to the seven gates' of the rose garden (a phrase reminiscent of one which appears in *De leone viride* and in Lacinius) is an 'aqua fortis' made of three 'herbs', which turn out to be green vitriol, saltpetre and alum.[61] A *Practica vera alkimika* states at the outset that four 'species' pertain to the work of the elixir, mercury, sulphur, vitriol and saltpetre, and it proceeds with a detailed description of the production of the same acid (nitric).[62] A *Compositum de compositis* attributed to Albertus Magnus and two works attributed to John of Rupescissa, an apocalyptic preacher well-known in the fourteenth century for his role in the anti-Papal reformist movement, take the same line. The philosopher's sulphur is 'Roman vitriol', according to Rupescissa's *Liber lucis*, but he is interested in its 'spirit', which is indicated by his recipes to be nitric acid.[63] Rupescissa's other work, *De confectione veri lapidis philosophorum*, and the pseudo-Albertine *Compositum* agree that the humidity or spirit drawn from saltpetre and Roman vitriol is really the philosopher's sulphur.[64]

From the twelfth-century *De aluminibus* to the *Testamentum* of Raymond two centuries later we find alchemical writing replete with rationalizations about spirits, 'middle minerals', and corrosive elixirs, which suggest experimentation with the mineral acids as elixirs. Only in the fourteenth century does the matter come out into the light, but it seems less likely that this delay was a matter of secrecy than that the mineral acids were not clearly identified as discrete substances prior to this time. Even in the latest of these works

[60] For example in the *Correctorium alchemiae* attributed to Richard of England (d. 1252) (in BCC, Vol. 2: 266–75), and the *Speculum alchemiae* attributed to Roger Bacon (in TC, Vol. 2: 377–84 [English trans. in pseudo-Roger Bacon, 1931]). These works are almost certainly spurious.

[61] TC, Vol. 2: 441–59, esp. 452. On the date and author see D. W. Singer, CLAM, No. 166, and Thorndike, HMES, Vol. 3: 180.

[62] TC, Vol. 4: 912–34. On the date and author see D. W. Singer, CLAM, No. 169, and Thorndike, HMES, Vol. 3: 692.

[63] BCC, Vol. 2: 84–7, esp. 84a. On the conception of vitriol as a 'middle mineral' between the elements and the metals John was cited by the influential seventeenth-century theorist, J. J. Becher (1703: 723, 84). On John of Rupescissa, see below, p. 210 ff.

[64] *De confectione*, in BCC, Vol. 2: 80–3. *Compositum de compositis*, in TC, Vol. 4: 825–41.

it remains uncertain that any mineral acid other than nitric was known, and the properties even of that acid were but vaguely recognized. The idea that there was but one elixir (or, at least, that only one was important) led to a complication in the process for its production, with a corresponding obscuration of its chemical character. The chlorides, nitrates and (probably) sulphates, of which we find traces in *De aluminibus* and related works, are less evident in the fourteenth-century tracts. Thus the fourteenth-century Latin alchemist seems to have fully sensed for the first time the potentialities of the mineral acids, at the expense of much which had been brought to light by the 'practical' alchemists of the twelfth and thirteenth centuries.

The fifteenth century

It has often been remarked that there was in the fifteenth century a diminution, both qualitative and quantitative, in the literature of gold-making alchemy.[65] Prescriptions for mineral acid elixirs continued to appear,[66] and the theory of philosophical sulphur was reiterated, but confidence that there was any connection between the two is little evident. The century was one of copyists and of collectors, and even the collectors seem to have sensed the impropriety of juxtaposing theory and practice. The collection of Arnold of Brussels (1473–90) is almost exclusively practical,[67] and that of Lacinius as rigorously theoretical.

Arnold and Raymond proved to be the last great names in Latin alchemy. The alchemical works attributed to them were probably over a century old when Lacinius wrote, but he can find no one later (excepting Petrus Bonus) worth mentioning. Lacinius betrays a decline in alchemical morale, for he admits that the idea is abroad that some of the leading authorities are in contradiction. He denies this. 'Only to inexperienced and superficial readers,' he tells us, 'can

[65] Thorndike, HMES, Vol. 4: 332. Ganzenmuller, (1938): 36.

[66] See, for example, *Das Buch der heiligen Dryfaldigkeit* in Ganzenmuller, 1956: 231–71) and the *Liber florum Geberti* (ibid.: 272–300). The 'blood of the green lion' esteemed by the most famous British alchemist, George Ripley (1415–90), was probably a mineral acid (Ripley, 1893. cf. Minderer, 1617, 19).

[67] W. J. Wilson, 1936.

there appear to be any disagreement among the different exponents of this Art. From Hermes, who calls the dissolved body a perennial water which coagulates mercury, down to the latest Sage, they are all in wonderful substantial harmony.'[68] It is to demonstrate this that he provides the summary statement of the teaching of Arnold, Raymond, al-Rāzī, Michael Scot and Albertus to which reference has been made.

One of the few in this century who touched upon both theory and practice was Bernard Trevisan,[69] who reveals himself to be a decided rarity, a sceptical alchemist. His studies, he tells us, began when a book of Rasis (al-Rāzī) fell into his hands, and continued with a perusal of the usual hierarchy of authorities. Particularly interested in 'waters of life thirty times rectified with their faeces until they became so acrid that no glass could contain them', he consumed twelve or fifteen years and much money in such investigations without result. He speaks of spending years making calcinations of alums, coperosas (vitriols), atraments, and other things, separating elements, etc., but concludes that it was all in vain.[70] His scepticism, however, has its limits, and he thinks he sees the cause of failure in the deviation of this practice from the 'way of nature'. Noting that corrosion alienates bodies from the metallic species, he enters upon what purports to be a solution to the problem, but which seems to lean heavily on the now venerable Arnold.[71] Trevisan was not to be the founder of a new school.

Insofar as the nascent publishing industry of the fifteenth century may be supposed to reflect the tastes of the time, it would appear that alchemy was not a popular subject. This is the more surprising since the popularity of other occult subjects clearly continued. No *incunabula* edition has been found of any of the Albertine alchemical works, whereas his *De mineralibus* and *Di mirabilis mundi* were printed, respectively, four and five times; and another of his attributions, *Liber agregationis* (on marvellous experiments with herbs, stones, and animals) was printed no less than fifty times in the fifteenth

[68] Lacinius, 1546: 180. 1894: 389.
[69] On his identity, see Thorndike, HMES, Vol. 3: 611–27. We have from him two writings, a *Librum de secretissimo philosophorum opere chemico* (BCC, Vol. 2: 388–99) and an *Epistolae duo ad Thomam de Bononiae, medicum* (BCC, Vol. 2: 399–409).
[70] BCC, Vol. 2: 389, 400.
[71] Ibid.: 399, 400, 408.

century![72] It is only encountered in manuscript half as often as is the *De alchimia*.[73]

Others of our reputed authorities on alchemy similarly appear among the *incunabula* only in other connections: Michael Scot in his *Liber physiognomiae* (21 editions), Raymond Lull in his writings on the mechanization of logic (*Arbor scientiae*, 2 editions, and *Ars brevis*, 5 editions), and Arnold of Villanova in his books on wine (10 editions) and alcohol (1 edition). Even the 'father of alchemy', Hermes Trismegistus, is represented only by non-alchemical works (of which there were 9 editions). Of truly alchemical writings we find very few, Geber's *Summa* and *Liber investigationis* (1 edition)[74] being possibly the first appearance of alchemy in print, and the only significant one in the fifteenth century.

The absence of alchemy from the *incunabula* is probably not to be attributed to a reluctance to give wide circulation to the secrets of the Art. Manuscripts were common enough, and alchemists seem later to have been positively eager to publish. It is probably to be attributed to the decline of alchemy in the fifteenth century, which occurred, as luck would have it, just when the printed book became available. Alchemy was to survive this accident, however, and printed works came out in increasing volume from the mid-sixteenth century, to reach a veritable flood in the following century. Nor did the devotees of the Art fail to attempt the preservation in print of the wisdom of the ancients on this subject. The collection of ancient alchemical writings has been a fashion from that time to the present day. Twice, in the *Theatrum chemicum* of Lazarus Zetzner (1659–61) and in the *Bibliotheca chemica curiosa* of J. J. Manget (1702), a heroic attempt was made at the assembly of the whole alchemical literature. Consideration of their contents, particularly of that of Zetzner, has much to tell us concerning the history of alchemy among the Latins.

Of about 200 works printed by Zetzner,[75] about half represent the writings of alchemists who lived in the sixteenth and seventeenth centuries, and these are mostly concerned with esoteric alchemy, indicating that the metamorphosis from exoteric to esoteric alchemy,

---

[72] Hirsch, 1950: 123–6.
[73] Thorndike, HMES, Vol. 2: 746–8. Kibre, 1942: 511–5.
[74] Compiled from Hirsch, 1950.
[75] The contents of TC are given in Ferguson, 1906: Vol. 2: 435–9.

which we have previously encountered in the corpus of Greek alchemy, had also occurred in Europe.[76] Of the remainder, the great majority are the works of the alchemists of the fourteenth century and earlier who have already been discussed here. It appears that Zetzner was no more successful than modern searchers of alchemical manuscripts in finding significant alchemists in the fifteenth century. The experiment in performing transmutation via the mineral acids had failed. Insofar as he was a chemist, the fifteenth-century alchemist sought new purposes for the science of matter. Although an occasional lapse into experimentation in gold-making was long characteristic of the chemist, the true gold-making alchemist ceased to be a factor in the history of the mundane science of matter.

[76] Cf. Waite, 1926. This is the phase of alchemy dealt with in the well-known recent study of psychology and alchemy by Jung (Jung, 1953). Jung makes little attempt to put the alchemical corpus in chronological order, and appears to have made nominal use of the works I have considered here. It seems to me that the great majority of European alchemists through the fourteenth century were exoteric, that is, were really concerned with gold-making.

Chapter Ten

Medical chemistry

IN medicine as in other scientific fields, medieval Europe was largely thrown upon its own devices. Hippocrates and Galen survived during the first Christian millennium as names attached to spurious or unimportant writings,[1] but the demand for healing survived the loss, such as it was, of the science of medicine. The practitioner turned increasingly to drugs. The numerous surviving medieval recipe books, which generally go under the name of 'antidotary', are made up of recipes concocted by mixing together many things, after a method which came to be known as 'polypharmacy'.[2] The germ of this already existed in Galenic medicine.

Dioscorides' book survived, at least in part, but its influence was greatly diluted. The sources of materia medica were rather indiscriminate, as is indicated by the name, *Medicina Plinii*,[3] of one of the more popular formularies, but this did not significantly alter the roster of substances used. It does not appear that much, if any, of the ancient materia medica was lost.

Greater continuity with antiquity was maintained by the Arabs, who included substantial portions of the works of Hippocrates, Dioscorides and Galen, among the earliest translations made at Bagdad in the ninth century. The Arabic pharmacopoeia appears to have been a considerable novelty when it was brought to Europe in the eleventh century. The first agent of this transmission was Constantine of Africa,[4] who was born a Moslem of North Africa,

---

[1] Cf. Durling, 1961: 232. Puhlmann, 1930.

[2] Sigerist, 1923. The most well known 'Antidotary' was that of Nicholas of Salerno (Nicholas, 1471, 1896).

[3] Pliny, pseudo, 1509. This is an antidotary organized according to diseases.

[4] On Constantine see HMES, Vol. 1: 742–59.

educated at Bagdad, and ended his life in 1087 as a Christian monk of Monte Cassino. Among the novelties of Constantine's *De gradibus simplicibus* was the considerably greater prominence he gave to mineral materials. They had appeared in the antidotaries as occasional but somewhat uncommon ingredients of complex recipes. Constantine, however, analyses such staples of the later medical chemistry as mercury, antimony and vitriol, in terms of the Galenic balance of qualities (hot, cold, wet and dry, in varying degrees), and mentions certain specific applications for them.[5]

The Bagdad-educated Constantine seems to have been unaware of more important pharmaceutical innovations which took place in Spain about the time of his birth. In 948 the Cordovan Caliph, 'Abd-al-Rahman III, received a gift of Greek manuscripts from the Byzantine Emperor, Constantine VII, among which was a copy of Dioscorides's *Materia medica*. The Arabic translation made in Bagdad about 850 was incomplete and defective, and the Caliph's Hispano-Jewish physician, Hasdei ibn Shaprut, with the assistance of a linguist provided by Constantine, undertook the translation of the new manuscript into Arabic.[6] The work was continued by subsequent court physicians, among them Ibn Juljul, physician to Caliph Hisham II (reigned 976–1009), and perhaps Abulcasis (Khalaf ibn-'Abbas al-Zahrāwī, d. *c.* 1013), one of the most distinguished medical men of Arabic Spain.

Ibn Juljul, like Agathodaimon and Bālinus, appears to be a missing link in the history of science. His works are listed as a commentary on Dioscorides, a book on drugs *not* in Dioscorides, and a history of physicians and philosophers of his time in Spain. None of these has been translated, and only the history has been published. Not only is Ibn Juljul cited in connection with medical chemistry by such as the author of *De aluminibus* and by Michael Scot, but Albertus Magnus and George Agricola were to regard him as an authority on the natural formation of minerals.[7]

---

[5] Constantine of Africa, 1536: 381–4. Constantine may have been the translator rather than the author of this work.

[6] This is related in the medical bio-bibliography of Ibn abī Usaibi'a (*c.* 1242), under the biography of Ibn Juljul. I have used the French translation of Silvestre de Sacy, 1810.

[7] On Ibn Juljul see Sarton (IHS, Vol. 1: 682) where other references are given. Silvestre de Sacy, 1810, is a French translation of his biography by Usaibi'a. Ibn Juljul's *The generations of physicians* has been published (in Arabic) by Fu'ad Sayyid (Cairo, 1955). The reference to

The writing of Abulcasis on materia medica was translated, however, and, under the name *Liber servatoris*, was to be one of the most popular tracts on medicines among the Latins. The *Liber servatoris* is a translation of the twenty-eighth book of Abulcasis' comprehensive medical treatise *al-Tasrif*[8]. It is a treatise on the *preparation* of medicines from all three kingdoms, for the most part by sublimation and distillation. Moreover, Abulcasis moves minerals from their usual position as a kind of addendum to the beginning of the book. His *Liber servatoris* was to achieve an influence in Latin pharmacy similar to that exercised by the *De aluminibus* on Latin alchemy, yet Abulcasis was not a medical chemist, in the sense in which this became the denomination of a sect among the Latins, for he draws no conclusions pertinent either to medicine or chemistry from his recipes. Nor does he appear to have had that recipe for corrosive sublimate which was known to the author of *De aluminibus*, and which was to be of such moment in both medicine and alchemy.[9]

---

a Latin manuscript of his treatise on drugs not in Dioscorides mentioned in Holmyard and Mandeville (1927: 37 note) is apparently a mistake. On the comments of Albertus and Agricola on Ibn Juljul, see below, p. 161 n 43, and p. 317.

[8] Hamarneh and Sonnedecker, 1963: 28. Latin versions, of which I have used those of 1471 and 1623, are from an earlier Hebrew translation (GKW, Vol. 1: 50).

[9] The *De aluminibus* and virtually all subsequent early works which describe the preparation of corrosive sublimate prepare it as a sublimate from three ingredients, mercury, vitriol or alum, and common salt or sal ammoniac. Abulcasis sublimates mercury and colcothar (vitriol) and claims to get a white sublimate (1471: 13r–13v). He also sublimates mercury and sal ammoniac (Ibid.: 13v–14r). This could have yielded some corrosive sublimate, but he is vague on the result and does not seem to regard it as anything of importance.

There is also 'an acute medicine' obtained by sublimation, with an alembic, of five ingredients, which the Latin translators Simon Januensi and Abraamo Judaeo name as yellow arsenic (orpiment), live chalk (quicklime), mercury, sal ammoniac, and 'alchalizimar'. The product is called 'adhicbardic'. The translators were obviously defeated by some of the Arabic words. Dr Sami Hamarneh has been good enough to assist me in comparing the Latin with the Arabic text in Istanbul manuscript Ali Amiri 2854. It appears that adhicbardic is a transliteration of the Arabic *al-Dik bau-Dik*, 'boiler over boiler', and probably refers to the alembic. The five ingredients of the Arabic text are yellow arsenic, mercury, sal ammoniac, Zinjar (verdigris) and al-Nawrah (a paste of yellow arsenic and quicklime used as a depilatory). Alcalizimar would thus equal to equal zinjar, reducing rather than increasing the likelihood that corrosive sublimate could be a product of this recipe (but see note 24 below).

The matter deserves further study, for Abulcasis was to be cited as an authority on corrosive sublimate by such sixteenth-century authorities as A. M. Brasavola (1537: 430–1) and Conrad Gesner (1555: 393).

Distillation

Abulcasis says that distillation is used to make rosewater, and also by 'the alchemists', as indeed it had been during something more than a millennium since the venerable Maria the Jewess. But Abulcasis does not reveal what the alchemists were doing with it. Abulcasis, himself, distilled, in addition to rosewater, such organic materials as vinegar and olive oil,[10] but apparently not wine. When it comes to the mineral kingdom he speaks only of sublimation, and it does not appear that he knew the mineral acids.[11]

That Abulcasis did not know alcohol and the mineral acids despite his evident concern with precisely those manipulations which were to lead to their discovery lends credence to the theory that improved distillate cooling was requisite to the discovery of those substances. He describes clearly his apparatus for sublimation, which consisted of a pair of dishes fitted mouth-to-mouth, and that for distillation, which was a typical alembic.[12] He makes no particular reference to condensate cooling, but it is evident that his alembic was capable of condensing water and higher boiling liquids. The absence of reference to cooling as a problem suggests that there may simply have been no awareness of the existence of liquids of lower boiling point than water.

If condensate cooling was the key to the discovery of alcohol, the matter was further complicated in the case of hydrochloric and nitric acids by the need for an appropriate recipe. Sulphuric acid, however, required neither a recipe, since it is a product of the destructive distillation of vitriol or alum, nor efficient condensate cooling, since its boiling point exceeds that of water. It does, however, require the use of apparatus capable of withstanding corrosive materials at high temperatures, a capability which was purely fortuitous in early alchemical apparatus.[13] Nevertheless, this

[10] He distills 'sea onions' (scilla), vinegar (modus albificandi acetum), and olive oil, under the name 'oleum de lateribus' (oil of bricks) (1471: 30. 1623: 245r–246v). The phrase 'as you distill rosewater' occurs repeatedly.

[11] Brasavola (1537: 214) and Gesner (1555: 393) cite Abulcasis on a distillate from vitriol (sulphuric acid?), but this is not supported by Liber servatoris.

[12] Abulcasis, 1471: 14. 1623: 242.

[13] Robert Boyle, who was surely in a far better position than had been the medieval alchemist to obtain satisfactory apparatus, frequently speaks of the inability of his glass to stand severe conditions. Glass apparatus was usually specified in medieval recipes for the acids.

characteristic was to some extent also required of the apparatus for distilling 'oil of bricks', and the importance Abulcasis and his successors attached to this process suggests an awareness on their part of the utility of apparatus improved in this direction.[14]

An inquiry into the history of 'alcohol' quickly reveals that the term, which is obviously from Arabic, referred, in its early usage, to 'kohl' (antimony sulphide).[15] Not until the mid-sixteenth century did it come into its modern signification. Our alcohol, when it was first known, went under a variety of other names, of which 'aqua vitae' was probably the most common, and 'aqua ardens' the most definitive. Then as now alcohol came in various grades. Even more difficult terminological problems beset the inquirer into the history of the mineral acids. It is not difficult to determine whether a particular reference to 'alcohol' refers to antimony sulphide or aqua ardens, but 'acetum' was an ancient term for vinegar, which is, after all, an acid. The literature is moreover full of references to 'strong waters', 'acute waters', 'mineral spirits', etc.[16] long before these terms could have signified, as they did later, one or another mineral acid.

Unequivocal recipes for alcohol emerge in the twelfth century, both in the recipe books of practical chemistry[17] and in the writings of the Salernian physicians.[18] Only at the end of the thirteenth century, however, do we find numerous references to it. Peter of

[14] Abulcasis calls oil of bricks 'a secret of the philosophers' (1471: 39r. 1623: 246v). By 1623 other authorities have raised it to 'oleum sapientiae & perfecti magisterii, & benedictum, & divinum, & sanctum' (Mesuë, Jr., 1623: 193). On oil of bricks see further, pp. 207-8.

[15] Lippmann, 1954: 31-2, summarizes the literature on the history of kohl and alcohol.

[16] See above, pp. 140, 164, 172.

[17] The following recipe appears in the twelfth-century version of the *Mappae clavicula*: 'De commixtione puri et fortissimi xknk cum iij. qbsuf tbmkt, cocta in eius negocii vasis, fit aqua, quae accensa flammans incombustam servat materiam.' (*Mappae clavicula*, 1847: 227 recipe ccxii). Berthelot's suggestion (in CMA, Vol. 1: 61) that this represents a recipe for alcohol is generally accepted. Another recipe appears in the thirteenth-century recipe book of Marcus Graecus (1842-3: 497): 'Aquam ardentem sic facies: recipe vinum nigrum spissum et vetus et in una quarta ipsius distemperabuntur unciae II sulphuris vivi subtilissime pulverazati, lib. II tartari extracti a bono vino albo, unciae II salis communis; et subdita ponas in cucurbita bene plumbata et alambico supposito distillabis aquam ardentem quam servare debes in vase clauso vitreo.'

[18] Puccinotti, 1855, Document VI, discusses a 'Compendium Salerni' of 78 chapters in the library of the Ospidale di Santa Fina in Sangimignano. Chapter 31 describes the production of alcohol (aqua ardente) as follows: 'Aqua ardens ad modum aqua rose sic fit [De aqua rosea is the preceding chapter] Vini rubri libra una in cucurbita ponatur et libra una salis affricani rubri perfecti item et salis comunis cocti in olla rudi, et dragm. quatuor

Spain (d. 1277), Thaddeus Alderotti (d. 1303), Arnold of Villanova (d. 1311), and Vitalis of Furno (d. 1327), all refer to alcohol, as 'aqua ardens', or 'aqua vitae', and as a well-known substance. They represent a period when alcohol was 'known', not when it was discovered. Peter of Spain, a Portuguese polymath who ended his life as Pope John XXI, included alcohol among (twelve) miraculous waters in his *Tractatus mirabilis aquarum*.[19] This was more or less contemporary with the *Consilia medicinalia* of the Florentine physician Thaddeus Alderotti, which speaks of aqua vitae as a medicine in common use, and makes perhaps the first reference to the special arrangement for condensate cooling (*serpente*) which we believe to have been the key to the discovery of alcohol.[20] The works in which alcohol is mentioned by Arnold[21] and Vitalis[22] were probably written a little later.

---

tartari in cucurbita ponantur cum vino prefato et ventosa superponatur. et aquositas descendet per nasum ventose. et colligetur quam poteris adstricte unde non habeas flammam neque perdicionem substancie. . . .'

Lippmann (1922) holds this to be a work of the mid-twelfth century. Another twelfth-century recipe for alcohol may be that in Puff von Schrick (1481: 12) if, as Sarton suggests, the real author was the early-twelfth-century Bartholomew of Salerno (IHS, Vol. 2: 239).

[19] Thorndike, HMES, vol. 2: 500–01. The work has not been printed.

[20] Puccinotti, 1855, Document II, lists the 156 chapters of the *Consilia medicinalia* from Vatican Latin MS 2418. The last is 'De virtutibus aqua vite'. Lippmann (1914) has found the following two recipes for alcohol in this manuscript.

(1) 'Recipe vini rubei vel albi optimi fortissimi . . . vini in vase noto decem mensuras ponas et diligenter clauso. Distilla cum igne lento; aquam, quae praeter primum vaporem exierit, collige; ardet enim. . . .'

(2) 'aquae vite; quae alio nomine dicitur ardens, fac fiere vasa duo de cupro, quorum unum sit ad modum cucurbite cum alembico, ubi distilletur aqua rosata, hoc excepto, quod istud vas sit totum unum et non habet canale intus habet tamen rostrum. in summitate eius sit unum foramen magnum ad modum digiti, per quid res distillanda intromittatur. Aliud sit sicut una cucurbita sine alembico equales per totum et infra se contineat canalem conclusum serpentiuum, serpente illud totum a sumitate usque ad fundum. Caput vero superius serpentis sit extra vas per 3 vel 4 digitos. . . .'

Thaddeus's only printed work, *De regimine sanitatis*, mentions wine but not alcohol (1477), but he also wrote a special book on alcohol, *De virtutibus aqua vitae quae etiam dicitur aqua ardens*, with which I am not acquainted. Lippmann reports that a thirteenth-century manuscript of this exists (1914: 379).

[21] 1585: 833 A–E (*De vinis*). Arnold also wrote a book on the medical uses of alcohol (Arnold of Villanova, 1477).

[22] Vitalis describes the production of alcohol as follows: 'Quaedam aqua vocatur aqua ardens, quae hoc modo fit. Recipe vinum bonum ac forte, purum, rubeum, et pone in alembico, et distilla lento igne. Sic fit aqua rosacea. Et exibit per sublimationes aqua ardens et si saepius distilletur, quanto plus distillabitur, tanto erit subtilior et utilior. . . .' (1531: 12).

According to the date – late thirteenth century – which has been assigned to the author of the treatises of the Latin Geber, these writers would be his contemporaries. Geber was the first alchemist to describe clearly the production of a mineral acid, nitric, and this acid was also known to Vitalis.[23] Peter of Spain may also have known some kind of an acid.[24] Vitalis further reveals that alcohol was in use as an alchemical elixir as well as a medicine,[25] and thus reveals the extent of the confusion between medicine and alchemy in his time. But it seems that alcohol was probably the prior discovery, for nearly all of our early sources connect the process for its manufacture with that for rosewater, and this we know to have had a continuous history extending back to the springtime of Arabic science.

There is one further curious circumstance to note in connection with the introduction of the mineral acids, namely that Abulcasis' process for making the somewhat mysterious 'oil of bricks' was the prototype of later processes for acid production. In later writings, oil of bricks was typically the product of a partial destructive distillation of olive oil, the prototype of the 'empyreumatic' oils, evil smelling counterparts to the pleasant smelling 'essential' oils. But Abulcasis, who prepares it by distilling 'oil' from new bricks, does

[23] Vitalis describes the production of nitric acid as follows: 'Est insuper alia quaedam aqua omnia solvens corpora, haec ita fit. Accipe sal petrae lib 1 corprosse lib 1 ita simul terantur, & misce in praedicta aqua ardenti & pone in urinali super cineres & distilla ad ignem cum bono vino. Primam aquam accipe per se, & postquam tota illa aqua fuerit distillata, iterum pone in urinali quemadmodum prius, & distilla secundo, illa secunda aqua si guttatim fundatur super pannum de blanqueto, facit illum croceum. Haec aqua omne metallum, cunctaque ferrilia solvit seu liquefacit. Chalybem, argentum, cuprum, plumbum, aurum & similia. Solvit praeterea mercurium & quosvis lapides calcinatos, omniaque corpora calcinata.' (1531: 13).

[24] In his *Thesaurus pauperum* Peter produces from sal ammoniac, vitriol, yellow arsenic, and verdigris, a distillate which 'penetrates bones and all metals', and 'cauterizes like fire'. (1497: Bk 4, Ch. 9). This is surely derived from Abulcasis' recipe for 'an acute water' (see note 9 above), but leaves out the mercury! According to Thorndike Peter's *Tractatus Mirabilis aquarum* also includes recipes for 'waters' of salt (sal gemme) and vitriol (copose) (HMES, Vol. 2: 500–1). Authors of the sixteenth century imputed knowledge of the mineral acids to their predecessors more extensively than modern students have been able to confirm. According to Conrad Gesner (1555: 393), Abulcasis and Franciscus de Monte (Francesco di Piedemonte?) knew sulphuric acid.

[25] It conserves meat from putridity, *congeals mercury*, *whitens copper*, cures wounds, paralysis and other ailments. Its odour kills reptiles, and 'above all it induces joyousness in men' ('hominem super omnia reddit hilarem') (Vitalis, 1531: 12. My italics). The alchemists of the sixteenth century still believed in the power of alcohol to induce metallic transmutation, according to the Italian metallurgist Biringuccio (1942: 347).

not identify it precisely as olive oil, and the recipe continues to vary
as it appears in works of the next several centuries. This can be seen
in the popular and much commented upon materia medica of
'Mesuë, Jr'. He makes oil of bricks by distilling 'oleum rorismarini'
(oil of rosemary) with *old* bricks, but one of his commentators
points out that it should be olive oil and another says that Dioscorides
distilled 'naptha' in this way and that Mesuë's process was already
known to al-Rāzī.[26] He further adds that the 'chemical philosophers'
call an oil from such a process 'the perfect magistery', and that he,
himself, has seen a single drop of it instantly penetrate a (marble or
metal?) slab on which it has accidentally fallen.[27]

That the empyreumatic oils were 'acid' – judged principally by
taste – was long a matter of interest to chemists, but they were
making mineral acid mixtures by the same process in the sixteenth
century, and probably much earlier, for Abulcasis, himself, said the
process was known to the alchemists.[28] Since bricks are made of
'aluminous' clays they would to some degree serve the purpose of
vitriol or alum in yielding acid upon heating with salt or saltpetre.
'Old' bricks, if incrusted with salt, as was often the case, would
require no saline addition. Recipes for such acids, under various
names, occur in the works of J. B. Porta, Libavius, Beguin, Croll
and Glauber, and by this time it is clearly a process for the production
of hydrochloric acid.[29]

Latin pharmacology

The year 1471 marked a milestone in the history of Latin pharmacy,
for it saw the publication, in Venice, of three fundamental works on

[26] Mesuë, Jr., 1623, embodies a number of commentaries. The two cited here are 'Chri.',
who may be Guillaume Chretien (d. 1560) and an undesignated commentator who seems
from the context to be Giovanni Costeo (d. 1603). The relevant passages are on folio 193v.

[27] Loc. cit. The passage reads, 'Vidi enim his oculis guttam cuiusdam olei fortuito cadentem
lectisternia omnia quae multiplicia erant momento penetrasse, & lecti fundum, quod ex
asseribus invississe.' Ducange, MIL, reports that *lectus* (bier) also signified in medieval usage
a platform for bearing trophies, and defines *lectisternum* as 'lectus apparatus et instrumentum'
I have assumed that it here signifies something which could be 'pierced' by an acid, an
assumption which is supported by the similar phrase in John of Rupescissa (see below, p. 213).

[28] Abulcasis 1471: 38v. 1623: 246v.

[29] Porta, the earliest source known to me, calls it 'an aqua fortis or oil out of salt' (1589:
197 [I do not find it in the 1569 edition of this work]). Similar recipes occur in Libavius
(1597: 342), Beguin (1620: 131), Croll (1609: 149) and Glauber (1651: 9).

materia medica. Two of them were the *Antidotary* of Nicholas of Salerno and Abulcasis' *Liber servatoris*, but it was the third, the 'Grabbadim [of] Ioannis Nazareni Filii Mesuae' which was to enjoy the greatest popularity among the Latins. It appeared, as the *Grabadin* of 'Mesuë, Jr.', in about 30 editions (with some variance in title) between 1471 and 1623, during which time it accrued a mass of commentary by Latin editors.

The origin of this work is in dispute. Its title comes from the Arabic transliteration of the Greek word for tablet or short treatise (γραφίδιον), and was a common Arabic name for works on materia medica. But this work has not been found in an Arabic version. There had been an eminent Bagdad physician of the ninth century named Mesuë (senior), but authorities have not connected the *Grabadin* with him or with his family. Leo Africanus (fl. *c.* 1500–50) held it to be the work of another Bagdad physician, Māsawayh al Mārdīnī (d. 1015), but modern opinion has been that it may be a European forgery, perhaps of the thirteenth century.[30]

Whereas Abulcasis' book is organized according to the sources of its remedies, and oriented towards 'simples', that of Mesuë, Jr. is organized in the Galenic tradition of compounded drugs (electuaries, opiates, etc.). Against the old-fashioned *Antidotary* of Nicholas and the radicalism of Abulcasis, Mesuë was the clear choice of the Latins. In the course of its career it accrued 'supplements' from the learned Italian Peter of Abano (1250–1315) and from Francesco di Piedemonte (d. 1319), and commentaries by the anatomist Mondino de Luicci (1275–1327), Ch. G. de Honestis of Florence (late fourteenth century), Joh. Manardus of Ferrara (1461–1536), physician to the Count of Mirandola and of the King of Hungary, Jacques Dubois Sylvius (1478–1555), Professor at the College de Trigueir, Paris (and Vesalius' teacher in anatomy), and Giovanni Costeo (d. 1603), Professor at Turin and Bologna.[31]

But the preference for Mesuë over Abulcasis did not dispose of

[30] Sarton, IHS, Vol. 1: 728–9. See also Leclerc, 1876, Vol. 1: 504–7 and BL. I have used Mesuë, Jr., 1471, 1502, 1568, and 1623.

[31] The 1502 edition, called 'Canones universales', contains the comments of Mondini. That of 1568 is an 'Opera' edited by Costao. The 1623 edition is also an 'Opera' . . . with the observations on the first three books of Mondini, Honesti, Manardi, and Silvii. In fact, it also includes those of Costaeo and 'Chri.', whom I am unable to identify. The French physician, Guillaume Chretien (d. 1560) is a possibility.

chemistry, for the commentaries betray an awareness of Mesuë's deficiency in this regard. In addition to those already indicated in connection with oil of bricks, both Manardus and Sylvius note that the chemists had, since Mesuë, greatly augmented the number of 'oils', and the latter decries both their lack of scientific rationality (*ratione scientibus*) and their tendency to introduce 'metallic calxes' into remedies. None of the commentators on Mesuë's book are conspicuous advocates of chemistry, the less so because 'the alchemists' whom they frequently mention had already launched an independent school of therapy.

This is revealed in the writings of Hieronymous Brunschwygk (fl. 1500), a surgeon and apothecary of Strassburg who published several books on the distillation of materia medica. Brunschwygk's materia medica was apparently derived from the herbal *Hortus sanitatus* (1485) of Johann von Cube, but differs not only in its preoccupation with distillation, but in the name 'quintessence' which is usually given to the product. A few minerals appear among the 'herbs', and there are some mineral quintessences, including nitric acid. But Brunschwygk is not here following Abulcasis or Mesuë. He acknowledges his model to be John of Rupescissa.[32]

John of Rupescissa was a countryman of Arnold of Villanova and Raymond Lull, and to a considerable degree their spiritual heir. Menendez y Palayo has called the three 'the triumvirate of Catalan science in the fourteenth century'.[33] John, who lived a generation after the other two more famous Catalonians, was a member of the Franciscan order who was best known for his apocalyptic preaching. His activities in this line caused him to spend a considerable part of his life in prison, and the few definite dates (1345, 1346, 1349) which can be associated with him are connected with these incarcerations. Like Arnold and Raymond he was reputed by later writers to have been involved in both medicine and alchemy, and extant works on both topics bear his name.[34] His one medical – actually pharmaceu-

---

[32] Brunschwygk, 1512, esp. 267, 276.

[33] 1880, Vol. I: 500.

[34] The alchemical works have been discussed above, p. 196. The authenticity of John's two alchemical and one medico-chemical tracts has not been made a subject of special concern. In her study of his career, Bignami Odier (1952) accepts the medical work, *De consideratione*, but declines to discuss the alchemical works, referring us to Thorndike (HMES, Vol. 3: 347–69), where they are accepted as genuine. Bignami Odier is particularly interested in

tical – work is a remarkably original tract called *De consideratione quintae essentiae* (On the consideration of the fifth essence).

This work begins with a paean in praise of the medical efficacy of alcohol. John tells us that, since a body cannot be preserved from corruption by things which are themselves corruptible, we must seek that which is related to the four qualities as heaven is related to the four elements. He conceives spirit of wine [alcohol] to be that which he seeks, and gives it the fitting name of fifth essence. He describes several processes for distilling wine, and, despite his attribution of superlative therapeutic powers to the fifth essence obtained, he proceeds to make it better still by extinguishing heated gold in it, which he calls 'fixing the sun in our sky', and which subsequently became a common procedure (although by no means the only one) for the preparation of the medicine, 'potable gold'.

John may have been the first to give to alcohol the name fifth essence, or 'quintessence', to use the more usual term. Whether or not this was the case, he goes on to bring the quintessence decisively within the sublunary sphere by declaring that it is not only obtainable from wine, but from all other things as well. In this generalizing the quintessence as a chemical species he was propounding a doctrine which was to assume great importance in the chemistry of the sixteenth century. For among the things which he chooses from which to extract quintessences, he mentions herbs and animal matter cursorily and then proceeds to a more detailed account of the quintessences of minerals, particularly of mercury, antimony and gold. Mercury is sublimed with vitriol and salt in the now familiar process for corrosive sublimate. Antimony (the sulphide) is imbibed with vinegar (acetum) and the resulting concoction is distilled. The vinegar is said to pass off, and following it the quintessence of antimony, in the form of 'blood red drops'.[35] The quintessence of

---

John's role as would-be prophet in the tradition of the apocalyptic Joachim of Fiora, and *Liber lucis*, one of the alchemical works, begins with a Joachimite prophecy (BCC, Vol. 2: 84a). The numerous manuscripts of the alchemical works appear all to be fifteenth century or later, and we have a fifteenth-century reference from Trithemius (cf. Partington, 1938) to John as a writer on medicine and alchemy (cf. Multhauf, 1954-1).

[35] John of Rupescissa, 1549: 100. 1561: 103-4. 1856: 10. The recipe also appears in the writings of Ulstad (1550: 30 misnumbered 36), and Gesner (1554: 155, 174). It was very probably a red variety of the starting substance, antimony trisulphide, which was later known as kermes mineral (cf. Macquer, 1778, art. 'antimoine').

gold is not a distillate or sublimate, but the supernatant layer from the imbibition of amalgamated gold with vinegar or urine.[36]

Obscure though this chemistry may be, we have here a treatise which, to quote Thorndike, 'possessed a marked individuality both in expression and arrangement, distinguishing it from other medieval alchemical treatises'.[37] He adds that 'it created a correspondingly profound and wide impression', as indeed it did, for if we follow the succession of later and more familiar writings in medical chemistry we find at the heart of the matter John's concept of the quintessence and its application above all to mercury, antimony, gold, and, finally, the mineral acids. John's treatise exists in manuscript versions in Latin, English, Italian and Swedish, and was printed in the sixteenth century in Latin and French. But before this the contents had been taken over as the basis for better known chemical works, notably by Philip Ulstad and Paracelsus, whose works entitled, respectively, *Coelum philosophorum* and *Archidoxies*, both written about 1525, are clearly much indebted to John's book on the quintessence. A variant version attributed to Raymond Lull had appeared, and by the mid-sixteenth century it seems to have been considered doubtful who was the real author. Not many after Brunschwygk gave credit to John of Rupescissa, and scarcely anyone did after the appearance of that stormy petrel of medical chemistry, Paracelsus.

The fruits of distillation chemistry manifested themselves in three fairly distinct literary genres in the sixteenth century, writings from the 'reformed alchemists' descended from John of Rupescissa, pharmaceutical writings in the tradition of Mesuë, Jr., which had become conventional among physicians, and those do-it-yourself formularies, the 'books of secrets', which then attained their greatest popularity. By the middle of the century authors of whatever persuasion were borrowing freely from all three sources, and the distinction between them was becoming decidedly blurred. The medical man did not need to believe John's notion that the quintes-

---

[36] It is not surprising that gold has a very long history as a remedy. Darmstaedter (1924) has traced the history of its use in internal medicine, as 'potable gold'. Oddly enough he does not mention John of Rupescissa, but makes much of Ulstad, Paracelsus, and Gesner (in his book of secrets), all of which are medico-chemical descendants of John.

[37] Thorndike, HMES, Vol. 3: 355-6.

sence is related to the qualities as Aristotle's fifth element is to the other four in order to see the importance of distillation. In the words of Conrad Gesner (1516–65), one of the most important naturalists of the century and author of a book of secrets, 'it teaches of those medicines which are not taken whole or in substance, but applied in the purer parts, that is, in liquors, oils, or juices secreted or abstracted through distillation or other artificial methods'.[38]

Most impressive of all were those corrosive distillates of which, as John said, a single drop could instantly pierce the hand.[39] In the sixteenth century this quintessence was joined by waters, oils, and what-not from what was probably the most popular mineral raw material in pharmacology, calcanthum or vitriol (iron sulphate). The account of Winter von Andernach (1478–1574), another leading figure in the biological sciences in the sixteenth century, is clearer than most. In his book on materia medica he speaks of the preparation, through distillation, of a water and an oil, 'the crasser spirits of calcanthum', and of the more subtle liquor, quintessence. The crasser spirits may further appear in the form of the vulgar oil, red oil, sweet oil, or as 'vitriolated sulphur'.[40]

'The alchemists', whom Abulcasis had credited with special knowledge of distillation, are still in possession of that reputation in the time of Gesner, who follows an impressive array of quintessences, waters, and oils from all of the three kingdoms with a few remedies 'non-alchemical, that is, not distilled or sublimated'. While we cannot set aside this impressive contemporary testimony to the alchemist's finesse with the alembic, he is more readily distinguished from the other distillers of Gesner's time by his ideology. While others simply joined quintessences to other entities – oils, waters, spirits, etc. – resulting from chemical manipulation, the medical alchemist adhered to John of Rupescissa's conception of the quintessence as a veritable elixir of life. But in the sixteenth century he began the attempt to establish a heirarchy of quintessences, and to find a place in the scheme for lesser substances, and began to evolve into the medical chemist.

[38] 1555: Argumentum.
[39] John of Rupescissa, 1549: 109. 1561: 112. 1856: 8. I suspect that the similarity of this statement to that in Costeo's comment on Mesuë, Jr. (see above, p. 208) is not accidental.
[40] 1571: 677–80.

In 1527 the city of Basel found itself with a town physician who was to shake the foundations of the newly reconstructed temple of medicine, Paracelsus (1493/94–1541).[41] In modern times he has very nearly become a mythological figure, but the monumental reputation for good or evil which he has come to enjoy is in large part derived from his adoption as a 'patron saint' of occultism and from scholarly delving into his literary legacy, which was first gathered together in 1589, nearly a half century after his death. In 1527 he had published nothing. He was an unconventional physician famed for semi-miraculous cures, which were thought to be connected with his profession of an unconventional doctrine of chemical therapy.

Although the doctrine was not new, the supposition was well founded. Paracelsus is known to have written in about 1525 the work called *Archidoxies*,[42] which has been mentioned as the capstone of the writings in the tradition of John of Rupescissa. While obviously dependent (without acknowledgement) upon these earlier writings, *Archidoxies* renovated the tradition in attempting to differentiate the various categories of substances with which this school was concerned. The nature of this endeavour is indicated by the subdivision of the work:

Book 1. On the prologue and microcosm
Book 2. On the separation of the elements
Book 3. On the quintessence
Book 4. On arcana
Book 5. On magisteria
Book 6. On specifics
Book 7. On elixirs
Book 8. On external medicines (extrinsica).

All books except the first are concerned with generalizations about and recipes for chemical medicines, and the medicines are not a very great expansion of those advocated by John of Rupescissa. The quintessence is divested more unequivocally of its association with alcohol and with preservative properties. Preservative properties are associated by Paracelsus with 'elixirs'. It is not clear what

---

[41] On Paracelsus' biography see R. Julius Hartmann, 1904; Pachter, 1951; Pagel, 1958.
[42] Sudhoff, 1926. I have used the edition of Sudhoff, 1922–33, Vol. 3: 93–200, and the English translation of Waite, 1894, Vol. 2: 3–93.

'separation of the elements' had to do with medicine, especially as Paracelsus conceived it, but 'that which, apart from separation or any preparation of the elements, can be extracted out of things', was to become one of his favourite categories of medicine, under the name *magisteria*. The *arcana* appear to be, as the name implies, secret remedies, typical of those with which the books of secrets abounded, and it is probably from them that Paracelsus derived the idea for such a category.

One is largely reduced to speculation in explaining the categories of *Archidoxies*, for Paracelsus, himself, is unclear, and there is little evident reason for the assignment of the recipes to the categories where we find them. The processes for separating elements and those for preparing quintessences are not fundamentally distinct if, indeed, they are even superficially different, and it is anything but clear how his quintessences differ chemically from his lighter 'elements'. Nor is the importance which magisteria were to attain apparent from *Archidoxies*, for the extracts and distillates which made up his magisteria are also little different from the elements and quintessences.[43] Nor do the drugs of *Archidoxies* correspond very well to those advocated by Paracelsus in his other writings. Nevertheless the curious idea of classifying quintessences and related chemical entities which we find in *Archidoxies* was to bear fruit in the end in the form of the first system of classification of substances which was essentially chemical rather than mineralogical.

Medico-chemical therapeutics

The question of the use of remedies of mineral origin, which is at the heart of 'medical chemistry', is a complex one, involving such auxiliary questions as that of the rationale of the pharmacopoeia, the question of the actual use of drugs, and that of the meaning of the term 'preparation' when referred to a drug.

The consistency with which mineral materials appear in drug lists has already been noticed. We have not heretofore given serious consideration to the question of their actual use, but it would appear from Dierbach's study of the drugs of the Hippocratic physicians that virtually the whole armoury of known minerals were on

[43] Multhauf, 1956: 336–40.

occasions recommended[44] even by that group, which had been given a special name ($\varDelta \iota \alpha \tau \eta \tau \acute{\iota} \varkappa \eta$) to distinguish it from another school of physicians ($\varphi \alpha \varrho \mu \alpha \varkappa \varepsilon \upsilon \tau \iota \varkappa \acute{\eta}$) which was addicted to the use of drugs![45] Moreover their use is not restricted to external medicine. We even find in a Hippocratic treatise a recipe incorporating arsenic bisulphide (sandarach) for internal use.[46]

Nevertheless minerals made up a small part of the pharmacopoeia, and it is beyond dispute that mineral-based remedies were not prominent in classical medicine. This leads us to the conclusion that there is no special significance to the mention of mineral remedies, or even to their internal administration. Drugs were used sparingly by the Hippocratics, and the Galenists, although they relied on them more heavily, usually compounded drugs according to their supposed qualitative composition (hot, cold, wet and dry in varying degrees), and this scheme was based primarily on botanicals.

Probably the fundamental deviation of the Arabic physicians from Galenic medicine, and one which was full of significance for the history of chemistry, was the movement of the Moorish physicians from Galen to Dioscorides, which was initiated by those involved in the new tenth-century translation of the latter. Their preference for simple over compounded drugs involved the abandonment of a multitude of Galenic preparations, which were nearly all vegetable based, leaving them with Dioscorides, one of whose five books was devoted to minerals.[47]

But minerals seem always to have had greater significance as remedies among the Arabs. Constantine of Africa had taken the trouble to adapt minerals to Galenic pharmacology by assigning to them the necessary qualitative gradations.[48] Perhaps this was a consequence of the Arabs' concern with external diseases, such as

---

[44] Dierbach (1824: 239–57) gives reference in Hippocratic prescriptions to alum, salt, natron, chalk, the arsenic sulphides, sulphur, clay, lead, iron, and copper, most of them in several varieties.

[45] Celsus, 1935–38, Vol. I: 6–7 (*De medicina*, Proomium, 9).

[46] For example, as a cathartic in *On wounds* ($\pi \varepsilon \rho \iota \ \check{\varepsilon} \lambda \varkappa \omega \nu$) (Hippocrates, 1839–61, Vol. 6: 420–1). Dierbach, 1824: 256, gives other references. Aristotle knew the poisonous character of sandarach (*Historia animalium*, 604b).

[47] The Arabs were criticized by the prominent sixteenth-century pharmacist, A. M. Brasavola (1537: 45) for having curtailed the materia medica. On this matter see also L. Levin, in EI-2, art. Akrabadhin.

[48] Constantine of Africa, 1536: 381–2.

ophthalmia and skin diseases. Antimony, which is not at all prominent in Greek pharmacology, is said to have been recommended for ophthalmia by the Prophet himself, and turns up regularly in Arabic literature on eye diseases.[49] The Arabs pioneered in this field, as they did in dermatology, and in the latter field we find early mention of ointments containing sulphur and mercury.[50] By the time of Abulcasis the external use of these substances was obviously a major concern of the Moslem physician. But of the internal administration of minerals there is no more indication in the writings of the Arabs than there was in those of their predecessors. Evidence of this comes to light among the Latins of the late fifteenth century who were faced with a disease of a notoriety, if not of a virulence, which was unprecedented, syphilis.

This dread disease 'appeared' in Europe just before 1500, and seems soon to have attained epidemic proportions, although its infamy may have led to some exaggeration of its incidence. The inability of the medical profession to cope with it gave a field day to the 'empirics', and led many a Galenic physician as well into unprecedented experimentation. It was natural to utilize the mercury- and sulphur-containing salves to treat its external manifestations, but their internal use as well is soon indicated by the rise of a con- troversy over mercury as a remedy for syphilis.[51]

If the proponents of medical chemistry profited from the use of minerals against syphilis, they were probably not involved in the quarrel over the use of mercury, for the sect of medical chemists scarcely existed in the early sixteenth century. Brunschwygk, who is the only prominent physician of the time to mention John of Rupescissa, does not seem to have been involved in syphilis therapy, and Paracelsus was to take a very conservative view of the efficacy of mercury for this disease.[52]

[49] See Browne, 1921: 12. The importance of antimony in the treatment of eye diseases can be seen in the seven-part collection assembled by Pansier (1903–33).

[50] Friedman (1938) mentions both in connection with al-Tabari (fl. 970).

[51] Mercury appears as a remedy for syphilis in the first printed tract on that disease, the *Consilium* of Konrad Schellig (1495/6) (Sudhoff, 1925). It was used internally by the early sixteenth century.

[52] In *On the French disease* Paracelsus is generally critical of the use of mercury (cf. Paracelsus, 1922–33, Vol. 7: 169), and in *Sieben defensiones*, reacting against 'supposed and fictious physicians' who have accused him of giving poisons as medicines, he declares, 'you anoint patients with quicksilver . . . you fumigate with its cinnabar, you wash with its

The peculiar character of medical chemistry revolves around the third question which was posed at the beginning of this chapter, that of the preparation of drugs. Preparation among the Galenists signified the mixing of 'simples', that is of drugs supposedly possessing a single quality, in such a manner as to achieve a desired compound of qualities. The medical chemist reversed this, and saw preparation as the separation of the 'impure' from the 'pure'. It was not the intention of John of Rupescissa simply to prescribe internally what others were using externally. His objective was the separation of the medically efficacious portions from the inert or deleterious portions of drugs. The tendency of medieval Galenic medicine to agglomerate complex mixtures was an invitation to such an innovation, and Roger Bacon had long since recommended the adoption of 'alchemical' methods in the preparation of drugs. From the fourteenth century, distillation was the alchemical method par excellence, and was always the favourite of medical chemists. It seems very likely that the ultimate justification for John's proposal was the discovery of alcohol, an agreeably 'therapeutic' substance which he took as a prototype for chemical medicines in general.

Purification of medicines was only part of John's objective, however. With him the idea of the elixir of life replaced that of the elixir as a catalyst for the transmutation of metals. This idea, which seems long before to have dominated Chinese alchemy,[53] had remained an undercurrent in the West. Earlier Western alchemists had noted that their elixirs could serve for the 'preservation of life', but made this a kind of secondary function. But for John, the life-preserving function of those elixirs became of primary importance even though their constituents were virtually identical with the transmuting elixirs of his contemporaries.

When all this is said, however, it must be remarked that it was the idea of separating the impure from the pure, rather than that of the elixir of life, which was to be central to medical chemistry. The panacea was to remain a fixture in medicine until the present day,

---

sublimate and do not wish people to say it is poison; yet it is poison and you introduce such poison into man' (Paracelsus, 1941: 22). There is ample evidence that it was the way in which mercury was used, and not the fact of its use, to which Paracelsus objected. See also note 74 below.

[53] Cf. Lippmann, 1954, art. Alchemie in China.

but from the time of Paracelsus most of the elixirs were to have specific purposes. The longevity promised by elixir-makers seems not to have had as much appeal to the West as it did to the East.

Drugs for specific purposes, such as emetics, purgatives, and antidotes, had been prominent enough in Galenic therapy, albeit outside of the system, and they were to become more prominent in medical chemistry. That Paracelsus' writings are a somewhat inconclusive guide to the drugs he actually used is partly because his recipes are characterized by the same vagaries as those of the alchemists who inspired him, but mainly because of his extensive and erratic use of specifics. His supposed fundamental work, *Archidoxies*, gives scarcely any indication of the purposes for which its recipes are intended, and most of his medical writings refer to *Archidoxies* only cursorily if at all. The perusal of several Paracelsian medical works suggests that his most popular remedies were vitriol and 'tartar' (the wine cask concretion, potassium tartrate) followed by 'laudanum', 'mummia', gold, antimony and mercury, in that order.[54] *Archidoxies*, however, gives little indication that medicines of particular importance are to be derived from vitriol and tartar, has little to say of antimony, and fails to mention at all such important Paracelsian remedies as laudanum and mummia.

His use of such substances as mummia and laudanum suggests that Paracelsus had no prejudice against non-mineral remedies, although it remains uncertain whether in these instances he adopted old remedies or merely gave old names to (more-or-less) new remedies. Mummia was a venerable remedy derived from corpses well preserved by embalming or by accident, but it has been reported that Paracelsus applied the word to other things, real and imaginary.[55] Laudanum was a somewhat more respectable remedy. Some of Paracelsus' fame comes from his reputation as the inventor of a

[54] See Multhauf, 1954. I have there compared the remedies of *Archidoxies* with those of several of Paracelsus' important treatises on disease, namely, *On the French disease*, *On the Diseases arising in Tartar*, *On the diseases that deprive man of his reason*, and *On the miner's disease*.

[55] Ambroise Pare (1510–90) gives a brief history of mummia, in explaining why he does not use it (Pare, 1952: 143–6). The eighteenth-century lexicographer, Dr James, held some of the other things to which Paracelsus gave the name mummia to be the marrow of bones, 'balsam of the external elements', manna, and water from the breath of a man, collected in a phial (1743–5: art. mummia).

process for ameliorating the causticity of opium and converting it into an effective anodyne, under the name of laudanum.[56] Here again there is a doubt, not that Paracelsus used opium, but that it was involved in his 'laudanum'. It may have been something else, in fact a variety of things, some of them mineral drugs.[57]

These peculiarities of his mummia and laudanum emphasize the stress given by Paracelsus to chemical preparation. He writes as though the raw material used was almost a matter of indifference. He even discourses at length on tartar, mercury, and vitriol as *causes* of disease, pointing out that a substance can be either a remedy or a poison depending on the mode of its preparation.[58]

Above all other substances, however, Paracelsus – at least in his books on therapy – resorted to vitriol. In one form or another, most commonly as the distillate, sulphuric acid, he recommends it for such various ailments as epilepsy, syphilis, dropsy, gout, and the miner's diseases. The list could be extended indefinitely. At one point he summarizes the powers of vitriol by referring them to 'one fourth of all diseases',[59] but the reader of his books would be likely to rate them even higher. His spirit or oil of vitriol is almost always further prepared, and the picture of Paracelsus as a physician who administered sulphuric acid internally needs to be ameliorated by consideration of his unfailing zeal for the mitigation of its acrimony. In one instance he claims to have given it 'the sweetness of honey and a brown colour' by what appears to be reflux distillation. In another he elicits from sulphuric acid a 'sweet oil of sulphur', and this one is somewhat more credible, for it appears to have been ether (diethyl ether, our 'ether', not Aristotle's).[60] Here again what

[56] Cf. Sala, 1618: 33–6.

[57] Thomas Thomson, 1830–1, Vol. 2: 147 note. Sigerist, 1941.

[58] Paracelsus, 1922–33, Vol. 11: 138 (*Sieben defensiones*). This is also the passage where he criticizes the use of mercurial remedies, which suggests that his rejection of mercury is not categorical.

[59] Ibid., 1941: 188 (*On the diseases that deprive man of his reason*). The same statement appears in *On natural things* (Paracelsus, 1922–33, Vol. 2: 147).

[60] The sulphur of vitriol 'is so sweet that chickens eat it and then fall asleep, but wake up again after some time without any bad effect. You should know that this sulphur can cure any illness which is to be cured by anodynes, without any bad after effects. It extinguishes pain and soothes the heat and painful diseases'. (*On the diseases that deprive man of his reason* [1525?], in Paracelsus, 1941: 205.) Paracelsus refers to this sulphur of vitriol on several occasions, but the nearest he comes to a recipe is where he remarks that 'a great thing' may

appears at first glance to be an example of medico-chemical extremism looks on closer inspection more like a significant modification of the heroic remedies of that sect.

The therapeutic phase of medical chemistry reached a crescendo of controversy in the seventeenth century, in what became known as the 'antimony war'. As is indicated, its therapy was by that time particularly associated with the use of antimony, from which a large number of real and imaginary chemical preparations had been drawn. The chemists were charged by their adversaries with causing the deaths of multitudes of patients, and there are at least a few case histories supporting the charge. But there are as many supporting the chemists' counter-charges against the bleeding practices of the Galenists.

This situation is anything but clear-cut. On the one hand the rise of the antimony controversy and of 'Paracelsian' medicine seem to coincide;[61] on the other hand neither Paracelsus' own writings nor the early literature of the antimony controversy associates him with the therapeutic use of this material – empirics, pharmacists, and even Galen himself are blamed, but not Paracelsus.[62]

This was an age of frightful medical problems and heroic remedies.

---

be accomplished by imbibing wine in vitriol and distilling the mixture (*On natural things*, in Paracelsus, 1922–33, Vol. 2: 154). Angelo Sala mentions it, and confesses that he has been unable to produce it (1618: 52). The first clear recipe for the production of ether from sulphuric acid and alcohol is practically contemporaneous with Paracelsus, from a younger man he may have known, Valerius Cordus (1515–44) (see Leake, 1925).

[61] The outbreak of the 'antimony war' was signalled by an attack on the substance by the physicians of the last half of the sixteenth century. Letters by Paris doctors condemning it were published in 1566 (Thorndike, HMES, Vol. 5: 479). The Senate of Augsburg issued a decree against it and other dangerous mineral remedies in 1588 (Darmstaedter, 1930: 68).

[62] Paracelsus was of course lumped by his medical contemporaries with the empirics. In 1530 the city council at Nuremberg, at the urging of the medical faculty at Leipzig, had forbidden the publication of Paracelsus' writings, and it is probable that Philip Melanchthon's letter of 1531 against 'medical empirics' refers to Paracelsus among others. But it does not name him, nor does the Augsburg decree of 1588, which contrasts physicians with 'empirici' and 'chymici populari'. (Thorndike, HMES, Vol. 5: 380. Darmstaedter, 1930: 68.) The early seventeenth-century chemist, Jean Beguin, mentions in connection with antimony three who were certainly not 'Paracelsians', Jerome Cardan, Julien Alexander, and Pierandrea Matthiolus, and remarks that Galen, Dioscorides, and other ancients had administered metallic and mineral things 'entirely crude' (1618: 12. 1620: 5. 1669: 4). Paracelsus' connection with the antimony controversy was undoubtedly in part that, as Gerard Dorn remarked (1568: 1), 'a treasury of medicine was prepared from the metals by the vulgar, but no physician knew of it before Paracelsus'.

But it can be said of the seventeenth-century medical chemist, as it can of Paracelsus, that he constantly emphasized the *preparation* of drugs as the key to therapy.[63] Chemical preparation, rather than the use of mineral remedies, was the essential innovation of the medical chemist. That Paracelsus applied it so often to minerals was, in part, a legacy of his alchemical lineage. In part it was a sign of his participation in the shift to Arabic Dioscoridean remedies which followed the breakdown of Galenic therapy.

The medical chemists as chemists

Down to the time of Paracelsus medical chemistry was pursued largely on the basis of such chemical data as had been inherited from the alchemists. The innovation of John of Rupescissa consisted mainly in the transfer of two anciently known materials, antimony sulphide and urine, from the 'dormant' to the 'active' shelf of the laboratory.

Antimony (sulphide) had been listed among drugs at least as early as Dioscorides, and had been given some prominence by the time of Abulcasis. In the hands of the medical chemists it was to be manipulated into a great variety of forms. By the end of the seventeenth century the repertoire of the chemist contained more compounds of antimony than of any other of our modern elements, and this process seems to have begun with the 'blood red drops' which John obtained by distilling it with vinegar.

Urine also appears in recipe books from the time of Dioscorides (and was certainly not then a new drug), and was consistently involved in the recipes of practical chemistry as well as of medicine. But its function in early recipes is almost never evident. It belonged to the mysterious realm of organic substances, and had virtually no chemical history. The Lullian *Testamentum*, and undoubtedly other fourteenth-century alchemical tracts, exhibits a dim awareness of the 'spirit' obtained through the distillation of urine.[64] This spirit

---

[63] The medical attack on antimony elicited in 1566 a reply from the Paris physician, Jacques Grevin, who was a leading authority on poisons. Neither Grevin nor the author whose work inspired him to write (Loys de Launay) takes a black-and-white attitude on antimony; on the contrary, both acknowledge the merits of chemical preparations of the substance (Thorndike, HMES, Vol. 5: 478–9).

[64] 'Accipe in nomine Domini urinam puerorum, qui ab octavo anno in duodecimum ultra non evadant quam urinam ex ipsis pueris mane ex lecto surgentibus collige, cuius magnam

was to become known as 'volatile alkali' and then as ammonia, and was to be used by the medical chemists to further extend their repertoire through the precipitation of metals from acid solution.

But medical chemistry rode in on a wave of enthusiasm for distillation, and John's interest in antimony and urine was only in the derivation of quintessences from them by distillation. The persistence of this prejudice in Paracelsus is evident, and in fact the only new synthetic substance indisputably assigned to him is a distillate (actually a sublimate) of antimony. This is antimony trichloride, later known as 'butter of antimony', but which he took to be a derivative of mercury and called 'mercury of life'.[65] There was an increasing awareness between Rupescissa and Paracelsus of those most important distillates, the mineral acids. Metallurgists knew two acids very well, one which dissolves gold (aqua regia, a mixture of nitric and hydrochloric acids) and another which dissolves silver (nitric acid), but they had no interest in other, metallurgically insignificant, acids. Paracelsus knew metallurgy, but his temperament knew no such limitations. He took guidance from the alchemists, who, as the Italian metallurgist, Vannoccio Biringuccio, had remarked in 1540, 'make an infinite variety of acids'.[66]

From the vantage point of modern chemistry we can say that Paracelsus was inhibited from discovering new substances by his distain for residues. The first generation of 'Paracelsians', that is, followers who appeared in the generation after his death, are similarly handicapped and seem moreover especially attracted to Paracelsus' more extravagant theoretical ideas. In due course, however, some reputable physicians became Paracelsians, often, it seems, because they had themselves experienced successful 'Paracelsian' cures.[67] From

---

quantitatem te habere oportet, quae vase vitreo putrefacienda est quam optime . . . [distil] . . . ac vase vitreo servabis quam optime occlusum, quod sal erit volatile. . . . Cave tibi a fumis, cum vas aperueris; sunt enim potentissimi' (BCC, Vol. 1: 829b–830a [*Testamentum*]). Lull calls it 'an animal spirit or mercury'. Kopp (1843–7, Vol. 3: 243) also found this spirit in John of Rupescissa's *Liber lucis*, where it is, however, even less clearly described than in the *Testamentum* (cf. BCC, Vol. 2: 85b–86b [*Liber lucis*]).

[65] Paracelsus, 1922–33, Vol. 3: 147–50 (*Archidoxies*).

[66] Biringuccio, 1942: 188.

[67] Adam of Bodenstein (1528–77), a professor at Basel who edited Paracelsus' *On the diseases that deprive man of his reason*, tells us that he was influenced to become a Paracelsian by a cure of tertian fever by 'spiritus vitrioli, liquor serapini, etc.' (Paracelsus, 1941: 137). The

about 1575 the number of professional physicians who favoured Paracelsian remedies was substantial enough to constitute a visible challenge to the practices of the ruling circles of medicine.

The defenders of Paracelsian medicine included a number of prominent physicians. Joseph Duchesne (1544–1609), also known as Quercetanus, was physician to King Henry IV of France. Theodore Turquet de Mayerne (1573–1655) was prominent enough to inspire the Paris medical faculty to promulgate a special decree of condemnation against him (1607) after which he found a post at the English court. Peter Severinus (1542–1602) was physician to the King of Denmark. Johann Hartmann (1568–1631) was physician to the Landgrave of Hesse-Cassel. From 1609 he held at Marburg what appears to have been the first Chair of Chemistry in any university. In addition to writing on medical chemistry he commented on the writing of his younger contemporary, Oswald Croll (1580–1609). Croll was physician to the Prince of Anhalt-Bernberg. Despite his short life his medico-chemical pharmacopoeia is perhaps the most comprehensible of a number produced by this group, a circumstance which may account for the fact that he is credited with a larger number of 'discoveries' than any other Paracelsian; although something must be credited to its augmentation, in later editions, by Hartmann.[68]

As is characteristic of the truly 'Paracelsian' pharmacopoeias, Croll's *Basilica chymica* begins with a long 'admonitory introduction' expounding Paracelsian medical theory, but virtually unconnected with what follows.[69] Then comes a collection of recipes, organized not after any theory whatever, but simply as cathartics, diuretics, diaphoretics, etc. which the Galenists had customarily appended, as 'entities', to their systematic lists of drugs. Croll omitted the systema-

---

King of Denmark's physician, Peter Severinus (1542–1602) began to read Paracelsus after hearing his remedies praised in Germany (Severinus, 1571: dedication). The celebrated Flemish physician and natural philosopher, J. B. van Helmont, turned from Galen after being cured of an itch by a sulphur ointment (Helmont, 1648–1: 320. 1662: 316 [*Scabies & ulcera scholarum*]).

[68] In the analysis of drug invention by Schröder (1957) Croll appears with Paracelsus and Beguin as the most important innovator. I avoid here the difficult question of the first mention of specific substances. Whatever his inventions, Croll, although he seems to have died before age 30, more than any other made the full range of new substances known (cf. Partington, 1961: 174–7).   [69] What follows is based on an analysis of Croll, 1609.

tic list, but does follow the section devoted to entities with another subdivided according to the parts of the body, where many of the same recipes are repeated.

Excluding a brief concluding section on 'confortiva' of vegetable origin, the recipes for entities number twenty-three. The number must, however, be taken as approximate, since some recipes contain as many as three separate prescriptions, and straightforward descriptions of chemical preparations are mixed with multiple-component mixtures and combinations of the two. The nature of Croll's chemical drugs, however, is not in doubt. Vitriol, saltpetre, common salt, and 'tartar' are the only salts mentioned, and each appears several times. The mineral acids appear altogether about twice as many times as do the salts from which they are derived, and in contexts which certify that Croll knew and distinguished all four, sulphuric, nitric, hydrochloric, and aqua regia.[70] These acids, plus the scarcely less active corrosive sublimate and butter of antimony (antimony trichloride), appear in about half of the recipes. Mercury and its compounds (both chlorides, the sulphate and red oxide) appear in a quarter of them. As far as his raw materials are concerned Croll was a true disciple of John of Rupescissa (whom he does not mention), but he differed from both John and Paracelsus in being free of their exclusive preoccupation with distillation and sublimation. The medical chemist of Croll's time was abandoning the quintessence, in his practice, if not in his theory. Croll was in tune with the future, and Hartmann's augmented edition, published thirty-four years later, although the number of recipes for 'entia' has more than doubled, differs little in the materials and types of process used.[71] The most important difference is a substantial increase in the number of recipes involving antimony, an indication, perhaps, of the advances made by the 'defenders' in the antimony war, in which the chemists were in fact on the threshold of victory by 1643.

The chemical history of mercury began about 500 B.C., with the discovery that the silvery metallic liquid (long called quicksilver) is

[70] Croll, 1609: 124, 149, 153, 186, 213. Although he differentiates the acids in some cases, in the first reference he speaks of the preparation of a single remedy (terpetum minerale) 'per spiritum nitri aliquoties cohobando, nonulli per spiritum salis communis, aquas fortes, oleum vitrioli. . . .' He makes hydrochloric and nitric acids by distillation of the salts with clay, and knows sulphuric acid both from vitriol and from sulphur (per campanum).

[71] I have analysed Croll, 1643, in some detail elsewhere (Multhauf, 1954–2).

produced by heating the pigment, cinnabar. The reverse process, in which cinnabar is produced by heating mercury with sulphur, must have been encountered by the alchemists who belaboured these materials so industriously, but the first clear description of it occurs only about A.D. 800. By the fifteenth century – and probably earlier – this 'vermillion' pigment was known to be identical to cinnabar,[72] but by this time the chemist's repertoire had acquired two additional alchemically fascinating red forms of mercury, which the modern chemist would reduce to one, mercuric oxide.

This red oxide of mercury, which is not found in nature, was to play a central role in the evolution of chemistry. It is chemically peculiar in that it forms when mercury is gently heated in air over a long period, and decomposes when more intensely heated. It is also formed by the thermal decomposition of the nitrates of mercury. Both processes are found in the writings of the Latin Geber,[73] and the discovery of these methods of 'reddening' mercury undoubtedly gave a fillip to late medieval alchemy. Subsequent to that we find mercuric oxide a prominent Paracelsian remedy for syphilis,[74] and finally, in the eighteenth century, it was mercuric oxide which was the principal source of the mysterious gas which Joseph Priestley was to call 'dephlogisticated air', and Lavoisier, 'oxygen'.

The differentiation of mercury compounds into mercurous and mercuric varieties was a development of modern chemistry. There

[72] According to the late fifteenth-century painter's recipe book of Cennini, 'cinabro' is made 'by an alchemical process performed in an alembic' (1899: 33-4. 1933: 24).

[73] The first is the presumed consequence of a process in which mercury is 'coagulated with long and constant retention in fire, in a glass vessel with a very long neck and round belly' (Geber, 1922: 156. 1928: 114 [Summa]). The second would be the 'most red' product of the sublimation of vitriol, saltpetre, and mercury, although it is necessary to suppose that the white nitrate, which does not sublime, was further decomposed by further heating to yield the red oxide, and that the 'most red' product was the residue rather than the sublimate (Geber, 1922: 176. 1928: 211 [De inventione]). One of the Lullian tracts (BCC, Vol. 1: 826) gives the latter process more clearly.

[74] Mercury preparations are not prominent in Paracelsus' writings, but a letter purportedly written by J. H. Operinus (1507-68), his one-time assistant, states that Paracelsus used 'praecipitati pulvere . . . as a purgative in all kinds of disease' (quoted in Sennert, 1676: 188). This was probably mercuric oxide, which Croll calls one of Paracelsus' 'great inventions and secrets' (1609: 129). It is prescribed for syphilis in De natura rerum, a Paracelsian work of questionable authenticity (Paracelsus, 1922-33, Vol. 11: 338 [this source also states that the remedy 'brightens up despondent alchemists']), and in a Paracelsian recipe book of 1656 (Paracelsus ?, 1656: 264). The encyclopaedist, R. James (1743-5, Vol. 1: lxxxiii) also assigns this 'quack' remedy for venereal disease to Paracelsus.

is a black (mercurous) as well as the red (mercuric) oxide, but the former is only prepared under controlled conditions, and was only identified in the eighteenth century. There was, however, an awareness, if not an understanding, of the two chlorides, of which corrosive sublimate (mercuric chloride) was an epochal discovery of the alchemists of Arabic Spain and calomel (mercurous chloride) a discovery of medical chemists of the early seventeenth century, perhaps of Beguin.[75] Although both are white, there is little difficulty in the preparation of either, and calomel corresponded to an urgent desideratum of medical chemistry, a relatively non-corrosive mercurial remedy. It was this which made possible its identification. That it was observed and differentiated at this time is surely due to a deliberate search by medical chemists for forms of mercury which were less violently active than corrosive sublimate. One is tempted to call calomel the first product of deliberate chemical research, and we are certainly justified in regarding its production as a milestone in the accomplishment of chemical synthesis requiring some control of physical and chemical conditions.

The history of the chemistry of mercury again raises the question of the sense in which we are to suppose that substances were 'known'. By heating mercury in air Geber tells us that he 'coagulates' it, and in the aforementioned thermal decomposition of the nitrate he 'prepares it most red'. The author of the De aluminibus explains similarly the reaction which led him to corrosive sublimate. We can be reasonably confident that *we* know what was made in these processes, but can we say that the substances were known to their 'discoverers'? Not until they turn up as commonplace medico-chemical remedies would it seem that we are assured that they were known. We can also be sure that Geber prepared the nitrate in one of his processes, since it is an intermediate in the process for mercuric oxide, but it is anything but clear that he knew it. The alchemists were interested in reddening and whitening mercury, and it is perhaps unreasonable to blame them for being satisfied with that accomplishment. It was the objective rather than the technique which was at fault.

The limitations of the alchemists as discoverers of new substances

[75] A recipe for calomel appears in Beguin, 1618: 355. 1669: 92. See also Urdang, 1948, and Schröder, 1957: 81–2.

are best shown by their failure to observe, in any meaningful way, the sulphates and nitrates. There was reason enough for confusion, as sulphuric and nitric acids were confused, and the compounds in question are both white and soluble, but it is still remarkable that they remained virtually unnoticed by several generations of alchemists who have left in their writings an endless series of recipes involving the dissolution of substances in sulphuric and nitric acids.

The medical chemist was almost in a worse case, for not only did he continue the preoccupation with reddening and whitening mercury, notwithstanding the fact that gold-making was no longer involved, but he devised the doctrine of quintessences which was antithetical to the cultivation of residues. He had, however, established a toleration of innovation, and with the decline of the quintessence among the late sixteenth century Paracelsians the nitrates and sulphates did at last emerge in the consciousness of the chemist. Beguin and Croll identified the sulphate of mercury,[76] and the mysterious 'Basil Valentine' knew the nitrate as well.[77]

The name 'antimony' dates from the end of the Latin Middle Ages.[78] Previously the sulphide ore was known as stibium (from οτίμμι) or, to the Arabs, as kohl. Antimony sulphide was a more ancient pigment than was the ore of mercury, and the archaeological discovery of lead antimoniate pigment (Naples yellow) indicates that it had an early chemical history. It is very probable that metallic antimony was produced in antiquity but confused with lead, yet the metal remained for all practical purposes unknown until the seventeenth century A.D. Elemental antimony is, in fact, ambiguous in its metallic character, and when it was defined as a unique substance in the seventeenth century it was given the not entirely inappropriate designator, 'semi-metal'.

Not only was antimony confused in its physical properties with

[76] Croll, 1609: 124. Beguin, 1618: 357. 1669: 93.

[77] Basil Valentine called it 'vitriol of mercury', having taken nitric acid for 'spirit of vitriol' (1769: 974). Croll does not give a recipe for the dissolution of mercury in nitric acid, although he makes passing reference to the possibility. In Beguin's recipes the process is merely an intermediate stage on the way to the red precipitate of mercury, or to a white precipitate obtained by adding common salt. The latter was calomel.

[78] The name was perhaps introduced by Constantine of Africa (Lippmann, 1919: 639. Dufrenoy, 1950).

lead, but its early chemical history is inextricably confounded with that of arsenic and bismuth, and if metallic antimony was taken in antiquity for a kind of lead, its compounds were in all probability taken for forms of arsenic. Arsenic and antimony are now known to belong to a chemically similar group of elements of which the third member is bismuth. Each forms no less than three series of oxides and salts, and hence involves a chemistry of a complexity quite beyond the powers of the chemist prior to the nineteenth century. That they became known at all may be attributed to the use of the ores of arsenic and antimony as pigments, and to the subsequent discovery of the Greek alchemists that the arsenic ores are both chemically active and susceptible to sublimation.

Each of these three pigments, orpiment, realgar and antimony (sulphide) oxidizes when 'roasted' to give off an oxide as a white sublimate, and these oxides were known by the early Christian era. It was arsenic trioxide, the product of roasting either orpiment or realgar, to which the name 'arsenic' was originally applied. I have suggested that this material was the key to much of the alchemical rationalization of Agathodaimon and Zosimos. Antimony trioxide seems to have been known to Dioscorides, but did not become sufficiently important to deserve a name of its own until the seventeenth century, at which time it became known as 'flowers of antimony'.[79]

Through its trioxide arsenic had a continuous chemical history from the time of the Greek alchemists, but arsenic compounds were often regarded as peculiar manifestations of sulphur and this confusion was never resolved in antiquity or the Middle Ages. The apparent indifference of the early alchemists to antimony may be due to its confusion with arsenic. The elements arsenic, antimony and bismuth are characterized by similar chemical properties, with decreasing activity from arsenic to bismuth. The 'metallic' properties, on the other hand, are least in arsenic – in fact modern chemistry considers it a non-metal – and greatest in bismuth. Bismuth is a relatively rare element, but seems to exist in nature as a native metal more commonly than in the form of an ore.[80] Under the circumstances of a confusion of the oxides of the arsenic-antimony-bismuth group

[79] Dioscorides, 1934: 632-3 (Bk 5; 99). Basil Valentine 1893: 93-4. Croll, 1609: 132.
[80] Mellor, 1922-37, Vol. 9: 589.

with sulphur, and of their elemental metallic forms with lead, the group remained an enigma until the nineteenth century.

Nothing was of greater moment for the future of medical chemistry than the selection of antimony as a basic medicinal substance. It is clear that John of Rupescissa recommended some of the alchemist's favourite materials as sources of medically efficacious quintessences, but antimony (sulphide) had not been a favoured material among alchemists. John, himself, does not mention it in his *Liber lucis*. We can only advance certain speculations for its introduction. His home was near the area, Auvergne, which was to be the principal source of antimony in western Europe. Perhaps its power of separating gold and silver was known there, although this first comes to our attention in the fifteenth-century German assayer's manual, *Probierbüchlein*. Perhaps the prominence of the material in contemporary works on materia medica led John to experiment with it. In any case, his book on the quintessence seems to mark the beginning of its spectacular career in chemistry and medicine.

The physiological activity of antimony is midway between the violence of arsenic and the mildness of bismuth, which was almost too gentle to be noticed in those heroic times. Antimonial remedies were seldom specifics. While they were sometimes touted as 'universal' medicines, they were usually used, according to the most respectable medical conventions, for the evacuation of noxious humours – that is, as purgatives. In this they were probably more effective than any remedy previously known. Much of the difficulty encountered by the medical chemists over antimony may have been due to the fact that, as its compounds had earlier been obscured by those of arsenic, so the arsenic compounds now became confused with those of antimony.[81] Some of the most gruesome legends of the enemies of medical chemistry may stem from the commission of this error by the swarm of empirical healers who in the sixteenth century adopted minerals as staples of folk medicine.

A comparison of the elucidation of antimony by the sixteenth- and seventeenth-century medical chemists with the ancient Greek alchemist's elucidation of arsenic indicates that a significant, if unspectacular, advance had been made in the chemist's command over his materials. The Greek alchemist had roasted the arsenic ores

[81] Cf. Boerhaave 1741, Vol I: 132; Erdmann, 1902: 375.

and recognized the white sublimate (arsenic trioxide) as a discrete substance (albeit a variety of sulphur). Further manipulation had brought about the reduction of the oxide into a black substance, again a sublimate, which we recognize as the element. The alchemist, however, at this point betrayed his exclusive interest in colour change, and although he went on to produce other colour changes with arsenic – and hence prepared other compounds – he never isolated or identified any of them. When the gold-making potentialities of these manipulations had been explored and found wanting he lost interest in the whole matter.

Perhaps the medical chemist was more fortunate in his objective, which was at least less readily shown to be unattainable. In any case he did not lose his interest in antimonial compounds prepared along the way. If John's experiment in preparing 'blood red drops' by distilling antimony sulphide with vinegar remained chemically inexplicable, the white sublimate (antimony trioxide) which John's successors obtained by the distillation of antimony sulphide alone was to become a staple of medical chemistry. Their effort towards its 'improvement' had the effect of producing the maximum possible number of varieties. They succeeded in defining not only a large number of compounds of antimony, but an even larger number of mixtures of various sorts. The ore was roasted, for example, but not to the point of sublimation, in which case it melted into a mixed sulphide-oxide mass which was long prescribed as a medicament under the name 'glass of antimony'. From this, 'corrected glass of antimony' was derived by treatment with sulphuric acid. If the ore was more thoroughly roasted the product was antimony's 'golden sulphur', 'liver' or some such, and if this was again cooked with 'tartar' yet another medicine revealed itself, 'tartar emetic' (potassium antimonyl tartrate). This is still in use, and has proven the most durable of the antimonial drugs.

There are several amorphous forms of the sulphide such as 'kermes minerale',[82] and a higher sulphide (antimony pentasulphide) which has been known as 'golden sulphuret of antimony', or 'antimonial

---

[82] Amorphous antimony trisulphide may exist in a variety of colours, from dark lead-grey to bright red. 'Kermes minerale', named from its resemblance to an animal insect drug, kermes, is a bright red variety obtained by subliming antimony sulphide ore with ammonium chloride or by dissolving and reprecipitating the ore from alkaline solution. John of Rupe-

panacaea'. Other series were begun by reacting the ore with corrosive sublimate or saltpetre. The first case yielded 'butter of antimony', discovered by Paracelsus, and an oxychloride called 'powder of Algaroth', obtained by the addition of water to butter of antimony. The second case, in which the ore is ignited with saltpetre, yielded potassium antimoniate, called 'diaphoretic antimony', and this in turn became the source of antimonic acid (or 'materia perlata') when acted upon by a mineral acid.[83]

This does not exhaust the list of seventeenth-century preparations of antimony which have been identified by the investigators of modern times, not to mention those which have eluded identification. The pre-existing confusion of chemical nomenclature was compounded as the chemistry of antimony evolved, but at least the activities of the chemist in his laboratory could no longer be called unproductive.

Paracelsian biology

Like 'Ptolemaic' cosmology, the 'Galenic' medicine of the sixteenth century was an impressive but delicate structure which suffered a general collapse when one of its apparently minor props was removed. Copernicus, whose *De revolutionibus orbium coelestium* was published in 1543, had no criticism to make of most aspects of the system to which his innovation referred. Similarly, Andreas Vesalius, whose *De humani corporis fabrica* was published in the same year, gave incontestable demonstration of error in Galenic anatomy without touching on other aspects of Galenic biology and medicine.[84]

In both astronomy and medicine the correction was nevertheless ultimately to prove fatal, although this was a century in becoming evident. The morbid condition of the Ptolemaic and Galenic systems

scissa's 'blood red drops' were probably merely this modification of antimony trisulphide. As late as 1720 the French government reportedly bought a recipe for such a preparation (cf. Mellor, 1922–37, Vol. 9: 512–18).

[83] On the antimony preparations of the medical chemists see Schröder, 1957, and for a nearly contemporary analysis of the recipes of a great many authorities see Salmon, 1706: 324–48.

[84] Copernicus and Vesalius did not reject Ptolemy and Galen in the way that the anti-Peripatetics rejected Aristotle. They merely sought to improve on Ptolemy and Galen. See Kuhn, 1957: 180–4, Durling, 1961: 245, Pagel and Rattansi, 1964.

was not only long obscured by the frenetic attempts of 'conservatives' to maintain the ancient doctrines, but there was a conspicuous lack of alternatives. In medicine, however, there was an alternative, had the physician been inclined to look for it. It was part of the legacy of Paracelsus, who had died two years before the publication of Vesalius' work.

Paracelsus was already celebrated for his cures, for his vitriolic criticism of conventional medicine, and, if we may judge from his early publication, as an astrologer. But to the world at large he was only 'a figure in the news', for the major portion of his writings remained unpublished at his death. In the latter half of the century one after another publication was put into print by his disciples until in 1589 the first of several 'Opera omnia'[85] revealed that Paracelsus had indeed essayed a whole system of medicine to set against the Galenists. This system, which was far more exotic than Paracelsus' chemical medicines, became an unfailing appendage to almost every book on chemical medicine,[86] but an appendage virtually unconnected with the pharmacy expounded in the body of the book. It was a sort of badge of the Paracelsian.

Paracelsus' criticism of conventional medicine began in therapy, which was the *raison d'être* of medical chemistry and where the syphilis epidemic had laid bare the weakness of the Galenists. Although he was actually more cautious than many of the Galenists in the use of specific remedies for syphilis, he emphatically believed that specific diseases require specific remedies, and this was an idea which struck at the foundations of Galenic medicine. The whole corpus of Galen was just becoming known in Europe in the time of Paracelsus, and his animus was first directed against the influential Avicenna. But the Arabs, themselves, were Galenists, and Paracelsus' criticism shifted smoothly enough to Galen himself.[87]

---

[85] Paracelsus, 1589–90. In general I have referred to Sudhoff's collection of the works of Paracelsus (Paracelsus, 1922–33), but occasionally to English translations (Paracelsus, 1893. 1941). The dates which are given for Paracelsus' various works are taken from Sudhoff, 1926.

[86] See, for example, Dorn, 1568, Croll, 1609, Du Chesne, 1614, Planis-Campy, 1629. Each of these recipe books contains an appended discourse on Paracelsian theory.

[87] On Galen in Renaissance Europe see Heinrichs, 1914 and Sarton, 1955. Paracelsus was to declare that his beard was more learned and his shoelace more experienced than Galen (1922–33, Vol 8: 65 [*Paragranum*]) but his consignment of Avicenna's *Cannon* to the fire (Sudhoff, 1936: 50) probably came first.

Paracelsus resembles Galen, himself, in his zest for controversy, and in his willingness to construct a framework encompassing the whole of medicine and biology as a support for his pathology. His framework, however, rather reminds one of the mines with which he was so familiar. Without a plan it is almost impenetrable, and Paracelsus left no plan. Explored from within it seems to be constructed erratically, one section connecting unexpectedly with another, or, more often, terminating obscurely in some cul-de-sac. Its main lines can be most plausibly sketched by comparing it to the system of Galen.

Whereas Peripatetic natural philosophy provided the basis for the Galenic system, 'alchemy', meaning essentially that alchemy which was as interested in medicine as in gold-making, was the basis of Paracelsus' system. The four humours are replaced by 'mercury, sulphur, and salt'. He seems to have inspired the addition of 'salt' to the traditional parents of the metals with a view to providing a substratum for the somewhat contradictory qualities of inert solidity and acidity.[88] Paracelsus sometimes speaks of a kind of 'humoural pathology' of mercury, sulphur, and salt,[89] but this is a passing notion. He usually picked a cause of disease to suit the occasion. His objective, after all, was to show that disease was *not* the consequence of humoural imbalance. In his contradiction of the Galenic system he went so far as to argue that disease, not health, is the normal human condition.[90] If Galen's framework of physiology was flexible, that of Paracelsus might be called elastic. It was not allowed to interfere with his conception of the specificity of disease. He saw the 'incurable' diseases as sacrifices made to preserve the Galenic system, and made no such concessions to his own.

The biological system behind Paracelsus' medicine was minimal,[91] and the adherance to it of Paracelsian physicians seems almost an act of piety. There is more than a little evidence that they neither understood it nor made use of it. And yet it did serve an important

---

[88] Paracelsus, 1922–33, Vol. 6: 121; Vol. 11: 154. Cf. Pagel, 1958: 154, Hooykaas, 1948–49.

[89] Ibid., Vol. 9: 101–13 (*Opus paramirum*, Bk 2, Chs. 4–6).

[90] Ibid., Vol. 10: 288–90 (*Grosse Wundarzney*, Bk 2, Tract. 2, Ch. 2).

[91] Some of it may of course be lost. According to Sudhoff (1926), only half of Paracelsus's medical writings have been preserved, and only three books from a planned comprehensive work on internal pathology and therapeutics. The latter three are Bk 6, on tartaric diseases, Bk 7, on 'diseases that deprive man of his reason', and Bk 9, on 'contractures'.

function in justifying a chemical approach to medicine. Whereas the supposed corrosiveness and acridity of the biles, and their formation in a 'fermentation' process, remained anomalies within the Galenic system, they provided the key to the Paracelsian system. In the seventeenth century the Galenists were still labouring to convince themselves that digestion could be caused by heat, that the conspicuous presence of acrid 'humours' in disease could be explained in terms of a balance of hot, cold, wet and dry, and that the other qualities of those humours, such as acidity, were incidental.[92] The Paracelsians extricated themselves from this dilemma by denying that heat is the cause of digestion, by regarding digestion as the work of an 'internal chemist', the *archaeus*, and by identifying (vaguely) the body's superfluities with acid and alkaline substances.[93]

The modern student of Paracelsus' physiology and pathology may derive some comfort from the knowledge that his puzzlement is shared by a detached and relatively unbiased contemporary. Daniel Sennert (1572–1637) was a contemporary of 'the Paracelsians' who brought the chemical doctrines to the attention of the world at large. He agreed that a knowledge of chemistry is essential to the physician, but finds the chemical doctrines of physiology and pathology shading from incomprehensible to reprehensible. He seems to know them chiefly from Severinus and Duchesne. From consulting the works of the latter, he concludes that salt is supposed to be the 'radical principle' of the liver, that the celebrated heat of the heart is produced by the calorific effect of a liquor of sulphur, and that the ætherial character of mercury makes it the spiritual principle of the brain. Severinus, on the other hand, seems content to dismiss the corporeal man as a product of the four elements, and stresses the importance of the fifth essence 'ex firmamento' in his constitution. Sennert finds this intolerable, and expostulates that the trouble with Paracelsus and Severinus is that they prefer faith in obviously absurd and paradoxical dogmas to reason.[94] Sennert's

[92] See below, p. 290ff.

[93] As Croll saw it, digestion involves the separation of the food into mercury, sulphur, and salt, 'as is evident in the three principal waste substances. Superfluous salt is separated through the urine, sulphur is separated out and discharged through the intestine, mercury or liquor occupies the place of nutriment.' Tartar, 'coagulated by the spirit of salt', is also a waste product. (Croll, 1609: 73).

[94] Sennert, 1629: 245, 1676: 238–9 (Ch. 15).

inability to avoid such outbursts of indignation is characteristic of his discussion, a weakness which many modern students of Paracelsus will find it possible to excuse.

Concerning the humours, Sennert concludes that the 'tria prima' (mercury, sulphur and salt) have replaced them, too, and cites Severinus' claim that anatomy has revealed 'many species' of mercury, sulphur and salt. Paracelsus' rejection of the humours, however, is said to have come from his inability to find them in the macrocosm! Sennert is particularly incensed at the chemist's determination to downgrade the importance of blood, by allocating its functions and qualities to such Paracelsian entities as 'balsam'. He finds the Galenic explanation more plausible.[95] Sennert fails altogether to find any reasonable connection between all this and disease. He finds various chemical doctrines on this subject, involving the trià prima, the five Paracelsian 'entia' (*Dei, Astrale, Naturalia, Spirituale, Veneni*)[96] and various specific substances such as tartar. He decides that Paracelsus has confused the symptoms and causes of disease.[97]

[95] Sennert, 1629: 247–8, 1676: 239.

[96] Ibid., 1629: 268–74, 1676: 244–5 (Ch. 16). The Paracelsian 'entia' are discussed in *Volumen medicinae paramirum*, an early work of about 1520, which has been translated into English from Paracelsus, 1589 by Leidecker (Paracelsus, 1949). It is interesting to compare this five-fold division with the 'five eternal substances' of al-Rāzī (God, soul, matter, space, and time), but it is probably not significant. *Paramirum* is a treatise on five-fold divisions, and there are others, on five kinds of poisons, five kinds of sulphur, etc.

[97] Sennert, 1629: 252, 1676: 240 (Ch. 18).

Chapter Eleven

Chemistry and natural philosophy

IN 1500 the Italian Renaissance had left its infancy far behind. Petrarch and Boccaccio had been dead for a century and Dante and Giotto for a century and a half. The 'great powers' of the peninsula, Florence, Milan, and Naples, fell almost together between 1494 and 1504 under invasions from France and Spain. But neither life nor learning ceased. The twenty-one-year-old Alexander Achillini of Bologna returned in 1484 to his native city after a sound Scholastic education in Paris. He spent the rest of his life, with the exception of a stay of about two years in Padua, teaching philosophy and medicine. He wrote on most of the old topics, the elements (which he held not to be 'totally' corrupted in a compound), natural minima, substantial forms, proportional velocities in motion, and anatomy.[1] He even sponsored the printing of Avicenna's book *De congelatione et conglutinatione lapidum* (attributing it to Aristotle). It does not appear that his career suffered any greater inconvenience than an academic quarrel with Pietro Pomponazzi (1462–1524) at Padua, which may have induced him to leave that place.

A quarrel between a philosopher who taught medicine (Achillini) and a physician who taught philosophy (Pomponazzi) would seem natural enough, but the quarrel is supposed to have been quasi-

---

[1] On Achillini see Munster, 1933, and HMES, Vol. 5: 37–49. The *De congelatione*, in a version called *De mineralibus*, is in Achillini, 1528: xlviiir– to l–r. His *De elementis* contains the argument about forms (Achillini, 1568: 154–5).

theological – Pomponazzi's defence of the 'true' teaching of Aristotle on the soul against Achillini's alleged Averroism. Achillini left Padua in 1508, but he and Pomponazzi were again to be colleagues, for the school was closed by the war between France and Venice in 1509 and Pomponazzi followed Achillini to Bologna two years later. Achillini was in the last year of his life, but Pomponazzi, although a year older, still had another fourteen years on the faculty at Bologna, during which his writings ranged as widely as had those of Achillini, covering, among other things, intension and remission, nutrition and augmentation, incantations, and meteorology. Pomponazzi found others with whom to quarrel, including the deceased Swineshead and Marliani, and a younger colleague, Agostino Nifo (1473–1546).[2]

Pomponazzi's controversies with Achillini and Nifo illustrate the fluidity of Scholasticism at the end of the Middle Ages. Pomponazzi had defended Aristotle against the Averroism of Achillini.[3] Nifo, who in his youth had incurred the Averroist stigma, recovered his orthodoxy by defending Thomas Aquinas against Pomponazzi's 'Alexandrism' (from Alexander of Aphrodisias) on the immortality of the soul. Nifo and Pomponazzi had been colleagues at Padua in the 1480s, but wars, plagues, and other misadventures interrupted Nifo's life (but not his writing!) for the next decade, after which he turned up at the University of Salerno. He spent most of the rest of his life teaching there and at Naples, except for a brief term at Pisa. Despite the harassments of life in Italy in the first half of the sixteenth century, Nifo was an even more prolific writer than had been Achillini and Pomponazzi. In addition to numerous commentaries on Aristotle and Averroës, he left such other works as his defence of the immortality of the soul against Pomponazzi, a book on demons, and a commentary on Ptolemy's astrology (for medical students).[4]

Achillini, Pomponazzi and Nifo had at least one foot in the Middle Ages, but among their students we find some who were

[2] On Pomponazzi's philosophy see Douglas, 1910. On Pomponazzi and science see Thorndike, HMES, Vol. 5: 94–110. Kristeller, 1961: 165 n. 73. Cassirer, 1964: 81–3, 103–9. Wilson, 1953, discusses Pomponazzi's criticism of Swineshead.

[3] On the relativity of the designators 'Aristotelian', 'Averroist', and 'Alexandrism' in the Renaissance see Kristeller, 1964: 75–6.

[4] On Nifo see HMES, Vol. 5: 69–93. Melson, 1960: 64–72.

men of the new age, such as Girolamo Fracastoro (1478–1553) and Julius Caesar Scaliger (1484–1558). Fracastoro, a one-time student of Pomponazzi (and a classmate of Copernicus), is known principally for his poem on venereal disease (to which he gave the name 'syphilis'), although another book suggesting the 'germ' theory of disease was more important. He belonged to the landed gentry, and rode out the political storms of sixteenth-century Italy as a physician in Verona. He was, however, an intellectual virtuoso, and wrote on physics and astronomy as well as on medicine, and even spent a brief period as professor of logic at Padua.[5] Scaliger, who studied under both Pomponazzi and Nifo at Bologna, was the more familiar Renaissance type, a wandering polymath who lived by wit and fortune. His early life was dominated by the latter, for, though poor, he grew up at the Imperial Court, engaged for a time in military adventuring, and flirted with the monastic life, all prior to his appearance as a student at Bologna. Once there this elderly (about 30) student embraced the humanistic movement, through which he became acquainted with the works of Galen and Hippocrates and came to regard himself as thereby qualified to practise medicine. In the 1520s he made a visit to France, which subsequently became his home. There he not only practised medicine, but taught it! He had Rabelais and Nostradamus among his pupils.[6]

Scaliger is mainly remembered for his controversy with a younger man, Girolamo Cardano (1501–76), who had the temerity to undertake to write a highly original cosmology, his *De subtilitate* (1550). Cardano was about seventeen years younger than Scaliger, and lived at a time when northern Italy had fallen into a political chaos from which it never emerged in his lifetime. We find him in the 1520s a student at Pavia and Padua, from which he graduated in medicine in 1526. Sixteen years of intermittent practice in his home town of Milan followed, and after that a professorship of medicine at Pavia from 1542 until the intermittent military closing of that university caused him to abandon the post. Both Cardano and Scaliger were possessed by that avidity for 'fame' which characterized the Renaissance man, and it was the younger man who first achieved

[5] On Fracastoro, see Charles and Dorothea Singer, 1917. Thorndike in HMES, Vol. 5: 488–97.
[6] On Scaliger see Hall, 1950.

239

it, not as a physician or philosopher, but as a mathematician. By the time of his *De subtilitate* he was well known throughout Europe.[7] He was a fit target for Scaliger, who had in 1531 made himself 'known' – and not entirely without credit – as an adversary of the humanist dictator, Erasmus. Scaliger's attack on Cardano's *De subtilitate*, published in 1557, seems to have had a similar inspiration, an instinct for iconoclasm.

That the wide learning of the Renaissance Peripatetics brought them into closer contact with mundane nature is indicated by their commentaries on the *Meteorology*, where Pomponazzi and Nifo attempted to make some improvement on Aristotle's chemistry.[8] For a detailed picture of the extent to which chemical data had entered the sphere of Peripatetic natural philosophy, however, we must go to Cardano's attempt to penetrate more deeply into the 'subtlety' of nature.[9] His *De subtilitate* is a cosmological work beginning with 'principles', and proceeding through the heavens, light, mixtion, minerals, plants, animals, man, demons and angels, to God. Thus it more nearly resembles in its organization Balinūs' cosmology than Aristotle's. Nor does he hesitate to tamper with the Peripatetic system, which he finds in need of up-dating. He reduces the elements to three, claiming that fire is either a mode of motion or mere burning air. He expands the doctrine of motion by adding to the Aristotelian up-and-down motions two other 'natural' motions, the avoidance of a vacuum and its opposite, the resistance of bodies to mutual penetration, for both of which he furnishes examples from experience. And he adds another 'unnatural' motion, the attraction exhibited by the magnet and amber.[10]

[7] On Cardano see Morley, 1854, Cass, 1934, and Eckman, 1946. His fame as a mathematician came from his *Ars magna* (1545). Of the very numerous editions of *De subtilitate* I have used two, 1556 and 1559.

[8] Pomponazzi, 1563, is a book of 'doubts' about various doctrines in the *Meteorology*, with some reference to specific chemical and medico-chemical problems, including the internal use of mercury in venereal disease. Nifo's commentary on the *Meteorology* (Nifo, 1547) similarly brings a modicum of chemical evidence into the argument. Among other things it held alchemy to be useless (inutilem). See also Melson, 1960: 69. These matters are dealt with by Achillini in his *De elementis* (Achillini, 1545: 90r–148v), which is a Scholastic commentary on generation and corruption which seems to be devoid of references to chemistry. But we have noted (note 1 above) that Achillini edited a chemical work.

[9] 'Est autem subtilitas, ratio quedam qua sensibilia a sensibus, intelligibilia ab intellectu, difficile compraehenduntur' (Cardano, 1559: 9. 1556: 1).

[10] Cardano, 1556: 5v–6. 1559: 17–18 (Bk. 2).

Cardano's enterprise for the improvement of Aristotle is reminiscent of Albertus Magnus's attempt to 'complete' the Stagirite. It proceeds less through the application of reason, as had been the practice among Cardano's immediate predecessors, than through 'experience' of one kind or another. As experience usually relates to terrestrial physics rather than to astrophysics, so Cardano finds less to say of larger cosmological questions than to those of inorganic nature, a subject to which he gives a degree of attention unprecedented among philosophers. Moreover he brings together aspects of the science of matter which had been kept awkwardly separated by those who had retained the format of the Aristotelian works (*Meteorology, On generation and corruption*, etc.). Although he gives some attention to the differentiation of generation, crasis, mixis, etc., he tends to short-cut the ancient arguments by giving the name 'mixtion' to all changes in matter, and the name 'mixta' to compounds of whatever degree. As will be subsequently related, this puts him in a position to attempt a classification of minerals. He retains the idea of the involvement of form, which he sees as the key to the action and passion involved in change, but again he avoids deep involvement in theoretical questions in favour of a more extended analysis of familiar terrestrial phenomena. In the autobiography Cardano wrote about twenty years later he remarks that he did not deal in his books on nature with certain 'questionable arts', among which he includes chemistry (*chymica*). But, in fact, he had dealt quite comprehensively with that questionable art, including some of its most questionable features.[11]

Paracelsus' enterprise entailed an attempt to construct a cosmology in which Renaissance Neoplatonism is amalgamated with chemistry,[12] although it is evident in the theoretical perambulations of his followers that they found his system hard to discover. Some of them shared in the effort to integrate chemistry with respectable philosophy, and the character of their effort is revealed in an essay by Gerard Dorn (flourished late sixteenth century), a second

---

[11] Cardano, 1654: 130. 1962: 168 (Ch. 39). In addition to his *De subtilitate* he also dealt with chemistry in his *De rerum varietate* (Cardano, 1557).

[12] This has been touched upon by Strunz (in Bugge, 1929–30, Vol. 2: 96) and Cassirer (1964: 110–11) but has not been developed in detail, to my knowledge. After Helmont this enterprise seems to have ended with the chemical and mystical aspects of Paracelsian thought taking different directions.

generation Paracelsian who may have studied with some who had actually known the great man. A physician, Dorn translated some of Paracelsus' writings from German into Latin, wrote with relative sobriety on Paracelsian remedies, and compiled one of the first of many 'dictionaries' to elucidate the peculiar Paracelsian terminology. Like Paracelsus himself, Dorn denied gold-making but still managed to achieve celebrity (perhaps only posthumously) as an occult alchemist. Dorn too aspired to philosophy, and in addition to the tract considered here he wrote others designed to replace the pagan and Arabic philosophies with a Christian Aristotelianism.[13]

Shorn of the pyrotechnics which characterized the founder, the Paracelsian philosophy appears rather like a chemical adaptation of Scholasticism, and Dorn's *Chymisticum artificium naturae* (1568)[14] is essentially a chemist's commentary on Aristotle. Dorn accepts the two terrestrial exhalations, but disagrees on the doctrine of generation and corruption. He argues that since the imperfection which necessarily characterizes the sensible world manifests itself in a susceptibility to corruption, it is absurd to say that the corruption of one thing is the generation of another – as though good fruit could come from bad seed. He goes further, and finds the Peripatetic doctrine of generation and corruption contradictory in its own terms, for the conception of corruption as 'a privation of forms', he points out, is not well suited to account for a simultaneous generation of some other form-bearing thing. Indeed, he concludes, the question of generation and corruption is much in need of further inquiry, since the Schools entertain a variety of interpretations involving such ideas as the obscuration of forms, mutual transmutation or compounding (mixtione) of the elements, an influx of celestial form, or a revelation of a hidden one.

[13] Dorn, whose name appears regularly on lists of alchemists, is a very obscure personality. Partington (1961: 159–60) provides the fullest account of his career. The number of his attributed works is uncertain, but seems to be about ten. They range from the Paracelsian dictionary to several alchemical tracts which appear in Vol. I of TC. On the basis of these, Jung (1953) gave Dorn an important place in esoteric alchemy, a role quite different from the one I have given him, but we have consulted different works [!]. I agree that there is little if any chemistry in the tracts which Jung has used. Partington says that Dorn 'abandons the attempt at transmutation', but Jung thinks that it never was his objective. Clearly Dorn warrants further study.

[14] What follows is from Dorn's discussion of 'generation and corruption', in Dorn, 1568: 31–47.

But where Dorn undertakes to differentiate natural corruptions and generations from those which are artificial, no Peripatetic could have been more solicitous of the principle of substantial forms, which turns out to be the cornerstone of his analysis. Corruption in nature he regards as a degenerative transformation incompatible with the Peripatetic notions of privation and interaction between extremes. He admits two kinds of corruption, a transmutation in which the species is retained and a transformation in which it is not, for species depends upon form. In generation hidden forms are revealed, or a passive form is concealed by an active one, a process which he considers manifest in meteorological and biological phenomena, although the generation of minerals and metals he holds to be more complicated (*longe diversa*).

Speaking of artificial corruptions and generations, he admits that chemistry cannot draw out the 'simple elements', by which he apparently means something simpler than fire, air, water and earth, since he subsequently claims that at least three of them can be separated by artificial generation and still later holds all four to be resolvable by artificial corruption. But the task of chemistry, he says, is merely to seek to answer such questions as what 'nature' underlies the compound body, and here he again refers to form. In such operations of artificial corruption as 'subtilization' and 'mundification', preparation is merely made for the reception of form. Were it otherwise, he thinks gold, for example, could be made from all metals. In artificial generation the pre-eminent operation is distillation, which is the key to the investigation of latent forms, and this is the most important study of the natural philosopher, for it reveals how the celestial virtues raise the crass inferior elements to the uses of medicine.

Although all this had begun among the Peripatetics, Renaissance philosophy had developed other sources of inspiration which had little connection with Aristotle. One of these was the famous German savant, Nicolaus of Cusa (1401–64), who recovered the work of that obscure ninth-century Neoplatonist, John Scotus Erigena, by way of Master Eckhart (d. 1327), a successor of Roger Bacon and Albertus Magnus at Paris. Nicolaus made their doctrines part of his own, a mystical philosophy of nature which had immense influence in the sixteenth century, although not among those who cared about chemistry.[15] Another source of Neoplatonism was in Florence, where a 'Platonic academy' was established in the mid-fifteenth century to collect and exploit the wisdom of learned Greek refugees from tottering Byzantium. The ornament of this academy was no Greek, but a native of Florence, Marsilio Ficino (1433–99), whose 'Platonism' included not only Neoplatonism, but extended to the astrological fringe where he found a body of (non-alchemical) writing associated with the redoubtable Hermes Trismegistus.[16]

In eschewing Aristotle and his kind of philosophizing these thinkers cultivated Plato, but this is not to say that their conception of nature was particularly Platonic. As a 'humanist' natural philosopher Ficino was only peripherally interested in nature at all, but the recovery of ancient literature of whatever sort became a major objective of the Italian humanists, and in its further development the doctrines of the Presocratics, Pythagoreans, Epicureans and Stoics were all reinstated.[17] Separated from their niches in the structure of Aristotelian philosophy, but not reconstructed in their entirety, these fragments of natural philosophy in a sense reconstituted the environment of Presocratic thought. But those who cultivated them were intent upon criticizing Aristotelian philosophy, not in reconstructing it. With the publication in 1565 of the De natura rerum of Bernardino Telesio (1509–88) these anti-Aristotelians finally generated a cosmology of their own.

Telesio was born to a noble family of Cosenza, near Naples.[18] Protected from many of the evils of life in sixteenth-century Italy, he studied in Rome and Padua (where he took a doctor's degree in 1535); but he was not immune to trouble and finally returned to

[15] On Nicolaus of Cusa see Bett, 1932, and Gandillac, 1941. His influence on philosophy and cosmology was through his book De docta ignorantia (Nicolaus of Cusa, 1954), which is a work of theoretical Neoplatonism. It is curious that he wrote in another work, Idiota de staticis experimentis (Nicolaus of Cusa, 1944), what is perhaps the most acute prescription for the pursuit of experimental science (including chemistry) to appear before modern times. It appears to have had little if any influence.

[16] On Ficino see Kristeller, 1943 and Marcel, 1958. His most important philosophical work, Theologica Platonica (1474 – I have used Ficino, 1559), has nothing specific on the mineral kingdom. Kristeller calls it 'a natural history of the soul'. On the Hermetic writings edited by Ficino see Festugiere, 1950: 106–8, 112–23.

[17] See Kristeller, 1956: 26.

[18] On Telesio see Rixner, 1820. Van Dusen, 1932. Kristeller, 1964: 91–109.

the family home where he engaged in study and teaching. His *De natura rerum* is an anti-Peripatetic cosmology based on the idea of an interaction between a celestial heat and a terrestrial cold, an idea for which it has been held particularly indebted to a remarkably improbable source, the anti-scientific Presocratic, Parmenides. Much attention is given by Telesio to the substitution of his heat-cold ideology for various elements of Peripatetic dogma, but, except in biology, he gives short shrift to terrestrial matters and fails to penetrate to the level of subtlety upon which Peripatic arguments were conducted. He even neglects to differentiate the three kingdoms of nature. The key to his conception of chemistry is his observation that heat may either rarefy (as water which is boiled) or condense (as salt in the same water), but he appears to regard the possible variety of things as altogether too great for practical differentiation.[19] In biology, however, he comes firmly to grips with the problem of digestion, and if he fails to add much to its solution, he does show himself well informed and eager to improve the Galenic theory along the same quasi-chemical lines as were pursued by the most learned physician of his time, Jean Fernel.[20]

Telesio's cosmology had a great vogue among the most illustrious Italian philosophers of the late sixteenth and early seventeenth centuries, notably on Francesco Patrizi (1529–97), Giordano Bruno (1548–1600), and Thomas Campanella (1568–1639). These unfortunate philosophers suffered both from the general misfortunes of their homeland and from the official disapproval of their tendency to radical pantheism, but despite all this each managed to publish a work on cosmology. As far as chemistry is concerned their views are not significantly different from those of Telesio, but it must be said that they do not merely repeat him. Patrizi uses chemical evidence to refute the Peripatetics, and while not a very convincing refutation, it certifies some familiarity with the subject by Patrizi.[21] Campanella professes to speak with some authority on metallurgy, and to have the

---

[19] Telesio, 1586: 21–4 (Bk 1, Chs. 14–5).

[20] See below, p. 291ff.

[21] On Patrizi's philosophy see Kristeller, 1964: 110–26. Rixner (1823: 21–183) summarizes Patrizi's *Nova de universis philosophia*, where his analysis of minerals appears on p. 178. Francis Bacon called Patrizi one who 'sublimed the fumes of the Platonists' (1857–74, Vol. 4: 359 [*De augmentis*, Bk 3]).

key to gold-making, although he does not appear to refer to alchemy by name.[22] If chemistry was peripheral to the interests of the anti-Aristotelians and of little significance in their writings, it remains noteworthy that even in their indifference they show themselves to be conversant with some particulars of the mundane science of matter. Clearly some acquaintance with chemistry was mandatory to the natural philosopher of the Renaissance.

New cosmologies

By 1600 'the Schools' no longer had much to do with philosophical research and speculation, but Scholasticism continued to be an issue, for no other philosophy had produced a teachable doctrine. The seventeenth-century innovators, however, were to have better luck than had their predecessors of the previous century, in explanation of which there are as many reasons as there are differences between a century still dominated by the spirit of the Middle Ages and one infused with that of modern times. It is curious, and probably not insignificant, that this age of developing nationalism in politics also witnessed the development of philosophies of nature associated with particular nations, with Descartes in France, Francis Bacon in England, and Paracelsus in Germanic Europe. Italy, on the other hand, although the traditional fountainhead of philosophical adventuring, seems to have abandoned even Telesio, and in reaction to have reverted to the defence of the expiring Scholasticism.

From the point of view of the science of matter the most conspicuous difference between the writers of the sixteenth century and their successors is the advent of 'particulate' philosophies. The classical exposition of that philosophy, Lucretius' *De natura rerum*, was among the works popularized by the humanists,[23] but it is questionable that the seventeenth-century particulate philosophies had their origins in atomism. There were other precedents. In the

---

[22] Rixner, 1826: 128–34, from Campanella's *Realis philosophiae epilogisticae*. On Campanella see also Blanchet, 1920.

[23] Although probably never lost, Lucretius' book was given new life through the discovery of a manuscript in 1414 by the humanist Poggio Bracciolini. It was published in 1473 (Stones, 1928: 445–6).

sixteenth century both the Peripatetics and their adversaries were accustomed to speaking of minima,[24] and both this term and the Anaxagorean 'seed' were as commonplace as 'atom' even in the terminology of the avowed atomist.[25] An acceptance of the void is a better criterion for identifying the atomist, but even those who accept both atoms and the void, notably Bruno and Helmont, make little use of the void and tend to make atoms a *continuum*.[26] Up to the mid-seventeenth century, when Gassendi did for Epicurus what the humanists had done for Lucretius, particulate philosophies were irresolvable mixtures of the ideas embodied in the sum-total of ancient ideas of particles.[27]

Even without being 'atomistic', however, the particulate theories brought about a substantial modification of Aristotelian doctrine. Scaliger had in this connection raised the question of the Aristotelian dictum that 'mixtion is the alteration of the mixables to a unity' and suggested rather that it is 'the motion of the minima of bodies to mutual contact, that they may make a unity'.[28] This proposal, which aroused the opposition of at least some of the Peripatetics,[29] was to provide the key to the theoretical innovations of the seventeenth century. Francis Bacon (1561–1626) proposed the examination of

[24] On the use of the term minima by Peripatetics see Wilson, 1956: 94ff., Wilson, 1953: 356, and Melson, 1960: 64–9. Minima were used indifferently with atoms by Bruno and others. One of the arguments put forward in 1646 by a French enthusiast for atomism, J. C. Magnen, was that minima, under different names, appear in nearly all physics (Stones, 1928: 459).

[25] In *De triplici minimo et mensura* Bruno defines minima as '*cuius pars nulla est, prima quod est pars*', and atom as '*minimum longum, latum atq. profundum corporis*' (1591: 145). On the whole Bruno's minima resemble Fracastoro's 'seeds' and Leibniz's 'monads' as much as atoms, and in his exposition of them he seems most influenced by Plato and Telesio (cf. D. W. Singer, 1950: 72–5. Stones, 1928: 450–1). In Bruno's behalf it should be said that he was primarily interested in the infinitely large, and allows his contradictions to accumulate in his commentary on the infinitely small.

[26] Discussing Aristotle's arguments against infinity in *De caelo*, Bruno says that 'the infinite universe may be regarded as a single continuum', and illustrates this by the example of mud. 'Since the concourse of atoms of earth and the atoms of water is beyond our sensible apprehension, these minima are called neither discrete nor continuous, but form a single continuum which is neither water nor earth but is mud.' (Bruno, 1950–1: 287 [*On the infinite universe and worlds*]). On Helmont see below, p. 251. Some, such as Francis Bacon, accepted atoms while rejecting the void.

[27] Pre-atomist particulate theories are discussed at length in Melson, 1960. He sees David van Goorle (1592–1612) as the first 'true atomist' of modern times.

[28] Scaliger, 1557: 143v.

[29] E.g. the Jesuits of Coimbra (Collegio Conimbricensis, 1599: 353–5).

'forms' in terms of particles in motion,[30] and such an examination was to be made by several of the leading natural philosophers of the seventeenth century.

Francis Bacon must be accorded the role of the pioneer advocate of a recasting of natural philosophy, and in calling for a philosophy based on experiment he made himself the patron of those who followed. Nearly a generation elapsed between his death and the outburst of natural philosophy which was, if not finally to abolish Aristotle, at least to obliterate him by infinite dilution, as the Peripatetics had long sought to dispose of the durable drop of wine. The critical decade was that of the 1640s. The year 1644 saw at last the publication of the full-blown cosmology which René Descartes (1596–1650) had been withholding through the decade since Galileo's troubles with the Roman Curia. It also saw the publication of the undeservedly forgotten natural philosophy of Sir Kenelm Digby (1603–65) contained in his *Two treatises of bodies and men's souls*, and the death of J. B. van Helmont (1577–1644) whose *Origins of medicine (Ortus medicinae)*, published four years later by his son, was scarcely less universal in its claims, its title notwithstanding, than was the cosmology of Descartes. The decade had begun with the dissemination, at least in England, of the anti-Aristotelian ideas of 'the German Bacon' (or German Boyle), Joachim Jungius,[31] and ended with the revival of Epicurean atomism by Pierre Gassendi. Thus was made available to such as Robert Boyle, then in his early twenties, a whole library of 'modern' natural philosophy to serve as a background for his own observations on the subject, which began to appear a little over a decade later.

Only Cartesianism among the new philosophies of nature exhibits the coherence and internal consistency of a unified doctrine, and it alone was essentially the product of a single mind. Descartes's career as a free-lance soldier and philosopher is familiar enough not to require repetition here. Although his *Principles of philosophy* was not published until 1644, his ideas were already fairly generally

[30] Marie Boas, 1952–1: 440.

[31] On Jungius see Wohlwill, 1887, and Partington, 1961: 415–22. Although Jungius' opinions were known to Boyle (see below, p. 255) he seems to have had little influence. His disputations on the elementary constituents of natural bodies (Jungius, 1887) constitute a resumption of the ancient argument between the Aristotelians and Stoics. They were out of the mainstream of seventeenth-century thought, although not necessarily behind it.

known. He had written them into a book called *Le monde* in 1629–33, but refrained from publishing it, probably out of caution inspired by the condemnation of Galileo in the latter year. He did, however, publish parts of it, and a partial account of the application of his system to chemical phenomena appeared in 1637, in his treatise on meteorology (*Meteora*).

The rejection of received doctrine reached totality in the philosophy of Descartes, who resolved to construct a science of nature *de novo*. He vows that he will receive no principle in physics which is not also received by mathematics – a promise which he thinks he can fulfil because he has taken geometry – extension – as his foundation. He calls the universe uniform, boundless, and one, and fills it with a 'matter' defined only as that which possesses geometrical qualities. But he sees that matter as divided into innumerable little bodies of diverse size and shape, constantly moving and by their motion forming the phenomena of the sensible world. These particles range in size from those of gross matter down to those of the finest emanations such as light.[32] Indeed, 'space' itself, since it has extension, is also necessarily a substance.[33] As Descartes takes up the questions which had confounded his predecessors his ingenuity proves a match for almost any problem. He manages to differentiate his particles from those of Epicurus or Plato.[34] His particles swirl in vortices, a regular movement which does not prevent their assuming at times the forms of the Peripatetic elements, the Paracelsian principles, and the multitudinous forms of the sensible world. He admits that he lacks the convenience for carrying out the experiments requisite for the verification of his reasoning,[35] but his countrymen of the next generation were quite prepared to remedy this defect. Nicolas Lemery, perhaps the most influential chemist of the last half of the

[32] Descartes, 1902: 202–13, 231–39 (*Meteora*, Ch. 1). 1905: 52, 59, 78 (*Principia philosophiae*, Pt 2, Princ. 21, 22, 34, and 64).

[33] Descartes, 1905: 45–6 (*Principia philosophiae*, Pt 2, Princ. 10–11).

[34] Atoms are philosophically defective, in contradicting both the human imagination and the powers of God (Descartes, 1905: 51 [*Principia*, Pt 2, Princ. 20]). Thus Descartes denies independently both atoms and the void. As to Plato, his particles are made of triangles which somehow form in space, while Descartes's space represents a kind of ultimate subdivision of his particles.

[35] 'Quae fortasse singula descripsissem hoc in loco, si varia experimenta quae ad certum eorum cognitionem requiruntur, facere hactenus liquisset.' (1905: 242 [*Principia*, Pt 4, Princ. 63]).

seventeenth century, provided a Cartesian explanation for almost every process known to medical chemistry.[36] As Cartesianism took possession of the Paris Academy of Sciences, most successful of the new academies, this particulate philosophy enjoyed a period of prosperity and influence scarcely known since the Aristotelianism of ancient times.

Descartes was a younger contemporary of Helmont, whose labours took place in a small town near Brussels at the same time that Descartes was working in happy seclusion not far away in Holland, although it does not appear that they knew each other. Helmont published little in his lifetime, and his reputation was largely posthumous. His book *Ortus medicinae*[37] climaxed a century-long quest of the Paracelsians for a cosmology satisfying to the chemist, but Helmont resembles Paracelsus himself more than he does the Paracelsians, in his predilection for innovations in medicine and philosophy. The two men were remarkably alike in their disdain for their academic contemporaries, their impatience with the fantasies of traditional theory coupled with a bland confidence in even more fantastic theories of their own, and in their construction of a peculiar combination of religion, philosophy, and empirical science. But Helmont was no 'follower', and among the fantasies which he rejected were those of Paracelsus.[38]

Helmont's reputation never seems to have rested on his contributions to therapy. Boyle esteemed him as an experimenter whose

[36] See the recipes in Nicolas Lemery 1677, 1686, 1698, 1701 and other editions. The first edition was in 1675.

[37] Helmont, 1648-2 (*On the passive deception and ignorance of the humoralist scholars*), was apparently published just before his death. It was republished with the *Ortus medicinae* (Helmont, 1648-1) which his son issued posthumously. The English translation (Helmont, 1662) contains both of the above, with others, in continuous pagination. Chapter and paragraph numbers in the translation correspond to those in Helmont, 1648-1 and 1648-2, except that the chapter numbers in the English version are given incorrectly in the text, although correctly in the index. There are French (Helmont, 1670), German, and Dutch versions which are substantially different. On this see further in Partington, 1961: 213-4.

[38] The ninth chapter of *Ortus medicinae* is on 'The ignorant natural philosophy of Aristotle and Galen', and this is only the beginning of his differences with them. He is gentler with Paracelsus (although he calls him stupid, among other things), but he criticizes him frequently enough, on his failure to observe 'gas' (Ch. 14: para. 30. Helmont, 1648-1: 72. 1662: 69), on the elements (ibid.), on Paracelsus' doctrine of tartar (Chs. 33 to 37. Helmont, 1648-1: 233-57. 1662: 229-53), on digestion (Ch. 31: 71. Helmont, 1648-1: 223. 1662: 219), etc. Helmont more often criticizes Paracelsus for contradicting himself than for being wrong.

criticism of the traditional systems of elements furnished much grist for the mill of the 'sceptical chymist', and although Helmont had his own strange conception of elements Boyle seems not to have held it against him. More recent writers have praised Helmont's use of the balance and of a sort of thermometer, his introduction of the word 'gas', and his substitution of a chemical theory of digestion for the traditional thermal theory.[39] Helmont would probably have preferred to be remembered for his chemical philosophy of nature, for he gives his intention to compose a new philosophy as the necessity which requires him to 'break down almost all things that have been delivered by those that went before'.[40] Those he most feels the need of breaking down (*rescindere*) seem to be the systems of Galen, Paracelsus, and 'the Schools', whose errors he tirelessly points out along the way.

Helmont was the first natural philosopher to resort consistently to experimental evidence, which is not to say that he relies on it exclusively. His attitude often seems not very different from that of the Peripatetic, Themistius, in Boyle's *Sceptical chymist*, who explains that the Peripatetics gather experiments 'rather to illustrate than to demonstrate their doctrines . . . to satisfy those that are not capable of a nobler conviction'.[41] Helmont uses up most of his experimental energies to prove that an elementary 'water' is the basis of 'all things', but this is no impediment to cosmological excursions as bold as those of Descartes. Although his experiments 'prove' that a great many things are made of water, he has no hesitation in grafting onto it the Paracelsian cosmology (such as it was) by generating the principles, mercury, sulphur, and salt, out of water. He uses atomism when it suits him, even accepting the void, but such Peripatetic concepts as substantial form are replaced not by atomic conceptions but by no less than three new emanations, which he calls Magnall, Blas and Gas,[42] and which perform the functions of form and a great deal more.

Although there is no doubt that Helmont was a competent chemist – for his time – he *uses* chemistry rather than explaining it. His

[39] There is a large literature on Helmont. See Strunz, 1907, Metzger, 1936, Partington, 1936, and Pagel, 1944.

[40] Helmont, 1648–1: 41. 1662: 37 (Ch. 8, Sec. 2).

[41] Boyle, 1772, Vol. 1: 469 (*Sceptical chymist*).

[42] 1648–1: 66–86. 1662: 63–86 (Chs. 14 to 17).

account of the chemistry of gold, for example, demonstrates its resistance to permanent change, but his reason for doing so is to explain by analogy what he believes to be characteristic of his elemental water; he does not conclude that gold might be an element![43] In general his experiments are devised to meet such purposes, sometimes flying straight in the face of the facts.

That Helmont's influence was relatively short lived, and that his was the last 'chemical' philosophy, is probably due less to its very considerable defects than to the fact that chemical considerations henceforth became so commonplace among natural philosophers that there was no occasion for a special chemical philosophy. In the 1660s we find Boyle excepting the philosophy of the leading chemical philosopher of the age, Helmont, from his general criticism of the philosophy of 'the chemists', while simultaneously laying the groundwork for an equally chemical – 'corpuscular' – philosophy. Indeed there is some question as to whether there really was an independent chemical philosophy in the minds of most philosophers. The idea that the 'chemical' and 'Peripatetic' were two opposed philosophies was perhaps the creation of Boyle in his *Sceptical chymist*, where he seems to differentiate Peripatetics from chemists solely on the ground of adherence to the four elements of Aristotle or the three principles of Paracelsus. Boyle scarcely names any particular person as the adherent of either doctrine. In his dialogue the Peripatetics have their spokesman in Themistius and the chemists theirs in Philoponus, but although the book deals for the most part with 'experiment' (more accurately, demonstration), and consequently gives most of its attention to the chemists, Philoponus is practically mute. In any case, chemistry had moved to the centre of the stage in natural philosophy and from the later seventeenth century there was no longer any peculiarly chemical philosophy. The fluidity of the situation was such that the natural philosophy which was to be most influential among the chemists themselves of the next generation was to be that of that conspicuously non-chemical personage, Descartes.[44]

Other Englishmen had flirted with atoms and corpuscles since

---

[43] 1648–1: 68. 1662: 64 (Ch. 14, Sec. 6).

[44] In 1646, two years before the publication of Helmont's book, Cornelius van Hogheland of Leyden published a tract on the economy of the animal body giving a chemical analysis and crediting it to Descartes (Hogheland, 1686: 26–49).

Francis Bacon had proposed examining forms through particles in motion. One of them was the picturesque Sir Kenelm Digby, a gentleman philosopher who achieved that status through a successful career in piracy, after which he 'retired to study alchemy'. Although he did claim success in gold-making he was more interested in medical chemistry and was something of a Paracelsian, although the sect had become largely diffused in his time. He gave much attention to the promotion of his 'powder of sympathy', a quasi-magical medicine which is thought to have been green vitriol (ferrous sulphate). Despite these questionable activities he is found among those who founded the Royal Society and, as we see in his *Two treatises*, among the would-be improvers of natural philosophy.[45]

The first of Digby's two treatises, 'On the nature of bodies', came about somewhat accidentally. He intended, as he tells us, to write on the soul, but found that the introduction had grown into an independent treatise.[46] Despite this inauspicious beginning, Digby's book is remarkably rational and eclectic, taking into consideration the writings of Aristotle, Galen, Gilbert, Galileo, Harvey, and Descartes. He is concerned to avoid the approach of 'the Schools', where 'unto all questions concerning the proper nature of bodies and their operations, it is held sufficient to answer, they have a quality or a power to do such a thing. And afterwards they dispute whether this quality or power be entirely distinct from its subject or no, and how it is separable or inseparable from it, and the like'.[47] He regards his explanations as 'far different' from those of Aristotle, but the Stagirite is nevertheless his most common authority, and Digby's treatise has usually been regarded as an attempt to reconcile Aristotle with the new science of Galileo, Gilbert and Harvey.

Like Descartes, Digby begins with 'quantity' – meaning 'bulk or magnitude' – which seems to him the first and most obvious affection of a body, and from that he goes on to consider rarity and density, the elements, light, motion, gravity, chemical compounds (mixed bodies), attraction, electricity and magnetism. He, too, is led by the force of logic to conclude that the world is composed of particles, for if the compounded bodies which are its commonest

[45] The most recent biography of Digby is Petersson, 1956.
[46] Digby, 1645: preface.
[47] Loc. cit.

manifestation were to be continuously subdivided we would necessarily arrive finally at bodies which are not compounded. He recognizes that such unlimited subdivision raises the question of the beginning and end of a body's existence, and holds that 'the first conjunction of parts in these bodies of least size' is made 'by the force of quantity'. He believes the smallest elementary particles to be those of fire. The other elements have larger particles because of 'compactedness', which proceeds from density, which 'means to be less divisible'. Further conjunctions, between different elements, proceed from quantity and density together.[48] On this basis Digby proceeds to construct the compounded bodies of the sensible world.

With Helmont and Digby we have reached the borderline between natural philosophy as an essay in cosmology and as a less ambitious undertaking – a system of physical science. In their writings astronomy has been reduced to a topic even more incidental than chemistry had been in the writings of Aristotle. Helmont seems still to retain pretensions to universality (although it should be remembered that his *Origins of medicine* was a collection put together posthumously), but Digby's claims are decidedly more modest, and it is no accident that he rarely appears among authorities significant in the history of cosmology.

In such works as Cardano's *De subtilitate* such peripheral topics as light, electricity and magnetism had bulked ever larger, being virtually independent treatises, and the majority of the writers Digby was trying to reconcile, Gilbert, Galileo and Harvey, had already turned from cosmology to these special topics. Most of the writing of Boyle and Newton was to be in this new tradition, and it is a measure of the decline of cosmology that Newton, despite his brilliant conquest of virtually all of the requisite topics, preferred to found a philosophy rather than a cosmology. Even Aristotelianism and Cartesianism were reduced to 'philosophies' by one of the French encyclopaedists of the end of the eighteenth century, who compared the 'Newtonian philosophy' with 'the Cartesian, the Peripatetic, and the ancient corpuscular [atomism]'.[49]

[48] Loc. cit. 145–7.

[49] Naigeon, 1791–an. 2 (1793–4), Vol. 3: 365 (art. Newtonianism). As noted in the preface, I have used the term 'cosmology' in this book as best characterizing that sector of philosophy within which the science of matter lay. The term, however, is a modern one, and was scarcely used by the authors with which I am concerned.

Boyle, who deserves a place in the history of this 'Newtonian philosophy', enjoyed some substantial advantages over his predecessors, in his possession of the publications of Descartes, Helmont and Digby, in his familiarity with the superior expositions of atomism by Jungius and Gassendi, and, above all, in working after the diffusion of acceptance of Torricelli's barometric experiment of 1643 as an experimental demonstration of the existence of the void.[50] Boyle was in large measure freed of the burden under which virtually all respectable philosophers of previous generations had laboured, the necessity of avoiding atomism by admitting particles but not the void. He regarded Cartesianism and atomism, outside of their 'metaphysical notions', as a single philosophy, and eschewing those notions – which derived from their un-Baconian a priori character – he called his the 'corpuscular' philosophy.[51]

This was Newton's starting point, and although his writings on corpuscles were scanty compared to Boyle's, they were important, and the corpuscular became part of the Newtonian philosophy, and particularly as it bore on chemistry. Both Boyle and Newton attributed chemical action to a mixture of atomic and Cartesian shapes, 'Newtonian' attraction, and 'sociability' (meaning affinity).[52] The resultant confusion muted the incipient conflict between Cartesians and Newtonians, for the French found 'corpuscularianism' quite compatible with Cartesianism,[53] and the English showed little reluctance to fill in the blanks in Newtonian philosophy with Cartesian particles and fluids.[54] Together the two doctrines found

[50] On Boyle's acquaintance with the work of Descartes and Gassendi, see Marie Boas, 1958: 26–7. Boyle was apparently introduced both to Gassendi and to the Torricellian experiment in 1648. Although many long denied that the experiment proved the existence of the void, Boyle accepted it by 1557–8 (Marie Boas, 1958: 43. Partington, 1961: 502. Middleton, 1964: 33–56).

[51] Boyle, 1772, Vol. 1: 355. See also Marie Boas, 1952–1.

[52] On the simultaneous involvement of shapes, Cartesian and atomic, attractions, and 'sociability' in the analysis of chemical reactions by Boyle and Newton see Kuhn, 1951 and 1952, and Marie Boas, 1952–2. The papers reported in Newton, 1958: 249–58, show Newton attempting, with difficulty, to escape from Cartesianism.

[53] See Metzger, 1923: 266–77.

[54] Such important chemists as Thomas Willis and John Mayow were strongly influenced by Descartes, but Cartesianism was mainly felt among English chemists through Nicolas Lemery, whose Cours de chymie was translated in 1677 by Walter Harris and on three subsequent occasions to 1720. Fontenelle reported that Lemery had forty Scotsmen among his students in a single year (see his Éloge to Lemery, English trans. in Farber, 1961: 152).

ample resources to relieve them of such Peripatetic impedimenta as forms, qualities and elements. Thanks to Gassendi, and above all to Torricelli, they were even able to opt for atoms and to dispense with minima, Aristotle was accordingly buried, although his 'ether' long remained, like a ghost, to haunt the Newtonian philosophy.

Chapter Twelve

The rise of the chemist

THE sixteenth century saw the emergence of a printed literature of practical chemistry beginning with the appearance, shortly after 1500, of several short tracts – the *Berg und Probierbuchlein* – which had circulated in manuscript among the German miners. This metallurgical literature culminated within a generation in the *Pirotechnia* of the Italian metallurgist, Vannoccio Biringuccio (1480–1538), a treatment of metallurgy and much of practical chemistry so comprehensive and circumstantial that it remained up-to-date for nearly two centuries.[1]

The celebrated metallurgical literature of the sixteenth and early seventeenth century may, however, owe more to the invention of printing than to any innovation among metallurgists. Although Biringuccio was certainly a practical man he was rather a manager than a craftsman. The son of a minor official of Siena, he was principally occupied as the superintendent of the arsenal and saltpetre works of the local prince, and the contents of his book was derived as much from observations made in his travels as from his own experience.[2] Of the subsequent authors of similar works – all

[1] There were ten editions of *Pirotechnia*, in Italian, French, and English, between 1530 and 1678. That there was no Latin or German translation helps account for the greater popularity of Agricola and Ercker, both of whom depended upon Biringuccio. According to Cyril S. Smith, Agricola copied in extenso from *Pirotechnia*, as did the Spanish authority, Perez de Vargas (*De re metallica*, 1569). Smith speaks of C. A. Schlüter, *Gründlichen Unterricht von Hütte-Werken* (1738) as the first book which 'begins to surpass the utility of those written by the great sixteenth century metallurgists' (see Smith's introduction to Biringuccio, 1942 and Ercker, 1951).

[2] On Biringuccio see Otto Johannsen in Bugge, 1929–30, Vol. 1: 70–84, and Cyril S. Smith's introduction to Biringuccio, 1942.

of whom were heavily dependent upon Biringuccio – George Agricola (1490–1555) was a learned physician, A. A. Barba (fl. 1640) a priest, and Lazarus Ercker (d. 1593) a mining official trained in medicine. They represent not a craft tradition but a rising interest of the community of learning in the arts,[3] which was to culminate in the foundation of the seventeenth century scientific societies.

Outside of metallurgy it is even more difficult to discover the craftsman himself putting pen to paper, and the printed literature is on the whole so slight as to suggest that the practical chemist continued to depend upon manuscripts – where he required a written record at all. There can hardly be any doubt of this among the goldsmiths and colour-makers, for it appears that what I have called the *Compositiones* treatises, which exist in many manuscripts postdating the invention of printing, were not printed at all until they attracted the attention of art historians about a century ago.[4] There is a printed literature on glass-making, dating from the *L'arte vitraria* of 1592 by Antonio Neri (d. 1614), who was no glass-worker, but a Florentine priest.[5] While it should be added that virtually the entire content of the medieval technological literature was absorbed into the literature of the 'books of secrets' which began to appear in print in the middle sixteenth century, few, if any, of these owed their existence to the literary proclivities of any craftsman.[6] Nor is it easy to suppose that any practical chemist would have found it practical to filter out the *regula* of the fine and practical arts from the multitude of medical recipes with which they were mingled in these books. The books of secrets, which fell from the printing presses in a veritable deluge for

[3] On the large literature on Agricola see Darmstaedter, 1926, and Wilsdorf, 1956. On Barba see HMES, Vol. 7: 258–60. On Ercker see Armstrong and Lukens, 1939, and Cyril S. Smith's introduction to Ercker, 1951. Koch, 1963, gives a general history of this genre of literature.

[4] No early printed versions of these tracts are mentioned in Berger's comprehensive history of painting techniques (Berger, 1912).

[5] On Neri see Ferguson, 1906, Vol. 2: 134–5. His book was the basis of subsequent seventeenth-century works by Kunckel and Christopher Merritt.

[6] In his 'Notes on some books of technical receipts, or so-called secrets', written in 1882 (republished in Ferguson, 1959, Vol. 1: 3–21), John Ferguson begins with reference to a series of the most popular authors, Levin Lemne, Conrad Gesner, Jean Liebaut, George Baker, Don Alessio Ruscelli, Gabriello Falloppio, Leonardo Fiorovanti, Giovanni B. della Porta, and Leonardo Locatelli. All can be identified as physicians except Porta and the little known Ruscelli, who were typical Renaissance intellectual virtuosi. Both of them attempted to found learned academies.

about a century, bespeak the emergence of the literate layman, if not of the 'gadgeteer'.

But all this in no way argues against the perseverance of the practical chemist, nor does it in fact demonstrate his alienation from the general cultural elevation of the time. He appears less as a literate craftsman than as a Renaissance virtuoso of curious learning and eccentric talents. Leonardo da Vinci and Benvenuto Cellini, rather than Agricola, Neri, or even Biringuccio, are prototypes of the literate craftsmen. This may be illustrated from the lives of Bernard Palissy and Leonhard Thurneysser, whose careers also reveal the potentialities of chemistry as a livelihood in the sixteenth century.

Palissy,[7] who was slightly the elder, was born at the beginning of the century in a small town southeast of Bordeaux. Although presumably of low birth, he managed to acquire sufficient education to master the rudiments of the demanding trade of surveyor. He seems, in fact, to have been a life-long student. He interested himself in chemistry during youthful travels which carried him as far as Germany, and spent some time as a maker of stained glass windows, but in the late 1530s he settled as a surveyor in Saintes, north of Bordeaux. About 1545 we find him in charge of mapping the nearby salt works in connection with the establishment of the gabelle (salt-tax) by King Francis I.

Palissy became a prosperous burgher of Saintes, but about 1555 he interested himself in the production of porcelain, and entered a long period of experimentation during which he impoverished himself and his family like a true inventor, before finally developing the style of 'rustic pottery' for which he became famous. In the meantime he had added to his problems by embracing Calvinism, and in 1562 his workshop was sacked and he was arrested. That he was an important personage is indicated by the fact that the governor of Saintes interceded with the crown and secured his liberation by having him attached to the Royal household. Ultimately this led to his removal to Paris, where, in 1566, he was put to work on the embellishment of the Tuileries gardens.

Palissy continued educating himself in Paris. He formed a 'cabinet of curiosities', reputedly the first natural history collection in France,

[7] On Palissy see the introductions by Paul A. Cap, to Palissy, 1844, and by Aurele la Rocque to Palissy, 1957.

and from 1575 to 1584 offered lectures in 'natural history and physics'. A group of his writings had been published in 1563 under the title *Recepte veritable*, and in 1580 he published his *Discours admirables*, which may represent his lectures. Both are somewhat disorganized collections, falling generally in what would today be called economic geology, but they include notices on many of the conventional chemical topics. In 1588 a resurgence of religious persecution in France put the now aged Palissy in the Bastille, and he died there two years later.

Thurneysser[8] was born in Basel in 1530, the son of a goldsmith of that city. In 1548 the young Leonhard found it expedient to make a sudden departure from Basel when it was discovered that he had sold some gilded lead bricks as bars of gold. During the next decade, largely spent in wandering about Europe, he became a mining expert and secured employment in that capacity with the Archduke Ferdinand of Austria. The German rulers were at this time eagerly seeking to expand their mineral industries, and Thurneysser's duties included visitations as distant as England and North Africa. During this period of continued wandering he interested himself in Paracelsus and in medical chemistry, on which he began publishing highly esoteric books about 1570.[9] At the same time he transferred his employment to Brandenberg, where he became personal physician to the Elector, Johann Georg. Attending to the royal ailments, selling remedies (and cosmetics) of his own concoction, and advising the Elector on such practical matters as the production of alum and saltpetre,[10] made Thurneysser a wealthy man in the 1570s, but then came a sudden reversal of fortune which left him again an impecunious wanderer. This turn of events seems to have resulted from the accumulated opposition of professional and personal enemies; that he was a controversial figure is indicated by the inclusion in one of his books of a portrait showing himself trampling his adversaries. Some misadventure in gold-making may also have been involved, for we find him spending most of the last decade of his life, which

[8] On Thurneysser see Moehsen, 1783, Kopp, 1886, Vol. 1: 107-24, and Bugge, 1944. The latter is a fictionalized biography.

[9] Moehsen, 1783, mentions 26 published (and 11 unpublished) works. Ferguson (1906, Vol. 2: 450-5) mentions 20. Their esoteric character owes much to his addiction to the use of Greek and Hebrew titles, and to the occasional use of languages as unusual as Ethiopian.

[10] Kopp, 1886, Vol. 1: 115.

ended in 1595, as an itinerant gold-maker in Italy. A nail, the point of which Thurneysser had transmuted for Cardinal Ferdinand de Medici in 1586, was long exhibited in Florence.[11]

The careers of Palissy and Thurneysser seem to have run the gamut of possibilities for employment in chemistry, including practical chemistry and mining, medicine and pharmacy, alchemy, and teaching. The notoriety of the employment of alchemists by Renaissance princes has overshadowed the less romantic opportunities offered the practical chemist. The chemist may well have been expected to serve both functions, just as the court astronomer was expected to cast horoscopes, but even Thurneysser, despite his bent for the occult, seems to have been valued by the Elector of Brandenberg more for his knowledge of the production of alum and saltpetre than for gold-making.

In the seventeenth century chemical employment came to centre on pharmacy, for this was the great era of medical chemistry. Not very different from the personal circumstances of Palissy and Thurneysser, however, were those of the lives of such important chemists of the next century as Angelo Sala (1576?–1637)[12], Johann R. Glauber (1604–70?),[13] Otto Tachenius (d. c. 1700),[14] Johann Kunckel (1630–1703),[15] and Johann J. Becher (1635–82).[16] All of these were men of humble birth and all were self-trained and devoted themselves to the various chemically oriented occupations already mentioned, in careers no less precariously pursued – they lived during the Thirty Years War – than had been those of Palissy and Thurneysser.

That Sala and Becher on occasion taught medicine is indicative of

---

[11] Kopp, 1886, Vol. 1: 90–1. The nail was in a repository of antiquities near the Court of Justice in Florence in 1664, where it was seen by John Evelyn, who said 'it plainly appears to have been but sother'd' (1959: 106 [*Diary*, Oct. 24]). John Ray, who also saw it in 1664, called it 'counterfeit, and not neatly either, the iron and the gold being but bunglingly joined together' (1738, Vol. 1: 286). This was also the opinion of Tachenius (1677: 114) and Georg Wedel (1675–6), who saw it a little later. My colleague, Silvio Bedini, who has guided me in the history of this nail, reports that his recent (1963) exploration of Italian collections has failed to turn it up.

[12] On Sala see Capobus, 1933.

[13] On Glauber see Gugel, 1955 and Pietsch, 1956.

[14] On Tachenius see Partington, 1961: 291–6.

[15] On Kunckel see Maurach, 1933, and Ganzenmüller, 1956: 192–202.

[16] On Becker see Hassinger, 1951.

the status of medical chemistry in Germany, for their interests were primarily pharmaceutical. Their careers, and those of the others just listed, revolve around a medical chemistry which was verging on the industrialization of drug production. Sala learned his chemistry in Venice, spent some time in its rival manufacturing centre, Amsterdam, and wrote a series of books on the principal medico-chemical materials, vitriol, antimony, tartar, opium, etc. Tachenius's *Hippocrates chymicus* (1666), although ostensibly a theoretical work, is most important for the light it casts on the industrialization of drug production in Venice, in which he was himself engaged. Glauber operated a manufacturing establishment in Amsterdam, and his *Philosophical furnaces* (1646–48) was the first comprehensive treatise on industrial chemistry outside of metallurgy. Kunkel, although his frequently interrupted career seems to have alternated between the practice of pharmacy and that of alchemy, is best known as an authority on glass-technology, and ended his life as Minister of Mines to the King of Sweden.

Becher, however, had the most varied career. He was the son of a Lutheran minister at Spire, left fatherless at the age of thirteen, but who nevertheless managed to educate himself while supporting his mother and three brothers by the practice of several handicrafts. He began editing and writing books at the age of nineteen and was still at it on his death twenty-eight years later, having covered such various subjects as alchemy, the promotion of German colonization in America, and, of course, chemical theory, where Stahl gave him immortality by adopting his system of elements. Although he was a theorist in chemistry and a one-time professor of medicine (Mainz), Becher's involvement in 'practical' matters seems to have differed from that of the others chiefly in the scale of his ambitions. He appears repeatedly in connection with promotional projects, among which were a government monopoly in the cloth trade at Munich, the establishment of a silk factory in Vienna, a 'psychological community' at Mecklenberg-Gustrow, and a scheme presented to the Dutch government to recover gold from the sands of Holland. Just before his death he appeared as a mine inspector in England.

This was finally the period which saw the appearance in Germany of the works of Basil Valentine, the last of the remarkable series of apparently imaginary personages who played so prominent a role in the early history of chemistry. Scholarship has transmuted this supposed fifthteenth-century German monk into one or more obscure Germans of the seventeenth century who wrote under this pseudonym, on alchemy, medical chemistry, and other topics.[17] But even when he is moved to the period 1602–51, when the most important writings attributed to him appeared, Basil retains an importance as an innovator in chemistry comparable to that of the more tangible Germans just listed. A number of those innovations will be subsequently mentioned, without, however, seriously attempting to determine Basil's priority in this group.

As these careers indicate, Germany was an exporter of chemists, and while it can hardly be doubted that the practitioner enjoyed a more tranquil existence elsewhere there are few opportunities to test the assumption. After Biringuccio, Tachenius seems to have been the most notable chemical practitioner in Italy, and Glauber was pre-eminent in Holland. Germans, some of whom influenced Robert Boyle in the direction of chemistry, were prominent among those who founded the Royal Society of London.[18] Only in France, where we find a series of independent chemical practitioners from about 1610, was there a substantial group of chemists outside of Germany, and their significance is principally in their involvement in the teaching of chemistry.

Palissy's lectures on 'natural history and physics', from 1575 to 1584, would seem to deserve a place in the history of the teaching of chemistry, if their content is fairly represented by his *Discours admirables*. But while chemistry tended everywhere to be the hand-maiden of pharmacy, the connection was especially close in France. Sedan and Montpellier seem to have been centres of the teaching of chemistry,[19] but the centre of French chemistry was to be – notwithstanding the unyielding opposition of the medical faculty –

[17] On Basil Valentine and the problem he has presented to historians of chemistry, see Partington, 1961: 183–203.

[18] Samuel Hartlib, Theodore Haak, and Henry Oldenberg were the most famous (see Stimson, 1940). Of Boyle's laboratory assistants (on whom see Maddison, 1955) two of the most important, Peter Sthael and A. G. Hanckwitz, were Germans.

[19] On chemistry at Montpellier see Astruc, 1767 and Germain, 1882, I have found nothing more than passing mention of the Protestant academy at Sedan, where Le Fevre and de Maets, among other chemists, studied. Its foundation, apparently in the 1570s, is barely mentioned in Peyran's history of Sedan, where it is indicated that the school flourished during the period (1598–1685) when the Edict of Nantes was in force (Peyran, 1826: 161–2).

Paris. The first chemical teacher of more than local importance was Jean Beguin (fl. 1605–15),[20] who offered lectures in Paris towards the end of the first decade of the seventeenth century. His course dealt with the production of chemical medicines, and his *Tyrocinium chymicum* of 1610 was to be the prototype of numerous French textbooks through the remainder of the century. Beguin died before 1620, but his book was to go on through fifty editions before the end of the seventeenth century.[21] The tradition continued, and found its most successful practitioner in Nicolas Lemery (1645–1715),[22] who, after offering lectures for several years in Montpellier, brought them to Paris in 1672, where he is said to have lectured to great crowds, not only of his countrymen, but of foreign visitors, and even women.

But before the middle of the century chemistry had found a tolerant institution in Paris, at the King's botanical garden (Jardin du Roi).[23] This predecessor of the famous Museum d'Histoire Naturelle was proposed to the King in 1618 by Jean Riolan, a prominent member of the Paris Faculty of Medicine. Riolan, who was a violent anti-Paracelsian, had in mind only an herb garden, but when the Jardin was actually established in 1635 its organization was determined by the king's personal physicians, who looked on chemistry with more favour. In 1648 a demonstrator of chemistry was engaged, in the person of Guillaume Davisson (William Davidson), a Scotch Paracelsian. He was succeeded in 1651 by Nicolas Le Fevre (1615–69), and he in turn by Christopher Glaser, who served from 1660 to 1671. But although this post was to be occupied in the next century by many of the most famous chemists in France, the seventeenth-century incumbents remained rigorously

[20] On Beguin see Patterson, 1937, Thorndike, HMES, Vol. 8: 106–16, and Multhauf in Farber, 1961: 67–79. Kent and Hannaway (1960) have recently shown that Beguin's material is in part copied from Libavius.

[21] I have not seen the first (unauthorized) edition of 1610 nor Beguin's first edition of 1612. I have used the editions of 1618, 1620, 1656, and 1669. According to Patterson (1937) the latter, an English translation, is taken from the 1612 edition. Beguin, 1618, is also from the 1612 edition, edited with additions by Johann Hartmann, under the name Ch. Glückradt. Beguin, 1620, in French, is an expansion of Beguin's own French edition of 1615 by J. L. de Roi. Beguin, 1656, is descended from a 1634 edition by J. G. Pelshofer, which was based on two editions of 1618, Hartmann's and another of Johannes Barth. See further in Patterson, 1937 and Thorndike, HMES, Vol. 8: 106–16.

[22] On Lemery see Cap, 1839, and the Éloge of Fontenelle (1715–1).

[23] On the history of chemistry at the Jardin du Roi see Contant, 1952.

practical chemists, concerned with little more than laboratory instruction in medical chemistry, and played a surprisingly slight role in the development of the science.

Little more significant was the first chair of chemistry at a European university, the chair of 'iatrochemistry' established at Marberg in 1609 and occupied for about seven years by Johann Hartmann, who has already been mentioned as an important Paracelsian physician.[24] But there was at least one earlier instance of academic chemistry in Germany, for Andreas Libavius (d. 1616)[25] probably offered lectures on that subject at Rothenberg an der Tauber from about 1592. Although Libavius had previously been Professor of history and poetry at Jena, he was already busily engaged in the compilation of a series of gigantic tomes which were to make him one of the most prolific chemical writers of all times. And although oriented towards medical chemistry these books are quite unlike those of Hartmann and the French chemists. Libavius' books would not be very useful as recipe books, for the recipes are buried in a mass of erudition and theorizing. He was clearly concerned to know the meaning of it all, and he pursues this meaning through the innumerable volumes of the Peripatetics and Paracelsians, adding the evidences of his own laboratory and amassing a heap of ore and slag which few, if any, successors have had the courage to rework.[26]

An intellectual successor to Libavius appeared in Daniel Sennert (1572–1637), who was professor of medicine at Wittemberg from 1602 until his death.[27] Only two of Sennert's numerous works deal with chemistry, but they reveal a comparable erudition and an equal propensity for amassing evidence beyond the point of his ability to rationalize it. However, Sennert, unlike Libavius, seems to have been an influential teacher of chemistry, for he can be connected with most of the leading German professors of chemistry

[24] See above, p. 224. See also Thorndike, HMES, Vol. 8: 116–18, and Ganzenmüller, 1941. Hartmann edited the works of two more important chemists, Beguin and Croll.

[25] On Libavius see Darmstaedter in Bugge, 1929: 107–24, Multhauf in Farber, 1961: 67–79, and Partington, 1961: 244–67.

[26] Partington (1961) seems to have revealed for the first time the scope of Libavius' literary production. He mentions 22 titles. Kopp (1843–47) had mentioned only 4, Ferguson (1906) mentioned 9 and Darmstaedter (in Bugge, 1929) listed 7. I have only used 3 (see bibliography), but they are the most important.

[27] Sennert deserves a biography. He is considered, from three points of view, in Lasswitz, 1890, Vol. 1: 436–54, Thorndike, HMES, Vol. 7: 203–17, and Partington, 1961: 271–6.

into the early eighteenth century. One of his students was Guerner Rolfinck (1599–1673), whose laboratory, opened at Jena in 1641, has been called the first university laboratory.[28] Rolfinck was a celebrated anatomist, but also professor of chemistry at Jena from 1641 to 1673. He was succeeded in this post by one of his students, Georg W. Wedel (1645–1721), who was the teacher of Friedrich Hoffmann (1660–1742) and Georg E. Stahl (1660–1734), teachers at Jena and two of the most famous chemists in Germany in the early eighteenth century. Another of Sennert's followers was Jacob Barner (1641–86), who was one of no less than three professors of medicine at Leipzig (the other two being Michael Ettmuller [1644–83] and Jean Bohn [1640–1718]) who wrote on chemistry and perhaps lectured on it.[29]

Chemistry was of little consequence in universities outside of Germany. It achieved some kind of official status towards the end of the century, at Montpellier (1673), Oxford (1683), Utrecht (1694), Leyden (1702), and Cambridge (1703), but these dates represent in each case the termination of a kind of infiltration extending over several decades.

Medicine was again the excuse for the introduction of chemistry. The hostility towards chemistry which prevailed at the University of Paris was, not surprisingly, ameliorated at its institutional rival, Montpellier, but mainly in the toleration of apothecaries who lectured on chemistry. Lemery and other prominent Paris chemists owed much of their education to the Montpellier lecturers. Such lecturers were inextricably involved with the university, for the faculty of medicine had been given the duty of fixing ordnances for the local apothecaries as early as the fifteenth century, and was later given the task of presiding at the examination of apothecaries.[30] The university, moreover, established a chair of 'surgery and pharmacy'

[28] See Partington, 1961: 312–14. There is a biography by his pupil, Georg Wedel, which I have not seen (*Vita W. Rolfinkii*, Jena, 1674).

[29] Barner wrote a medical work, *Forerunner of the new Sennert* (*Prodromus Sennerti novi*, 1674) but could hardly have been Sennert's student (cf. Partington, 1961: 377) if, as appears, he was born four years after Sennert's death.

[30] See Germain, 1882. On a visit to Montpellier in 1664 John Ray remarked that 'The number of apothecaries in this little city is scarce credible' (1738, Vol. 1: 389). The Paris professor, Jean Riolan – as antipathetic to chemistry as to Montpellier – classed chemistry among the 'mechanic arts' which made it possible for 'young barbers and surgeons of Paris, having little Latin, to be received as doctors in Montpellier' (1651: 179–80).

in 1597, and a number of persons, including Nicolas Lemery, seem to have given chemical lectures there; but these were apparently unofficial, for the teaching of chemistry at Montpellier is dated from 1673, when Jean Matte La Faveur was appointed Royal demonstrator of chemistry. The faculty objected to the irregularity of lectures in a subject for which there was no professor, with the result that a chair of chemistry was established two years later.[31]

In England we find one of Boyle's German assistants, Peter Sthael (d. c. 1675), lecturing at Oxford from 1659 to 1664, but official chemistry began at that institution only in 1682, when Elias Ashmole included a laboratory in his new museum and Robert Plot (1640–96), whose contributions to science were principally in natural history, was appointed professor of chemistry.[32] Cambridge had been the home of some of England's more celebrated alchemists (John Dee, Samuel Norton), and was the scene of Newton's feverish chemical experimentation, but not until 1683 does it seem to have had a chemical lecturer. This was a self-trained Italian chemist, John Francis Vigani (d. 1713), who began to give private lectures in Cambridge in that year and persisted until the university gave him the title of professor in 1703.[33]

Chemical instruction seems to have proliferated in Holland in the 1660s.[34] An apothecary named Carolus L. van Maets (Dematius) was lecturing at Utrecht in 1668. At the instigation of François de la Böe Sylvius (1614–72), perhaps the most famous medical teacher of the later seventeenth century – and a zealot for chemistry – Leyden established a chemical laboratory 'in the corner of the botanical garden', and Maets came there as first 'demonstrator' in 1669.[35] On Maets' death (1690?) the position of 'prefectus laboratorii

[31] Astruc, 1767: 69. Germain, 1882. The chair was not given to La Faveur, but to one of the Professors of Medicine!

[32] On Sthael see Turnbull, 1953. On chemistry at Oxford see Robert T. Gunther, 1923–45, Vol. 1: 1–86. On Plot see ibid., Vol. 8: 2–12, 333–418, and F. S. Taylor, 1949, where it is shown that Plot practised alchemy.

[33] On chemistry at Cambridge, see Gunther, 1937: 217–38. On Vigani see Peck, 1934 and Coleby, 1952.

[34] On chemical teaching in Holland see Jorissen, 1919. Thorndike, HMES, Vol. 8: 163–5. Partington, 1961: 236–8.

[35] On Sylvius see Frank Baker, 1909 and Baumann, 1949. Hirsch, BL, is not clear as to when Sylvius began teaching at Leyden, but Ray (1738, Vol. 1: 30) lists him with the medical faculty in 1663.

chymico' was given to Jacob Le Mort, who had been Maets's assistant and may have begun his chemical studies under Glauber. Le Mort's successor (in 1714) was to be one of the most notable figures in eighteenth-century chemistry, Hermann Boerhaave (1668–1738), but although Boerhaave was a student at Leyden from 1684 he seems not to owe his chemical instruction to Maets or Le Mort, but to another Leyden chemist, one Mr Stam.[36] In the meantime Utrecht acquired, in 1694, the services of another excellent chemical teacher, Johann C. Barchausen (1666–1723).

One further factor in the seventeenth-century establishment of the chemist remains to be considered, the scientific society. This institution grew out of the genesis of a personal interest in the arts and sciences among some of the princes who employed artisans and scientists. Perhaps the earliest of these scientist-princes was Wilhelm' IV, Landgraf of Hesse from 1567 to 1592, who was a patron of such early luminaries of the scientific revolution as Tycho Brahe and Joost Burgi, and who joined them in astronomical observations and assembled a collection of instruments. His son Mortiz (Landgraf from 1592 to 1627) extended this interest into chemistry,[37] and other princes followed suit, including Ferdinand and Leopold da Medici, patrons of the famous Accademia del Cimento, whose interest in chemistry is certified by surviving documents.[38] Another laboratory was maintained by the Duke of Orleans, brother of Louis XIV of France,[39] and in England King Charles II had one in the Royal Palace.[40] That these laboratories left no mark on the history of chemistry is less important than the fact that they existed, for they bespeak an interest in science which was to lead some of these illustrious princes to lend more significant support to its pursuit.

[36] On Boerhaave see Burton, 1746. Burton calls Stam 'an eminent chemist then at Leyden', and says that Boerhaave had been giving private courses in chemistry for 14 years, when he succeeded Le Mort (Op. cit.: 16, 37).

[37] On Landgraf Wilhelm IV see Kirchvogel, in Artelt, 1953: 12–18. On the interest of his successor in chemistry see Kirchvogel, 1954.

[38] A 'fonderia farmaceutica' seems to have existed in the Medici household from the time of Cosimo I. (Cf. Targioni-Tozzetti, 1852: 208, 239.) Chemical apparatus is mentioned in an inventory preserved as MS Guardroba No. 509, Archivio di Stato di Firenze.

[39] Ornstein, 1928: 55–6.

[40] It is mentioned by Pepys (1953, Vol. 3: 335), Sorbiere (1666: 67) and Sprat (1667: 149). The important French chemists Nicolas Le Fevre and Moise Charas, both refugees from religious persecution, worked in this laboratory (see Partington, 1962: 17, 27).

There were also among educated persons in the more advanced countries informal associations for scientific discussion and experiment, the earliest of which was a club for experimentation in natural science organized at Naples towards the end of the sixteenth century by G. B. della Porta. The most famous was the Accademia del Cimento, which existed in Florence from 1657 to 1667, and which was the scene of pioneering experimental work in physics and meteorology.[41]   The Medici brothers supported this undertaking, which commanded the talents of Toricelli and others of Galileo's students. The understandable difficulty of maintaining over an extended period such a combination of princely favour and scientific virtuosity is sufficient to account for the ephemeral character of this and most other early scientific societies. Some did survive, however, and have indeed done so to the present day, notably the Royal Society of London and the Académie des Sciences of Paris.

An interest in chemistry is decidedly less conspicuous among the members of the more successful societies than it is on the part of some of their royal patrons. Both the Medici and King Charles II dabbled in chemistry, but the scientific virtuosi who assembled under their patronage were more addicted to what King Charles described with some disappointment as 'weighing air'.[42] Chemists had been considerably more prominent in the two informal groups which had been meeting intermittently at London and Oxford since about 1645 than they were in the Royal Society as finally constituted.[43] In France chemists seem to have been in ill repute even among those who initiated the meetings leading to formation of the Académie. Marin Mersenne, who had used an 'alchemist' as the butt of his critical analysis of the science of the time,[44] was the principal moving spirit, and associated mainly with mathematicians and physicists. When in 1666, however, it occurred to Colbert, the famous minister of Louis XIV, to emulate the English in forming a royal scientific

[41] On the Italian societies see Ornstein, 1928: 73–90.

[42] According to Samuel Pepys' diary, under Feb. 1, 1663/4 (Pepys, 1953, Vol. 1: 482).

[43] Such chemists as Robert Child, Benjamin Worsley, George Starkey, Peter Sthael and Frederick Clodius (cf. Marie Boas, 1958: 24–5) were not taken into the Royal Society. A. G. Hanckwitz was in 1729, and, curiously, so had been the Jardin du Roi chemist, Le Fevre, in 1663, at which time he was a Protestant refugee working in the King's laboratory. Hanckwitz published one paper in the *Philosophical Transactions*, Le Fevre, none.

[44] Mersenne, 1625, Bk 1.

academy, he preferred 'skilled men' to 'scholars', and did include two chemists among its initial twenty-one members, the king's physician, S. C. DuClos (d. 1715) and an apothecary, Claude Bourdelin (1621–99).[45]

The earliest attempt at a German society,[46] the 'Societas Ereunetica' of Rostock, apparently predates anything similar outside of Italy, but it lasted only from 1622 to 1624. Its founder, Joachim Jungius (1587–1657)[47] was a distinguished botanist, but ranged over the whole of the sciences and has in modern times been esteemed for his general views on natural philosophy. He was no less distinguished than the progenitors of the English and French societies, Bacon and Mersenne, but found, as did most of his successors in Germany, that the scientific society could not flourish under the political and social circumstances of central Europe in the seventeenth century. Another German society was established in 1651, the 'Collegium naturae curiosorum', and this one still exists today, under the name 'Academia Caesarea Leopoldina' which it adopted in 1687 to secure the favour of the Austrian Emperor. This society, however, was loosely organized to the degree that its headquarters moved about with the homes of its presidents and its functions scarcely extended beyond the publication of a learned journal. In 1672 a society in imitation of the Florentine academy was established at the University of Altdorf, under the name 'Collegium curiosorum sive experimentale'.

In terms of the number of chemists, university teachers, and the number of scientific societies, Germany gained a conspicuous ascendency in Europe in the course of the seventeenth century. There was scarcely a more propitious environment than existed at the University of Altdorf in the 1680s, where there was an astronomical observatory and laboratories for physics and chemistry, and where the Professor of Physics, Johann Christopher Sturm (1635–1703), headed the Collegium curiosorum sive experimentale while the chemist, Johann Moritz Hoffmann (1653–1727), was president of the Collegium naturae curiosorum.[48] If the published remains of

[45] See Bertrand, 1869: 1–4. Ornstein, 1928: 145–7, also gives a list of the first members.
[46] On German societies see Ornstein, 1928: 165–97.
[47] On Jungius see Wohlwill, 1887, and Partington, 1961: 415–22. The fundamental account is C. G. Guhrauer, *Joachim Jungius und seine Zeitalter*, Stuttgart and Tübingen, 1850, which I have not seen.
[48] See S. Günther, 1881.

these years are not especially significant, they are hardly inferior to those contemporaneously issued in London and Paris, but the German effort, as events proved, had reached its apogee. Neither the universities nor the societies were able to sustain an expansion of scientific research. Sturm's society faded away with the death of its founder, the journal of the Collegium naturae curiosorum passed into other hands, and Altdorf lapsed into the status of a provincial German university.

The relative absence of the anti-Paracelsian prejudice which reigned in medical faculties elsewhere favoured the establishment of chemistry in the German universities, but had far less consequence for the science of chemistry than might be expected. The number of universities in Germany, in consequence of the religious conflicts of the time, increased in the seventeenth century from seventeen to thirty-nine,[49] but they were very small, and staffed by faculties burdened with a heavy load of variegated duties. Thus at Jena, Rolfinck taught anatomy, surgery, botany and practical medicine, as well as chemistry. Like almost all German professors of chemistry, his principal title was that of Professor of Medicine, and as the century advanced German professors of medicine compensated for their tolerance of Paracelsianism with an increasing hostility to the acid–alkali doctrines of François Sylvius. In chemistry the books of the German professors, with the sole exception of Stahl, became sources of important but incidental observations which were left to be harvested by others. But if chemistry was in the German universities pursued less effectively than one might expect, they were certainly in this regard not behind the universities in the rest of Europe. It was the scientific society which was to prove the most effective environment for chemistry as for the other sciences, and although Germany produced the majority of chemists it was the failure of Germany to develop, prior to the mid-eighteenth century, a scientific society comparable to those in London and Paris which primarily accounts for their failure to play a larger role in the genesis of the science of chemistry.

The Royal Society of London also failed to reach its potentiality in chemistry, for although it numbered among its members such notable chemists as Boyle, Digby, Mayow and Newton, only the

[49] Ornstein, 1928: 226–7.

first of these published anything on chemistry in the *Philosophical Transactions*. Boyle published twenty-four chemical papers in the *Transactions* between the first issue and his death in 1690, and was its most prolific chemical author. After him come the zoologist Martin Lister (1683?-1712) and a physician-chemist, Frederick Slare (1647?-1727), neither of whom has been given more than a footnote in the history of chemistry. Most of their papers were on organic chemistry.[50] Thus the *Philosophical Transactions* gives a surprisingly poor reflection of chemistry in England during the seventeenth century, and was, if anything, even less significant in this science during the early part of the following century. It is well known that the Royal Society received little financial support from its royal patron and was essentially an association of gentlemen, but this hardly accounts for the failure of such as Digby and Newton to publish in its transactions. Comparing the Royal Society with the Paris Academy one is struck, as George has pointed out, with the almost total lack of pharmacist members in the London group;[51] for it was the members of the Paris Academy who were professionally connected with pharmacy who gave a continuity to its chemical studies which finally gave them the respectability of natural philosophy in the eighteenth century.

Although Colbert had sought out skilled men rather than scholars for the Académie des Sciences, and had provided them with a financial support contrasting markedly with the conditions obtaining in London, the history of chemistry in the early days of the Paris Academy was much like that in London. DuClos and Bourdelin had little more impact on science than did Lister and Slare, and there was no Boyle in Paris. But a crucial event in the history of chemistry came in the last decade of the century, when the Académie des Sciences began the systematic appointment of the leading chemists of France. Since its establishment in 1666 only one additional chemist had been appointed, another of the king's physicians, Pierre Borel. Then, in 1692, it appointed the seventy-four-year-old Moyse Charas, who had been Glaser's successor as chemist at the Jardin two decades earlier, and in 1694 added the newly designated Jardin demonstrator, G. F. Boulduc. In 1699 even Lemery was appointed.

[50] Cf. George, 1952. Only 6 or 7 papers by all three men were on inorganic chemistry.
[51] Ibid.

The motivation for this sudden interest in chemistry may have been the influence of an appointee of 1691, Wilhelm Homberg (1672–1712).[52] Born in Java of German parents, Homberg held degrees in law (Leipzig) and medicine (Padua), had studied physics with Otto von Guericke and chemistry with Boyle, and was to make chemistry his special subject at the Paris Academy. Although he died at the age of forty, Homberg's contributions were to rival Boyle's in volume, and were moreover not to remain similarly isolated, for from this time the chemical demonstrators of the Jardin du Roi were usually members of the Academy, and they established the dialogue of continuous investigation which has characterized modern science. Their enumeration reads like a roll-call of fame in French chemistry, including Louis Lemery, E. F. Geoffroy, Pierre Macquer, H. M. Rouelle, and A. F. de Fourcroy, the last two being Lavoisier's teacher and one of his principal collaborators.

[52] On Homberg see Fontenelle, 1715-2.

Chapter Thirteen

On matter and its changes

AMONG the earliest Greek philosophers a universal materialism was the principal obstacle to the elucidation of questions of the nature of matter and the causes and mechanism of its changes. From this natural philosophy was liberated by Plato and Aristotle, but from the point of view of the modern science of matter they went too far; for in the dichotomy they established (in different ways) between heaven and earth, they put matter in one and the causes of its changes in the other, giving the two aspects of the fundamental problem of chemistry a separateness which persisted for over two thousand years. The attempt of the alchemists to heal this dichotomy smacked as much of pre-Hellenic primitivism as it did of philosophical innovation, and remained throughout the Christian era an unfulfilled hope, in natural philosophy as well as in gold-making. The natural philosopher had finally to rescue himself from the dilemma.

The improvement of Aristotle's rationalization of the theory of the nature of matter proved a problem of immense difficulty, and arguments about it proved to be remarkably circular. Rejection of the four elements was almost invariably qualified. Some in denying them simply reverted to the question of the primal material and, as we see from the ancient atomists to Descartes, used the four elements as intermediate, but still somehow fundamental, building blocks in the formation of 'things'.

Others, notably the chemists of all varieties, tended to relegate the four elements to limbo, without denying them, and postulated principles, posterior to the elements and admittedly made of those elements. One would not suppose that Aristotle would have found much to disagree with in either of these modifications of his theory.

Humanist learning put the Europeans of the sixteenth and seventeenth centuries in possession of the bulk of ancient literature on natural philosophy and gave them a full awareness of the extent of ancient differences of opinion. The Swiss polymath Conrad Gesner found that there had been eight systems of elements between Thales and Empedocles![1] Liberated from the illusion of the monolithic character of ancient philosophy the Peripatetics and their adversaries alike set themselves to reshuffling the elements of Aristotle. Cardan reduced them to three, claiming that fire is either a mode of motion or mere burning air. Telesio decided that there were only two, which he called heat and cold, and Helmont, although he admitted two elements, managed to derive 'all things' from water.[2]

The practical chemists were not without opinions on this question, which consistently came up in the introductory chapters to their textbooks. They were generally less dogmatic, probably because of a lesser concern with ancient philosophical controversies. Jean Beguin finds an intuitive correspondence between the chemist's mercury, sulphur and salt, and a series of traditional triads, body, soul and spirit, bitter, sweet and acid, etc.[3] His editors generally expanded this excellent idea. Hartmann (Glückradt) added the Platonic God, Ideal, and sensible worlds (Deum, Exemplar, et Materia). De Roi pointed out that 'nothing is more necessary in all of the arts and sciences than a recognition of their principles', and added that the physicist and physician each have their own principles (respectively, matter and form, and the four elements), so why should the chemist not enjoy his own, namely the three principles?[4]

[1] 1586: 29.

[2] Cardano, 1556: 20v.–21v. 1559: 46 (Bk 2). Helmont, 1648–1: 105–9 (Ch. 9). Telesio, 1586: 2–4 (Bk 1, Ch. 1).

[3] Beguin, 1669: 22. This is an English translation of the 1612 edition (see above, Ch. 12 n. 21).

[4] These additions to Beguin's text appear in Beguin, 1618: 49–50 (Hartmann's ed.) and Beguin, 1620: 26–30 (de Roi's ed.).

It had long been supposed that analysis by fire should enable the chemist to obtain the Paracelsian principles, and his inability to demonstrate this, especially with metals, was to be the source of much of Boyle's scepticism. Beguin observes that chemical analysis of mista yields, in addition to mercury, sulphur and salt, two others which the chemists had not regarded as principles, namely phlegm and *terra damnata* or *caput mortum* – that is, earth.[5] This is perhaps our earliest reference to what became towards the end of the seventeenth century the most popular system of elements, and which was the most radical and influential innovation in the doctrine of elements since the alchemists of antiquity. It was far more empirical than the system of Paracelsian principles, being based directly on the supposition that destructive distillation divides a substance into its elemental components.

The theory of five elements marks a significant intrusion of the chemist into the arena of theory. Beguin refers to the 'fact', which was a commonplace among chemists, that the 'principles' are not really simple, for each contains some of the others (mercury contains the substance of sulphur and salt, etc.), and he differentiates these three from the other two products of destructive distillation, water and earth, on the ground that the latter two *are* simple. On this peculiar distinction the five-element theory was to be stranded for a generation, a delay which undoubtedly owed something to the 'condemnation of 1624'.

In August 1624 it became known in Paris that five 'theses' were to be defended at the house of a nobleman, François de Soucy, denying the primal material, substantial forms, privation, and holding the sublunary world to be made of two 'elements', earth and water, and 'mixts' of five entities, earth, water, mercury, sulphur and salt. The hearers were dispersed at the order of Parliament, and one of the principals, Etienne de Clave, was arrested.[6] In referring with approval, in the following year, to the condem-

---

[5] Beguin, 1669: 23–4, and in all other editions known to me. I have translated as 'chemical analysis' a phrase which appears in the Latin editions as '*spagyrica mistorum αναζοιχειωσει*' and in the French as '*la spargerique resolution des mixtes*'. Cardano had earlier claimed his three elements to be the products of analysis by distillation (1556: 21v [Bk 2]).

[6] On the condemnation of 1624 I have relied on Mersenne, 1625: 78–83; Mersenne, 1932: 167–8 (Editor's annotation); and on Thorndike, HMES, Vol. 7: 185–7, where reference is made to other sources unavailable to me.

nation of these 'alchemical' ideas, Mersenne added his disapprobation of such philosophical innovators as Patrizi, Basso, and Gorlaeus.[7] Thus the distinctly chemical notion of the five elements was joined together with atomism and other anti-Peripatetic ideas.

Basso had referred to the five elements in 1621, but had rejected earth and water as 'useless'.[8] The chemists Davisson and Glaser were to do the same, the former calling earth and water useless and the latter naming mercury, sulphur and salt as 'active' and water and earth as 'passive'.[9] But we find a more-or-less full acceptance of all five as elementary, in a meaningful sense, by Willis (in 1659), whom Stahl credits with originating the system,[10] and, although Boyle mentioned the system (in passing) as being as defective as that of the 'vulgar chymists',[11] it was accepted by Le Fevre and Lemery.[12] It was consistently demonstrated through the distillation of organic matter, with the collection of the appropriate (real or imaginary) fractions, and was, as Boyle said, as defective as the Paracelsian system. But it was at least empirical,[13] and required as an answer to criticism of its application to the mineral kingdom only a change of the names. This was accomplished by Becher and Stahl.

Becher wavered between systems of two, three, four, and five elements,[14] and his final conclusion remained beclouded until clarified by Stahl. Their five elements were called air, water, terra fluida, terra pinguis, and lapis fusilis.[15] Here was a system relatively impervious to criticism of its application to the mineral kingdom in

[7] Mersenne, loc. cit.

[8] 1621: 35–6.

[9] Davisson, 1660: 360–1. Glaser, 1673: 6.

[10] Willis, 1659: 3–4 (De fermentatione, Ch. 1). Stahl, 1730: 4.

[11] That is, as the three-element system. He (rightly) felt that ignition might in some cases result in synthesis rather than analysis (1772, Vol. 1: 544–5 [Sceptical chymist]).

[12] Le Fevre, 1664: 19–20. Nicolas Lemery, 1677: 4.

[13] It was the method of analysis by dry distillation, which was used in the analysis of organic materials as late as the time of Fourcroy—that is, the end of the eighteenth century (see Nierenstein, 1934).

[14] For an analysis of Becher's complex and inconsistent doctrine of elementary composition see Kopp, 1875: 201–10; Partington, 1961: 643–7; and Hassinger, 1951.

[15] On the involved reasoning which leads Stahl to these 'principles' see Stahl, 1746–7, Pt. 1: 3–8. 1730: 3–12. After alluding to the five elements, he reverts to consideration of the number of principles which the multitude of mixta may logically be supposed to require. Logic is interrupted by his preference for Becher, whose theory of the composition of terrestrial bodies he reports to postulate an elementary water and three 'earths' (Becher's elementary 'air' was as intangible as Helmont's). Stahl thinks four more than necessary, but

part because of its avoidance of the use of identifiable names such as mercury and sulphur and in part because it provided three 'earthy' elements against one in the earlier system. The terra pinguis became the celebrated phlogiston, and this 'phlogiston theory', as is well known, achieved nearly universal acceptance in the eighteenth century and was only put down by the followers of Lavoisier after a vigorous debate.

We may suspect, however, that the success of the phlogiston system owed something to a general decline of interest in the question of elements. In the light of his own subsequent work, we must assume that Boyle's conclusion, in the *Sceptical chymist*, that we do not know what the elements of bodies may be, carried the implication that it doesn't much matter. Like Becher, who said that everything on earth is compounded and that compounds (*composita*) are 'earths' produced through the mixture of simpler 'species of earth',[16] Boyle, and most chemists after him, was principally interested in the constitution and interrelationship of compounds.

The compounded substance

In their arguments on mixis and crasis the Stoics and Peripatetics of late antiquity came nearer to the establishment of a tenable theory of the compounded substance than did any of their successors through the sixteenth century. But they did so only on the most abstract level. The question of compounding was naturally involved in confusion by the relativity of the concept of element, and the chemical examples of either party were the easiest point of attack by the other. As more chemical examples were introduced by al-chemists, physicians, and natural philosophers, the confusion itself was compounded.

The ancients, to whom chemistry was but one aspect of a multi-faceted problem, had worried about which of a number of terms signifying mixture should be held to describe that transient mixture, the chemical compound. The writers of the Middle Ages accepted one of these terms, mixis (mistio), and took a different approach

accepts it 'till time shall make further discoveries'. Chemists continued to derive independently what were essentially the same five elements (cf. Barner, 1689: 14–34).

[16] 1669: 43.

to the explanation of the transformation of one substance into another. They assigned it to a change of 'form', and were led by the further pursuit of this line of thought to consider the smallest possible particle of a substance, beyond which it could not maintain its form. This was their 'natural minimum'.

The combination of ancient and 'modern' learning tended to produce a strange compound in the mind of the Renaissance scholar. The additional burden placed on Aristotle is already indicated in Pomponazzi's book of 'doubts' concerning the fourth book of the *Meteorology*, where he shows himself to be troubled by the problem of reconciling Aristotle with 'the alchemists' not only on such traditional questions as the coagulation of oil and the Peripatetics' multiple digestions, but on others such as the distillation of bricks and the physiological action of mercury taken internally.[17] Gesner, in his treatise on classification, differentiates the elements, meteorological phenomena, and chemical compounds as simple, mixed, and perfectly mixed bodies, but when he takes up mixtion he denies that it is involved in such phenomena as burning wood or animal digestion.[18] In the writing of Agricola and Cardano, however, these questions were finally taken out of the context of the commentary on Aristotle (although not out of the environment of Aristotelian thought) and, no less important, out of the context of organic phenomena. They gave special attention to the classification of the various 'mista' found in mineralogy.

Agricola's *De natura fossilium*, published in 1546, is characterized by perspicacious speculation on the origin of ore deposits and by an unprecedented clarity in its description of specific minerals which has led Hoover to call it 'the first attempt at systematic mineralogy'.[19] Accepting the Peripatetic four elements and the Aristotelian subterranean exhalations, Agricola differentiates 'minerals' from the exhalations which form them, on the one hand, and from mixtures (in our sense) on the other, on the ground that 'minerals are solidified from particles of the same substance, such as pure gold'. He subdivides minerals, thus defined, into 'simple' (earths, congealed

[17] Pomponazzi: 1563: 'Doubts' 46, 96, 105.

[18] This contradiction arises in the fact that he is in the first instance concerned to separate 'hexis' (on which see above, p. 74) into several degrees, and in the second to differentiate mixis, alteration, and generation (Gesner, 1586: 19–21, 110–2).

[19] In his Introduction to Agricola, 1912.

juices, stones and metals) and 'compound' minerals.[20] As a system of classification this is a modest advance on Avicenna and Albertus. Its merit resides largely in Agricola's subsequent care in the description of individual minerals. In its physico-chemical basis it scarcely represents any advance at all, for his 'compound' minerals would appear to be compounds of simple minerals which are themselves compounds of the two exhalations which are in turn compounds of the four elements. But in turning these rationalizations to bear directly on the mineral kingdom Agricola at least moved the discussion fully into the consideration of inorganic chemical phenomena.

Cardano makes use of Agricola's book in his own discussion of the same topic, which appeared four years later. All mista, declares Cardano, are either earthy, as are stones and plants, or watery, such as milk and oil, or completely (plane) mixed, as are animal bodies. He decides that there are four kinds of mista in the earth, namely Agricola's 'simple' minerals, earths, juices, stones and metals. He further differentiates them according to their state (solid or liquid) and susceptibility to melting, and goes on to find eleven 'genera' of these four types, which he arrives at by simply combining them, the last being a juicy, stony, earthy metal![21] Although he digresses to pay his respects to the Peripatetic dogma on the composition of minerals out of the four elements (notwithstanding his denial of one of them), and to the notion of minerals as organic beings, his subsequent discussion of particular minerals remains within the context of his classification of mista. The specific minerals mentioned are the traditional ones, although Cardano remarks that he sees no reason why there should be fewer minerals than there are plants, which he numbers at about 500 kinds.[22]

Agricola's system continued to satisfy the mineralogists into the eighteenth century,[23] but innovation continued among the natural philosophers. In the seventeenth century Digby continued, in a

[20] Agricola, 1955: 17 (Bk 1).

[21] Cardano, 1556: 98r. 1559: 184 (Bk 5).

[22] 1556: 105v. 1559: 199 (Bk 5).

[23] Writing in 1714, the English authority, John Woodward, changed Agricola's system only superficially, dividing 'congealed juices' into 'salia' and 'bitumena', which Agricola had also done on a subordinate level of classification, and adding 'mineralia' (Agricola's mixed minerals) to the primary list of classes, which thus became six. Mercury, which Agricola had made a metal, is returned to the mineralia by Woodward, and a few other substances are shifted, for unknown reasons since he does not rationalize his classification (Woodward, 1714).

highly original manner, Cardano's attempt to classify minerals in terms of the four elements. He observes that there are several degrees of solidity in mixed bodies, and holds them to be based on solid particles of earth 'glued' together by water. If fire or air were the basic body, he perspicaciously remarks, compounds would either be continuously consumed or would be invisible. He proceeds to discuss the relative dominance of the elements in bodies. If water is the basis and earth predominant over the other two we get something like mud, dirt, honey or butter. If air is in excess in a watery compound the result is an inflammable oil, but if fire predominates, it will be such as a wine or distilled spirit. Taking earth as the basis and water predominant he sees the product as metal. If air is predominant the product is exemplified by the soil called mould, and if fire predominates in an earthy compound, it is a coagulated juice ('the succi concreti of the Latins') such as all kinds of salts, nitres, sulphurs and bitumens.[24]

These theories appear in a context of mineralogy, but are not significantly different from those voiced by chemists when dealing with the same subject. Dorn thought the formation of 'salts, chalcanthum, and various species of alum' to be incidents in the complex process of metal formation.[25] But the chemist in the sixteenth century was becoming less concerned with mineralogy and with naturally occurring materials. He was typically a medical chemist and was discovering in this period that artificial materials had become predominant in his repertoire. Such was the ideology of medical chemistry, however, that its practitioner had not thought of himself as dealing with simple and compounded substances, but with materials of varying degrees of purity. He dealt with the separation of the pure from the impure. By the heirs of John of Rupescissa the process of distillation was exploited to produce a hierarchy of increasingly pure substances terminating in the quintessence.[26] This ideology tended to carry the medical chemist into regions of fantasy akin to alchemy, but from these he was brought back to earth by the Paracelsians.

Paracelsus, in *Archidoxies*, attempted to systematize the un-

[24] Digby, 1645: 154–7 (Ch. 14).
[25] Dorn, 1568: 42.
[26] See Multhauf, 1956.

systematizable. In addition to quintessences it dealt with elements, arcana, magisteries, specifics, and elixirs, all of which were names given by earlier medical writers and alchemists to their favourite preparations. Elixirs had been the goal of the alchemists until the Latin Geber, who had seen fit to call most of his preparations magisteries. While the Rupescissans sought quintessences, the authors of books of secrets preferred, naturally enough, arcana. If their magisteries, quintessences, elixirs, arcana, and even elements, were often identical, that was a problem for the future to work out. The century after Paracelsus, however, witnessed the discovery of new substances at a rate which taxed the chemist's ability to name them, let alone to attend to their classification.

An important step was nevertheless taken by Libavius, who managed to reconcile the terminology with the fact that the majority of the additions to the chemist's armoury were not the spirits and quintessences dear to the heart of the distilling chemist, but were to be found among the residues despised by the ideology of separating the pure from the impure. Examining the Paracelsian categories Libavius found it convenient to distinguish:

1. Magisteries, or chemical species extracted from all extraneous material, worked to remove the external impurities, and 'exhaulted'.

2. Extracts, or what is extracted from solid bodies, leaving behind 'the crassness of the elements'.

3. Composite species, or that which is compounded from the prepared simple substances.[27]

Most of the lore of distillation chemistry appears in the second category, and here we find the waters, oils, and quintessences of his predecessors described in detail, in greater detail, in fact, than any of them had offered. But even the quintessence, although he calls it 'a mysterium exalted to the purity of the celestial nature', is rigorously restricted to its proper place, and that not a very prominent one, in his system of classification. A few salts also appear among the extracts, but it is chiefly among the magisteries that we find the roster of synthetic salts prepared by acid dissolution, to which the medical chemist owed the major part of his discoveries.

[27] Libavius, 1597: 85, 242, 409.

Libavius' *Alchimia* might be described as a *tour-de-force* on the chemistry of the mineral acids, and residues abound among the products of processes where he uses the acids variously to render the metals potable, powdered, fixed, volatile, calcined, vitrified, transmuted, and converted into 'crocus'.[28] Libavius' heroic effort to classify all of this led him into complexities equally cumbersome, but less imaginary, than those into which the distillation chemists had fallen. His contemporaries of a more practical and less theoretical bent, such as Beguin, found a solution sufficient to their needs in a loose system of naming artificial substances haphazardly from the raw materials involved, the process used, or the physico-chemical properties of the product. Most of the chemical textbooks of the seventeenth century were laboratory manuals of practical chemistry which emphasized proper techniques and left classification largely to the reader. As a rule dissolution yielded a liquor, volatilization a spirit, vitrification a glass, calcination a calx and precipitation a precipitate, but there were plenty of exceptions. Colours and textures led some substances to be known as 'flowers' or 'butters', or they became 'diaphoretic' or 'sudorific' from their observed physiological effects. The name of a supposed discoverer was often attached to his discovery. It was a century's accumulation of such substances which inspired the effort of Lavoisier and his associates to reform the nomenclature at the end of the eighteenth century.

On the cause and mechanism of change

The rise of Greek philosophy marked the expulsion of a host of celestial influences which earlier cosmogonists had seen as the causes of terrestrial events. To replace them various mechanisms were devised, through which a single divine agency could be supposed to power the world. Although plausible as an explanation of astronomical events such a mechanism proved inadequate to explain the multiplicity of mundane changes, and the Greek cosmologists found it necessary to readmit celestial influences and intangible fluids in increasing numbers as they attempted to penetrate the nature of 'things' in greater detail. They also found empirical evidences for

[28] Libavius, 1597: 91–8, 105–6, 111–3, 133–4, 144–5, 148–54, 158–60.

the existence of intangible fluids, in phenomena which we attribute to the gaseous state of matter, in electricity and magnetism, and, above all, in light. I have given these fluids and influences the generic name, emanations.

The dual role of emanations as matter and as energy led to the continuous reformulation of the concept. Aristotle had been relatively decisive in giving the role of energy to his 'contrarieties', hot, cold, wet and dry, and the role of matter to the four elements. By the time of the Jābirian alchemists, however, the Aristotelian contrarieties seem to have the place of matter, and are acted upon by the energies of celestial influences. The approach of Avicenna and the Latin Scholastics, on the other hand, through the intension and remission of forms, led finally to the conversion of an originally static concept into an emanation combining matter and energy, the 'substantial form'.

So firmly was Peripatetic causation associated in the sixteenth century with substantial forms that their denial became a sort of badge of the anti-Aristotelian. It was a cardinal point with Telesio, and Bruno, always something of an extremist, called form imperfect and corruptible, a perversion of matter, which is excellent and divine. Lest this give form more of a role than he intended, he adds that it loses its being when separated from matter.[29] Under this assault the idea of form underwent a transformation into something like its modern signification. Cardano tended to abandon form when he discussed specific materials.[30] Scaliger gave it something like its modern meaning,[31] as did Libavius, who merely admits that some phenomena, such as the malleability of metals, might better be referred to form than to any more specifically chemical cause.[32]

But the casting out of substantial forms raised again the question

[29] Telesio, 1910–23, Vol. 1: 107–11 (Bk 2, Ch. 1). Bruno, 1950–2: 157–8.

[30] It is the basis of his theory of mixtion (1556: 102r. 1559: 193 [Bk. 5]), but when discussing specific substances he tends to speak of genera, species, or 'kind', rather than of form (1556: 108v–120r. 1559: 204–25 [Bk 5]).

[31] He analyses mixta in terms of 'modes, grades, or species', and only brings in form where he tries to explain the sense in which a compound can be said to be one continuous body (1557: fols. 144–5 Exerc. 101 [De mistione, etc.]).

[32] He declares 'chemical species', rather than essentia, extracta, mysteria and the like to be the proper subject of chemistry. In consequence, 'form' appears in his system under the category of magistery of figure, polish, etc. (see Libavius, 1597: 90–91. 1615: 4).

of the cause of chemical change, and this problem had very much to do with the equivocal character of the particulate theories of the sixteenth and seventeenth centuries, as in their consistent amalgamation of 'atoms' and 'seeds'. The complicated 'minima' of that strident anti-Peripatetic, Bruno, were, among other things, 'the primordial force'.[33] Scaliger denied the involvement of 'the stars' in mineral formation,[34] and the chemist, Davisson, settled for 'a vital principle ordered by a mechanical science',[35] but most natural philosophers reintroduced emanations to fill the void left by the departed substantial forms. Telesio had already resorted to Stoic pneumatism in giving the role of substantial forms to 'spiritus'.[36] In the seventeenth century Gassendi and the pioneer of geology, Nicolaus Steno, continued to find emanations indispensable,[37] and in proportion to his success in casting out substantial forms, even Boyle found it necessary to multiply emanations.[38]

The continuing role of emanation in cosmology may be further illustrated from Helmont and Descartes. Although Helmont makes all things of water, and gives no role to his elementary air, he is not at a loss for its equivalent. As already noted, his void is not quite 'nothing', but is an emanation which he calls 'Magnall' or 'Blas'. He owed much to Paracelsus, and not least his penchant for coining bizarre names. One which no longer seems so bizarre was his third

[33] Bruno, 1591: 135–6. (*De triplici minimo*, Bk 4, Ch. 2). Cf. Stones, 1928: 450–1. Michel, 1962: 157.

[34] Scaliger, 1557: fol. 168 (Exerc. 106 [*Quae de metallis*]).

[35] 'Mixti motor, est principium vitale, scientia mechanica instructum' (Davisson, 1660: 401). Similar references to 'scientia spiritum mechanicorum', etc. also appear in his 'textbook' (Davisson, 1640–2, Pt 2, Ch. 25).

[36] Cf. Telesio, 1586: 341–2 (Bk 8, Ch. 21) and elsewhere.

[37] The objective of Steno's *Canis carchariae dissectum caput* (1667) is to disprove the alleged mineral origin of fossils through a '*vis plastica*'. He speaks of the formation of true mineral bodies in terms of chemical precipitations, 'as we see in metals, where one metal dissolved in acid may be precipitated if another metal is added', but he adds that 'what the variety of diet brings about in the humours of the microcosm the changes of the sun and moon and other various changes might be able to produce in the humours of the earth. This is shown by Gassendi . . .' (Steno, 1958: 29–31 Garboe's trans.). Gassendi's concurrent opinion is in his *Syntagmatis philosophici*, Pt 2, Bk 3, Ch. 6 (Gassendi, 1727, Vol. 2: 121).

[38] Boyle's *Origins of forms and qualities* is an almost modern treatise on this topic. Yet even in this work he alludes to the 'invisible and heterogeneous bodies', 'unheeded agents', and 'swarms of steams and effluvia' (1725: 279, 284, 290) to which he has frequent recourse throughout his writings in explaining phenomena. See also note 49 below.

emanation, 'Gas'.[39] He attributes the apparent rarefaction of air on heating to expansion of the Magnall, but on the whole explains meteorological phenomena through Gas, as the material cause, and Blas as form or the efficient cause, these being the only two causes he acknowledged.[40]

Coming down to earth, Helmont is inclined to view all bodies as being generated by the action of seeds or ferments, and that they are made of water he has demonstrated in his famous willow tree experiment.[41] But he finds it necessary to contend with the Paracelsian principles dear to the hearts of so many chemists. He admits that they are the products of the analysis of bodies by fire, but holds that they are also made of Gas (which is in turn made of water), although he ponders the inability of Paracelsus' celebrated universal solvent, the alkahest, to reduce mercury, sulphur and salt to water, and admits that his statement is an hypothesis, like the eccentrics of the astronomers, intended to meet the weakness of our understanding.[42]

In general emanations became more numerous but less prominent in proportion to the specificity of the mechanism of a cosmology. Aristotle himself only brought in emanations where his combination of circular and up-and-down motions failed. An attempt to further elaborate the mechanism is evident in Cardano, who added several new motions, 'natural' and 'unnatural',[43] in Telesio, who revived the rarefaction and condensation of Anaximines, and in Descartes, who availed himself of the vortex motion long since espoused by Anaxagoras. As both the most eminent critic of Peripatetic 'occult causes', and the most industrious of cosmologists, Descartes's success in the abolition of emanations through mechanization is worthy of special consideration.

[39] These three entities are dealt with in *Ortus medicinae*, Chs. 15–17 (1648–2: 73–86. 1662: 70–86). After a series of experiments (including some with the vacuum pump) proving the existence of a vacuum, he concludes that the pores in the air nevertheless contain a 'sheath', the *Magnall* (1648–2: 87. 1662: 85 [Ch. 17, paras. 21–2]). Blas comes from the stars (ibid.) and Gas, in most cases, signified water vapour (cf. 1648–2: 82. 1662: 79 [Ch. 16, para. 11]).

[40] 1648–2: 82. 1662: 79 (Ch. 16, para. 12).

[41] 1648–2: 32–39. 1662: 27–34. (Ch. 6). On the willow tree experiment see 1648–2: 109. 1662: 109 (Ch. 20, paras. 4–5).

[42] 1648–2: 74. 1662: 71 (Ch. 15, para. 8).

[43] 1559: 17–8. 1556: 15 (Bk. 1).

The particles of which Descartes composes the universe move in a vortex, or rather a complex of vortices, and in the course of that motion they wear each other down, like grains of sand. In the heavens this celestial abrasion fills the interstices with filings which accelerate in subordinate vortices and form the matter of the sun and stars, a matter very fluid and mobile, resembling flame.[44] At the other extreme the vortex motion brings heavy particles to the centre, as manifested in that phenomenon we call gravity. That the universe is not finally reduced altogether to an incandescent powder can be attributed to the fact that he introduced degrees of gradation, favoured particle sizes, which correspond to what other philosophers have called elements. Of these there are three, two forming the sun and stars and a third the planets and earth, but the third is further subdivided into three gradations equivalent to the Peripatetics' air, water and earth.[45] Through the complex manipulation of these elements, and taking full advantage of the fact that he has not defined them restrictively, Descartes undertakes to account for the full range of natural phenomena, from astrophysics to terrestrial meteorology and geochemistry.

Continuing with 'suppositions', which he hopes to make credible by their 'simplicity and plausibility', he takes up the structure of terrestrial bodies.[46] He has ample building materials at hand, for air, water and earth 'are composed of innumerable little bodies of diverse size and shape', mingled with other particles of varying fineness, representing vapours and exhalations of terrestrial origin as well as the 'subtle matter' which transmits light and heat. Water particles are long and smooth and never get entangled, as do the irregular particles which form air. Closely intertwined, the latter form solid bodies such as wood. Salt particles differ from those of water in being rigid rods, and so shaped as to pierce the tongue, giving the sharp taste which we experience in sea water. Below these particles of sweet and salt water we find heavier particles, of irregular figure, pressing together and sometimes breaking, leaving fissures through which seep not only the terrestrial fluids but the subtle

[44] Descartes, 1905: 104–7 (*Principia*, Pt 3, Princ. 49–53). Descartes's terms for the abraiding process are '*atteruntur*', and '*eraditur*'.

[45] Descartes, 1902: 233 (*Les meteores*, Disc. 1). 1905: 220–31 (*Principia*, Pt 3, Princ. 52. Pt 4, Princ. 33–45).

[46] Descartes, 1902: 233 (*Les meteores*, Disc. 1).

material of celestial origin to which subterranean generations may be attributed.[47]

As he proceeds, Descartes finds increasingly less need to involve such emanations. The motion of his particles continues within the earth's interior, constrained, but exercising powerful effects among a multitude of gross particles densely packed. Descartes supposes a stratification whose principal elements are a crust and below it a denser layer which resembles the modern conception of the 'mantle'. Below this denser layer intense pressures produce among these gross particles some of smooth and slippery figure, which we know as quicksilver. Where the denser layer meets the lighter crust parts of salt and such are caught in pores of the denser layer and sharpened and polished like knives until they assume the character of the 'corrosive juices', although if they are less hard they are extruded into many slender and flexible branches which are finally carried away and deposited in the crust in the forms of sulphur, bitumen, and the like.[48] Thanks to these 'knives', 'flexible branches', and some sponge-like particles – and to the fact that they had little interest in pneumatic chemistry – such Cartesian chemists as Nicolas Lemery were able to get away from emanations almost altogether.

On the prevalence of emanations most chemists were in full agreement. If the 'ascending and descending vapours' and the 'celestial virtues' which Dorn combines to account for the complex generations in the mineral kingdom are reduced by Boyle to 'subterranean steams', Boyle remains so convinced of their importance that he believes that even that most fixed metal, gold, should be susceptible to vaporization.[49] Dorn expressed the general opinion of chemists, in holding that, in his 'separations', the chemist can so surpass nature

[47] Descartes, 1902: 239–64 (Les meteores, Disc. 2–3). 1905: 213, 239, 245–6 (Principia, Pt 4, Princ. 23, 58, 69–72). Descartes' dependence on his 'peculiar notion' of a materia subtilis was remarked upon by Boyle in the preface to his Treatise on the origin of forms and qualities (1772, Vol. 3: 11–12).

[48] Descartes, 1902: 263–4 (Les meteores, Disc. 3). 1905: 239–42 (Principia, Pt. 4, Princ. 58–62).

[49] 'Effluvia' seem to have been among Boyle's favourite topics. On effluvia in the formation of metals, and on metals as sources of effluvia, see Boyle, 1725, Vol. 3: 76–7 (Suspicions about some hidden qualities in the air). 1772, Vol. 3: 284 (Notes about the atmospheres of consistent bodies); Vol. 5: 68 (An experimental discourse of some unheeded causes of the insalubrity of the air);503 (A previous hydrostatical way of estimating ores).

in 'subtilization' as to reach the 'ethereal bodies' and 'latent forms'.[50] Nearly a century after him we find Sennert disposed to regard odour not only as a test for the presence of the Paracelsian principles in metals, but also as proof that they are animated bodies, since 'all bodies which have spirit may be said to live',[51] and Digby, who followed Galileo in assigning the cause of corporeal operations to 'local motion', concerned himself with the motions of 'magnetic currents of atoms' and an 'aereal salt' which he regarded as the origin of all vegetables and minerals.[52] John Mayow's preoccupation with the latter entity has a more respectable place in the history of chemistry, through his prevision of the role in nature of the gaseous element, oxygen, and it can hardly be doubted that the seventeenth century frequently verged on the discovery of gases. That this discovery had another century to wait may owe much to the confusion which continued to reign between real and imaginary emanations.

Organic change

The impact of Renaissance innovation on the microcosm was analogous to that on the macrocosm, as the monument of Galenic physiology suffered indignities comparable to those contemporaneously meted out to Aristotelian physics. Galen's physiology, too, contained the seeds of its own destruction, for despite his celebrated assignment to heat of the role of cause in organic processes, the explanation of digestion, and the functions of the humours, had come out of his systematization of physiology and pathology with chemical connotations; for he involved 'fermentation' in the former and gave two of the latter – the biles – properties of a distinctly chemical nature.[53] The Paracelsian reformation scarcely improved on Galenic physiology by assigning digestion to the 'archaeus' ('an internal chemist'), and in replacing the humours by mercury,

[50] 1568: 44. Less philosophic chemists, of course, continued to use the term 'quintessence' (cf. Biringuccio, 1942: 340–1).

[51] 1629: 109. 1676: 207 (Ch. 9). This is part of a passage in which he adopts the views of 'recent chemists', extending the Peripatetic criteria of life, which recognized only motion.

[52] Digby, 1669: 233.

[53] Galen, 1916: 209–15.

sulphur and salt. As Sennert remarked, 'Philosophy is calling things by their names, stomach stomach, liver and cooking power also by their names. It is not to mock everything and to confound different things.'[54] But as the Peripatetics and their adversaries alike had set about the improvement of Aristotle's doctrines so did they also of Galen's, and with a comparable result, the evolution of something more nearly resembling our modern theories.

In medicine as in natural philosophy the conservatism of the sixteenth-century Peripatetics and Galenists was only relative, and far less than the critics of tradition would lead one to suppose. Thus we see the leading Galenist of the century, Jean Fernel (d. 1558), contending valiantly with the weaknesses of the Galenic system. In his book, *On the function and humours*, he reveals that the solution to the problem of digestion has been made even more difficult by accretions from folklore, which pondered such questions as the inability of the lion, despite its well-known hot temperament, to digest iron, which the ostrich easily manages, and how the (cold) fish is able to digest at all. Here Fernel is unable to improve much on Galen. He attempts to elucidate the difference between the coction of the stomach and simple cooking by emphasizing that the former case involves an 'innate spirit' as well as a 'peculiar natural heat', and he finds the supposed blood-making process of the liver analogous to the fermentation of the wine vat. At least this clarified the question of the biles, for he points out that in this process deposits appear like those in the wine vat, one the black or melancholy bile which goes to the spleen to be stored, and the other the yellow or choleric bile which is stored in the gall bladder. These biles are 'natural'; they are the primary mixta of organic bodies. He expresses surprise at the persistence of questions about their origin, since the powers of nature are known to be manifold, and he attributes their differentiation to differences in material and in grades of heat.[55]

As to the reputedly noxious character of the biles, he says that the idea that they are pernicious derives from their confusion with some similar but essentially different fluids. He notes that there is an acid in the stomach which the liver and veins will not accept, and also that the austere and acerbic crasser part of the melancholic humour, if

[54] Sennert, 1629: 252. 1676: 240 (Ch. 16).
[55] Fernel, 1567: 116-7, 121-4.

the spleen cannot ameliorate it, will cause eructations at the mouth of the stomach. These are manifestations of several different 'melancholies' which are to be distinguished from that mild humour suited to nourishment which the Greek doctors called 'black juice' rather than 'black bile', and also from the humour of the gall bladder, which should be called 'black humour' [the yellow bile?]. In contrast to these there is a humour which is burning or putrescent with unnatural heat and possesses acid, acerbic or acrimonious qualities as though it had been converted to ash. This, which is properly called black bile, is altogether unnatural. But the matter is more complicated, for it is of three kinds. Putrescence or intense heat reduce the melancholic juice or humour, as it were, to a cinder which is acrid and mordant, although he does not think this altogether equal to 'the cinder from burned wood', for the humours cannot be so completely divested of their liquorous character. Another kind, said to derive from yellow bile, is altogether the most pernicious black bile, and is more malignant even though that from the melancholic bile may be more acrid. It is this bile [as the Hippocratic physicians had said] which falling on the earth seems to ferment and effervesce, eroding and ulcerating the earth. The third acrid black bile, which passes without further description, arises from phlegm.[56]

Almost simultaneous with Fernel's discussion another appeared from the pen of Telesio, whose cosmology, De rerum natura (1565), was particularly oriented towards the elucidation of the organic kingdoms. Despite his antagonism to Peripatetic thought Telesio found no alternative to Aristotle and Galen on animal digestion, and we find him reduced to improving on them through a liberal application of 'spirits'. He admits that the stomach 'cooks' the food for the liver, but thinks that the motions of the esophagus and stomach represent the rejection of portions of the food which they 'sense' to be improper to nutrition. This sensing is the work of 'a great quantity of spirits', whose involvement in the work of the stomach is so fundamental that Telesio is led to class that organ as part of the nervous system.[57]

Telesio, too, finds it necessary to contend with the problems of sharp or acrid fluids in the system and with the biles. Hunger and

[56] Fernel, 1567: 132–4.
[57] Telesio, 1586: 236–8 (Bk 6, Ch. 7).

thirst, he claims, have their origin in acid juice (acido succo) poured into the stomach from the spleen. When the stomach is empty the acid acts on the spirit in the fibre of the stomach, causing hunger and then a movement which helps break up the food. The chyle still contains impurities when it reaches the liver. A thick, black, sour bile is drawn off by the spleen, and a thick, yellow, bitter (amara) bile passes to the gall bladder. A thin substance passes off as urine. There is also an ash-like substance which must be removed, but he does not say where it goes and seems to regard it as the source of stoney concretions in the body.[58]

The works of Fernel and Telesio show that theories of digestion and the humours had been complicated in two directions, one anatomical, in the involvement of additional organs, and the other chemical, in the differentiation of the properties of the two biles into acid and alkaline.

The significance of this may be better understood by comparison with the modern theory of digestion, which involves the successive action on food of a series of biochemical entities called enzymes, in the mouth, stomach and intestines, aided by muscular contraction of these organs. In the stomach gastric juice secreted from tiny glands within the stomach walls contains hydrochloric acid and a protein decomposing enzyme, pepsin. These partially digest the food which then passes to the small intestine (duodenum) where it encounters bile from the liver (and gall bladder, in which bile is stored during non-digestive periods) and performs a function in connection with the digestion of fats. The bile duct also brings pancreatic juice, through smaller passages leading to the pancreas. This alkaline juice stops the action of pepsin and introduces three enzymes which act on starches and fats, and continue the digestion of proteins. Finally a juice from the walls of the intestine completes the process and the products of digestion are absorbed by the intestinal walls and diffuse into the blood or lymph of the circulatory system.

The ancients knew all of these organs, but gave them various significance, not only because of an imperfect understanding of their inter-relationship, but because of the nature of ancient anatomical studies. Aristotle mentions most of them in his book, *On the parts of animals*, where, since he is concerned with comparative anatomy, he

---

[58] Telesio, 1586: 239-40 (Bk 6, Ch. 9).

is particularly interested in the sizes and shapes of the organs, and their absence altogether in some animals. In most animals, he reports, the liver is not supplied with a gall (bladder), nor do they invariably have the spleen.[59] The involvement of these 'auxiliary' organs in digestion was a matter of much uncertainty. Modern physiology gives to the pancreas something like the function assigned by the ancients to the spleen, which is physically connected to the circulatory and not to the digestive system. The ancients were obviously not clear on the duct connections of either of these organs. That Galen made the spleen a part of the digestive system is perhaps in consequence of his criticism of Erasistratus for denying any function to the organ. Galen's own vagaries on the gall bladder made this organ a focus of anti-Galenism in the seventeenth century.

The more definitive assignment of functions to the spleen and gall bladder by Fernel and Telesio is connected with their differentiation of the biles into acid and alkaline fluids. The fact that modern physiology gives acids and alkalis a role in digestion gives great importance to this innovation, which is usually credited to Helmont. Nor does the discovery that Fernel and Telesio anticipated him necessarily deprive Helmont of his claims, for the acid and alkaline biles remained little more than pernicious fluids in the writings of his sixteenth-century predecessors.

The conclusion that certain body fluids have acid or alkaline properties was hardly reached on significant chemical grounds. Taste remained in the sixteenth century the most commonplace criterion of the differentiation of substances, but there was no consistent terminology for differentiating the bitterness, astringency, or acrimony of such materials as vinegar, soda, quicklime, and alum. Pliny had called both vinegar and natron 'acrimonious' (Bks 31: 115, 34: 116). The sourness and bitterness (acidam, acerbam, acrimoniam) of black bile continued in Fernel and Telesio to be its principal characteristic, and they tend to use other words (mordax, amara) to indicate an alkaline bile, but they are not altogether consistent and we would be hard put to understand their meaning were it not for the fact that one is associated with effervescence and the other compared to the acrimonious salt in wood ash.[60] There is no doubt

---

[59] Aristotle, 1912: 670a–b, 676b–677a.
[60] Fernel, 1567: 133–4. Telesio, 1586: 243 (Bk 6, Ch. 12).

that they attribute acid qualities to one of these pernicious biles and alkaline to the other, but until Helmont this seems to have had little significance either to chemistry or physiology. In particular no reference is made to acid-alkali neutralization. It seems to reflect an attempt to further elucidate the 'fact' (in the context of Galenic biology) that there are two pernicious biles and that two organs are to be accounted for.

Helmont's innovation was in applying to digestion the chemical fact of the mutual neutralization of acids and alkalis, which was a discovery of his own time.[61] He postulates a six-stage digestion, but of these the last four are as vaguely described as is the third digestion of 'the Schools', and his controversy with them really concerns only the first two. Where they had arrived at the notion of 'innate heat' acting in the stomach, followed by 'fermentation' in the liver – and were troubled by an unexplained intrusion of bilious acidity – he gave the acidity a positive function in the stomach and then neutralized it with alkali in the intestine. 'There is indeed,' declared Helmont, 'a sharp, vital, and spiritual ferment in the spleen, whereby the stomach cocteth . . .', but 'the ferment conceived in the cream of the stomach is pernicious in the intestine'.[62] This was, of course, the principal obstacle to the involvement of acidity in digestion, and Helmont's major innovation was in his claim to have observed 'that a sour cream (acidus cremor) in the duodenum doth straightway attain the savour of salt, and doth so willingly exchange its own sharp salt into a salt salt. No otherwise almost than as the vinegar which is most sharp hath forthwith (through red lead) put off its former sharpness, and doth presently change into an aluminous sweetness; . . . or when a sharp distillation (acidum stagma) is drunk up in an alcali salt.'[63] It is the ferment of the gall through which this 'sharp salt of the stomach is changed into a salt salt'.[64]

Although Helmont explained his chemical physiology by analogy

[61] See Glauber's reference to the mutual killing and nullification of acid and alkali (below, p. 300). Since this appeared only in 1647, it was later than Helmont. The most recent and comprehensive account of the beginning of titrimetric analysis (Madsen, 1958) regards Boyle, in his Experiments and considerations touching colours (1664 – Madsen says 1663) as the pioneer student of the neutralization reaction.

[62] Helmont, 1648-1: 83 (also in 1662: 1029).

[63] 1648-2: 209. 1662: 207 (Ch. 31, paras. 6-7).

[64] 1648-1: 213. 1662: 210 (Ortus medicinae, Ch. 31, 27).

to reactions of inorganic substances, it does not appear that he saw the mutual neutralization of acids and alkalis as a reaction of transcendent importance. Neither did Boyle, for although he ventured the opinion that 'the generality of former physicians . . . have taken a great deal too little notice of the saline (if I may so speak) and sulphurous properties of things', he also found it necessary to write a tract against the 'dewllists', as he called them, who gave too much importance to the acid-alkali reaction.[65] These 'dewllists' were a new school of physicians who rationalized Helmontian chemical physiology by divesting it of its mystical and vitalistic elements, and who finally worked out a theory connecting diseases and remedies on the purely chemical basis of acid and alkaline properties.

The principal ornament of this group was François de la Boë Sylvius. Sylvius' theory of digestion[66] was no mere extension of Helmont's, although it added up to much the same thing. He gave the decisive role in the digestion of the stomach to saliva, which he identified as a 'ferment', but he retained the alkalinity of the bile, which he indeed identified as 'calcined lye salt', and, relying on the investigations of one of his students, he found a corresponding 'acid' in the pancreatic juice.[67]

Sylvius tells us that his doctrine is based upon experience, not upon the teachings of any master, old or new. He exemplifies this by describing three 'experiences': the first, the 'spontaneous separation of the parts' at the conclusion of vinous fermentation, as evidenced by the emission of volatile spirit; the second, the formation of a precipitate when solutions of salt of tartar and vitriol are mixed; and the third, the precipitation of a metal from solution by the addition of another metal having a greater affinity for the solvent. He sees in the first the escape of a portion of the 'acid spirit' along with the volatile spirit, in the second a 'desertion' of sulphur by the acid spirit of

[65] *Reflections on the hypothesis of acid and alkali* (1772, Vol. 4: 282-92).

[66] On Sylvius and his system see Baumann, 1949.

[67] F. Sylvius, 1680: 13-4. This appears to be a curious episode. Sylvius' remarks were first published in 1663 and his student's (Regnier de Graaf, 1641-73) account of the pancreatic juice came out only in the following year. Graaf says that his objective had been 'avoir une recherche de laquelle depend en quelque facon la gloire de nostre Maistre commun' (Graaf, 1666: preface), and proceeds by reviewing opinions on the use of the pancreas, concluding with, and accepting, that of Sylvius, which held the pancreas to be the source of stomach acid, since he could not attribute that acid to the 'bitter' gall nor to the 'insipid' saliva (ibid. 33). Modern research has found the pancreatic juice to be alkaline.

vitriol, and in the third a scale of differing affinities of the metals for acid spirit. His interpretation of all three reactions in terms of 'acid spirit' reveals the dominant pattern in Sylvius' application of experience to the interpretation of physiology. One of the most important publicists in support of Harvey's theory of the circulation of the blood, he claimed as the cause of that circulation a periodic acid-alkali interaction in the ventricles of the heart![68]

The immense, if transitory, influence of Sylvius' system owed much to its compatability with contemporary mechanistic ideologies. G. A. Borelli (1608–79), a leading exponent of a mechanical school known as 'iatromathematics', undertook to explain the old question of the strange digestive powers of certain animals by arguing that their stomachs 'act by pressure, like a wine press', but admitted this implausible in some animal stomachs (e.g., shell fish), and there had recourse to 'a very potent ferment (acting) much in the same way as corrosive liquids corrode and dissolve metals'.[69] The Cartesian chemist, Nicolas Lemery, in undertaking to explicate the reactions in which he produced chemical medicines, found so plausible the picture of pointed acid particles and porous alkalis that he ended by classifying everything upon which an acid could act, including the metals, as alkaline.[70] Since effervescence, rather than the indicator reaction (which was known to Boyle as early as 1664), was the accepted test for acidity, such a classification was as natural outside as within the Cartesian circle. The doctrine of Sylvius, which saw most diseases as due to imbalances in the body's numerous acid-alkali interactions, was perfectly adapted to the prescription of the same old chemical remedies under a new theory of counteracting acid diseases with alkaline remedies and the reverse. But the biochemical system of Sylvius was to prove short lived. It was too successful, and was scarcely erected before its very proponents began to quarrel on some fundamental points, notably on the differentiation of acids and alkalis. Originality is an eternal aspiration of man, and some of the chemical physicians sought it by reversing the whole system, claiming to have discovered that all which had been classified

[68] Sylvius, 1680: 13–4, 17.

[69] Borelli, 1685: 290 (Prop. 192). Sennert had recorded this idea long before (cf. Sennert, 1676: 221).

[70] 1677: 10–21. Lemery held 'earthy matters' to be alkalis and, like Mayow, found an 'acid salt' in the air.

as acid was really alkaline.[71] Extravagant controversies in which one physician's medicine was another's poison quickly brought down this too hurriedly constructed edifice in the early eighteenth century, leaving medicine much as it had been before. The effect on chemistry, however, was more profound.

If the enthusiasms of the acid-alkali physicians were most immediately felt in biology, their effect was hardly less in mineralogy, where they provided an alternative, which cosmological writers had been unable to discover, to the all-persuasive emanations. The idea of the involvement of acids in mineral formation had been one of the notions of the medieval alchemists which remained palatable to such as Agricola, who made 'the corrosive action of subterranean waters' a key to his theory of mineral formation. But the mineral acids were only vaguely thought of as prototypes of 'corrosive waters' until the mid-seventeenth century, when they also rose to prominence in the writings of the physicians of the acid-alkali persuasion. Sylvius seems to have been exceptional in restricting his opinions to medicine, but in his confusion of fermentation with effervescence[72] and his habitual reliance on evidences from inorganic chemistry he opened a door to cogitation on mineralogy which others were not to ignore. Thomas Willis, the leading English representative of the school, wrote a book designed to show the universality of fermentation,[73] to which he attributed as many physiological processes as had Sylvius plus such others as the natural formation of minerals. Effervescence was the hallmark of fermentation and acid a consistent accompaniment, although he developed this in detail only in relation to biology. In the same vein the self-styled Helmontian, William Simpson, discovered that the seminal principles with which Helmont's elementary water is endowed are to be identified as 'acid' and 'sulphur', and finds this appropriate for explaining much of mineral phenomena.[74] Thus even conserva-

---

[71] Cf. Colbatch, 1698: Preface, x.

[72] Sylvius states that effervescence resulting from the combination of acid spirits and lixivial salts is altogether·different from fermentation (1680: 12 [*Disputationum III, De chyli mutatione in sanguinem*]), but his concept of effervescences is broad enough. He sees body heat, for example, as the result of an effervescence between the acid spirit of lymph and 'the bitter lye salt of bile' (ibid.: 51 [*De febribus altera*] Ch. 44).

[73] *De fermentatione*, in Willis, 1695: 1–62.

[74] Simpson, 1677: 34–5.

tive chemists found every reason to explain subterranean chemistry in terms of acids, and the more venturesome (e.g. Becher and Stahl) went so far as to claim the 'universal acid' (of vitriol) to be the agent of mineral formation.[75]

[75] This is one of the main arguments of Becher's *Physica subterranea* (Becher, 1669). See also Stahl, 1746–7, Pt 1: 10, 50. 1730: 15, 78, and Barner, 1689: 533–5.

Chapter Fourteen

Affinities

THE idea of affinities is rooted in that of sympathies and antipathies, which may have found its earliest expression in the
Presocratic, Empedocles,[1] but it is probably much older, for it lies
at the basis of magic and astrology.[2] It was no less basic to the
doctrine of macrocosm and microcosm, both in Hellenistic times and
in the European Renaissance,[3] and was involved in medicine from
the Roman era to Stahl.[4] Aristotle touched upon it where he discussed
the aptitude of 'things' for interaction and concluded (*On gen.*,
323b) that an agent and a patient could not be either absolutely 'like'
or absolutely 'unlike', but must be in one sense identical and in
another unlike one another.

In 1546 Fracastoro published a book on sympathies and antipathies, in which he considered, in a theoretical and essentially
Peripatetic way, the sympathy between 'affinia', or 'similia'.[5]
Although theoretical, his discussion is related to mixtion, and this
became a commonplace topic in the next century, when Sebastian
Basso saw 'aptitude' as critical to the formation of mixta,[6] Jungius
used such terms as familiarity, aptitude and affinity in what was

[1] Aristotle, pseudo, 1955: 379. Kirk and Raven, 1957: 191.

[2] Thorndike, HMES, Vol. 1: 84–6. Cumont (1911: 171–2) calls it 'a belief as old as human
society'.

[3] D. J. Furley, introduction to pseudo-Aristotle, 1955. Andreas, 1948: 608. Pagel, 1958:
297–301.

[4] Cf. Allbutt, 1921: 52–3, 353–5. Thorndike, HMES, Vol. 1: 86–7. Sprengel, 1815–20,
Vol. 5: 263.

[5] Fracastoro, 1546: 3v–6r. (Ch. 5, De attractione & motu similium ad similia.)

[6] 1621: 341, 334.

clearly a search for a new terminology,[7] and the French atomist, J. C. Magnen, reportedly postulated a sympathy between atoms.[8]

There was also an increasing conviction among chemists in the seventeenth century of the desirability of appending to a recipe some reference to the character of the reaction, which they generally rendered in anthropomorphic terms. The interaction of acids and alkalis often reminded them of 'antagonism' and 'combat'. Glauber spoke of the precipitation brought about by the addition of alkali to a solution of gold in aqua regia as a 'killing' of the alkali and the nullification (*zunicht gemacht*) of the acid, rendering them 'powerless' to hold dissolved materials.[9] The liberation of ammonia from sal ammoniac by an alkali reminded both Thomas Willis and John Mayow of a severing of chains or bonds.[10]

Substances were sometimes more friendly. Mayow observes that the combination of sulphur with alkali 'would appear to result not so much from any antagonism as from their mutual affinity . . .'[11] Glauber had made a similar observation in his analysis of the familiar process for making butter of antimony (antimony trichloride), where he found that the 'spirit' in corrosive sublimate 'prefers' (*griefen lieber an*) antimony, leaving the mercury (of the sublimate) to 'conjugate' with the 'sulphur' of the antimony (sulphide).[12]

Aided by a series of mistakes, Glauber succeeded in making a general principle of this. He began with the observation that whereas the 'acid spirit' of nitre (nitric acid) dissolves many metals, nitre could also be made to yield 'a clear and fiery liquor' which could dissolve that material which he considers the antithesis of a metal, sulphur. His clear and fiery liquor was potash, which he obtained by igniting saltpetre (nitre) with charcoal and allowing the product to liquefy through deliquescence. But considering it a product of nitre, he goes on to discover in this phenomenon the key to many ancient riddles.

[7] Wohlwill, 1887: 65 (quoting Jungius' lectures on physical topics, *Doxoscopiae physicae minores*, a posthumous collection).

[8] According to Stones, 1928: 459.

[9] 1658–9, Vol. 2: 125. 1689, Pt 2: 46 (*Philosophical furnaces*).

[10] Mayow, 1674: 225–7. 1926: 155–6 (*De sal nitro*, Ch. 14). Willis, 1674–5, Vol. 1: 211. The phrase recurs frequently in both authors.

[11] 'ab affinitate mutua' (Mayow, 1674: 238. 1926: 164).

[12] 1658–9, Vol. 2: 23. 1689, Pt 1: 8 (*Philosophical furnaces*, Pt 1). Thomas Willis (1674–5, Vol. 1: 65) and Isaac Newton (1931: 382 [*Opticks*, Query 31]) were to analyse this reaction in almost the same terms.

' 'Tis evident that every nature doth lovingly embrace its like and is willingly conjoyned therewithall. . . .' If none of the three principles (mercury, sulphur and salt) dominates in a substance, then either the acid spirit or the fixed salt of the nitre will dissolve them, but if sulphur is severed from mercury and salt the spirit of nitre will not dissolve it, but its 'sulphurous liquor' will.[13] This leads him to postulate a system in which mineral sulphur is the 'beginning' and gold the 'end'. The 'fixed liquor' has dissolving powers at the prior extreme and the acid at the other. What the liquor dissolves the acid precipitates, and vice versa; 'thus what the sister can't do the brother can', and he is finally led to the conclusion that he has discovered in nitre the long sought universal solvent of Paracelsus.[14]

In later editions of his work, however, Glauber seems to have withdrawn this enthusiastic conclusion and reverted to the question of affinity. He notes that 'middle subjects' such as lead, tin, iron, copper, mercury and silver, 'partaking of both the sulphurous and mercurial natures', are dissolvable by both nitrous solvents but in varying degrees of difficulty depending on their composition. 'The acid spirit doth more easily dissolve one subject than another according as it is of more affinity with, or remote from, its own nature. And therefore every chemist may easily know the nature and properties of every metal and mineral by the dissolving them with these two, viz. liquour and acid spirit. Note well,' he concludes, 'I have (by this means) found out what metals and minerals are of nearest affinity with gold, and this kind of inquiry is far more certain and safer than the reading of many books.'[15]

But Glauber's scheme was vitiated by a few mistakes which, if understandable, were fatal,[16] and the further development of the

[13] 1658–9, Vol. 1: 51. 1689, Pt 2: 99–100 (*Spagyrica pharmaceutica*. The preparation of animals and vegetables by the fiery liquor of nitre).

[14] 1658–9, Vol. 1: 53–5 (*Spagyrica pharmaceutica*). This is not in the corresponding passage in Glauber, 1689.

[15] 1689, Pt 2: 100 (*Spagyrica pharmaceutica*). Packe's translation. This is not in Glauber, 1658–9.

[16] He appears to have been the first to describe the product of the ignition of saltpetre with charcoal, which was still identified as a peculiar alkali in the late eighteenth century (see below, pp. 331, 347), although Newton identified it with salt of tartar in 1692 (Newton, 1958: 256. [*De natura acidorum*]). That his scheme led him to identify aqua fortis as the solvent of gold must be attributed to over-enthusiasm, since he shows elsewhere an understanding of

ideology of affinities was interrupted by an interlude in which all 'occult' explanations were disposed of by the more plausible mechanisms of the Cartesians. They had indeed met brilliantly the problem of varying reactive powers, with a doctrine which gave acids the form of pointed particles and everything on which they could act a porous, sponge-like form. The way in which their imaginations worked on this is illustrated by Lemery's explanation of the dissolution of gold in aqua regia and its precipitation by an alkali, a process on which we have already seen the views of Glauber. The dissolution of gold is 'a suspension in which the points of the aqua regia support the particles of metal in the phlegm', much as a piece of metal is supported in water if it is attached to the end of a piece of wood. The 'fermentation' which occurs when the alkali (oil of tartar) is added to the solution 'enfeebles' the points of the aqua regia, because the hardness of the gold particles is such that the points only penetrate them superficially and are easily shaken loose.[17] Even Boyle was overwhelmed by such reasoning, and found it necessary to admit in his own attempts to elucidate the corpuscular philosophy by experiment the influence of 'a determinate figure of the corpuscles, answerable to that of the pores of the body by them to be dissolved', or 'the fitness of the shapes of the component particles to fasten to each other'.[18]

A severer test, however, was presented by the fact that reactive powers are limited in curious and unpredictable ways, a fact which emerges most frequently from the literature in connection with acid dissolution of the metals. 'Why', asked Davisson, the chemist at the Jardin du Roi, 'does the corrosive faculty of strong waters act by election? Why do they consume and dissolve hard things like stones and metals but leave soft things like wax? . . . Whence this kind of sympathy and antipathy?'[19] Attempts to answer the query most often took the form of a commentary on a celebrated question; why does aqua regia dissolve gold but not silver, while aqua fortis dissolves silver but not gold? Davisson, himself, holds that aqua fortis dissolves

---

the relationship of these substances. The facts that his fiery liquor of nitre was no form of nitre, and that aqua fortis does not dissolve gold, nullifies his scheme, to say the least.

[17] Nicolas Lemery, 1677: 58–9.

[18] 1772, Vol. 1: 369 (*A physico-chymical essay, containing an experiment relating to saltpetre*), and 414 (*The history of fluidity and firmness*).

[19] 1640–2: 212 (Pt 3, Ch. 31, *De aquis fortibus*).

only feminine metals and marchasites, like silver and bismuth, while aqua regia dissolves only masculine metals like gold and antimony. He also thinks that there is in gold a 'metallic sulphur' which is antagonistic to aqua fortis.[20] Lemery believed it more probable that aqua regia could not dissolve silver because 'the edges of the spirit of nitre, being magnified by the addition of salt, slide over the pores of silver, not being able to enter into them by reason of the disproportion of their figures'. They do, however, easily enter the larger pores of gold. The 'subtle points' of aqua fortis, on the other hand, fit the pores of silver, but are too small in proportion to the pores of gold to act on that body.[21]

Boyle seems to have accepted this, or at least not attempted to replace it. But out of the study of gases, which he initiated, where repulsion played a prominent role, and of Newtonian physics, with its connotation of attraction between material bodies, came a modification of the affinity idea which was uncomfortably close to the no longer fashionable sympathy and antipathy. Newton called it 'sociability' stemming from principles of 'according and receding'.[22] Although Newton was notoriously reluctant to publish his views on chemistry, he did on several occasions take note of the differential action of aqua regia and aqua fortis on gold and silver, and shows himself concerned to substitute 'sociability' or attraction for the Cartesian mechanism. He was not successful, however, and even admits that his explanation was occult.[23] Only after the majority of chemists had become Newtonians, in the nineteenth century, did it come to seem less so.

Closely related to the selective dissolution of metals by acids was the selective replacement of one metal by another, in solution. An example of this in which copper is replaced from copper sulphate solution by iron was one of the most notorious of chemical reactions, for it was commonly believed to be an experimental demonstration

[20] 1640–2: 211–2 (Pt 3, Ch. 31, De aquis fortibus). See also Metzger; 1923: 48–50, and Read, 1951: 18.

[21] 1677: 350–1.

[22] 1958: 251 (letter to Boyle, dated Feb. 28, 1678–9).

[23] 'There is a secret principle in nature. . . .' (ibid.). Newton also touched on the subject in his De natura acidorum of 1692 (Newton, 1958: 256–8) and in the famous query 31 of his Opticks (Newton, 1931: 382–3). On Newton's conception of acid dissolution of the metals see Kuhn, 1951 and Boas, 1952–2.

of the transmutation of iron into copper. The process was practised by the miners of Central Europe for the production of iron vitriol by casting pieces of iron into 'vitriolate' drainage waters. Chemists were generally more interested in a by-product, the copper which was precipitated in the process, and such as Minderer and Canepario, both authorities on vitriol, regarded it as a transmutation motivated by some kind of affinity between the iron and (copper) vitriol.[24]

During the first half of the seventeenth century the supposed iron-copper transmutation[25] was exposed as a replacement by iron of copper pre-existing in the solution, although many chemists continued to believe in it. About 1640 the replacement reaction was explained by both Helmont and Jungius in a manner compatible with the ideology of affinities, but without accepting the theory of metallic transmutation. Helmont declared that the vitriol waters contain 'atoms' of copper which 'change place' with the iron, while Jungius held that the iron presents the 'spirit of sulphur' in the vitriol with a combination for which it has a greater sympathy.[26] Lemery characteristically opposed affinities as vitalistic, declaring that they seemed to give intelligence to the 'points' of aqua fortis, and held rather that the 'phlegm' detaches little pieces of iron which 'swim about' knocking the points of aqua fortis loose from the copper.[27]

This was stretching things too far for any but the most zealous Cartesian, and when it came to this type of reaction most chemists remained content to think that the iron enjoys a particular affinity with aqua fortis, whether through points or some other property. That it was a *type* reaction seems to have been evident from the time the iron-copper transmutation was first challenged by Angelo Sala, for he cited similar replacement reactions – precipitation of silver by copper, copper by iron, etc. – as proof that the vitriol was merely a solution of copper.[28] By 1663 we find the chemically-oriented physician, François de la Boë Sylvius, remarking that the metals

[24] Minderer, who thinks it no accident that iron and copper are also known as Mars and Venus, declares that 'omne ferrum mediante vitriolo facili negotio in aes transeat' (1617: 9). Canepario considers the change (commutatio) a demonstration of the old principle that vitriol is the medium between stones and metals (1660: 203-9). Both these authorities use the word 'affinity' in this connection.

[25] See below, pp. 316-17.

[26] Helmont, 1648-2: 292. 1662: 695. Wohlwill, 1887: 57-8, quoting Jungius' *Doxoscopiae*.

[27] 1677: 69.

[28] 1647: 399-400. This was written about 1618 (see below, p. 316).

generally replace one another from their solutions in an acid in accordance with their relative 'affinity' for that acid.[29] In 1669 Becher spoke of a successive replacement of one metal by another in this reaction, and by the time of Stahl (1723) this had been extended to cover most of the common metals.[30]

The Systematization of affinities

Despite the Cartesian orientation of that body it was the Paris Academy which was to bring about the further development of this line of thought. While chemistry in the *Transactions* of the Royal Society of London sank in the first half of the eighteenth century to an even lower level,[31] the *Memoires* of the Académie des Sciences, from 1692, published in increasing numbers important papers from the best chemists in France, a practice which continued until the emergence of the specialized chemical periodical at the end of the eighteenth century. It is perhaps appropriate that the Paris Academy had begun its exploration of chemistry under the inspiration of a report of Boyle's 'aenigma' of a sweet salt composed of ingredients more acrid than brine and more sour than vinegar, and which does not colour syrup of violets either red, as do acid salts, or green, as do alkalis.[32] In reporting on this in 1667, DuClos notes the existence of other similar salts from corrosive ingredients, but makes no generalizations, as he scarcely could since he managed to conclude that Boyle's aenigma was 'sweet crystals of common salt prepared with vinegar or honey'.

[29] 1680: 14. (*Disputationum medicarum, II*). He mentions it as analogous to the digestive processes in which some substances are assimilated and others rejected.

[30] Becher, 1669: 228. Stahl, 1746, Vol. 1: 26. 1730: 40. This, according to Partington (1961: 661), is identical to the 1723 edition of Stahl's book, which I have not seen.

[31] In the first half of the eighteenth century the *Philosophical Transactions* printed fewer chemical papers per issue than it did in the seventeenth century. Such important chemists as John Keil and Stephen Hales published only one paper each, while the most prolific chemical author, with 26 papers, was Francis Hawksbee, whose importance to chemistry can be gauged by the fact that he is principally remembered as an electrician (see George, 1952).

[32] DuClos, 1667 (*Histoire*). The *Memoires* of the Paris Academy during this period were preceded by an *Histoire* – separately paginated – in which the contents of the *Memoires*, plus some work not reported there, was summarized. This was done by the Perpetual Secretary, who from 1666 to 1697 was J. B. Duhamel (1624–1706). The work of Duclos reported here appears only in the *Histoire*.

The real birth of chemical research in the Paris Academy appears to date from the appointment of Homberg. He began the publication of papers on chemistry in the Memoirs of the Academy almost immediately upon his arrival in Paris, and they continued to appear until they totalled fifty-one by the time of his death. Many of these were interrelated articles on inorganic chemistry, and their continuity was not broken by his death but was continued by his successors in the Academy. The pharmacist E. F. Geoffroy published seventeen between 1700 and 1725, many of which continued the investigations of Homberg, whose lectures Geoffroy had probably attended. Beginning in 1706, similar papers began to appear from Louis Lemery, the son of Nicolas and chemist of the Jardin du Roi, and twenty-four of these had appeared by 1736. J. F. Rouelle's first paper appeared in 1744, and those of his student, Lavoisier, began to appear in 1768, thus carrying the studies begun by Homberg into the era of modern chemistry.

Articles on a sort of 'recipe chemistry' exemplified by DuClos's cogitations on Boyle's aenigma were typical of chemistry in the French Academy up to the time of Homberg, including the contributions of Nicolas Lemery and Pierre Borel, both of whom became members of the Academy late in life. It was Borel, however, who was emboldened, shortly before his death, to 'propose an essay to judge the mortification of acids by alkalis',[33] and the inadequacy of his proposal is rather technical than conceptual. Despite Boyle and DuClos he does not consider pigment colour changes as an indicator of the 'mortification point', but proposes to measure 'the force of the alkali' by precipitating it with a measured solution of vitriol or corrosive sublimate. Time was his unit of measurement, and he thinks vitriol to be better since it precipitates more slowly.

Homberg resumed this question in 1695, and taking up the force of acids, he first attempted to determine wherein that force resides.[34] 'Acid spirits', he holds, are nothing but 'volatile salts dissolved in an aqueous liquor', and observing that the dissolving power of an acid with various metals varies with the water content of the acid he recommends that experiments be conducted to obtain the acid

---

[33] Borel, 1688 (*Histoire*).
[34] Homberg, 1695.

spirits in a concrete form. But he subsequently decides that 'art' cannot separate the 'useless phlegm' from the active particles 'swimming' in it, and devises two methods for obtaining a measure of their force, by comparing their relative weights, and hence acid content, with an aerometer (specific gravity bottle) of his own invention, and through salt of tartar (potassium carbonate), 'a powerful alkali which avidly charges acid liquors'. Against an ounce of tartar he measures 'all that it can carry' of each of the acids.[35]

This, too, ends inconclusively, but in the next year (1700) Hom-. berg came forward with a third essay,[36] this time to measure the force of alkalis – although he points out that 'if the force of acids consists in a power of dissolving that of alkalis consists, so to speak, in being dissolvable, and the more they are the more perfect the genre'. Believing that aqua fortis and aqua regia represent 'the two principal kinds' of acid (apparently for no better reason than their differing dissolving powers over gold and silver), he undertakes to discover their equivalent acidities. He subjects them both to 'dephlegmation' (evaporation) until he obtains equal volumes which have equal weights. His aerometer then informs him that they are one-fifth heavier than river water, and he concludes that this excess represents in both cases the weight of the acid spirits. Having acids 'of equal force' he then measures the different quantities of a series of alkalis necessary to 'absorb' each of the acids. The result, as far as the alkalis are concerned, was a conclusion that some alkalis are dissolved 'feebly' and 'with less effervescence' because of the presence of a fatty or oily material in their constitution. More decisive is his correlative conclusion with regard to the acids, for he finds that in every case aqua fortis dissolves nearly twice as much alkali as does aqua regia. Thus aqua fortis, he concludes, has smaller but more numerous particles – twice as many cutting edges, as Fontenelle put it in considering this *memoire*.[37]

This leads Homberg to consider further experiments. He proposes to measure the time required for the reactions and ponders measuring the relative effervescence. The latter carries him altogether out of

[35] Homberg, 1699.

[36] Homberg, 1700.

[37] In the *Histoire* accompanying Homberg, 1700. The Perpetual Secretary of the Academy from 1699 to 1739 was the celebrated Cartesian philosopher, Bernard le Bovier de Fontenelle (1657-1757).

his subject, for he observes, to his surprise, that slaked lime (calcium hydroxide), which he had supposed to be quicklime (calcium oxide) deprived of its active volatile alkali, has lost none of its alkaline powers. He decides that the active principle of quicklime must consist of fire particles rather than alkalinity.

Much of Homberg's difficulty stems from his inability to make a clear differentiation between the several mineral acids and between the various alkalis. This is evident in the long essay on salts which he published in 1702.[38] Having failed (as had others) in attempts to isolate the 'acid salts', he decides that the salt principle cannot be isolated. A believer in the system of five elements analysed by fire, he decides that only three of them, mercury, water and earth, can be isolated, and that the other two, sulphur and salt, cannot. This leads him into hopeless difficulty, since he believes the several acids to be salts differentiated by their content of different kinds of sulphur. Thus neither the salt principle common to all acids nor the sulphur principle which differentiated the kinds of acids can be isolated!

It was at least possible to isolate the alkaline salts. Homberg shows himself to be well acquainted with the differentiation of solidifiable salts on the basis of their crystal forms, but in the cases of the alkaline salts this is largely nullified by their hydroscopicity. He was moreover confused by the Cartesian conviction that all materials upon which acids may act are alkalis, and was imbued with the conviction that alkalis, even those which are called 'fixed', may be volatilized. And, finally, in the experiments referred to above he speculates that the two acids chosen may exemplify two noxious acids of the body, and chooses in consequence to explore 'alkalis' common to medicine, such as 'crab's eyes', coral and pearl, in the hope that his work may be useful to medicine![39] In consequence of all this he was even more frustrated in his study of alkalis than he was in regard of the acids.[40]

One who seems to have attended Homberg's lectures as a boy was finally to hoist the science of chemistry onto a higher plateau where it was to remain for the next half century. This was E. F.

[38] Homberg, 1702.

[39] Homberg, 1700: 64–5.

[40] We know by hindsight that the alkalis proved more difficult to differentiate than did the acids. See below, p. 347.

Geoffroy (1672–1731), son of a Paris pharmacist and himself a pharmacist and one-time chemist at the Jardin du Roi.[41] Admitted to the Academy in 1700, Geoffroy offered the members for nearly twenty years the usual series of small chemical papers and then, in 1718, published one of the epochal papers in the history of chemistry, his 'Table of the different "rapports" observed in chemistry between different substances'.[42] Geoffroy saw the common features of his own and his predecessors' explorations of reactions between acids and alkalis, acids and metals, sulphur and metals, etc. Most of the 'hidden movements which follow the mixing of bodies' depend upon the circumstance that some materials have 'more rapport', or disposition to unite, than others. He finds it possible to arrange most of the substances with which chemists were accustomed to experiment in tabular form, in columns which compare the order of the rapport of the substance below with the substance which heads each column.

Commenting on Geoffroy's table, Fontenelle declared[43] that the fact that a body united to another quits it to unite with yet another which it prefers is a thing 'the possibility of which has not been divined by the most subtle philosophers and of which the explanation is still not easy'. One supposes that the second substance is more suitable to it, but what principle of action can one conceive for this? Sympathies and antipathies seem appropriate, but they leave unexplained such facts of chemistry as the differences of degree of the disposition to unite, for a body which abandons a second for a third, abandons the third for a fourth, and so on. It is these dispositions which Geoffroy calls rapports, and a greater disposition is a greater rapport. His table enables one to predict the effect of mixing substances and considers the different forces which materials have for interacting. The more chemistry is perfected, he correctly predicts, 'the more Geoffroy's table will be perfected in its comprehension and organization'.

The chemist still harboured the yearning for the mathematization of his science. To his comment on Geoffroy's table Fontenelle wistfully added: 'If physics cannot arrive at the certainty of mathematics,

[41] On Geoffroy see Max Speter in Bugge, 1929–30, Vol. 1: 221–7.
[42] Geoffroy, 1718.
[43] In the *Histoire* accompanying Geoffroy, 1718.

would it not at least be better to imitate a mathematical order? A chemical table is by itself a spectacle agreeable to the spirit as would be a table of numbers ordered following certain rapports or certain properties.' Time was to prove that he had more reason for optimism than he seems to have realized.

Chapter Fifteen

Metal industries and the science of metals

IN the previous chapter I have examined the state of chemical science in the first decades of the eighteenth century. In this chapter and the next my objective is the state of practical chemistry and the status of knowledge of some of the most familiar processes. It was apparent from the evidences of practical chemistry in antiquity that certain substances were produced in large, if not precisely definable, quantities. In the sixteenth century we begin to encounter detailed accounts of the production of the same substances, the metals and materials used in building, glass-making, food preservation, the production of textiles and leather. The seventeenth century offers a few statistics on the quantities produced, and occasional reflections on its significance to science.

We can trace a decline and revival of metallurgy in western Europe through industrial archæology, aided, from the late fifteenth century, by a more-or-less continuous literary record. The decline is especially evident in Britain, where mines worked in Roman times seem to have been abandoned, and where in some cases – e.g., iron-working – technology relapsed to a more primitive stage. The revival of British iron-working came at the end of the Middle Ages, when the average size of the 'bloom' (product of a single furnace operation), which had remained about the same for a thousand years, increased from 30 to 300 pounds in a single century, the fifteenth.[1] Evidences of revival, from what was probably a less drastic

[1] Tylcote, 1962: 296–7.

decline, are considerably earlier on the continent, where the opening of some of the most famous mining centres can be traced to the tenth century, and where the blast furnace was commonplace by the middle of the fifteenth.[2]

The introduction of the blast furnace was the touchstone of the ascendency of European metallurgy. There are three basic commercial forms of iron; wrought iron, cast iron and steel. Wrought iron is produced by hammering a spongy mass of iron mixed with impurities (the bloom) which is the product of the primitive furnace. Cast iron comes molten and relatively pure from a high-temperature, forced-draught (blast) furnace. Steel, a compound of iron and carbon, was known in antiquity as a product of the re-working of iron in a charcoal forge. As the most useful form of iron it was continuously improved by empirical methods.

The blast furnace seems to have been known in China 1500 years earlier than in Europe, and the European iron industry was generally inferior to that of Asia during the Middle Ages,[3] but during the fifteenth, sixteenth and seventeenth centuries the Europeans brought about a general reversal of this inferiority. This development seems to have been due principally to the mechanization of metal-working processes, beginning with the improvement of conditions of reduction in the iron furnace through the use of water-powered bellows, a development which led to the modern blast furnace and made it commonplace in continental Europe by 1500. Further innovations leading to the water-powered tilt-hammer and rolling mill were encouraged by the fact that the cannon provided an urgent market for cast iron just at this time.[4] A general mechanization of the iron industry took place in the sixteenth century, a renovation, the impetus of which extended to the mechanization of the hauling processes of the mine. By 1700, much of what we credit to the 'industrial revolution' had been accomplished.[5]

The ancient prejudice in favour of gold and silver, in which all other metals were in a sense by-products of the search for these precious metals, still prevailed to some degree in the sixteenth

[2] Wertheim, 1962: 57.

[3] See the comparisons of European and Oriental iron-working in Needham, 1956; Smith, 1960: 144, 40ff.; Wertheim, 1962: 44–78; and Hartwell, 1962.

[4] Cf. Wertheim, 1962: 63–7.

[5] Cf. Mumford, 1934.

century, and of these two metals we have the fullest indications of production. It appears that world production of gold almost doubled between 1500 and 1700, and that 1800 saw about three times as much gold produced as had been produced annually three centuries earlier; but this was probably the slowest rate of increase in production of any metal. Silver production increased almost nine-fold between 1500 and 1600, the reason of course being the discovery of America, the mines of which were responsible for nearly 95 per cent of the silver produced in 1600![6] European production had actually undergone a substantial reduction.

The earliest production records for specific mines come from two of the most important copper mines, at Fahlun (Sweden), from 1633, and Mansfeld (Germany), from 1688. During the subsequent period up to 1800 these records indicate that the two mines together accounted for 1,200 to 1,300 tons of copper per annum.[7] Sweden produced about 23,000 metric tons of iron in 1683, at which time, and for a century thereafter, it was the leading producer. Both Swedish and English data indicate that iron production was about ten times that of copper in the seventeenth and eighteenth centuries, after which the proportion of iron to copper rose rapidly until it had attained nearly 1000 by the middle nineteenth century.[8] But this development does not belie the fact that the production of both metals was already 'industrialized' in the seventeenth century.

There appears to be no early systematic statistical record of the production of lead, tin and mercury. As a by-product of silver, lead had probably always been produced in larger quantities than were wanted, but in the seventeenth century there is plenty of evidence that it was widely and deliberately produced.[9] Tin, as it had since antiquity, came principally from Britain, where production averaged about 6,800 tons per annum in the seventeenth century. It sub-

---

[6] See production statistics in Neumann, 1904: 184–5, 228.

[7] Fahlun produced 1,336 metric tons in 1683. Its production rate subsequently declined, while Mansfeld rose until in 1800 Fahlun produced 587 and Mansfeld about 700 metric tons (Neumann, 1904: 110). World production of copper in 1800 has been given by Robert Allen (1923: 1) as about 10,000 tons.

[8] This is based on the statistical tables in Neumann, 1904: 51–3, 109–11.

[9] See Neumann, 1904: 133–6, and, on the uses of lead, C. S. Smith and R. J. Forbes, 1957.

sequently decreased, in part due to the competition of East Indian tin imported by the Dutch, but probably mainly because its principal application, for the making of pewter, was being undermined by a change in fashion of household wares, in which pewter was being replaced by porcelain and related ceramics.[10]

Our statistics on the production of mercury come after the development of the first large-scale industrial demand, which dates from the introduction, in the New World, of the amalgamation processes for the extraction of gold and silver.[11] The mine at Fruili in the territory of Venice was reportedly producing it at the rate of about 130 tons (256,000 pounds) per year in 1663, and had been increasing its production at the rate of about 10 per cent per annum.[12]

About sixty years later the ancient Spanish mine at Almadén was found by a visitor to have some 1,250 tons (25,000 quintals) of mercury in its warehouse, and this was described as the mere residue of a larger quantity which had been shipped away in that year (1717).[13]

Antimony and bismuth were also produced on a sufficient scale in the sixteenth century to attract the attention of writers on metallurgy, who indicate that both were produced commercially.[14] This coincided with the emergence of antimony as the favourite remedy of medical chemistry and, probably more important, with its application in an alloy for type-metal.[15] The uses of bismuth, beyond medicine, are less clear. Zinc was not mentioned by metallurgical writers before 1617, but it was probably already imported. Henceforth it was both produced in Europe and imported from the East Indies, and found increasing use in the direct fabrication of brass.[16]

---

[10] Clow and Clow (1952: 293) speak of the replacement in the eighteenth century of the 'eotechnic' table furnishings, wood and pewter, by the 'paleotechnic' glass and pottery.

[11] On the amalgamation processes see Hoover's note in Agricola, 1912: 297–300.

[12] Pope, 1665.

[13] Jussieu, 1719: 335.

[14] Agricola speaks vaguely of the production of both antimony and bismuth (1912: 428, 433), on the latter of which Ercker (1951: 275–8) gives some detail. In his monograph on the history of bismuth Lippmann (1930: 37) calls J. H. Pott's *Observationes et animadversiones de Vismutho* (1739) the first step in scientific research on the substance.

[15] Biringuccio, 1942: 374. See also the editor's notes to Moxon, 1958: 379–80.

[16] On the history of zinc see Beckmann, 1846, Vol. 2: 32–45.

The science of metals

No question in chemistry had a longer history than that of the formation of metals, and perhaps in no question was the theorist less successful in improving on Aristotle. Exoteric alchemy had posed the problem differently, in adding to it the question of the formation of metals by 'art', but with little effect. In the sixteenth and seventeenth centuries, one's position on mineral formation had little to do with a belief in transmutation of the metals by chemical methods, and one's belief in the possibility of artificial transmutation had scarcely more to do with his attitude towards alchemy. Gregorius Reisch, writing at the end of the fifteenth century, stated with unusual clarity what was probably the most common opinion, that metallic transmutation is possible, but alchemy false.[17]

By 1500 Latin alchemy was increasingly turning to occultism or charlatanry, but everyone who touched on chemistry still found it necessary to have an opinion on the gold-making art. The encyclopaedist, Polydore Vergil, was somewhat original in dwelling on its legality, which he finally supported.[18] The prominent French physician, Symphorien Champier, was forthright in arguing that a denial of alchemy implies a denial of both artificial and natural transmutation.[19] His assertion that the metals were so created by God and remain unaltered was only popular among those who had no real interest in chemistry (or by reformed alchemists),[20] for not only did it cost the chemist a goodly part of his territory, but it seemed contradicted by 'eye-witness' accounts of the growth of metals in the earth. More common were opinions which rejected alchemy (Leonardo da Vinci), or at least condemned it (Biringuccio, Agricola), while accepting the traditional theories of metal formation in nature.[21] And finally, there were those who denied alchemy but

---

[17] 1504: Bk 9, Ch. 25.

[18] 1868: 237–41. See above, Ch. 7 note 49.

[19] Champier, 1533: fols. 31v–39r.

[20] Partington (1961: 268), mentions a one-time alchemist, Nicolas Guibert, who finally concluded that metals are species and cannot be changed. Agricola of Nettesheim may have been a similar case (see Thorndike, HMES, Vol. 5: 132–3).

[21] Cf. MacCurdy, 1939: 69, 142–3, and elsewhere. Agricola, 1912: Preface and notes on p. 46. Biringuccio, 1942: 35–43 and note on p. 26. The Spanish authority, Barba (1674: 71–3), adhered to the alchemical view of mineral formation and the transmutability of metals.

none the less gave instruction for its practice. Such a one was Cardano, who saw no reason why metals cannot change their substance, since they can change their colour and weight, and who, moreover, was familiar with the supposed 'transmutation' of iron into copper as well as with a successful demonstration of gold-making which he had witnessed in Venice. But although he gives some instructions on how to go about gold-making, he takes a dim view of the practicality of transmutation, considers the activities of gold-makers a blemish on the otherwise admirable art of chemistry, and thinks that even the best artificial gold is imperfect in substance and colour.[22] One regrets that no one adopted the suggestion of Marin Mersenne, that 'academies' of alchemists be established to regulate their activities.[23]

Much publicity was given in the sixteenth and seventeenth centuries to a supposed experimental demonstration of metallic transmutation by the metallurgists of central Europe, who were accustomed to converting 'vitriolate' mine drainage waters into useful (iron) vitriol by casting scraps of iron into those waters. This reaction involved the dissolution of the iron and deposition of copper – since the drainage of copper mines contains copper sulphate. It was very generally regarded as a 'transmutation' – though not by the metallurgists, according to Helmont[24] – and its disproof was something of a landmark in seventeenth-century chemistry. Angelo Sala, who held, about 1618, that the copper was already present in the vitriolate waters,[25] may have been the first to cast doubt on it. Sennert disproved it experimentally between 1629 and his death eight years later, although he did not regard this as conclusive evidence against the possibility of metallic transmutation, in which

[22] 1556: 124r–125. 1559: 235–6.

[23] Mersenne, 1625: 105–6.

[24] 'viri metallarii vix agnoscentes' (Helmont, 1648–2: 692. 1662: 695).

[25] Sala is led into the question in considering 'the artificial preparation of vitriol after the description of Oswald Croll in *Basilica Chymica*' (from iron or copper and sulphur, cf. Croll, 1609: 218–20) He considers the supposed iron-copper transmutation analogous to laboratory processes in which a metal is dissolved in aqua fortis and then 'reduced' (precipitated) by another metal, using several examples (Sala, 1647: 399–400 [*Anatomia vitrioli*]). Sala wrote this, as he says, about nine years after the first publication of his *Anatomia vitrioli* in 1609. That belief in the iron-copper transmutation continued to be widespread may be due to ignorance of Sala's work, but is more probably a reflection of the conservatism of tradition.

he continued to believe.[26] The exposure of the supposed iron-copper transmutation was an important step in the development of the theory of affinities – and hence in the science of chemistry – but it does not seem to have seriously impaired the theory of transmutation.

When theories of metal generation were formulated outside of the context of alchemy, they were little influenced by metallurgy. While some, such as Palissy and Sennert, held that the Peripatetic exhalations constituted an insufficient explanation of metal formation, and had resort to the principles mercury and sulphur,[27] others, even some chemists,[28] held the exhalations to be sufficient. Cardano supposed the theory that metals are made of mercury and sulphur to have originated in observation of the sulphurous fumes and silvery liquids which appear in the smelting process, but points out the incompatibility of sulphur and mercury in terms of the Aristotelian doctrine of like acting on like, and also notes that the two substances are not found together in nature. He concludes that metals are not made of mercury and sulphur, although he admits some similarity.[29]

The most influential writers were even more anachronistic. Agricola's opinion, that metals are made of the elements earth and water, in proportions known to God alone, was reached after a lengthy discussion of the views of Albertus Magnus and Ibn Juljul ('Gilgil of Maretania')![30] Becher, who stressed the equivalence of the four elements and the three chemical principles, gives his authority as Thomas Aquinas, in his commentary on the *Meteorology*![31]

The extent to which the mechanical cosmologies of the seventeenth century escaped from this can best be appreciated from a

[26] In the 1629 edition of his *De consensu* Sennert remarked that transmutation was experimentally demonstrated in the 'fountains' of Hungary and at Goslar, where iron was transmuted into copper (1629: 10). In later editions (cf. Sennert, 1676: 182) he has inserted a passage saying that he has prepared such a water by the dissolution of copper in 'aqua ex vitriola et sale communi facta'.

[27] Palissy brought in a good many other factors as well, in his *Treatise on metals and alchemy* (1957: 80–110). It is not quite certain that the views expressed in Sennert, Culpepper and Cole, 1659: 152, are Sennert's.

[28] E.g. Michael Sendovogius (1615: 11).

[29] Cardano, 1556: 124v–126. 1559: 235–7 (Bk 6).

[30] Agricola, 1956: 168–75 (*De ortu*, Bk 5).

[31] BCC, Vol. 1: 310b (*Oedipus chymicus*).

consideration of the views of Descartes and Digby. The former put himself to the trouble of deriving from his shaped particles the three Paracelsian principles, because it was Descartes's opinion that the true cause of metals in mines is an interaction of these three, where corrosive juices running in the pores of the dense inner crust of the earth become enveloped by small branches of the sulphurous or oily material and are then pushed into the crust by quicksilver which has been agitated and rarefied by heat. As the sizes and figures of the particles of the dense layer differ, so do the metals.[32]

Almost simultaneously we find Digby cogitating the same question. Having outlined his conception of the formation of solid bodies by varying compositions of the four elements, he proceeds to subterranean events, and sees heat extracting humours from bodies in the earth and these 'steams' collecting and condensing in some hollow place. They then flow where subterranean fissures allow, gathering 'loose parts' along the way, and finally coming to rest in some low place where they are by concentration of heat digested into a metal. He reports that miners who have come upon such unfinished metal deposits, 'by their experience knowing after how many years they will be ripe, they shut them up till then'.[33]

Perhaps the most striking evidence of the retarded state of metallurgical science is the lack of an improved differentiation of individual metals and alloys beyond that which had been achieved in antiquity. Attempts to modify ancient tradition were inconclusive, to say the least. Biringuccio lists six 'metals', gold, silver, copper, iron, tin, and lead. Agricola remarks that this is the traditional number, but disagrees with 'writers' and 'alchemists' whom, he says, have denied mercury to be a metal. He admits mercury, grey lead or bismuth 'which was unknown to the older Greek writers', and finally 'smelted stibnite' (antimony), but he is not much in advance of Pliny (whom he cites) on 'the genius of lead minerals' which he lists in one place as three, lead, tin and bismuth, and in another as four (adding antimony). He also thinks brass may yet turn out to be a metal of natural occurrence.[34]

[32] Descartes, 1905: 242 (*Principia*, Pt 4, Princ. 63).

[33] 1645: 161. In an incidental reference to the alchemists he remarks that they 'profess to make spirits so etherial and volatile that being poured out of a glasse from some reasonable height, they shall never reach the ground' (ibid.: 155).

[34] Biringuccio, 1942: Bk 1. Agricola, 1955: 18–19, 178–81.

Agricola failed to induce his contemporaries to abandon the ancient dogma of seven (rather than six, as he says) metals to which both Cardano and Ercker adhered.[35] But they were either indifferent to the question (Ercker), or confused (Cardano), and it was Biringuccio, who regarded mercury and antimony either as 'mineral deformities and monstrosities among metals' or as 'materials about to reach metallic perfection which have been hindered from doing so by being mined too soon', who set the pattern for the future. He included mercury and antimony in a group of 'semi-metals', a class which included sulphur, 'marcasite', salts, vitriols, and other things, and which very nearly corresponded to Pliny's 'other things' found in mines.[36] In the eighteenth century the class of semi-metals came to be restricted to the newly discovered metals, and they were given a distinctive, if uncertain, place in the scheme of chemical classification. Pierre Macquer, writing in the 1770s, included among 'metals' not only the metals 'properly so-called', but also the semi-metals, 'or all matter which have the essential metallic properties'. They are 'not very numerous'. The essential properties in question are malleability and resistance to 'destruction' by fire. Those metals possessing both, gold, silver and platinum, are 'perfect'; those possessing only the first, copper, iron, tin and lead, are 'imperfect'; and those which lack both, regulus of antimony, bismuth, zinc, regulus of cobalt and regulus of arsenic, are merely 'metallic substances'.[37] Mercury makes a class separate from the others, and it has not quite ceased to be their 'parent'. The application of the analytical method of decomposition and recomposition – plus '[reflection] on the essential properties of metals' – has shown Macquer that the metals are compounded of 'the earthy element', and 'the inflam-

[35] Ercker, 1951: 4. Cardano, 1556: 120v. 1559: 226. Scaliger contradicts Cardano, who stresses the fusibility of metals, on the ground that there is in Mexico an 'orichalcum' which no fire has been able to liquefy (1557: 134v [Exerc. 88]). This was perhaps the first mention of platinum.

[36] Biringuccio, 1942: 91, and Bk 2, on semi-minerals.

[37] Macquer, 1778: arts. Metaux and metallisation. Three of these 'metallic substances' were essentially new to chemical literature in the eighteenth century. Zinc had been obscurely mentioned in 1617 as a metallurgical furnace by-product (Löhneyss, [1690]: 83v), and had been known much earlier in Asia and imported from there by the Dutch. Platinum had been found by the Spanish in the New World, mentioned by Scaliger (1557: 134v), but only generally noticed in the 1740s. Cobalt was discovered in Swedish ores in the 1730s, by Georg Brandt (cf. Weeks, 1956).

mable principle' (phlogiston). If, as he admits, the difference between the metals requires an additional ingredient, he thinks (with Becher and Stahl) that it is 'probably of a mercurial nature'.[38]

A principal difficulty in the elucidation of the metals seems to have been that the question was consistently considered in terms of gold, and so retained connotations of gold-making at a time when alchemy was increasingly discredited among the learned. A second inhibiting factor was the fact, only surprising from the modern viewpoint, that metals seem never to have been regarded as elements but, on the contrary, as the 'most mixed' of bodies. Hence the most sophisticated chemists tended to prefer the investigation of simpler substances.

There was also a third difficulty, in the increasing contrast between an empirical metallurgy not unworthy of comparison with the technology of modern times and a science of metals which was already regarded as fantastic. The magnitude of this contrast has tempted some to accord the practical metallurgist a superior scientific knowledge of metals, and the 'organized positive know-ledge' (as George Sarton defined science) in the works of Biringuccio, Agricola and Ercker is scientific, indeed, by comparison with any-thing which had appeared before on the subject of metallurgy. But quite aside from the question of the extent to which these writers can really be called 'practical metallurgists', we search this literature in vain for advances in that knowledge. It is not 'discoveries' which these metallurgical writers record, but a technological complex which, although sophisticated, had been virtually static throughout the Christian era and which was to remain so for another two centuries.

[38] Macquer, loc. cit.

Chapter Sixteen

Heavy chemicals

THE large-scale production of materials which would now be called 'heavy chemicals' can also be described in considerable detail from seventeenth-century sources. Some of these industries, such as those in common salt and sulphur, were purely extractive; other substances, notably (anhydrous) gypsum and quicklime, were produced by simple heating. The alkali, vitriol and alum industries were more complex in that they involved the differentiation of several members of a family. Other industries were concerned with exotic substances which had been unknown (at least in the West) in antiquity and were originally imported; these became the object of a concerted search for domestic sources in Europe. Of these, saltpetre, sal ammoniac, and borax seem to deserve inclusion among the heavy chemicals. A discussion of these materials, if it does not exhaust the heavy chemical industry of the seventeenth century, is certainly sufficient to characterize it.

The processes for production of these materials were generally simpler than were those for the metals, and ancient dogma exercised no comparable domination over their scientific consideration. There was in the eighteenth century, however, a modern dogma, that of Becher and Stahl, which provided the not-too-curious chemist with a systematic chemical explanation of all of these substances. All except sulphur are 'salts', which Stahl takes up as the first examples of 'mixed [bodies] consisting of earth and water', in the order, vitriol, alum, nitre, common salt, and sal ammoniac.[1] The order is not accidental, for he thinks that he sees in these five salts an affinity

[1] The following is from Stahl, 1730: 79–107. 1746, Pt 1: 50–67.

series which combines his system of elements with the theory that a primordial acid and a primordial alkali play fundamental roles in nature. Vitriol is the 'universal salt' (or, elsewhere, 'universal acid'), coagulated into a solid form by metals. Alum is next in the series, having the same 'saline principle' united to a different 'alkaline or earthy body', a chalky earth resembling limestone which is more difficultly separated by fire from the salt principle than is the metal in vitriol. The kinship between his salts becomes increasingly vague as he goes down the series. Nitre (saltpetre) differs in both components, 'an oily and saline volatile mixt' and a 'very subtle alkaline earth', but comes next because it is even more difficult to obtain its principles 'by resolution'. However difficult this may be, he finds no difficulty eliciting from it various spirits (nitric acid, nitric oxide) nor in reproducing nitre from aqua fortis and potash. Common salt has its alkaline earth (which he elsewhere identifies as his metalline earth principle) in common with nitre, and its other ingredient (the universal acid) in common with vitriol, and is reproduced by mixing its spirit (hydrochloric acid) with oil of tartar. With sal ammoniac he seems to have reached an opposite extreme from vitriol, since it contains the most fixed of all earths (which he obliquely identifies with potash) combined with 'an oily substance'.[2]

Stahl's system has clearly become unmanageable by the time it reaches sal ammoniac, and he passes on to a loosely organized discussion of other salts, animal, vegetable and mineral, among which we find those persistently mysterious substances, the alkalis. The 'fixed alkaline salt' (soda and potash) recurs repeatedly, for he thinks it differs 'both according to the difference of the plant and the difference of the operation'.[3] Quicklime is 'an artificial alkali' composed of 'a subtle corrosive earthy matter' with 'a grosser matter'. Borax, which like quicklime appears somewhat incidentally, is made up of the universal acid with a vitrifiable earth,[4] and common

[2] Stahl, like Paracelsus, seems to have baffled his followers almost as much as he does us. Saltpetre is 'ex oleoso & Oino volatile mixto' ('an oily and saline volatile mixt') according to his *Fundamenta chymiae dogmaticae et experimentalis* (1746–7, Pt 1: 56. 1730: 88), but according to Baumé (1773, Vol. 3: 593) Stahl held saltpetre to be a putrefaction product of vitriolic acid and the inflammable principle (phlogiston). These two statements are not contradictory, but are well indicative of the degree of precision characteristic of the 'phlogistonists'.

[3] 1730: 139. 1746, Pt 1: 85–6.

[4] 1730: 18, 150. 1746, Pt 1: 11, 91.

sulphur, he discovers after a lengthy research, is made of 'a saline corrosive astringent substance' and 'a black earth'.[5]

The further development of this can be discovered in the remarkably complacent pages of the chemical dictionary of Pierre Macquer, which was published on the eve of the overthrow of Becher and Stahl by Lavoisier. Although a follower of Stahl, neither Stahl's beautifully nebulous system of elementary constitution nor the abortive affinity series of salts prevents Macquer from following a less tortured path in his analysis of the most commonplace salts, a divergence which is facilitated by the presentation of his work in the form of a dictionary.[6] Common salt, saltpetre and sal ammoniac are all neutral salts composed of an acid and an alkali. Common salt is composed of marine (hydrochloric) acid and 'marine or mineral alkali'; saltpetre is composed of nitric acid (acide nitreux) saturated with 'fixed vegetable alkali'; sal ammoniac results from the union of hydrochloric acid and ammonia. Of the ingredients of these three salts there is only one, 'marine or mineral alkali', concerning which Macquer's identification would not agree with that of a modern chemist, and it is again in regard to the alkalis that he encounters his greatest difficulty. Where he treats of alkalis he classifies them as vegetable, mineral and volatile, but then shows himself to be as confused as Stahl, taking 'fixed alkali of nitre' as a distinct substance, leaving 'fixed alkali of tartar' unclassified, and confounding the carbonates of sodium and potassium generally. He finally takes comfort in his conviction that all alkalis are composed 'of acid, of earth and of a little phlogiston'.[7]

Where he refers to 'acid' as though it were elementary, Macquer, following Becher and Stahl, refers to vitriolic (sulphuric) acid, 'the simplest of all acids and consequently the simplest of all saline substances'.[8] Combined with copper, iron or zinc this

---

[5] 1730: 156. 1746, Pt 1: 95.

[6] His textbook (Macquer, 1764) seems greatly deficient to the dictionary in clarity, a circumstance which seems to me to owe more to the difference in format than to the lapse of seventeen years between the two, for the opinions expressed are in most cases almost identical.

[7] Macquer, 1778, arts., sel nitreux, sels marin, and a series of articles on alkalis. The expansion of the repertoire of the chemist, which we find in the tables of Lavoisier's *Traité* of 1789, is already in large part visible in these articles.

[8] Ibid., art., acide vitriolique. Becher and Stahl were in turn following, in some degree, John of Rupescissa whom Becher cites on the universal acid (1669: 91) and on vitriol as a 'middle' principle (1703: 723 [*Theses chymicae*]).

acid yields a vitriol; combined with argillaceous earth it yields alum.

The only mystery Macquer seriously admits relates to borax. He believes borax to be a neutral salt, but confesses his inability to say more because of the general ignorance of its origins which were a closely guarded secret of the Dutch and the Venetians who imported it. His confidence reaches its opposite extreme in relation to quicklime. Chemists, he says, 'have long been embarrassed' by the phenomena of quicklime and the calcareous earth from which it is derived. The theory, which he attributes to Stahl, that they are to be explained on the ground that calcareous earth is 'strongly disposed to enter into the saline combination' and that quicklime is the fulfilment of this disposition, has been 'completed' by Black's discovery of 'fixed air' (1754), showing that 'the volatile principles . . . may be separated from the fixed earthy principles'. This, Macquer concludes, makes it 'one of the most satisfactory [theories] in chemistry'.[9]

Stahl and Macquer tell us less about the contemporary state of scientific knowledge of the heavy chemicals than they do of the difficulty of establishing a general synthesis of chemistry in the eighteenth century. The heavy chemicals, however, are among the materials on which they are most fully informed and in which they are most interested. It appears to be as true in their time as it was in antiquity that the substances of commercial importance are also those with which the natural philosopher is most concerned; to which it should be added that it also remains true that virtually all known substances were of commercial importance, for the discoveries which had by 1750 increased the number of known substances several fold were largely made in the continued pursuit of new medicinal materials.

For an accurate picture of the status of chemical science at the end of the seventeenth century and the beginning of the eighteenth it is necessary to trace the history of individual substances, and this must further be done for a number of materials, for science has a considerably firmer grasp of some than of others. A systematic study of all substances which could be called 'known' is by no means out of the

---

[9] Macquer, 1778., arts., borax and chaux terreuse. In his textbook, apparently written before Black's work, Macquer was equally delighted with the correspondence between his own experimental evidence 'that there is no saline matter in the composition of lime', and 'the illustrious Stahl's opinion' (Macquer, 1764, Vol. 1: 38–43).

question, for the number was still by modern standards severely limited.[10] It is, however, beyond the scope of the present work. I have chosen to illustrate the state of chemical science through the heavy chemicals, as constituting a limited and workable group and one which also casts an especially interesting light on the relationship between science and technology. In choosing substances produced on an industrial scale we are not abandoning medicine, for without exception these materials continued to have medical application. Nor is the medically oriented chemist eliminated. If there were by this time chemists not exclusively devoted to medicine – of which Boyle is the classic example – most of the chemists retained the medical orientation, including those who concerned themselves with the heavy chemicals.

I will consider the heavy chemicals in the order in which they were, in the sense of modern chemistry, clearly understood. Common salt, gypsum, saltpetre, sal ammoniac and borax were best understood, at least in the sense that they were subject to the fewest misconceptions. Vitriol was about as well understood but entailed the additional difficulty of the involvement of analogous substances, among which were the alums. What one might expect to have been the best known substances, sulphur, quicklime and soda, were actually the most mis-understood. In them resided much of the mystery which was to be unravelled in the course of the chemical revolution.

Common salt

Common salt was in all probability the first 'industrial chemical', and was produced in remote antiquity by three methods which remain in use today; the solar evaporation of sea water, the boiling down of brines, and the mining of salt deposits. The first of these was the most important, and the medieval ascendancy of sun-poor northern Europe brought with it a crisis in the economy of salt, a crisis stemming not only from an increase in population, but also

[10] In his *Traité de chimie* Lavoisier calculates that 1,152 'neutral salts' are possible from the action of acids on the three (known) alkalis, four earths and seventeen metallic substances; but he lists the acids as no less than forty-eight, including nineteen organic acids and 'seventeen metallic acids hitherto imperfectly known, but upon which Mr Berthollet is about to publish a very important work'. Lavoisier adds that only about 'thirty species of salt' were known 20 years before (1790: 166–8).

from the spread of the practice of preserving food (e.g., herring) by salting.[11]

The trade in salt produced from sea water in the neighbourhood of Venice, was important in the rise of that commercial state, and salt remained, in the great age of Venice, one of its more important products.[12] France, too, became a major supplier. It not only had a Mediterranean coast, but also introduced salt production on the Atlantic coast, which became towards the end of the Middle Ages a principal source of supply for the herring fisheries.[13] Less fortunate regions had to resort to the improvement of the expensive process of boiling down brines. Pliny (Bk 31, Ch. 7) had reported the Germans to be producing salt by casting salt water over burning coals. By the tenth century they seem to have begun the improvement of that process, which we find described by Agricola, in which brine is heated in a 'salt-pan' of iron or lead fitted to a specially constructed furnace.[14]

Mineral salt had been known in central Europe since antiquity, and the production of some mines in the seventeenth century was enormous. A mine near Cracow was described in 1670 as one of the best revenues of the king of Poland, and it was probably not less productive than the mine near Eper, Hungary, which was reportedly producing over 6,500 tons (50,000 tuns of 268 pounds) annually in 1730.[15] Great Britain, however, remained an importer, and depended upon foreign sources for over two-thirds of the 40,000 tons consumed annually in the first half of the sixteenth century. From 1560 salt-pans were introduced in increasing numbers and were finally adapted to use with coal as fuel. By 1690 only one-fourth of the 130,000-ton annual comsumption was imported.[16]

[11] See Nenquin, 1961, and on the salting of fish, Cutting, 1958. Forbes reports that the salting of herrings was invented by a Fleming, Wm. Beukelszoon, about 1330 (in Chas. Singer et al, 1954–8, Vol. 3: 22).

[12] Bauer, 1930.

[13] Cf. Hauser, 1927. This is the area described by Palissy, and where he was employed (1957: 136–45).

[14] Fester, 1923: 78. Agricola describes several methods of salt production in De re metallica, Bk 12 (1912: 545–58).

[15] Anonymous, 1670, and Brückman, 1730. Here and subsequently I have expressed production data in English tons or 2,000 lb., but have also given them in parentheses as they appear in the sources.

[16] Nef, 1932, Vol. 1: 178–9.

The production of salt was not a chemical problem, and the substance entered the purview of the chemist chiefly as the prototype of one of his 'principles'. His interest in this principle increased with his interest in the mineral acids, to which it was supposed to occupy some kind of primitive relationship. But that acid known as 'spirit of salt' (hydrochloric acid) was still in the eighteenth century the least known of the mineral acids. Although the chlorides of most of the classical metals were known, they were not known as products of this acid,[17] indeed the acid of common salt itself was thought to be that 'primordial' acid, sulphuric, the confused consequences of which we see in Stahl and Macquer. The emergence of an interest in the 'base' with which this primordial acid is compounded seems to be an early example of that pursuit out of curiosity to which we give the name 'pure science'. The event took place in 1736, when the French chemist Duhamel du Monceau published in the *Memoires* of the Academy a long and rigorously analytical *memoire* on the 'base' of common salt, which led him to the conclusion that the base is a soluble alkaline salt of bitter taste which he compares with soda; and it was in fact soda to which his analysis had led him.[18] The base of common salt remained a mystery until the emergence of electro-chemistry in the early nineteenth century.

Gypsum

Although it had been a major industrial chemical since antiquity, gypsum received little attention from chemists, perhaps because it had little vogue in medicine. Until the middle eighteenth century its history belongs rather to mineralogy than to chemistry. Its compo-

---

[17] See, for example, the 'old nomenclature' of the chlorides (muriates) as listed by Lavoisier, which includes such substances as martial sea salt (iron chloride), plumbum corneum (lead chloride), smoking liquor of Libavius (tin chloride), and of course sal ammoniac and the sublimates of mercury (Lavoisier, 1790: 253).

[18] Duhamel du Monceau, 1736. He (1) reacted salt and sulphuric acid, (2) ignited the product with charcoal, (3) treated this residue with vinegar, (4) alternately distilled and calcined this product. Duhamel viewed all this as 'transporting' the base of salt onto vitriolic acid, converting the acid to 'common sulphur', 'precipitating' said sulphur with vinegar and driving off the 'more feeble' vegetable acid leaving the base of salt. In fact the products of his four processes were probably: (1) sodium sulphate, (2) sodium carbonate, (3) sodium acetate, and (4) sodium carbonate. His description of the final product makes it quite clear that it was sodium carbonate (soda).

sition seems to have been inferred from its occurrence and its appearance, and it was accepted as an earthy substance related to lime and to the vitriols on mineralogical grounds alone. That it was a composition of the two was so far assumed that proof of it by Pott and Marggraf aroused no apparent interest, and it was in fact accidental. They were testing a theory, attributed to Stahl, that alum is a product of lime and sulphuric acid, and found that the product was instead gypsum. Henceforth the further elucidation of gypsum became a part of the problem of quicklime. It was on this neglected substance, however, that Lavoisier began his illustrious career in 1765.[19]

Saltpetre

The appearance of saltpetre in European literature at the end of the thirteenth century occurs in a recipe for gunpowder, and the rapid rise in demand for the substance in the fourteenth century is all too understandable. It seems to have been obtained from India by importation through Venice, but its mode of production did not long remain secret, and it was produced in Europe from about 1400. Until the development of the ammonia synthesis in the twentieth century saltpetre remained essentially a naturally occurring substance for the production of which every conceivable source was exploited. To the original Asiatic process of simply leaching 'manureal' soils some unknown European of the fourteenth century added an improvement which enriched those soils by treatment with a lime-potash mixture.[20] Although the peculiar salt occurring in the Chilean desert, which we know as sodium nitrate, had been known since the sixteenth century, it remained unexploited even after its identification in the seventeenth. Sodium nitrate is not useful in gunpowder, and only in the mid-nineteenth century was a process

[19] Marggraf, 1754: 32. The Paris Academy gave less attention to gypsum than to any other of the heavy chemicals. Jussieu, 1719, is essentially a mineralogical study. Lavoisier, (1865), if he contributed little to the science of gypsum, already exhibits the skill in research which was to revolutionize chemistry.

[20] That the European process was different virtually from the outset from the Indian process is an assumption resting on the fact that the earliest European references speak of 'saltpetre plantations' (or gardens) which signified, at least from the time of Biringuccio (1530) an enclosure for the treatment of saltpetre-bearing soil with potash and lime.

perfected for its economical conversion into potassium nitrate (saltpetre).[21]

Saltpetre was derived from human and animal refuse. In the Indian method of production the practitioner of the trade, having identified promising sources by a tell-tale crystalline efflorescence in domestic drains, visited them regularly, scraping up a thin layer of adjacent soil which he leached and finally evaporated to obtain the desired salt.[22] If this method was ever used in Europe it was improved upon very early, for a larger yield was obtained by layering the saltpetre-bearing earth with a lime-potash mixture in 'saltpetre plantations' through which water was allowed to percolate. This improvement results from the fact that potash converts to potassium nitrate the insoluble calcium salt which is the most persistent nitrate in the soil. After a first reference in 1405 accounts of saltpetre plantations become increasingly common in European literature.[23]

If the Indian saltpetre producer practised a curious trade, that of the European 'saltpetre hunters' was more bizarre, for they lacked the time or patience to follow the ancient ways of the Orient. The salt-petre industry of Europe was one of the strangest of enterprises. Armed with writs of legal authority the saltpetre hunters prowled the stables and refuse heaps of Europe, identifying by taste those which seemed promising.[24] Although the importance of saltpetre as a raw material for 'parting water' (nitric acid, for separating gold and silver) was not negligible, its military utilization provided the real impetus for the production of the substance. It entered into the cargos of the British East India Company as early as 1626, and in 1693 the Company contracted to provide the British Government with 500 tons per annum.[25] Indian methods were modified to European practice, and through the eighteenth century the Indian salt maintained an economic advantage which stifled attempts at domestic manufacture in Britain.[26] The domestic saltpetre hunter

---

[21] Donald, 1936.

[22] (Thevenot), 1665.

[23] The first mention is in Kyeser's *Bellifortis* of 1405. On this and subsequent references see Rathgen, 1928: 95–6.

[24] Cf. Beckmann, 1846, Vol. 2: 509–10.

[25] Anderson, 1862: 4.

[26] Cf. Beckmann, 1846, Vol. 2: 511. The improved Indian method is described by (Thevenot), 1665.

maintained himself in France, however – with strong government support – and justified himself with a prodigious effort which successfully offset the effect of the British blockade in the Napoleonic Wars.[27]

Saltpetre had been a staple reagent in the laboratory of the alchemist and medical chemist since the beginning of the fourteenth century, and, as the source of aqua fortis, it was one of the most commonplace raw materials in the pharmacology of medical chemistry. Although it can hardly be doubted that most of the nitrates of the classical metals were frequently made, there was little awareness in the seventeenth century that they constituted a class of substances. There was first of all the uncertainty as to whether aqua fortis originated in saltpetre or in vitriol (since it was made by distilling a mixture of the two), and such nitrates as those of tin, mercury and copper were called 'vitriols' by their respective discoverers, Libavius, 'Basil Valentine', and Boyle.[28]

Under such misnomers most of the common nitrates did, in fact, emerge in the seventeenth century. Libavius' systematic exploration of mineral acid reactivity also revealed a 'sweet calx of lead' which he crystallized from a solution of lead in aqua fortis.[29] Silver nitrate, and its property of blackening under sunlight, was reported by Angelo Sala in 1614, under the name 'crystalli Dianae',[30] and in 1675 calcium nitrate emerged – surreptitiously – when the German alchemist, C. A. Baldouin, prepared from chalk and aqua fortis his 'hermetic phosphorus', a luminescent substance which he believed to be Paracelsus's universal solvent.[31]

[27] A massive attack on the saltpetre problem by the scientists of France was signalled by Turgot's establishment of a 'Gunpowder Commission' in 1775. The Commission produced a voluminous study of the question (Académie des Sciences, 1786), and ultimately a great increase in domestic production of saltpetre (see Smeaton, 1962, 63). See also McKie, 1952: 125-31.

[28] Libavius, 1597: 386. 'Basil' obtained a 'very white vitriol' by evaporating a solution of mercury in aqua fortis (1769: 974). This was the intermediate, which the alchemists never seem to have discovered, on the way to 'whitening' or 'reddening' mercury. Boyle obtained a 'vitriol' of singular crystalline beauty from a solution of copper in aqua fortis (1772, Vol. 3: 58 ['Doubts and experiments touching the curious figures of salts.']).

[29] 1597: 151. Elsewhere he gives the name 'lead vitriol' to lead acetate (or perhaps carbonate) (ibid.: 386).

[30] Sala, 1647: 194-5 (Septem planetarum terrestrium spagyrica reconsio, 1614). François Sylvius used this poison internally, as a hydrogogue (for removal of water) (1680: 102).

[31] His report to the Royal Society of London (Baldouin, 1676) is, to say the least, obscure. For an analysis of it see Harvey, 1957: 321-2.

The prominence of crystal form in the specification of these substances seems to signify its emergence as a specific substance characteristic. The various crystals formed in aqueous solution were repeatedly remarked upon by the sixteenth century writers,[32] and crystal forms were familiar enough by the mid-seventeenth century to encourage both Davisson and Hooke to propose their systematic analysis.[33] If this was too ambitious an objective, the study of crystals did make possible some of the observations just mentioned, and others which were more remarkable. It was crucial to the analysis of the constitution of saltpetre, which was accomplished by both Glauber and Boyle. In what appears to be a deliberate example of 'pure research', the former reported dividing a sample of saltpetre into two parts, one of which he distilled with clay to yield an 'acid spirit of nitre', and the other of which he ignited with charcoal to give a 'liquor of fixed nitre'. He then combined the two and reported the product to be 'common saltpetre', a conclusion he clinched by the identity of its crystal form.[34] In 1685 the familiarity of this crystal form enabled the Leipzig professor of medicine, Johann Bohn, to believe that the 'cubic' (rhomboid) nitre he obtained by boiling common salt with aqua fortis was a different substance, and it was indeed sodium nitrate.[35]

The eighteenth century saw the restoration to the class of 'nitres' of many nitrates which had been classed as vitriols, but not until the end of the century do we find a general theory of the constitution of the class. Nitres were products of the 'acid spirit of nitre', but that acid (aqua fortis) was itself a product of nitre (saltpetre). Although the chemist suffered under a similar handicap in relation to the chlorides and sulphates, it seems to have given him the greatest difficulty in regard to the nitrates. Blithely assuming some understanding of sulphuric and hydrochloric acids, he proceeded to a reasonably successful ordering of their compounds. In the case of the nitrates, however, he faced up to the problem of first understanding the nature of nitre and its acid.

[32] For example, Biringuccio (1942: 94, 100, 112, 117) and Palissy (1957: 165).

[33] Davisson, 1640–42, Pt. 3: 184–209. Hooke, 1665: 85–8.

[34] 1689, Pt 1: 275 (*A treatise on the importance of salts, metals, and plants*). Boyle duplicated this research in his 'Physico-chymical essay . . . touching the differing parts and redintegration of salt-petre' (Boyle, 1772, Vol. 1: 359–76, esp. 360–1).

[35] Bohn 1685: Diss. 2, No. 7.

Those practical chemists (or spokesmen for practical chemists) Biringuccio, Agricola and Ercker, had been quite uncertain whether saltpetre is of animal, vegetable or mineral origin, although they were aware enough of the richness of manureal soils.[36] Two centuries later we find the celebrated Boerhaave, who held it to originate in the excrements of animals, in conflict with his English translator, Peter Shaw, who located saltpetre in putrefied vegetables.[37] By this time a fourth possible source had been added, the atmosphere, as a consequence of a large literature on the supposed 'aereal nitre', which is better known for its prevision of the discovery of oxygen than for its significance to the nitre question.[38]

An interesting discussion of the nitre question was published by Louis Lemery in 1717. The nub of the problem appears to be the fact, as he believes, that unlike most other salts there is no mineral source of nitre. He further reveals that a reaction against the chemical physicians of the acid-alkali doctrine, which led many persons to deny the existence of 'acids' in animals, had led to a corresponding denial of the animal origin of nitre. Both of these circumstances lend support to the aereal nitre theory, but Lemery has himself discovered that some plants contain a high proportion of nitre, and is led to postulate a theory that nitre follows a cycle through plants and animals.[39]

Reviewing in 1773 the numerous theories on the nitre question, Baumé reverts to a consideration of the factors requisite to its formation, the presence of calcareous earths, the accession of air and humidity, and an environment of animal and vegetable putrefaction, and concludes that nitre is a product of the interaction of all of these, 'which is all that one can say'. But Lavoisier was to solve the problem three years later, through the analysis of spirit of nitre in terms of the chemistry of gases, and by making that substance (nitric acid) rather than nitre the parent of the chemical family of nitrates.[40]

[36] Cf. Biringuccio, 1942: 404–09. Agricola 1912: 561–4. 1955: 44–5. Ercker, 1951: 291–306.

[37] Boerhaave, 1741, Vol. 1: 107–8. Shaw, 1755: 283–4.

[38] The most famous statement of this theory was put forward in John Mayow's *De respiratione* of 1668 and his *De sal nitrum* of 1674 (cf. Mayow, 1674 and 1926), on which see Patterson, 1931 and Partington, 1956.

[39] Louis Lemery, 1717.

[40] Baumé, 1773, Vol. 3: 589–98. For a summary of scientific opinion on saltpetre through 1776, and including Lavoisier's observations, see Académie des Sciences, 1786: 21–30.

Sal ammoniac and borax

Sal ammoniac and borax were among the more important exotic chemicals traded by the Italian mercantile cities, particularly by the Venetians, who not only imported them but maintained factories for their purification, thus effectively compounding the secret of their origin.[41] Both were originally products of the wastelands of central Asia, but the Arabs' discovery of an organic source of sal ammoniac ('hair sal ammoniac'), if it failed to improve their prospects in alchemy, at least led to the industrialization of the production of sal ammoniac. In the period now under consideration most European sal ammoniac came from Egypt, although production continued in central Asia, and the Dutch seem to have been importing it from the 'the Indies'.[42]

In 1620 Sala published an account of the synthesis of sal ammoniac from volatile salt (of urine – that is, ammonia) and the spirit of common salt (hydrochloric acid),[43] and a generation later Glauber demonstrated the analysis of the substance into these ingredients.[44] This background of theory seems to underlie the opinions of later seventeenth and early eighteenth century chemists (although they rarely mention Sala or Glauber) that 'natural' (that is, imported) sal ammoniac was somehow generated by solar action on salt-incrusted desert sands impregnated with camel urine, while 'artificial' sal ammoniac was obtained by boiling down and finally sublimating a mixture of five parts of urine, one of sea salt, and one-half part of chimney soot. This process was said to be practised at Venice and

[41] On the early history of sal ammoniac see Beckmann, 1846, Vol. 2: 396–406. On borax see Kopp, 1843–47, Vol. 3: 339–44 and Macquer, 1778, art., borax.

[42] The large-scale exploitation of natural deposits in Tartary, 'in the land of the Calmuks' is mentioned in the *Encyclopédie* (Vol. 14 [1765]: 914a) and also in nineteenth-century sources (cf. Barthold, 1928: 169). Dutch importation from 'the Indies' is mentioned by Claude Geoffroy, 1723.

[43] 'Si partem salis volatilis cum debita spiritus salis communis quantitate . . . misceas; sal inde armoniacum, eiusdem cum sale armoniaco vulgari qualitatis conficiens.' Sala, 1647: 246 (*Synopsis aphorismorum chymiatricorum*, 1620).

[44] After stating that sal ammoniac contains 'a common acid salt' and 'a volatile salt of urine' (which he equates to the spirit of sal ammoniac), Glauber says that they can be : eparated i one is 'mortified'. 'Lapis calaminaris and zinck,' which 'have a great affinity (Gemeinschaft) with all acid things', hold the former and set free the volatile salt (1658–9, Vol. 2: 136–8. 1689, Pt 1: 49 (*Philosophical furnaces*, Pt 2, Ch. 87).

elsewhere, and to be responsible for most of the sal ammoniac used in Europe.[45]

Towards the end of his life, Nicolas Lemery, whose chemical textbook had long given this process as practised at Venice 'and many other places', had second thoughts, and ventured the opinion that the Venetians really imported sal ammoniac.[46] His son, Louis, and his fellow-academician, Homberg, doubted that commercial sal ammoniac was a sublimation product, apparently on the ground of its being a crystalline substance. In this they were in disagreement with Claude Geoffroy,[47] and in 1720 Geoffroy triumphantly produced his vindication in no less than two circumstantial accounts of sal ammoniac production in Egypt, both of which described it as a sublimation product of soot from furnaces using camel dung as fuel.[48] Geoffroy was as interested in reconciling the process with the ancient urine-salt-soot formula as in proving that it involved sublimation, and, noting that the accounts received from Egypt mentioned some addition of urine and salt to the soot, he allowed himself to believe them to be the essential ingredients and went so far as to consider the soot useless. Unfortunately for his theory, however, subsequent accounts received from Egypt made it clear that urine and salt were not really added.[49] Far from being useless, the soot – which had represented only one-thirteenth part of the ancient recipe – turned out to be the only useful ingedient! Before this was clarified, Boerhaave had observed that coal soot was capable of yielding sal ammoniac,[50] and the first European sal ammoniac

---

[45] See Le Fevre, 1664, Pt 2: 302–3. Glaser, 1674: 234–5. Nicolas Lemery, 1677: 344. Boyle, 1772, Vol. 2: 225 (*The usefulness of experimental philosophy*). Le Mort, 1696: 19. Harris, 1708, Vol. 1: art., 'Sal ammoniac.' Fontenelle, 1716. Geoffroy, 1720. The process long predates the seventeenth century, however, going back to *The invention of verity* of the Latin Geber (1928: 205–6)!   [46] 1759: 765.

[47] Fontenelle, 1716 and 1720, resumes this controversy. Homberg, 1702: *Mem.*: 41 discussed sal ammoniac as a salt, and Louis Lemery, 1705, spoke of the same in connection with a crystalline 'natural sal ammoniac' found on Mt Vesuvius.

[48] Claude Geoffroy, 1720, prints the memoire he had not succeeded in printing in 1716, plus summaries of two accounts received from Egypt, from M. Lemere, the Consul at Cairo, and from a Jesuit missionary named Sicard.

[49] Duhamel du Monceau, 1735. The clearest account of the Egyptian process was that of Hasselquist, 1760.

[50] In his analysis of soot. Where he speaks of sal ammoniac, however, he seems to accept the traditional notions of the sources, both 'natural' and 'artificial', of the salt (Boerhaave, 1741, Vol. 2: 177–8, 206).

factory for which there is substantial evidence apparently used this process. This sal ammoniac works, established in Edinburgh in 1756 by James Hutton and James Davie, would appear to have been as empirical as were the Egyptian factories,[51] but it was followed only three years later by the first of a large number of truly synthetic processes which appeared in considerable numbers in the last half of the century.

While the academicians of Paris pursued a complex and often obscure dispute concerning the origin of sal ammoniac, coal soot seems to have occupied a different place in their thought, as a source of ammonia. Tournefort brought this forth spectacularly in 1700, as part of the exposure of the composition of a celebrated 'secret' remedy, 'the famous English drops', which turned out to owe their efficacy to 'the volatile spirit of crude soot'.[52] This spirit, which was ammonia, appeared as ammonium carbonate when it was distilled from coal, and in 1760 one of the academicians, Antoine Baumé, established a sal ammoniac factory utilizing the double decomposition of ammonium carbonate and magnesium chloride (bittern).[53] This was more probably the third than the second European factory, however, for it appears that a factory had been established at Brunschwygk the year before, by a brewer, Johann Gravenhorst. This works used the double decomposition of ammonium sulphate and common salt, a highly sophisticated process, but one which appears to have been suggested earlier in the 'Histoire' of the new Academy of Berlin.[54] The history of sal ammoniac thus seems to

[51] A description of the process is given, without attribution, by Clow and Clow (1952: 420). Playfair's biographical sketch of Hutton (1803) gives the impression that Davie played the more prominent part in developing the process, although it would be reasonable to surmise that Hutton learned of it when he was in Holland, where, according to a later report (Gren, 1782: 20–1), sal ammoniac was made of peat alone. Contemporary references to this and other early sal ammoniac factories indicate proprietary secrecy and depend upon hearsay and indirect evidence. Sal ammoniac is not, however, an inconceivable or even commercially infeasible product of coal soot (cf. Lowry, 1945: 1075).

[52] Tournefort, 1700. Martin Lister of the Royal Society of London had confided to Tournefort that this remedy was prepared by absorbing 'the volatile spirit of crude soot' in an essential oil. The power of medicine over chemistry is indicated by the frequency with which this remedy, which would appear to be the ancestor of our 'smelling salts', recurs in the literature of sal ammoniac.

[53] Baumé's process is described in Demachy, 1773: 120–3.

[54] The Gravenhorst process is described in Klaproth and Wolff, 1810–11, Vol. 3: 163–8. All of the chemical data necessary for this process could be found in an analysis of 'secret sal

place the beginning of the industrial revolution in chemistry in the mid-eighteenth century.

Borax remained essentially an exotic product for about a half century longer. The Dutch, who appear to have spear-headed the breaking of the Venetian monopolies, unravelled to some extent the mystery of borax, in that they discovered the process for purifying it.[55] But the real genesis of a native European industry stemmed from the late eighteenth century discovery of springs of 'sedative salt' (boric acid) in Italy. These were described by the Court Apothecary of Florence, Francis Hoefer, in 1778, but were not extensively exploited before the third decade of the nineteenth century, after which they superseded imported borax almost altogether.[56]

Like sal ammoniac, borax had commonly been thought an artificial material, a compound of familiar ingredients known only to the Venetians. Here again, however, the Paris Academy pioneered its scientific study. The origin of these investigations was a familiar one, the investigation of a newly popular medicinal substance. In this case the medicinal virtues were not imaginary, for the 'narcotic salt of vitriol', described by Homberg in 1702,[57] was boric acid. It led Louis Lemery to a deeper study of borax, according to a report by Fontenelle in the *Histoire* for the following year,[58] and to the conclusion that borax is a 'middle salt' (neither acid not alkaline) obtained from the East Indies, Persia, and Transylvania, and consisting of a 'saline salt', a 'urinous salt', and 'a little oily substance'. Not even Lemery himself was very satisfied with this, and twenty-five years later he was to proclaim borax the least known of all the naturally occurring salts.[59] Chemists commonly continued to think borax a product of vitriol or alum, even those who visited what was apparently the principal source of eastern exportation, in India.[60]

---

ammoniac' (ammonium sulphate) published in 1752 by Gravenhorst's countryman, Pott (cf. Pott, 1752: 67, 81). It would have taken an informed and imaginative chemist to dig it out, however.

[55] *Encyclopédie Méthodique*, 1789: 753. Fester, 1923: 88–9, 157, gives other references.

[56] Knapp, 1848–9, Vol. 1: 309–20.

[57] Homberg, 1702: 50–2. He obtained it by distilling a mixture of borax and the caput mortuum of vitriol.

[58] Fontenelle, 1703.

[59] Louis Lemery, 1728: 273.

[60] Cadet, 1766. Samuel B. Croll, 1743. The latter is a report from India.

Finally, in 1787, a British traveller explained that the 'borax of Bengal' was really imported to that place from Tibet, and gave a circumstantial (if secondhand) account of its production in what may have been the same region from which the Arabs had first obtained it.[61] Two years later the *Annales de chimie* printed the account of 'M. (Robert) Saunders' a visitor to the saline lake in Tibet where 'tinkal or borax' was produced.[62] It appeared in the same issue of that journal which reviewed the *Traité de chimie* of Antoine Lavoisier, in which 'the radical of borax' was listed among the elements.

Vitriol and alum

The confusion which formerly prevailed between these two classes of substance is understandable enough, since both are soluble sulphates of like taste and similar, although not identical, uses. Our conviction that both were known in antiquity hinges on: (1) their use in fixing vegetable dyes to cloth (mordanting), which could only apply to the alums, and (2) a test given by Pliny (the blackening of a solution by gall nuts), which could only apply to iron vitriol. But Pliny held this to be a test for 'alumen', indicating a confusion which was far from dispelled even in the early nineteenth century, when we find Rhee's Encyclopaedia describing vitriol as 'a greenish or yellowish-white, apple or verdigris green, or sky blue colour(ed)' substance of 'an acerbic metallic flavour', while alum is a substance 'of aluminous taste', which is simply the product of 'all those minerals which either contain alum ready formed or are capable of yielding this salt by the process of manufacture'.[63]

Iron and aluminium, the crucial elements in the historical development of the chemistry and technology of vitriols and alums, are among the most plentiful elements in inorganic nature. Iron occurs rarely in metallic form, but commonly in oxides and sulphides (pyrites), which are its ores. It is also widely distributed in chemically complex silicate rocks. Metallic aluminium does not occur in nature, and was unknown prior to its isolation by Wohler in 1827, although its existence was suspected a generation earlier. It took its name from

[61] Blane, 1787.
[62] Saunders, 1789.
[63] 1819, Vol. 27: art. vitriol, Vol. 1: art. alum.

alum, although it is of much wider occurrence, and is in fact the most plentiful metallic element in the earth's crust. Silicates of aluminium are the principal constituents of clay.

Chemically the vitriols and alums are sulphates, and the former are generated simply enough by the weathering of pyrites. Since, however, they are very soluble, they have little tendency to accumulate, except under special conditions. Such a condition existed in antiquity, in consequence of the early development of deep mining for copper. In these mines the weathering of copper sulphide ore led to the formation of copper (or blue) vitriol which gathered, and sometimes crystallized, in the waters which accumulated at the bottom of the mines. Iron vitriol was similarly formed from the ever-present iron pyrites, and iron (or green) vitriol was much more important in commerce. Thus arose on the one hand the custom of converting copper vitriol to iron vitriol (with the attendant 'transmutation' of iron to copper which I have often mentioned), and on the other the conviction, which the Romans seem to have held, that vitriol is basically a cuprous material. By the sixteenth century we find that the commercial demand for iron vitriol has exceeded the supply available from mine waters, and has led to the establishment of an industry in which pyrite is mined and artificially weathered.[64]

There is no aluminium pyrite in nature, but conditions for the formation of aluminium sulphate occur in the vicinity of volcanos, where the sulphuric acid which is a by-product of volcanic activity acts on the adjacent aluminous clays. Since iron is almost always present in clay as an impurity, iron sulphate is also formed, and the combination of the difficulty of crystallizing aluminium sulphate and the masking effect of iron salts make the former substance difficult to purify or even to detect. It was not identified as a discrete substance until the nineteenth century.

It is, however, a chemical property of aluminium that if sodium or potassium salts are present in the clay, and this is very often the case, the aluminium sulphate undergoes a further chemical change into the double salts, sodium aluminium sulphate or potassium aluminium sulphate, which are true alums. Sodium alum, because of its extreme solubility, is even more elusive than aluminium

[64] Cf. Biringuccio, 1942: 95–8. Agricola, 1912: 572–4. Ercker, 1951: 312–13.

sulphate,[65] but potassium alum has the peculiar property of forming large, spectacular crystals which not only reveal its presence, but yield the substance in a pure state. It is occasionally found as an efflorescence in volcanic regions, and this is believed to have been the source of the alum of antiquity, which was thus a material of natural occurrence.[66]

Among the most important medieval innovations in industrial chemistry were two processes for the manufacture of alum from 'aluminous' rocks. The first of these, which is vaguely dated 'about the tenth century', and assigned to the Arabic lands of the Middle East which had long been the principal source of natural alum, was simply an acceleration of the process in which natural alum was produced. In the composition of these aluminous rocks natural (potassium) alum forms with aluminium hydroxide a basic potassium aluminium sulphate known as 'alunite'. This insoluble mineral in turn becomes a component of more complex rocks, notably shales, but in some places it is found in a relatively pure state, and it was the artificial weathering of alunite which was taken up towards the end of the first millennium as a manufacturing process for alum. It involved the long exposure of heaps of 'alum stone' (alunite), fragmented mechanically or by roasting, after which the alum was leached out and crystallized. The product was 'ordinary' alum (potassium aluminium sulphate).

The second process is even more obscurely dated,[67] but it is more complicated and was probably later. Using shale as a raw material, it proceeds in much the same way as the first process, but the chemical character of shale is such that the solution leached from it does not readily crystallize. This process required a crucial invention, the addition of decayed urine which promoted the crystallization of what was in fact 'ammonia alum' (ammonium aluminium sulphate). If the alum known in Europe as 'alum of Yemen' is correctly identified as ammonia alum, it would appear that this process, too, was developed by the Arabs.

[65] The earliest references in Mellor (1922–37; Vol. 5: 332, 343) are to the preparation of aluminium sulphate by boiling ammonium alum in aqua regia, by H. V. Collet Descotils (1816) and the preparation of sodium alum by crystallization from the mother liquor of potassium alum when soap-boiler's lye, containing common salt, has been used in its preparation, by K. G. Wellner (1822).

[66] Chas Singer, 1948: xvii–xviii.   [67] Ibid., 'in the earlier middle ages'.

Both vitriol and alum were applied in unusual quantities in medicine, and were until the late eighteenth century indispensable ingredients (either one could be used) in the production of all of the mineral acids. The principal use of iron vitriol, however, was for its property, with oak galls, of giving a black colour, to inks, in dying, leather colouration, etc. Vitriol was imported to Europe, but the principal source seems to have been indigenous, the central European mining region. Vitriol was exported in quantity from Germany to Venice.[68] The principal use of alum was as a mordant, and with the expansion of the textile industry alum came to be a more important substance than vitriol. It was apparently not produced in Europe prior to the last half of the fifteenth century, but was exported from virtually every trading port in Western Asia and North Africa, and imported by every trading city in Europe.

Such was the importance of alum that, about 1275, the city of Genoa secured from the Byzantine Emperor Michael Paleologus the right to an alum works at Phocaea (Asia Minor), where the substance was manufactured from alunite. The production from this single source, which was one of many, has been set at about 780 tons (14,000 hundredweight) per annum.[69] Although Venice contested primacy in the alum trade, Genoa continued to operate the Phocaean works until its capture by the Turks in 1455. Shortly thereafter the Genoese, Giovanni di Castro, who had known the Phocaean alum works, discovered 'alum stone' at Tolfa in the Papal States, and about 1461 production began at this famous alum works, which was long to be a mainstay of the Papal treasury. A contract drawn up in 1465 spoke of a production of 1,500 tons per year, and the profit to the Papacy during the next five years is estimated at 100,000 ducats.[70] A vigorous attempt to maintain this monopoly commanded the talents of such clerical celebrities as the humanist Cardinal Bessarion, but it was to fail. Less than a century later Agricola's account[71] of the central European mines speaks of a variety of processes for preparing alum, including the second process mentioned above, utilizing

[68] Biringuccio, 1942: 98.

[69] Byrne, 1919–20.

[70] Singer, 1948: 143–4.

[71] 1912: 564–72. That alum was already produced in Germany in the previous century is indicated by the description of a process in the *Mittelalterliche Hausbuch* of 1480 (*Mittelalterliche Hausbuch*, 1912: xxiv).

ordinary shale as a raw material and producing ammonium alum. This process was subsequently practised all over Europe.

Vitriol had been since the time of al-Rāzī the name of a class of substances. The first foothold of science on the vitriol question would appear to have been the observation that vitriols are salts which can be obtained from any one of a number of metals by its dissolution in sulphuric acid. We encounter this observation repeatedly after about 1600, perhaps first in the writings of 'Basil Valentine'.[72] Inasmuch as the crystal forms of the sulphates provided a relatively easy criteria for their differentiation, the chemist was probably in a better position to establish a degree of scientific understanding in relation to the vitriols than in any other area of chemistry. That this did not happen is a measure of the gap which remained between the practice and science of chemistry.

Because of the backward-looking tradition of chemistry, the antiquity and abundance of the literature on vitriol was rather a hindrance than an advantage to the advancement of knowledge on the subject. Biringuccio was only able to conclude that vitriol has five properties, those of sulphur, alum, nitre or salt, copper, and iron.[73] The more learned Agricola was completely confused by the great variety of names, misy, sory, melantaria, chalcanthum, etc., which had come down through the centuries in the literature on this substance. The third of the trio of sixteenth-century mineralogical luminaries, Ercker, gives tests for both vitriol and alum, but in the former case it depends upon the combination of a sharp and sour taste with the property of giving a red colour to cleaned iron, and in the latter on a taste which puckers the tongue, and 'tastes something like vitriol'.[74] The state of the question nearly a century later is at least symbolized by the fact that it was still possible in the middle of the seventeenth century for Digby to present ferrous sulphate as his secret 'powder of sympathy', and for Glauber to make a 'miracle drug' out of sodium sulphate.

The vitriol-alum question too, was discussed by the chemists of

[72] 'Basil Valentine' gets vitriols from the sulphuric acid dissolution of 'any metal' (1769: 740), but he also obtains 'vitriols' through dissolutions of metals in other acids. Croll (1609: 218-9) gives recipes for making vitriols of iron and copper through their cementation with sulphur.

[73] 1942: 95.

[74] 1951: 313.

the Académie des Sciences, notably by Louis Lemery, who produced on the subject a series of memoirs of increasing length between 1706 and 1736. Beginning with an analysis of vitriol which led him to the conclusions 'Basil Valentine' had reached a century earlier, Lemery came next to the question of 'white' vitriol and finally to alum, both of which he more-or-less inaccurately concluded to be manifestations of the vitriol of iron.[75] Subsequent elucidation came from the Academy of Sciences in Berlin, which emerges in the 1740s as a centre of chemical research rivalling Paris. The pharmacist, Kaspar Neumann (1683–1737), Johann H. Pott (1692–1777), and Andreas S. Marggraf (1709–82), all followers or (in the case of Pott) actually students of Stahl, were to take great strides in mineral chemistry in numerous memoirs from 1727. Most of this lies outside the scope of the present study, but it may be noted that in 1743 Pott cleared up both the question of white vitriol, by showing that the term covered both anhydrous ferrous sulphate and zinc sulphate, and that of alum, the base of which he identified as a 'peculiar earth'.[76] The author of the articles on vitriol and alum in the Diderot *Encyclopédie* owed more to the chemists of Berlin than to those of Paris in his identification of white vitriol as a salt formed by the union of vitriolic acid and zinc, and alum as 'a true vitriol' combining vitriolic acid with 'an earth of which the nature is little known to chemists'.[77] But the next step was made by Lavoisier, whose studies of the combustion of sulphur led him to identify the 'vitriolic' part of vitriol as a combination of sulphur and oxygen and to give it the name, sulphate, which we still use. The corresponding part of alum remained a mystery, and appeared among his tentative elements.

Sulphur

Prior to the advent of gunpowder, sulphur appears, despite its prominence in chemical literature, to have been consumed only in small quantities, which were satisfied by local sources of this naturally

[75] See Louis Lemery, 1706, 1707, 1735–1 (on white vitriol), 1735–2, and 1736 (on alum).

[76] Pott, 1743.

[77] The article 'alum' appeared in the first volume (1751) and that on vitriol in the last (Vol. 17, 1765).

occurring and easily identifiable substance. Even in the mid-nineteenth century, when large quantities were used in gunpowder and for the manufacture of sulphuric acid, world production was only about 100,000 tons per year, and it was a commodity largely produced and used in Europe. Although the production of sulphur as a by-product of metallurgical smelting is found as early as Agricola (1546), this remained a very minor source of supply in the mid-nineteenth century, at which time ninety per cent of the world supply was coming from natural deposits in Sicily.[78]

There was little literary discourse about its production. As in the case of common salt, there was no problem from the point of view of technology. There were, however, scientific problems. The chemist held sulphur as one of his 'principles', and found it everywhere; but one of the consequences of this was that he found what he was pleased to call the 'vulgar' sulphur of nature almost an embarrassment, for it lacked some of the attributes of his sulphur principle. In chemical literature his attention to the vulgar sulphur was inversely proportional to the frequency of appearance of the word sulphur. The chemists of the eighteenth century seem very pleased to accept Stahl's dictum that sulphur is a combination of vitriolic acid and phlogiston.[79]

Quicklime

After common salt, quicklime was probably produced in antiquity on a larger scale than any other industrial chemical, for it became the principal ingredient of the mortar of building construction and was used in the production of glass and in the preparation of leather. Its importance continuously increased in the Middle Ages, as it found use in soap and textile production and as a fertilizer.[80] Its raw materials were, if anything, more commonplace than were those of common salt, and although it was not a naturally occurring substance and had

---

[78] Knapp, 1848–9, Vol. 1: 217–18. Liebig et al, 1859: 418.

[79] Cf. Ed. Vol. 15, art., soufre. Baumé, 1773. Vol. 1: 237. Macquer, 1778, Vol. 2, art. sulphur.

[80] The scale of the soap industry is indicated in the fact that the oft-told tale of the dissolution of the luckless workman (in this case 'a drunken man') who fell into the soap-factory vat was already current in the seventeenth century (cf. Tachenius, 1677: 9 [Ch. 4]). Quicklime was used as fertilizer as early as the sixteenth century (cf. Palissy, 1957: 210).

such different (although chemically identical) sources as limestone, chalk, and seashells, the simplicity of its production, by simple heating, and the distinctive burning ('caustic') property of the end product, banished doubt as to the identification of the common product as 'quick' lime (calx viva). It is probably in consequence of these factors that no statistics seem to exist on its production even into the mid-nineteenth century.

Quicklime was as recalcitrant as sulphur to scientific elucidation. Its most remarkable characteristic was its causticity (burning property, from the Greek καυστικός) and it remained the prototype of caustic substances to the degree that our caustic soda (sodium hydroxide) remained virtually unknown, being regarded as soda 'strengthened' by quicklime. There were a remarkable number of different views on the causticity of quicklime. It was the Peripatetic opinion, according to Boyle, that it was due to 'a supposed antiperistasis, or invigoration of the internal heat of the lime, by its being invironed by cold water', and Boyle attributed to Helmont the opinion that it reflects 'a conflict between some alcalizate and acid salts'.[81] The most common opinions, however, attributed the causticity of quicklime to an accession of something akin to fire, if not identical to it. They are usually brought forth as part of a discussion of causticization, that is, the production of caustic soda or potash by the action of quicklime on the appropriate alkali. 'Basil Valentine' had spoken of the preparation of caustic potash as a transferrence of the 'heat' in quicklime.[82] Boyle's own opinion was a characteristically tentative evocation of 'peculiar texture' and 'ignious effluvia', Mayow found the agent in his nitro-aereal particles, and Louis Lemery held the substance to be simply fire.[83] Stahl had, as usual, the 'last word', and was characteristically ambiguous. Where he discusses quicklime directly he regards it as a compound of 'a subtle corrosive earthy matter', and 'a grosser earthy matter', but elsewhere he suggests that a 'sulphurous acidity' gives acid character to a substance as it is present in excess and alkaline character as it is deficient, quicklime

[81] Boyle, 1772, Vol. 4: 245–6 ('Of the mechanical origin of heat and cold'). Antiperistasis was the famous Aristotelian doctrine of the motion of projectiles (*Physics*, 267a–b, *On the heavens*, 301b), but Aristotle also had other uses for it (see Solmsen, 1960).

[82] 1769: 71.

[83] Boyle, 1772, Vol. 4: 247–9 ('Of the mechanical origin of heat and cold'). Mayow, 1674: 222ff. 1926: 153ff. (*De sal nitro*, Ch. 14). L. Lemery, 1709: 410–12.

being an extreme case of the latter.[84] Thanks to Stahl's peculiar linking together of causticity and alkalinity in the character of quicklime it came as a surprise to the chemists of the eighteenth century to discover that when quicklime is slaked (converted by water to the non-caustic calcium hydroxide) it retains its alkalinity while losing its causticity.[85]

The controversy over the source of the causticity of quicklime became more heated after about 1720, when the 'water' of slaked quicklime became prominent as a medicine in England, and it was to inspire the mid-century doctoral dissertation of the Scotch medical student, Joseph Black. Black's researches established the first landmark in the chemical revolution, but not for any elucidation of quicklime, for Black had found it convenient to shift his interest from lime remedies to analogous preparations from magnesia. Quicklime remained a mystery to Black,[86] as it did to Lavoisier, who included it among his elements.

Alkali

Another Mediterranean-based industry of the Middle Ages was concerned with the production of alkali. This, too, had been industrialized in antiquity, and had involved several methods of production, the mining of (Egyptian) natron deposits and the leaching of various plant ashes. Unlike the vitriols the several alkalis had no generic name. Natron was an impure soda (sodium carbonate). The ashes of sea or shore vegetation yielded a purer form of soda, called by the Arabs 'kali' (hence alkali) and those of inland plants yielded potash (potassium carbonate), both of which were produced at various places. A dim recognition of the difference between soda

[84] Speaking of causticization, Stahl remarks that 'it seems rational that the fine sulphurous acidity adhering to a constituent part of the alkaline salt, should render the alkali more mild or sluggish, but by being separated from it, more sharp and intense'. (1730: 144. 1746, Pt 1: 88). Stahl's direct discussion of quicklime is found in 1730: 150. 1746, Pt 1: 91.

[85] Homberg's observations, noted above (p. 308) were continued in Homberg, 1719: 68–9. Guerlac (1957: 141–7) discusses similar observations made in Scotland, which were the background of Joseph Black's epochal discovery of carbon dioxide.

[86] On Black see Guerlac, 1957. Magnesia alba (magnesium carbonate) had been discovered about 1700, in the saltpetre refining process, as a deposit which resembled lime but was not identical to it (see Friedrich Hoffmann, 1755: 56).

and potash reinforced the natural tendency to regard alkalis from different sources as different substances, but although mineral alkali deposits were reportedly worked in Hungary from antiquity[87] the principal source from Roman times to the later Middle Ages appears to have been the Mediterranean littoral, where the production of soda from the marine plant, known in Europe as barilla, was a large-scale industry into modern times.

Europe's emergence from the 'Dark Ages' can be measured (in more than one sense) in terms of the increased utilization of soap and glass,[88] two manufactures depending upon alkali as a raw material. So great was the demand that a German visitor to Tripoli in 1573 reported that there were more tradesmen connected with the alkali and soap businesses than with all other trades together.[89] With the growth of the textile industry in the Low Countries we find the Baltic region also emerging as a major source of alkali, primarily potash. There was a Hanseatic warehouse for 'ash' in Bruges as early as 1360, and in the fifteenth century Danzig alone exported 600 to 700 tons (6,000 to 7,000 barrels) of potash and 2,400 to 2,600 tons (24,000 to 26,000 barrels) of Waidasche (raw wood ashes). This went principally to the Low Countries, for which 'Russia' remained three centuries later the most important source of alkali.[90] Spanish barilla remained important, to the degree that Parliament exempted it from the embargo during war between England and Spain (1717), although it was increasingly supplemented in that century by 'seaweed ash' from British (chiefly Scottish) kelp.[91]

Unlike the industrial chemicals discussed earlier, the alkalis were not easily identified, and they illustrate the greater difficulties which beset the scientific chemist as compared to the practical chemist who is concerned with the production of a few commodities. The scale of the alkali industry clearly implies a degree of 'standardization'

[87] Poutet, 1828: 15. Fester, 1923: 80.

[88] On the significance of glass in the medieval economy see Mumford, 1934: 124–31. The large scale of the soap industry of Venice was noted by seventeenth-century visitors such as John Ray (1738, Vol. 1: 172 [under the year 1663]). Marseilles reportedly had fifty soap works in 1708 (Martin, 1898: 300).

[89] Rauwolf, 1738: 24, says that several shiploads of soap and 'ash' were annually sent to Venice.

[90] Fester, 1923: 80–1

[91] Clow and Clow, 1947: 67–9. Sayre and Smith (1964) find that glass made with potash rather than soda was predominant in northern Europe from the 10th century.

adequate to the commercialization of production, but it was a localized standardization. The comparative merits of Waidasche, seaweed ash, and such other 'foreign ashes' as those of Marseilles, Castille, Venice, and 'Joppa',[92] were apparently for the purchaser to discover. It was more troublesome to the would-be scientist to be ignorant of the difference between alkalis, especially as he became aware that what appeared to be new varieties were coming to light, such as the 'alkaline salts' of tartar (potassium carbonate, from burnt wine lees), and nitre (potassium carbonate, from the 'detonation' of saltpetre with charcoal), and the curious volatile alkali (ammonia) from urine.

We have seen the difficulties these caused the chemists of the Paris Academy. They remained unresolved in Geoffroy's 'Table des rapports'. Boerhaave knew ten distinguishing marks of 'alkali', but held that it varied according to the kind of wood, and found wood alkali scarcely distinguishable from alkalis from the seashore plant, kali, from burnt wine lees (tartar), or from the various 'foreign ashes'.[93] He was little better off than had been Biringuccio two centuries earlier, who had been 'sure that salt can be extracted from anything that has a biting sharpness and that is converted into ashes by fire'.[94] Natron does not seem to have troubled these authors, for Biringuccio said that in his day 'there is no naturalist who knows it except by name', and Boerhaave claimed that alkali does not exist in nature. This is somewhat puzzling, for natron was familiar enough to others, for whom it added to the confusion, as may be illustrated in the views of the author of the article on 'alkaline salts' in the Diderot *Encyclopédie*. Writing in 1765, he declared that there were volatile and fixed alkaline salts, and of the latter, three kinds, an earthy alkali, which is 'natrum', a marine alkali, which is soda (soude), and the alkali of tartar.[95] With evident satisfaction, he then observes that 'in a way each realm of nature has its own alkali, the animal realm adopts the volatile, natrum belongs to the mineral, soda to the watery, and the alkali of tartar is the vegetable alkali'.

In Duhamel du Monceau's memoir on the base of common salt,

[92] Shaw, 1755: 288, mentions these as the common varieties in English commerce in the eighteenth century.

[93] Boerhaave, 1741, Vol. 1: 530-4.

[94] 1942: 112.

[95] D. J., 1765.

he had found it, as has already been noted in our discussion of common salt, an alkali resembling soda. He goes on to remark that this alkali 'does not produce all the effects of salt of tartar; it does not make a vitriolized tartar with oil of vitriol, but rather a Glauber's salt; it does not make with nitric acid "*un Saltpetre en aguilles, mais un Nitre quadrangulaire*"; finally, with the acid of sea salt it does not make a "digestive salt of Sylvius" (potassium chloride), but a cubic salt, or a true regenerated sea salt, which proves by its recomposition that this alkaline salt is the true base of sea salt.' 'Boerrhave', he adds, had wrongly claimed in his *Chemistry* that the digestive salt of Sylvius regenerated from oil of tartar and spirit of salt 'nearly resembled sea salt in form of its crystals and by some other properties, but that it was distinguished from it by some others'.[96]

This passage, written in 1736, represented the first milestone in the scientific differentiation of soda and potash. It serves as well to illustrate the jungle of terminological underbrush through which Lavoisier and his associates had to cut their way to reach the 'elementary' bodies, soda and potash, which the next generation was to reduce to sodium and potassium.

[96] Duhamel du Monceau, 1736: 224–5.

Summary and conclusion

B Y 1750 the science of matter was on the eve of the 'chemical revolution' which was to give it the shape it was still to retain in its essentials through the beginning of the twentieth century. The essence of this revolution was in the discovery that air consists of a mixture of substances in the gaseous state, and in a new and finally successful essay on the mathematization of chemistry, through quantitative analysis, accepting as final authority the evidence of the balance. These great events have been a principal preoccupation of students of the history of chemistry. Yet by the early eighteenth century a *science* of chemistry had emerged from a matrix of natural philosophy, medicine, alchemy, and technology. Our concern here has been with the formation of that science which was later reformed by the revolution of the late eighteenth century.

That the earliest evidence bearing on chemistry comes from technology is perhaps an accidental consequence of the superior durability in archaeological remains of the artifact over the theory, although the best evidence yet adduced for a theoretical background to early practical chemistry is far less substantial than the evidence of empirical influence in the earliest theories of matter. The first involvements of medicine with chemistry seem largely due to the indiscriminate use of materials as drugs and the consequent importance of the drug-list as a guide to the corpus of materials known – an indispensable piece of data to the early chemist as well as to the modern student of his works. Medicine, however, spans science and technology; in historic times it has drawn theory from natural philosophy and returned a contribution of empirical data from physiology as well as the chemical data embodied in the drug-lists. Thus as early as the classical era of Greece we can detect an already complex distribution of theory about matter and its changes, in natural philosophy, technology, and medicine.

Alchemy drew most of its content from these three, to which it added bits and pieces of Hellenistic magico-religious lore. The cement which held all of this together was an empirical innovation which was apparently developed by the alchemists themselves, the production of chemical change by prolonged sublimatory and distillatory processes. That alchemy exercised so fundamental an influence on the history of chemistry, however, resulted from the fact that, unlike the earlier fields of endeavour, alchemy made matter and its changes its central preoccupation. In its primitive form – exoteric alchemy, or gold-making – it bears a close resemblance to a science of chemistry, but that primitive form was remarkably evanescent. Alchemy seems to have risen and declined successively in each culture which received it, beginning in a close relationship to technology and with gold-making as a serious objective, and ending in an occultism (esoteric alchemy) which had little to do with gold-making or a science of matter. One might speculate that, had alchemy never 'happened', a science of chemistry might have arisen at an early date out of certain aspects of technology, natural philosophy, and medicine, the common features of which were already well recognized by Aristotle and Theophrastus. History, however, is concerned to discover what did happen.

In the first Christian millennium, alchemy gained equal status with natural philosophy, technology, and medicine as an art or science concerned with matter. There was a particularly close relationship between alchemy and medicine. The pharmacopoeia, rather than a literature of practical chemistry – which, indeed, scarcely existed – provided the alchemist with his repertoire of substances to work on. This fact in turn made the physician uniquely well equipped to practise alchemy, and many alchemists, if not the majority, were physicians. Alchemical theory also developed along medical lines, to the degree that the alchemist worked on the bodies of the imperfect metals like a physician on the ailing human body; but this seems rather a feature of mature than of primitive alchemy, and since 'mature' alchemy was characteristically verging on sheer occultism, the practice of alchemy as a 'healing art' was an abortive development as far as chemistry is concerned.

The direct contribution of alchemy to chemistry seems to have been minimal. That it has generally been credited with considerable importance is probably due to its immense indirect importance, firstly in the fact that through alchemy chemistry gained some semblance of independence in the spectrum of the arts and sciences, and secondly through the fact that it evolved into 'medical chemistry', which, in the European Renaissance, gave chemistry a secure and significant place in science; for medical chemistry was long regarded as a kind of conquest of medicine by alchemy. This reaction of alchemy on medicine stemmed from the introduction of new methods of preparing medicines, by the traditionally alchemical processes of distillation and sublimation. It was contemporaneous with a movement, internal to medicine, from the Galenic pharma-copoeia of compounded vegetable drugs to the 'simple' remedies of Dioscorides, including minerals. Both events apparently began in the far west of Islam, Spain and North Africa, and continued in Italy. Our knowledge of the Moslems who began it is clouded by the fact that we still know them largely through their Latin disciples, and we are not yet able to answer with much confidence the funda-mental question of whether the development began in alchemy or in medicine. The result was a new theory of the preparation of medicines (and alchemical elixirs) and, more important, the intro-duction of new artificial substances, the corrosive chlorides of mer-cury and antimony, and finally the mineral acids.

The twelfth-century transmission of science from Islam to the Latin West saw the simultaneous establishment in Europe of the alchemical and medical aspects of this movement. Western Europe apparently first learned of alchemy through this transmission, and the next two centuries saw the Latins go through a characteristic period of enthusiasm for gold-making by chemical methods. There-after alchemy made its usual turn to occultism, but unlike his predecessor in Antiquity and the Islamic Middle Ages, the Latin alchemist discovered an avenue of escape, through which many Latin alchemists – perhaps the majority – moved from gold-making into medicine. He 'discovered' the elixir of life; more specifically, he recognized the essential identity of both his procedures and his objectives with those of medicine. From the fourteenth century the philosopher's stone became the elixir of life and then simply a superior medicine. Shorn of virtually all its alchemical presuppositions, this ideology remained one of medical preparation by distillatory methods in which 'the pure' was separated from 'the impure', an appropriate contrast to 'polypharmacy', the Galenic ideology of medical preparation by multi-component mixture.

Galenic medicines, however, were based on a theory of physiology and pathology, while the 'pure' and simple remedies of medical chemistry were not. They were specific remedies, and after a few conspicuously successful conquests (more apparent than real) of notorious diseases they were found to be more hazardous without being more effective than the remedies they had replaced. But the medical chemist was an experimenter, and found in chemistry the power to discover new drugs faster than his critics were able to expose them. The result was a rapid expansion of the repertoire of the chemist from the latter part of the sixteenth century. Moreover, the medical chemist finally succeeded in discovering a plausible theory, in the presence, real and imaginary, of the phenomena of alkalinity and acidity, both in his remedies and in the metabolism of the human body. The resources of ingenuity in the medical chemist were far from exhausted at the end of the period here under consideration.

Through the sixteenth century natural philosophy continued to accommodate itself to the modifications in its sister discipline (medicine) and offspring (alchemy). In the seventeenth century, however, the pace of innovation finally exceeded the digestive powers of the natural philosopher. Descartes was the last to undertake a full explanation of the nature of matter and the causes and mechanism of its changes as part of a general cosmology. Thereafter natural philosophy, the ancient 'physics' of Aristotle, began to break up into its constituent parts, among which were fragments which were to become part of the philosophy of modern chemistry. The chemist, who had been hovering on the edge of the philosophical dialogue since the mid-sixteenth century, lost no time in seizing the opportunity afforded. He put aside some fundamental questions, such as the primal material and the weight or levity of the elements, and adapted others to problems arising more directly out of the materials themselves. It became unnecessary to combat 'forms' which were interpreted so as to approximate what we call the 'physical constants' of substances. Philosophical ramblings about sympathies and antipathies were transmuted into the doctrine of 'affinities'. The chemist had not abandoned philosophy, but had absorbed enough to suit his requirements. This was to be his 'science'; recalcitrant fundamental questions were henceforth to be set aside as 'philosophy'. As to alchemy, although he continued to ponder the transmutation of metals, the chemist came to regard alchemy as a different subject. The hoary practice of distillation lost its mystery when it became merely a method of analysis, and with the rise of the five-element doctrine theory and practice were joined, to gain a provisional solution of one of the most obstinate problems of the science of matter.

The spectacular growth of technology in the late Middle Ages had brought Europe, by the time of the Renaissance, in advance of antiquity in the traditional chemical industries, but it was the establishment of medical chemistry as a profitable occupation which above all made the chemist a member of a numerous and enterprising occupational group. Gaining a livelihood from the 'preparation' of substances, some of these inventive spirits realized, by the seventeenth century, that certain processes yielded 'artificial' substitutes for natural products. The best of them were able to demonstrate the identity of some artificial and natural substances, by experiments in disintegration and 'redintegration', and thus developed a primitive practice of analysis and synthesis. The reconciliation of this practice with the new chemical doctrine of elementary constitution was to be an accomplishment of the 'chemical revolution'.

By the end of the seventeenth century an awareness of the potency of such experimentation for both theoretical and practical chemistry had clearly emerged, not only among chemists, but among princes and governments who, during the preceding half-century, had come to enjoy, if not to appreciate, the potentialities of physics and astronomy. When, about 1700, chemistry was afforded in Paris an opportunity to take a place among the sciences receiving official sanction, the chemist was ready for the opportunity. Within less than four generations he had constructed the basis of the science as we know it.

Bibliography

ABULCASIS. 1471. *Liber servitoris.* Translatus (from Hebrew) a Sim. Januensi & Abraam Judaeo Tortuosiensi. Venice, N. J. Gallicum.

ABULCASIS. 1623. *Liber servitoris.* In Mesuë, Jr. 1623: fols. 240r–251v.

ACADÉMIE DES SCIENCES. 1786. *Recueil de mémoires et de pièces sur la formation et la fabrication du salpêtre.* Paris, Moutard (*Mémoires de mathématique et de physique,* Vol. 11).

ACHILLINI, ALEXANDER, ed. 1528. *Secreta secretorum Aristotelis.* Lugduni, A. Blanchard.

ACHILLINI, ALEXANDER. 1567. *Opera omnia.* Venice, H. Scotum.

ADAMS, FRANK D. 1938. *The birth and development of the geological sciences.* Baltimore, William and Wilkins.

AFNAN, SOHEIL M. 1958. *Avicenna, his life and works.* London, Allen and Unwin.

AGRICOLA, GEORG. 1912. *De re metallica.* Ed. and English trans. by H. C. Hoover and L. H. Hoover. London, The Mining Magazine.

AGRICOLA, GEORG. 1955. *De natura fossilium.* English trans. by M. C. Bandy and J. A. Bandy. New York, Geological Society of America (Special Paper 63).

AGRICOLA, GEORG. 1956. *De ortu et causis subterraneorum.* German trans. by Georg Fraustadt. In Agricola's

Ausgewählte Werke, Ed. by Hans Prescher, Vol. 3: 83–187. Berlin, VEB Deutscher Verlag der Wissenschaften.

AITCHISON, LESLIE. 1960. *A history of metals.* 2 vols. London, Macdonald and Evans.

AL-AHWANI, A. H. 1960. Jabir ibn Hayyan, (Arabic). *al-Majallah* (Cairo), 4.

ALBERTUS MAGNUS. 1890–99. *Opera omnia.* Ed. by Auguste Borgnet. 38 vols. Paris, L. Vives.

ALBERTUS MAGNUS ?. 1944. *Alchimia . . . inc. Calistenus unus de antiquioribus.* Ed. by Pearl Kibre. *Isis,* 35: 309–16. From BM Sloane MS. 3457, fols. 40r–50v.

ALBERTUS MAGNUS ?. 1949. *Alkimia minor . . . inc. dilecto in Christo patri. . . .* Ed. by Pearl Kibre. *Isis,* 32: 276–300.

Based on Venice, San Marco MS VI. 214 (A.D. 1427), fols. 180r–189v.

ALBERTUS MAGNUS ?. 1958. *Libellus de alchimia . . . inc. omnis sapientia a Domino. . . .* Ed. and English trans. by Sister Virginia Heines. Berkeley, Calif., University of California Press.

ALEXANDER OF APHRODISIAS. 1549. *De mistione.* Latin trans. by Angelo Canini. In Alexander's *Quaestiones naturales et morales.* Venice, H. Scotum.

ALEXANDER OF APHRODISIAS. 1936. *Commentary on Book IV of Aristotle's Meteorologica.* English trans. by V. C. B. Coutant. New York, Columbia University Press.

AL-FĀRĀBĪ. 1892. *Philosophische Abhandlungen.* Ed. and German trans. by Fr. Dieterici. Leiden, Brill.

AL-FĀRĀBĪ. 1900. *Der Musterstaat.* German trans. by Fr. Dieterici. Leiden, Brill.

AL-FĀRĀBĪ. 1916. *De ortu scientiarum.* Ed. by C. Baeumker. *BGPM* 19, Heft 3: 17–24. From BN Latin MS 14700, probably translated from the Arabic by Gundissalinus. Arabic source unknown.

AL-FĀRĀBĪ. 1953. *Catalogo de las sciencias.* Ed. and Spanish trans. by A. G. Palencia. Madrid, Consejo superior de investigaciones cientificas.
    Contains the Arabic text, Gerard of Cremona's Latin trans. (from Bibliothéque Nationale Lat. MS 9335, fol. 143–51), and a Spanish translation.

AL-KINDĪ. 1897. *Die quinque essentiis.* In *Die philosophischen Abhandlungen.* Ed. and commentary by Albino Nagy. *BGPM* 2, Heft 5: 28–40.

AL-KINDĪ. 1848. *Buch über die Chemie der Parfums und die Destillationen.* Ed. and German trans. by Karl Garbers. Leipzig, Brockhaus.
    Arabic title, *Kitab fi-kimiya al-itr wat-tasidat.*

ALLBUT, THOMAS C. 1921. *Greek medicine in Rome.* London, Macmillan.

ALLEN, ROBERT. 1923. *Copper ores.* London, John Murray.

AL-NĀDIM (AN-NADIM). 1951. *Kitāb al-Fihrist, tenth discourse.* English trans. by J. W. Fück. *Ambix*, 4: 88–109.

AL-RĀZĪ. 1937. *Geheimnis der Geheimnisse.* Ed. Julius Ruska. Q S 6: 83–226. From four Arabic and one Latin MSS.

ANDERSON, COL. WILLIAM. 1862. *Sketch of the mode of manufacturing gunpowder at the Ishapore mills in Bengal.* London, John Weale.

ANDREAS, WILLY. 1948. *Deutschland vor der Reformation.* 5th ed. Stuttgart, Deutsche Verlags-Anstalt.

ANONYMOUS. 1670. A relation concerning the sal gemme mines in Poland (by a curious gentleman of Germany). *PT*, 5: 1099–2002.

APELT, OTTO. 1886. Die Schrift des Alexander von Aphrodisias über die Mischung. *Philologus*, 45: 82–99.

APOLLONIUS OF TYANA. Twelfth century. *Liber de secretis naturae et occultis rerum causis.* Bibliothèque Nationale Latin manuscript 13951. 31 leaves. (*Inc. liber Apollonii de principalibus rerum causis, et primo de caelestibus corporibus et stellis et planetis, et etiam de mineriis et animantibus, tandem de homine.*)
    Used in microfilm through the courtesy of the Bibliothèque Nationale, Paris. This manuscript has been analysed by Nau, 1907.

ARISTOTLE. 1910. *Historia animalium.* English trans. by D. W. Thompson. Oxford, Clarendon (*Works*, Ed. by W. D. Ross).

ARISTOTLE. 1912. *De partibus animalium.* English trans. by Wm. Ogle. Oxford, Clarendon (*Works*, Ed. by W. D. Ross).

ARISTOTLE. 1922. *De generatione et corruptione.* English trans. by Harold H. Joachim. Oxford, Clarendon (*Works*, Ed. by W. D. Ross).

ARISTOTLE. 1929. *Physics.* Ed. and English trans. by P. H. Wicksteed and F. M. Cornford. 2 vols. London, Heinemann (Loeb classical library).

ARISTOTLE. 1933. *Metaphysics.* Ed. and English trans. by Hugh Tredennick. London, Heinemann (Loeb classical library).

ARISTOTLE. 1936. *Physics.* Ed. and English trans. by W. D. Ross. Oxford, Clarendon.

ARISTOTLE. 1941. *Les météorologiques.* French trans. with notes by J. Tricot. Paris, J. Vrin.

ARISTOTLE. 1953. *On the heavens.* Ed. and English trans. by W. K. C. Guthrie. Cambridge, Mass., Harvard University Press (Loeb classical library).
   Reprint of 1939 ed.

ARISTOTLE, pseudo. 1528. *Secreta secretorum.* Ed. by A. Achillini. Lugduni, A. Blanchard.

ARISTOTLE, pseudo. 1955. *On the cosmos* (De mundo). Ed. and English trans. by D. J. Furley. Cambridge, Mass., Harvard University Press (Loeb classical library).

ARMSTRONG, EVA V. and HIRAM S. LUKENS. 1939. Lazarus Ercker and his 'Probierbuch'. Sir John Pettus and his 'Fleta minor'. *JCE*, 16: 553–62.

ARNOLD OF VILLANOVA. 1477. *De aqua vitae simplici et composita.* Venice [Adam de Rottweil].

ARNOLD OF VILLANOVA. 1585. *Opera omnia.* Basil, C. V. Valdkirch.

ARRHENIUS, SVANTE. 1912. *Theories of solutions.* New Haven, Conn., Yale University Press.

ARTELT, WALTER, ed. 1953. *Index zur Geschichte der Medizin, Naturwissenschaft und Technik.* Munich, Urban & Schwarzenberg.

ASTRUC, JEAN. 1767. *Mémoirs pour servir à l'histoire de la faculté de médicine de Montpellier.* Paris, P. G. Cavelier.

AUGUSTINE, SAINT. 1912. *Confessions.* Ed. and English trans. by Wm. Watts. 2 vols. London, Heinemann (Loeb classical library).

AVICEBRON (IBN GABIROL, SOLOMON BEN JUDAH). 1895. *Fons Vitae.* Latin trans. by Johannes Hispanus, ed. by

Clemens Baeumker. *BGPM* 1, Heft 2–4.

AVICENNA. 1479. *Canon medicinae,* lib. 1–5. Latin trans. by Gerard of Cremona, ed. by Petrus Rochabonella. Padua, J. Herbort.

AVICENNA. 1927. *De congelatione et conglutinatione lapidum.* Ed. and English trans. by E. J. Holmyard and D. C. Mandeville. Paris, P. Geuthner.

AVICENNA. 1955–58. *Le livre de science* (Dânesh-nâmè). French trans. by M. Achena and H. Massé. 2 vols. Paris, Les belles lettres (Coll. Budé).

AVICENNA, pseudo. 1572. *De anima.* In *Artis chemicae principes, Avicenna atque Geber.* Basileae, Petrum Pernam. pp. 1–471.

BACON, FRANCIS. 1857–74. *Works.* Ed. and English trans. by James Spedding, Robert D. Ellis, and D. D. Heath. 14 vols. London, Longman, *et al.*

BACON, ROGER ?. 1603. *Sanioris medicinae magistri D. Rogeri Baconis Angli, de arte chymiae scripta. cui accesserunt opuscula aliaeiusdem authoris.* Francofurti, Schonuvetteri.

BACON, ROGER. 1859. *Opera quaedam hactenus inedita.* Ed. by J. S. Brewer. Vol. 1 (*Opus tertium, Opus minus, Compendium philosophiae*). London, Longman, *et al.*

BACON, ROGER. 1897-1. *Opus majus.* Ed. by J. H. Bridges. 3 vols. Oxford, Clarendon.

BACON, ROGER. 1897-2. An unpublished fragment of a work by Roger Bacon. Ed. by F. H. Gasquet. *English Historical Review,* 12: 494–517.

BACON, ROGER. 1909-1. *Un fragment inédit de l'Opus tertium de Roger Bacon.* Ed. by Pierre Duhem. Florence, Claras Aquas (Quaracchi), Collegio S. Bonaventurae.

BACON, ROGER. 1909-2. *Communia*

naturalium. Ed. by Robert Steele. Oxford, Clarendon (*Opera hactenus inedita*, fasc. 2–3).

BACON, ROGER. 1911. *Compendium studii theologiae*. Ed. by H. Rashdall. Aberdeen, University Press (British Society for Franciscan Studies, III).

BACON, ROGER, ed. 1920. *Secreta secretorum*. Ed. by Robert Steele. Oxford, Clarendon (*Opera hactenus inedita*, fasc. 5).
From Bodlian Tanner MS 116 (thirteenth century).

BACON, ROGER. 1928–1. *Quaestiones supra libros quatuor physicorum Aristotelis*. Ed. by F. M. Delorme and Robert Steele. Oxford, Clarendon (*Opera hactenus inedita*, fasc. 8).

BACON, ROGER. 1928–2. *De retardatione accidentium senectutis cum aliis opusculis*. Oxford, Clarendon (British Society for Franciscan Studies, XIV).

BACON, ROGER. 1962. *Opus majus*. English trans. by R. B. Burke. 2 vols. New York, Russell and Russell.
Reissue of 1928 edition.

BACON, ROGER, pseudo. 1931. *The mirror of alchemy* (Speculum alchemiae). English trans. by T. L. Davis. *JCE*, 8: 1945–53.

BAEUMKER, CLEMENS. 1890. *Das Problem der Materie in der griechischen Philosophie*. Münster, Aschendorff.

BAEUMKER, CLEMENS, ed. 1895. *Avicebron (ibn Gabirol), Fons Vitae*. BGPM 1, Heft 2–4.

BAEUMKER, CLEMENS, ed. 1916. *Alfarabi, Über den Ursprung der Wissenschaften (De ortu scientiarum)*. BGPM 19, Heft 3.

BAILEY, CYRIL. 1926. *Epicurus, the extant remains*. Oxford, Clarendon.

BAILEY, CYRIL. 1928. *The Greek atomists and Epicurus*. Oxford, Clarendon.

BAILEY, KENNETH C. 1929–32. *The elder Pliny's chapters on chemical subjects*. 2 vols. London, Arnold.

An English trans. of parts of Bks 2, 9, 19, 31, 35, and 36 of the *Naturalis historia*.

BAKER, FRANK. 1909. The two Sylviuses. *Bulletin of the Johns Hopkins Hospital*, 20 : 329–39.

BALDOUIN, CHRISTOLPH A. 1676. [Extract of a letter to Henry Oldenburg.] *PT*, 11: 788–89.

BARBA, ALVARO A. 1674. *The art of metals*. English trans. by R. H. Edward. London, S. Mearne.
The 1st (Spanish) ed. appeared in 1640.

BARNER, JACOB. 1674. *Prodromus Sennerti novi seu delineatio novi medicinae systematis*. Augsburg, T. Gobelii, J. Schonigkii.

BARNER, JACOB. 1689. *Chymia philosophica . . . cum brevi sed accurata & fundamentali salium doctrina*. Noribergae, A. Ottonis.

BARTHOLD, VASILII V. 1928. *Turkestan down to the Mongol invasion*. London, Luzac (E. J. W. Gibb Memorial Series. New Series V).

BARTHOLOMEW OF ENGLAND (BARTHOLOMAEUS ANGLICUS). 1494. *De proprietatibus rerum*.

'BASIL VALENTINE'. 1769. *Chymische Schriften*. 6th ed. Leipzig, J. P. Krauss.
A reprint of the 5th ed. of 1740. The 1st ed. was in 1677.

'BASIL VALENTINE'. 1893. *The triumphal chariot of antimony*. English trans. by A. E. Waite. London, Elliott.
'From the Latin ed. of Amsterdam, 1685.' The 1st ed. (in German) appeared in 1604.

BAUER, CLEMENS. 1930. Venezianische Salzhandelspolitik bis zum Ende des 14. Jahrhunderts. *Vierteljahrschrift für Sozial- und Wirtschaftsgeschichte*, 23 : 273–323.

BAUERREISS, HEINRICH. 1914. *Zur Geschichte des spezifischen Gewichtes im Altertum und Mittelalter.* Erlangen, Junge & Sohn.

BAUMANN, E. D. 1949. *Francois de le Boë Sylvius.* Leiden, Brill.

BAUMÉ, ANTOINE. 1773. *Chymie expérimentale et raisonnée.* 3 vols. Paris, Didot.

BAUR, LUDWIG, ed. 1903. *Dominicus Gundissalinus de divisione philosophiae.* BGPM 4, Heft 2–3.

BEARE, JOHN I. 1906. *Greek theories of elementary cognition.* Oxford, Clarendon.

BECHER, JOHANN J. 1669. *Actorum laboratorii chymici monacensis, seu Physicae subterraneae.* Francofurti, J. D. Zunneri.
    The 1st ed. appeared in 1667.

BECHER, JOHANN J. 1702. *Oedipus chymicus.* In *BCC,* Vol. 1: 306–67.
    First published in 1664.

BECHER, JOHANN J. 1703. *Physica subterranea.* Leipzig, J. L. Gledischium.
    Contains supplementary 'Theses chymicae'.

BECK, H. C. 1934. Glass before 1500. *Ancient Egypt* (1934): 7–21.

BECKMANN, JOHN. 1846. *A history of inventions, discoveries, and origins.* English trans. by Wm. Johnston. 4th ed., revised and enlarged by Wm. Francis and J. W. Griffith. 2 vols. London, Bohn.

BEGUIN, JEAN. 1618. *Tyrocinium chymicum.* Ed. by Ch. Glückradt. 4th ed. Regiomonti, J. Fabricium.
    Text from the 1st. (1612) ed., plus the notes of Glückradt (Joh. Hartmann) [Patterson, 1937].

BEGUIN, JEAN. 1620. *Les élémens de chymie.* Revues, notez, expliquez & augmentez par I.L.D.R.B.IC.E.M. [Jean Lucas de Roi, Baccal. Juris C. et Med.] Paris, M. le Maistre.
    A revision of Beguin's own 2nd ed. of 1615, which was in French [Patterson, 1937].

BEGUIN, JEAN. 1656. *Tyrocinium chymicum.* Wittebergae, A. Hartmann.
    Descended from a 1634 ed. of J. G. Pelshofer, which was based on two 1618 eds. of Ch. Glückradt and Jeramias Barth [Patterson, 1937].

BEGUIN, JEAN. 1669. *Tyrocinium chymicum; or, chymicall essayes.* London, T. Passanger.
    The 1st English trans., from the 1st ed. 1612 [Patterson, 1937].

BERGER, ERNST. 1912. *Beitrage zur Entwickelungs geschichte der Maltechnik.* III Folge. Quellen und Technik der Fresko, Opel-und Tempera-Malerei des Mittelalters. Munich, Georg D. W. Gallwey.

BERTHELOT, MARCELLIN. 1885. *Les origines de l'alchimie.* Paris, Steinheil.

BERTHELOT, MARCELLIN. 1889. *Introduction à l'étude de la chimie, des anciens et du moyen âge.* Paris, Steinheil.

BERTHELOT, MARCELLIN. 1893. *La chimie au moyen âge.* 3 vols. Paris, Imprimerie nationale (here abbreviated CMA).

BERTHELOT, MARCELLIN. 1906. *Archéologie et histoire des sciences.* Paris, Gauthier-Villars.

BERTHELOT, MARCELLIN P. and CHARLES E. ROUELLE. 1887–88. *Collection des anciens alchimistes Grecs.* 3 vols. Paris, Steinheil (here abbreviated, AAG).

BERTRAND, JOSEPH. 1869. *L'Académie des Sciences et les académiciens de 1668 à 1793.* Paris, J. Hetzel.

BETT, HENRY. 1925. *Johannes Scotus Erigena.* Cambridge, University Press.

BETT, HENRY. 1932. *Nicholas of Cusa.* London, Methuen.

BIDEZ, JOSEPH and FRANZ CUMONT. 1938. *Les mages hellénisés.* 2 vols. Paris, Les Belles Lettres.

BIGNAMI-ODIER, JEANNE. 1952. *Études sur Jean de Roquetaillade (Johannes de Rupescissa)*. Paris, Vrin.

BIRINGUCCIO, VANNOCCIO. 1942. *Pirotechnia*. English trans. of the 1st (Italian) ed. by Cyril S. Smith and Martha T. Gnudi. New York, American Institute of Mining and Metallurgical Engineers.

BLANCHETT, LEON. 1920. *Campanella*. Paris, Alcan.

BLANE, WM. 1787. Some particulars relative to the production of borax. *PT*, 77: 297–300.

BOAS, GEORGE. 1959. Some assumptions of Aristotle. *Trans. of the American Philosophical Society, NS.* 49, Pt 6.

BOAS, MARIE. 1952–1. The establishment of mechanical philosophy. *Osiris*, 10: 412–541.

BOAS, MARIE. 1952–2. Newton and the theory of chemical solution. *Isis*, 43: 123.

BOAS, MARIE. 1958. *Robert Boyle and seventeenth-century chemistry*. Cambridge, University Press.

BOERHAAVE, HERMANN. 1741. *A new method of chemistry*. English trans. by Peter Shaw, 2nd ed. 2 vols. London, Longman.
    The 1st ed. appeared in 1727, and was translated from the 1st Latin ed. of 1724. The latter was an unauthorized edition by Boerhaave's students.

BOETHIUS. 1918. *The theological tractates*. Ed. and English trans. by H. F. Stewart and E. K. Rand. London, Heinemann (Loeb classical library).

BOLL, FRANZ. 1894. *Studien über Claudius Ptolemäus*. Leipzig, Teubner.

BOREL, PIERRE. 1684. [Expérience sur les coagulations et sur les effervescences.] *Histoire de l'Académie Royale des Sciences*, Vol. 1 (1666–86, pub. 1733): 404–5.

BOREL, PIERRE. 1688. [Observation on the combination of acids with alkalis.] *Histoire de l'Académie Royale des Sciences*, Vol. 2 (1686–99, pub. 1733): 50.

BORELLI, GIOVANNI A. 1685. *De motu animalium*. Leyden, J. de Vivie, et al.

BOURDELIN, C. L. 1728. Mémoire sur la formation des sels lixiviels. *ASP*, année 1728, *Mém.*: 384–400.

BOYLE, ROBERT. 1725. *Philosophical works*. Ed. by Peter Shaw. 3 vols. London, W. & J. Innys, et al.
    'Disposed under the General Heads of Physics, Statics,' etc., and hence almost impossible to correlate with other editions of Boyle's works.

BOYLE, ROBERT. 1772. *Works*. 6 vols. London, J. & F. Rivington, et al. Ed. by Thomas Birch. First issued in 1744, in 5 vols. and with different pagination.

BOYLE, ROBERT. 1911. *The sceptical chymist*. London, J. M. Dent (Everyman's Library).

BRASAVOLA, ANTONI M. 1537. *Examen omnium simplicium medicamentorum, quorum in officinis usus est*. Lugduni, J. et F. Frellaeos.
    The 1st ed. appeared in 1536.

BREHIER, EMILE. 1951. *Chrysippe et l'ancien Stoicisme*. Paris, Presses Universitaires.

BREUIL, ABBÉ HENRI and HUGO OBERMAIER. 1935. *The cave of Altamira*. Madrid, Tip. de Archivos.

BREWER, J. S. 1859. *Fr. Rogeri Bacon Opera quaedam hactenus inedita*. Vol. 1 (ed. and introduction to [part of] *Opus minus*, *Opus tertium*, *Compendium philosophiae*). London, Longman, et al.

BRICKMAN, BENJAMIN. 1941. *An introduction to Francesco Patrizi's Nova de universis philosophia*. New York, Columbia University Press.

BRIDGES, J. H., ed. 1897. *The opus majus*

of Roger Bacon. 3 vols. Oxford, Clarendon.

BROWN, JAMES WOOD. 1897. *An inquiry into the life and legend of Michael Scot.* Edinburgh, David Douglas.

BROWNE, EDWARD G. 1921. *Arabian medicine.* Cambridge, University Press.

BRUCKMAN, FRANCIS E. 1730. An account of the imperial salt works of Soowar in upper Hungary. *PT,* 36: 260–64.

BRUNO, GIORDANO. 1591. *De triplici minimo et mensura.* Francofurti, J. Wechelum & P. Fischerum.

BRUNO, GIORDANO. 1950–1. *On the infinite universe and worlds.* English trans. by D. W. Singer. In D. W. Singer, *Giordano Bruno.* New York, Schuman. pp. 229–378.

Trans. from *De l'infinito universo et mondi,* Venice, 1584.

BRUNO, GIORDANO. 1950–2. *Concerning the cause, principle and one.* English trans. by S. Greenberg. In Sidney Greenberg, *The infinite in Giordano Bruno.* New York, King's Crown Press. pp. 77–173.

Trans. from *De la cause, principio et uno,* Venice, 1584.

BRUNSCHWYGK, HIERONYMUS. 1512. *Liber de arte distillandi de simplicibus.* Strassburg.

The 1st (German) ed. appeared in 1500.

BÜGGE, GUNTHER, ed. 1929–30. *Das Buch der grossen Chemiker.* 2 vols. Berlin, Verlag Chemie.

BÜGGE, GUNTHER. 1944. *Der Alchemist, die Geschichte Leonhard Thurneyssers, des Goldmachers von Berlin.* Berlin, Limpert.

BURNAM, JOHN MILLER. 1920. *A classical technology.* Boston, R. G. Badger.

BURNET, JOHN. 1930. *Early Greek philosophy.* 4th ed. London, A. & C. Black.

BURTON, WILLIAM. 1746. *An account of the life and writings of Herman Boerhaave.* 2nd ed. London, H. Lintot.

The 1st ed. appeared in 1743.

BYRNE, EUGENE H. 1919–20. Genoese trade with Syria in the twelfth century. *American Historical Review,* 25: 191–219.

CADET, LOUIS C. 1766. Expériences sur le borax. *ASP, année 1766, Mém.,* 365–63 (see also *Hist.:* 64–74).

CALEY, E. R. 1926. The Leyden papyrus X. An English translation with brief notes. *JCE,* 3: 1149–66.

CALEY, E. R. 1927. The Stockholm papyrus. An English translation with brief notes. *JCE,* 4: 979–1002.

CALEY, E. R. 1928. Mercury and its compounds in ancient times. *JCE,* 5: 419–24.

CALEY, E. R. 1946. Ancient Greek pigments. *JCE,* 23: 314–16.

CALEY, E. R. 1955. On the existence of chronological variations in the composition of Roman brass coins. *Ohio Journal of Science,* 55: 137–40.

CALEY, E. R. and D. T. EASBY, Jr. 1959. The smelting of sulphide ores of copper in preconquest Peru. *American Antiquity,* 25: 59–65.

CALEY, E. R. and J. F. C. RICHARDS. 1956. *Theophrastus on stones.* Columbus, Ohio, Ohio State University Press.

CANEPARIO, PIETRO M. 1660. *De atramentis.* London, T. Alestry.

Revision of a work first published in 1619.

CAP, PAUL A. G. 1839. *Nicolas Lemery.* Paris, Fain.

CAPOBUS, ROBERT. 1933. *Angelus Sala.* Berlin, Verlag-Chemie.

CARDANO, GIROLAMO. 1556. *De la subtilité.* French trans. by Richard le

Blanc. Paris, Ch. L'Angelier.
The 1st (Latin) ed. appeared in 1550.

CARDANO, GIROLAMO. 1557. *De varietate rerum*. Basil, Henricum Petri.

CARDANO, GIROLAMO. 1559. *De subtilitate*. Lugduni, G. Rouillium.

CARDANO, GIROLAMO. 1654. *De propria vita liber*. Amsterdam, J. Ravenstein.

CARRA DE VAUX, BERNARD. 1921–26. *Les penseurs de l'Islam*. 5 vols. Paris, Geuthner.

CASS, MYRTLE M. 1934. *The first book of Jerome Cardan's De subtilitate*. Williamsport, Penna., Bayard Press.

CASSIODORUS. 1656. *Opera omnia*. Geneva, P. Gamonetus.

CASSIRER, ERNST. 1964. *The individual and the cosmos in Renaissance philosophy*. English trans. by Mario Domandi. New York, Harper Torchbooks.

CELSUS, AULUS CORNELIUS. 1935–38. *De medicine*. Ed. and English trans. by W. G. Spencer. 3 vols. Cambridge, Mass., Harvard University Press (Loeb classical library).

CENNINI, CENNINO. 1899. *Il libro dell'arte*. English trans. by C. J. Herringham. London, Allen and Unwin.

CENNINI, CENNINO. 1933. *Il libro dell'arte*. Ed. and English trans. by D. V. Thompson, Jr. 2 vols. New Haven, Conn., Yale University Press.

CHAMPIER, SYMPHORIEN (SYMPHORIANO CAMPEGIO). 1533. *Annotatiunculae . . . Apologitica epistola*. Lugdunum.

CHARAS, MOISE. 1695. [*Sur la nature des sels*]. *Histoire de l'Académie Royale des Sciences*, Vol. 2 (1686–99, pub. 1733): 252–5.

CHEVALLIER, PAUL. 1948. *La Table d'Emeraude. Secret de la préparation de l'acide sulphurique. Biologie Medicale*, 37: LIX pp (entire issue).

CHILDE, V. GORDEN. 1952. *New light on the most ancient east*. 4th ed. London, Routledge and Kegan Paul.

CLAGETT, MARSHALL. 1941. *Giovanni Marliani and late medieval physics*. New York, Columbia University Press.

CLAGETT, MARSHALL. 1950. Richard Swineshead and late medieval physics. I. The intension and remission of qualities. *Osiris*, 9: 131–61.

CLARKE, JOHN. 1910. *Physical science in the time of Nero*, being a translation of the *Quaestiones Naturales* of Seneca. London, Macmillan.

CLOW, ARCHIBALD and NAN CLOW. 1947. The natural and economic history of kelp. *AS*, 5: 297–316.

CLOW, ARCHIBALD and NAN CLOW. 1952. *The chemical revolution*. London, Batchworth Press.

COGHLAN, H. H. 1940. Prehistoric copper and some experiments in smelting. *TNS*, 20: 49–66.

COGHLAN, H. H. 1942. Some fresh aspects of the prehistoric metallurgy of copper. *Antiquaries journal*, 22: 22–38.

COGHLAN, H. H. 1951. Notes on the prehistoric metallurgy of copper and bronze in the old world. Oxford, Pitt Rivers Museum, *Occasional papers on technology*, No. 4.

COHEN, MORRIS RAPHAEL and I. E. DRABKIN. 1948. *A source book in Greek science*. New York, McGraw-Hill.

COLBATCH, SIR JOHN. 1698. *Four treatises of physick and chirurgery*. 2 vols. 2nd ed. London, J. D. for Daniel Brown.

COLEBY, J. L. M. 1952. John Francis Vigani. *AS*, 8: 46–60.

COLLEGII CONIMBRICENSIS SOCIETATIS JESU. 1599. *In libros de generatione et corruptione Aristotelis*. 2nd ed. Moguntiae, J. Albini.

Compositiones ad tingenda. 1774. Ed. by L. A. Muratori, in *Antiquitates Italicae Medii Aevi.* Arettii, Michaelis. Vol. 4: cols. 673–722
    All editions and translations of this work are from the sole extant manuscript, Lucca Biblioteca Capitolare 490: fols. 217r–231r.

Compositiones ad tingenda. 1920. English trans. by John Burnham, in *A classical technology.* Boston, R. G. Badger.

Compositiones ad tingenda. 1932. Ed. and German trans. by Hjalmar Hedfors. Uppsala, Almguist & Wiksells.

CONCI, GIULIO. 1934. *Pagine di Storia della Farmacia.* Milano, Edizioni Vittoria.

CONSTANTINE OF AFRICA. 1536. *Opera.* Basil, H. Petrum.

CONTANT, JEAN-PAUL. 1952. *L'Enseignement de la chimie au Jardin Royal des Plantes de Paris.* Cahors, A. Coueslant.

CONYBEARE, FREDERICK C. 1927. *Philostratus' life of Apollonius of Tyana.* 2 vols. London, Heinemann (Loeb classical library).

COOPER, LANE. 1928. *A concordance of Boethius.* Cambridge, Mass., Medieval Academy of America.

CORBETT, JAMES. 1939. *Catalogue des manuscrits alchimiques Latin.* Brussels, Union Académiques Internationale.

CORNFORD, FRANCIS M. 1937. *Plato's cosmology. The Timaeus of Plato.* London, Kegan Paul.

COUTANT, V. C. B. 1936. *Alexander of Aphrodisias: Commentary on Book IV of Aristotle's Meteorologica.* New York, Columbia University Press.

CRANZ, F. E. 1960. *Catalogus translationem et commentariorum.* Vol. 1. Alexander of Aphrodisiensis. Washington, D.C., Catholic University Press.

CROLL, OSWALD. 1609. *Basilica chymica.* Francofurti, C. Marnium.

CROLL, OSWALD. 1643. *Basilica chymica* . . . aucta a Johan. Hartmanno. Venice, *sub signo minervae.*

CROLL, SAMUEL B. 1743. Extractus ex letteris eius de alcali nativo Indico et borace. *Miscellanea Berolinensia,* 7: 318–23.

CUMONT, FRANZ. 1911. *The oriental religions in Roman paganism.* Chicago, Open Court.

CUMONT, FRANZ. 1912. *Astrology and religion among the Greeks and Romans.* London, Constable.

CUTTING, C. L. 1958. Fish preservation. In *A history of technology,* ed. Charles Singer *et al.* Vol. 4: 44–54.

D. J. 1765. Article, sel, in *ED,* Vol. 14.

DANIEL OF MORLEY. 1918. *Liber de naturis inferiorum et superiorum.* Ed. by K. Sudhoff. *AGNT,* 8: 1–40.

DARMSTAEDTER, ERNST. 1922. *Die Alchemie des Geber.* Berlin, Springer.
    Includes a German trans. of five works; see Geber (the Latin), 1922.

DARMSTAEDTER, ERNST. 1924. *Per la storia dell' aurum potabile. Archeion,* 5: 251–71.

DARMSTAEDTER, ERNST. 1925. Liber misericordiae Geber. *Archiv für Geschichte der Medizin,* 17: 181–97.

DARMSTAEDTER, ERNST. 1925–28. Liber claritatis. *Archivo di Storia della Scienza* (after 1926, *Archeion*), 6: 319–30; 7: 257–65; 8: 95–103, 214–26; 9: 61–80, 191–208, 462–82.

DARMSTAEDTER, ERNST. 1926–1. Georg Agricola. Munich, Münchener Drucke (*Münchener Beiträge zur Geschichte und Literatur der Naturwissenschaften und Medizin,* Heft 1).

DARMSTAEDTER, ERNST. 1926–2. *Berg-, Probir-, und Kunstbüchlein.* Munich, Münchener Brucke.

DARMSTAEDTER, ERNST. 1930. *Paracelsus*

und die Einführung chemischer Präparat als Heilmittel, in Karl Sudhoff, ed. *Historische Studien* (Festgabe Georg Sticker). Berlin, Springer: 63–73.

DAUMAS, MAURICE. 1946. *L'acte chimique*. Bruxelles-Paris, Sablon.

DAVIS, T. L. 1926. The Emerald Tablet of Hermes Trismegistus. *JCE*, 3: 863–75.

DAVISSON, WM. 1640–42. *Philosophia pyrotechnica, seu cursus chymiatricus*. Paris, J. Bessin.

Pt I (14 pp.) and Pt II (pp. 15–487) are continuously paginated, and have an Approbatio dated 1635. Pt III (independently paginated 1–292) has an independent title page, *Curriculi chymici, de vocabulis chymicae operationi inservientibus*, and date, 1640.

DAVISSON, WM. 1660. *Commentariorum in . . . Petri Severini Dani Ideam medicinae philosophicae*. Hagae-Comitis, A. Vlacq.

De aluminibus et salibus. 1929. Ed. by Robert Steele. *Isis*, 12: 14–42. From BN Latin MS 6514 and BM Latin MS Arundel 164.

De aluminibus et salibus. 1935. German trans. by Julius Ruska (as *Das Buch der Alaune und Salze*). Berlin, Verlag Chemie.

Arabic version (Berlin Springer MS 1908), Latin, from John of Garland, *De mineralibus liber*, Basel, 1560, and German translation.

DE BROGLIE, LOUIS. 1955. *Physics and microphysics*. New York, Pantheon Books.

De coloribus et artibus Romanorum. 1849. English trans. in M. P. Merrifield, *Original treatises*. London, J. Murray. Vol. 1: 182–257.

From BN Latin MS 6741, dated 1431.

De coloribus et artibus Romanorum. 1873. Ed. and German trans. by Albert Ilg (as *Heraclius, von den Farben und Künsten der Römer*). Wien, Braumüller.

A critical ed. from eight manuscripts.

DEMACHY, JACQUES F. 1773. *L'art du distillateur d'eaux fortes* etc. Paris, Académie Royale des Sciences (*Déscriptions des arts et metiers*, Vol. 37).

DESCARTES, RENÉ. 1668. *Les principes. de la philosophie*. Paris, M. Bobin & N. le Gras.

DESCARTES, RENÉ. 1902. *Discours de la méthode & essais*. Paris, Leopold Cerf (*Oeuvres*. Ed. by Ch. Adam & P. Tannery. Vol. 6).

Reprint of the French ed. of Leyden, 1637.

DESCARTES, RENÉ. 1905. *Principia philosophia*. Paris, Leopold Cerf (*Oeuvres*. Ed. by Ch. Adam & P. Tannery. Vol. 8: 1–348).

Reprint of the Latin ed. of Amsterdam, 1644.

DIELS, HERMANN. 1893. *Über das physikalische System des Straton*. *Sitzungsber. der K. Preuss. Akad. der Wiss.* (Berlin), Phil.-Hist. Kl.: 101–127.

DIELS, HERMANN. 1959–60. *Die Fragmente der Vorsokratiker*. 9th ed. Ed. by Walther Kranz. 3 vols. Berlin-Charlottenburg, Weidmann (here abbreviated DK).

DIERBACH, J. H. 1824. *Die Arzneimittel des Hippokrates*. Heidelberg, K. Gross.

DIERGART, PAUL, ed. 1909. *Beiträge aus der Geschichte der Chemie* (Festschrift Georg Kahlbaum). Leipzig, F. Deuticke.

DIETERICI, FRIEDRICH H. 1876. *Die Philosophie der Araber im IX und X Jahrhundert. Fünftes Buch. Die Naturanschauung und Naturphilosophie*. 2nd ed. Leipzig, Hinrich.

DIETERICI, FRIEDRICH H. 1879. *Die*

Philosophie bei den Arabern in X Jahrhunderts. Pt II. *Mikrokosmos.* Leipzig, Hinrich.

DIETERICI, FRIEDRICH H. 1892. *Alfarabi's philosophische Abhandlungen.* Leiden, Brill.

DIGBY, SIR KENELM. 1645. *Two treatises, in the one of which, the nature of bodies; in the other, the nature of man's soule; is looked into,* London, J. Williams.

DIGBY, SIR KENELM. 1669. *A discourse concerning the vegetation of plants.* Spoken . . . at Gresham College, on the 23rd of January, 1660. London, J. Williams (printed as pp. 209–31 with 1669 ed. of *Two treatises*).

DIOGENES LAERTES. 1925. *Lives of eminent philosophers.* Ed. and English trans. by R. D. Hicks. 2 vols. London, Heinemann (Loeb classical library).

DIOSCORIDES. 1950. *The Greek herbal of Dioscorides.* English trans. by John Goodyear (1655), ed. by Robert T. Gunther. New York, Hafner. Reprint of 1934 ed.

DODWELL, C. R. 1961. *Theophilus, the various arts.* London, Nelson.

DONALD, M. B. 1936. History of the Chile nitrate industry, I. *AS,* I : 29–47.

DORN, GERARD. 1568. *Chymisticum artificium naturae,* theoricum et practicum. [Frankfurt.]

DOUGLAS, C. and R. P. HARDIE. 1910. *The philosophy and psychology of Pietro Pomponazzi.* Cambridge, University Press.

DU CHESNE, JOSEPH (also known as Quercetanus). 1614. *Pharmacopoea dogmaticorum restituta.* Venice, Jacobum de Franciscis.

DU CLOS, S. C. 1667. [Observation sur l'acid du sel marine, sur les differentes bases]. *Histoire de l'Académie Royale des Sciences,* Vol. I (1666–86, pub. 1733): 23–27.

DUFRENOY, M. L. 1950. The significance of antimony in the history of chemistry. *JCE,* 27: 595–97.

DUHAMEL DU MONCEAU, H. L. 1735. Sur la sel ammoniac. *ASP,* année 1735, *Mém.:* 106–16, 414–34, 483–504, (see also *Hist.:* 23–6).

DUHAMEL DU MONCEAU, H. L. 1736. Sur la base du sel marin. *ASP,* année 1736, *Mém.:* 215–32 (see also *Hist.:* 65–8).

DUHEM, PIERRE. 1909. *Un fragment inédit de l'Opus tertium de Roger Bacon.* Florence Claras Aquas (Quaracchi), Collegio S. Bonaventurae.

DUHEM, PIERRE. 1913–59. *Le système du monde.* 10 vols. Paris, Hermann (here abbreviated *SM*).

DÜRING, INGEMAR. 1944. *Aristotle's chemical treatise.* Meteorologica Book IV. Göteborg, Högskolas Årsskrift, Bd. 1, No. 2.

DURLING, RICHARD J. 1961. A chronological census of Renaissance editions and translations of Galen. *Journal of the Warberg and Courtwald Institutes,* 24: 230–305.

EASTON, STEWART COPINGER. 1952. *Roger Bacon and his search for a universal science.* New York, Columbia University Press.

EBBELL, BENDIX JOACHIM. 1937. *The papyrus Ebers.* Copenhagen, Levin and Munksgaard.

EBERT, MAX. 1924–32. *Reallexikon der Vorgeschichte.* 15 vols. Berlin, de Gruyter.

ECKMAN, JAMES. 1946. *Jerome Cardan.* Baltimore, Johns Hopkins Press (Supplements to the Bulletin of the History of Medicine, No. 7).

EDELSTEIN, LUDWIG. 1936. The philosophical system of Posidonius. *American Journal of Philology,* 57: 286–325.

ELIADE, MIRCEA. 1956. *Forgerons et alchimistes.* Paris, Flammarion.

Encyclopedia of Islam. 1908–38. 5 vols. Leyden, Brill (here abbreviated *EI-1*).

Encyclopedia of Islam. New Ed. 1,900 pp. Leyden, Brill (here abbreviated *EI-2*)

Encylopédie, ou dictionnaire raisonné des sciences, des arts et des métiers. 1751–65. 17 vols. Paris, various publishers (ed. D. Diderot & J. d'Alembert. Here abbreviated ED).

Encyclopédie méthodique. Arts et métiers mécaniques. 1782–91. 8 vols. Paris, Panckoucke.

Encyclopédie Méthodique. 1789. *Procédés d'industrie de chimie.* In *Arts et métiers mécaniques,* Vol. 6: 691–769.

EPICURUS. 1926. *The extant remains.* Ed. and English trans. by Cyril Bailey. Oxford, Clarendon.

ERCKER, LAZARUS. 1951. *Treatise on ores and assaying.* English trans. by A. G. Sisco and C. S. Smith. Chicago, University of Chicago Press.

 From the German ed. of Frankfurt a/M, 1580.

ERDMANN, HUGO. 1902. *Lehrbuch der anorganischen Chemie.* 3rd ed. Braunschweig, Vieweg.

ERNOUT, ALFRED and LEON ROBIN. 1925–28. *Lucrece, de natura rerum, commentaire.* 3 vols. Paris: Les Belles Lettres (Coll. Budé).

EVELYN, JOHN. 1959. *Diary.* Ed. by E. S. de Beer. London, Oxford University Press.

FARBER, EDUARD, ed. 1961. *Great chemists.* New York, Interscience.

FERCKEL, CHRISTOPH. 1927. Cantimpre über die Metalle. In Ruska, 1927–1: 75–80.

FERGUSON, JOHN. 1906. *Bibliotheca chemica.* 2 vols. Glasgow, Maclehose.

FERGUSON, JOHN. 1959. *Bibliographical notes on histories of inventions and books of secrets.* 2 vols. London, Holland Press.

FERNEL, JEAN. 1655. *Les VII livres de la physiologie.* French trans. by C. Saint-Germain. Paris, J. Guignard.

 The 1st (Latin) ed. appeared in 1542.

FERNEL, JEAN. 1567. *Universa medicina.* Paris, A. Wechelum.

 The 1st ed. appeared in 1554.

FESTER, GUSTAV. 1923. *Die Entwicklung der chemischen Technik bis zu den Anfängen der Grossindustrie.* Berlin, Springer.

FESTUGIÈRE, ANDRÉ J. 1944. *La révélation d'Hermès Trismégiste.* Vol. 1. *L'astrologie et les sciences occultes.* 3rd ed. Paris, Gabalda.

FICINO, MARSILIO. 1559. *Theologia Platonica, de immortalitate animorum.* Paris, A. Gorbinum.

 The 1st ed. appeared in 1482.

FISCHER, JOHANN KARL. 1801–08. *Geschichte der Physik.* 8 vols. Göttingen, J. F. Röwer.

FLÜGEL, GUSTAV L. 1857. Al-Kindi. genannt 'der Philosoph der Araber'. *Abhandlungen für die Kunde des Morgenlands,* 1: No. 2.

FÖRSTER, RICHARD. 1889. Handschriften und Ausgaben des pseudoaristotelischen Secretum secretorum *Centralblatt für Bibliothekswesen,* 6: 1–22, 67–76.

(FONTENELLE, BERNARD LE BOUVIER DE.) 1703. Analyse de Borax. *ASP,* année 1703, *Hist.*: 49.

 An account of work by Louis Lemery.

FONTENELLE, BERNARD LE BOUVIER DE. 1715–1. Éloge de M. Lemery. *ASP,* année 1715, *Hist.*: 73–82.

FONTENELLE, BERNARD LE BOUVIER DE. 1715–2. Éloge de M. Homberg. *ASP,* année 1715, *Hist.*: 82–93.

(FONTENELLE, BERNARD LE BOUVIER DE.) 1716. Sur l'origin du sel armoniac. *ASP,* année 1716, *Hist.*: 28–30.

(FONTENELLE, BERNARD LE BOUVIER DE.) 1720. Sur l'origin de sel armoniac.

ASP, année 1720, *Hist.*: 46–50. A continuation of Fontenelle, 1716.

FORBES, ROBERT JAMES. 1950. *Metallurgy in antiquity*. Leyden, Brill.

FORBES, ROBERT JAMES. 1955. *Studies in ancient technology*. Vol. 3. Leyden, Brill.

FORBES, ROBERT JAMES. 1957. *Studies in ancient technology*. Vol. 5. Leyden, Brill.

FOSTER, SIR MICHAEL. 1924. *Lectures on the history of physiology during the sixteenth, seventeenth and eighteenth centuries*. Cambridge, Cambridge University Press.

FOUGEROUX DE BONDAROY, A. D. 1766-1. Mémoire sur les aluminieres, alumiers ou alunieres de la Tolfa. *ASP*, année 1766, *Mém.*: 1–16 (see also *Hist.*: 16–21).

FOUGEROUX DE BONDAROY, A. D. 1766-2. Mémoire sur le giallolino ou jaune de Naples. *ASP*, année 1766, *Mém.*: 303–14 (see also *Hist.*: 60–64).

FRACASTORO, GIROLAMO. 1546. *De sympathia et antipathia*. Venetiis, Junta.

FRANCHET, LOUIS. 1911. *Ceramique primitive*. Paris, Guenther.

FRANKFORT, HENRI. 1934. *Iraq excavations of the Oriental Institute 1932/33*. Chicago, University of Chicago Press (Oriental Institute Communications No. 17).

FRANKFORT, HENRI, and H. A., J. A. WILSON, THORKILD JACOBSEN, and WILLIAM A. IRWIN. 1946. *The intellectual adventure of ancient man*. Chicago, University of Chicago Press.

FRIEDMAN, REUBEN. 1938. The story of scabies. *Medical Life*, 45: 163–76.

FÜCK, J. W. 1951. The Arabic literature on alchemy according to An-Nadim (A.D. 987). *Ambix*, 4: 81–144.

GADD, C. J. and R. C. THOMPSON. 1936. A middle Babylonian chemical text. *Iraq*, 3: 87–96.

GALEN. 1916. *On the natural faculties*. Ed. and English trans. by A. J. Brock. London, Heinemann (Loeb classical library).

GALEN. 1821–33. *Opera*. Ed. by K. G. Kuhn. 20 vols. Leipzig, C. Cnobloch.

GANDILLAC, M. P. DE. 1941. *La philosophie de Nicolas de Cues*. Paris, Aubier.

GANZENMULLER, WILHELM. 1938. *L'alchimie au moyen age*. French trans. by G. Petit-Dutailles. Paris, Aubier.

GANZENMULLER, WILHELM. 1941. Das chemische Laboratorium der Universität Marberg im Jahre 1615. *Angewandte Chemie*, 54: 215.

GANZENMULLER, WILHELM. 1955. Ein alchemistische Handschrift aus der zweiten Hälfte des 12. Jahrhunderts. *SA*, 39: 43–51.

GANZENMULLER, WILHELM. 1956. *Beiträge zur Geschichte der Technologie und der Alchemie*. Weinheim/Bergstr., Verlag Chemie.

GARBERS, KARL. 1948. *Buch über die Chemie der Parfums und die Destillationen von Yaqub B. Ishaq al-Kindī*. Leipzig, Brockhaus.

GASQUET, F. H. 1897. An unpublished fragment of a work by Roger Bacon. *English Historical Review*, 12: 494–507.

GATTERER, CHRISTIAN W. G. 1798–99. *Allgemeines Repertorium der mineralogischen, und salzwerkswissenschaftliches Literatur*. Giessen.

GEBER (the Latin). 1922. *Die alchemie*. German trans. by Ernst Darmstaedter. Berlin, Springer. Includes the *Summa perfectionis magisterii*, *De investigatione perfectionis*, *De inventione veritatis* and *Liber fornacum*, all from the Latin ed. of Nuremberg, 1541, and the *Testamentum*, from the ed. of Venice, 1542.

GEBER (the Latin). 1928. *Works*. English trans. by Richard Russell (1678), reissued with intro. by E. J. Holmyard. London, Dent.

Includes *Of the investigation or search of perfection, Of the sum of perfection, or of the perfect magistery, Of the invention of verity*, and *Of furnaces*.

GEOFFROY, CLAUDE J. 1720. Observations sur la nature et la composition du sel ammoniac. *ASP* année 1720, *Mém.*: 189–91.

GEOFFROY, CLAUDE J. 1723. Observations sur la nature et la composition du sel ammoniac. *ASP* année 1723, *Mém.*: 210–22, a continuation of Geoffroy, 1720.

GEOFFROY, E. F. 1700. Part of a letter from Mr. Geoffroy, FRS, to Dr. Sloane concerning the exact quantity of acid salts contained in acid spirits. *PT*, 22: 530–34.

GEOFFROY, E. F. 1718. Table des différents rapports observés en chimie entre différentes substances. *ASP*, année 1718, *Mém.*: 202–12 (see also *Hist.*: 35–7).

GEORGE, PHILIP. 1952. The scientific movement and the development of chemistry in England, as seen in the papers published in the Philosophical Transactions from 1664/5 until 1750. *AS*, 8: 302–22.

GERMAIN, A. 1882. *L'Apothicairerie à Montpellier sous l'ancien régime universitaire*. Montpellier, J. Martel.

Extrait des Mémoires de la Société archéologique de Montpellier.

GESNER, CONRAD. 1555. *Thesaurus Euonymi Philiatri*. Lugduni, B. Arnolletum.

The 1st ed. appeared in 1552.

GESNER, CONRAD. 1586. *Physicarum meditationum* annotationum et scholiorum. Tiguri, Froschoviana.

GETTENS, R. J. 1950. Lapis lazuli and ultramarine in ancient times. *Alumni*, 19: 342–57.

GIBBS, F. W. 1938. On 'nitre' and natron. *AS*, 3: 213–16.

GIBBS, F. W. 1939. The history of the manufacture of soap. *AS*, 4: 169–90.

GILSON, ETIENNE. 1955. *History of Christian philosophy in the Middle Ages*. New York, Random House.

GLASER, CHRISTOPHLE. 1673. *Traité de la chymie*. Paris, J. d'Houry.

The 1st ed. appeared in 1663.

GLAUBER, JOHANN R. 1651. *A description of new philosophical furnaces*, or a new art of distilling. English trans. by J.(ohn) F.(rench) D. M. London, Richard Coats for T. Williams.

The 1st (German) ed. appeared 1646–49.

Glauber, Johann R. 1658–59. *Opera chymica*. 2 vols. Frankfurt a/M, T. M. Götzens.

GLAUBER, JOHANN R. 1689. *Works*. English trans. by Christopher Packe. London, T. Milbourn.

Contains three parts separately paginated.

GMELIN, JOHANN F. 1797–99. *Geschichte der Chemie*. 3 vols. Goettingen, Rosenbusch.

GRAAF, REGNIER DE. 1666. *Traité de la nature et de l'usage du suc pancreatique*. Paris, O. de Varennes.

The 1st (Latin) ed. appeared in 1663.

GRABMANN, MARTIN. 1916. Forschungen über die lateinischen Aristoteles-Übersetzungen des XIII Jahrhunderts. *BGPM*, 17: Heft 5–6.

GRABMANN, MARTIN. 1918. *Die Philosophia Pauperum und ihr Verfasser Albert von Orlamünde*. *BGPM*, 20: Heft 2.

GRAY, D. H. F. 1954. Metal working in Homer. *Jour. of Hellenic Studies*, 74: 1ff.

GRAY, SAMUEL F. 1831. *The operative chemist*. London, Hurst, Chance, and Co.

GREENBERG, SIDNEY. 1950. *The infinite in Giordano Bruno.* New York, King's Crown Press.

GREGORY, THOMAS C. 1942. *The condensed chemical dictionary.* 3rd ed. New York, Reinhold.

GREN, F. A. C. 1782. [on sal ammoniac]. *Crelle's neusten Entdeckungen in der Chemie,* 7: 19–38.

GUERLAC, HENRY. 1957. Joseph Black and fixed air. *Isis,* 48: 124–51, 433–56.

GUGEL, KURT F. 1955. *Johann Rudolph Glauber.* Wurzburg, Freunde Mainfränkischer Kunst und Geschichte (Mainfränkischere Hefte, 22).

GULICK, N. 1938. *Bulletin of the American School of Oriental Research.* No. 71: 3ff.

GUNDISSALINUS, DOMINICUS. 1903. *De divisione philosophiae.* Ed. by L. Baur. *BGPM,* 4: Heft 2–3: 1–142.
A critical text based on 5 MSS.

GUNTHER, ROBERT T. 1923–45. *Early science in Oxford.* 14 vols. Oxford, printed for the subscribers.

GUNTHER, ROBERT T. 1937. *Early science in Cambridge.* Oxford, printed for the author at the University Press.

GUNTHER, ROBERT T. 1950. *The Greek herbal of Dioscorides.* New York, Hafner.
Reprint of 1934 edition.

GÜNTHER, SIEGMUND. 1881. Die mathematischen- und Naturwissenschaften an der Nürnbergischen Universität Altdorf. *Mitteilungen des Vereins für Geschichte der Stadt Nürnberg,* 3: 1–36.

HALL, VERNON Jr. 1950. Life of Julius Caesar Scaliger. *Transactions of the American Philosophical Society,* N.S. 40, Pt 2: 85–170.

HAMARNEH, SAMI K., and GLENN SONNEDECKER. 1963. *A pharmaceutical view of Abulcasis al-Zahrāwī in Moorish Spain.* Leyden, Brill.

HAMMER-JENSEN, INGEBORG. 1921. *Die älteste Alchemie.* Copenhagen, Host & Son (Det Kg. Danske Videnskabernes Selskab., Historiskfilologiske Meddelelser. IV 2).

HARDEN, DONALD B. 1956. Glass and glazes. In Sir Charles Singer, ed., *A history of technology.* Oxford, Clarendon. Vol. 2: 311–46.

HARRIS, JOHN. 1708–1710. *Lexicon technicum: or, an universal English dictionary of arts and sciences.* 2nd ed. 2 vols. London, Dan. Brown, et al.

HARTMANN, R. JULIUS. 1904. *Theophrast von Hohenheim.* Stuttgart und Berlin, J. A. Cotta'sche Nachfolger.

HARTWELL, ROBERT. 1962. A revolution in Chinese iron and coal industries during the Northern Sung, A.D. 960–1126. *Journal of Asian Studies,* 21: 153–62.

HARVEY, E. NEWTON. 1957. *A history of luminescence.* Philadelphia, American Philosophical Society.

HASKINS, CHARLES HOMER. 1911. The translations of Hugo Sanctelliensis. *Romanic View,* 2: 1–15.

HASKINS, CHARLES HOMER. 1922. Michael Scot and Frederick II. *Isis,* 4: 250–75.

HASKINS, CHARLES HOMER. 1924. *Studies in the history of medieval science.* Cambridge, Mass., Harvard University Press.

HASKINS, CHARLES HOMER. 1927. *The renaissance of the 12th century.* Cambridge, Mass., Harvard University Press.

HASKINS, CHARLES HOMER. 1928. The Alchemy ascribed to Michael Scot. *Isis,* 10: 350–59.

HASSELQUIST, FRED. 1760. The method of making sal ammoniac in Egypt. *PT,* 51: 504–06.

HASSINGER, HERBERT. 1951. *Johann Joachim Becher.* Wien, Holzhausens (Veröffentlichungen der Kommission für neuere Geschichte Österreichs, 38).

HAUSER, HENRI. 1927. Le sel dans l'histoire. *Revue économique internationale*, 19: 270–87.

HAWTHORNE, JOHN C. and CYRIL S. SMITH. 1963. *On divers arts*, the treatise of Theophilus. Chicago, University of Chicago Press.

HEFORS, HJALMAR. 1932. *Compositiones ad tingenda*, herausgegeben, übersetzt und philologisch erklärt. Uppsala, Almquist & Wiksells.

HEINRICHS, HEINRICH. 1914. Die Überwindung der Autorität Galens durch Denker der Renaissancezeit. *Renaissance und Philosophie*, 12: 1–80.

HELMONT, JOHANN B. VAN. 1670. *Oeuvres*. French trans. by Jean le Conte. Francofurti, Lyon, J. A. Huguetan et G. Barbier.

HELMONT, JOHANN B. VAN. 1648–1. *Ortus medicinae*. Ed. authoris filio, Francsico Mercurio van Helmont. Amsterdam, Elzevir.

HELMONT, JOHANN B. VAN. 1648–2. *Opuscula medica inaudita*. Amsterdam, Elzevir.
Bound with Helmont, 1648–1.

HELMONT, JOHANN B. VAN. 1662. *Oriatrike*. London, Lodowick Loyd.
An English translation of Helmont, 1648–1 and 1648–2, with continuous pagination, by John Chandler.

HERACLIUS. See *De coloribus et artibus Romanorum*.

HERRINGHAM, CHRISTINA J. 1899. *The book of the art of Cennino Cennini*, an English trans. of Cennini's *Il libro dell'arte*, with notes. London, Allen and Unwin.

HEYM, GERARD. 1938. Al-Rāzī and alchemy. *Ambix*, 1: 184–91.

HILLEN, CORNELIUS. 1955. *The early development of metal working in the ancient Near East*. Chicago, University of Chicago, (unpublished) doctoral dissertation submitted March, 1955.

HIPPOCRATES. 1839–61. *Oeuvres*. Greek text and French trans. by É. Littré. 10 Vols. Paris, J. B. Baillière.

HIRSCH, AUGUST. 1884–88. *Biographisches Lexikon der hervorragenden Aerzte*. 6 Vols. Wien u. Leipzig: Urban u. Schwarzenberg (here abbreviated BL).

HIRSCH, RUDOLF. 1950. The invention of printing and the diffusion of alchemical and chemical knowledge. *Chymia*, 3: 115–42.

HOEFER, JEAN CHRÉTIEN FERDINAND. 1842–43. *Histoire de la chimie*. 2 vols. Paris, Hachette.

HOFFMANN, FRIEDRICH. 1755. *Observationum physico-chymicarum selectiorum*. Naples, B. Gessari.
The 1st ed. appeared in Halle, 1722.

HOGHELAND, CORNELIUS VAN. 1686. *Cogitationes*. Leyden, J. Gelder.
First published in 1646.

HOLMYARD, E. J. 1923. The Emerald Table. *Nature*, 112: 525–6.

HOLMYARD, E. J. 1924. A critical examination of Berthelot's work upon Arabic chemistry. *Isis*, 6: 479–99.

HOLMYARD, E. J. 1925. A romance of chemistry. *Journal of the Society of the Chemical Industry*, 44: 75–7, 105–8, 136–7.

HOLMYARD, E. J. 1927. An alchemical tract ascribed to Mary the Copt. *Archeion*, 8: 161–67.

HOLMYARD, E. J. 1928. *The works of Geber*, Englished by Richard Russel, 1678. London, Dent.

HOLMYARD, E. J. 1935–36. Medieval Arabic pharmacology. *Proceedings of the Royal Society of Medicine*. Section of the History of Medicine, 29: 1–10.

HOLMYARD, E. J. and D. C. MANDEVILLE. 1927. *Avicennae de congelatione et conglutinatione lapidum*. Paris, Geuthner.

HOMBERG, GUILLAUME. 1695. Sur les esprits acides. *Histoire de l'Académie*

Royale des Sciences, Vol. 2 (1686–99, pub. 1733): 250–52.

HOMBERG, GUILLAUME. 1699. Observation sur la quantité exacte des sels volatiles acides contenus dans les différens esprits acides. *ASP,* année 1699, 3rd ed., *Mém.*: 44–51 (see also *Hist.*: 52–3).

HOMBERG, GUILLAUME. 1700. Observation sur la quantité d'acides absorbees par les alcalis terreux. *ASP,* année 1700, 2nd ed., *Mém.*: 64–71 (see also *Hist.*: 48–50).

HOMBERG, GUILLAUME. 1702. Essais de chimie. *ASP,* année 1702, 2nd ed., *Mém.*: 33–52.

HOMBERG, GUILLAUME. 1708. Mémoire touchant les acides et les alkalis. *ASP,* année 1708, *Mém.*: 312–23.

HOMBERG, GUILLAUME. 1719. Sur la force des alkalis terreux. *ASP,* année 1719, *Mém.*: 64–71 (see also the *Hist.*: 48–50).

HOOKE, ROBERT. 1961. *Micrographia.* New York, Dover.

Facsimile reprint of the 1665 edition published in London by Jo. Martyn and Ja. Allestry.

HOOVER, H. C., and L. H. HOOVER. 1912. *Georg Agricola, De re metallica.* London, The Mining Magazine.

HOOYKAAS, R. 1948–9. Chemical trichotomy before Paracelsus? *AI,* 2: 1063–74.

HOPKINS, ARTHUR JOHN. 1934. *Alchemy, child of Greek philosophy.* New York, Columbia University Press.

HOPPE, EDMUND. 1926. *Geschichte der Optik.* Leipzig, Weber.

HROZNÝ, BEDŘICH. 1953. *Ancient history of Western Asia, India and Crete.* English trans. by J. Prochazka. New York, Philosophical Library.

HUMBOLDT, ALEXANDER VON. 1849–58. *Cosmos:* a sketch of a physical description of the universe. English trans. by E. C. Otté. 5 vols. London, Bohn.

ILG, ALBERT. 1873. *Heraclius, von den Farben und Künsten der Römer.* Wien, Braumüller.

ISIDORE OF SEVILLE (Isidorus Hispalensis). 1472. *Etymologiae.* Augsburg, G. Zainer.

JĀBIR IBN HAIYĀN. 1925. *Liber misera-cordiae* (Kitāb al Uss, Book of Mercy). Ed. by E. Darmstaedter. *Archiv für Geschichte der Medizin,* 17: 181–97.

From Florence Riccardiana Latin MS 933.

JACOBI, RICHARD. 1941. Über den in der Malerei verwendeten gelben Farbstoff der alter Meister. *Angewandte Chemie,* 54: 28–9.

JAMES, ROBERT. 1743–45. *A medicinal dictionary.* 3 vols. London, T. Osborne.

JASTROW, MORRIS Jr. 1905–12. *Die Religion Babyloniens und Assyriens.* 2 vols. Giessen, Töpelmann.

JOB OF EDESSA. 1935. *Encyclopedia of philosophical and natural sciences.* Ed. and English trans. by A. Mingana. Cambridge, Heffer.

From Mingana (Syriac) MS 559, a copy made in 1930 of an original written in Caesarea in 1221.

JOHANNES SCOTUS ERIGENA. 1870. *Über die Eintheilung der Nature.* German trans. by Ludwig Noack (Books 1–3). Leipzig, Dürr.

JOHANNSEN, O. 1941. *Peder Mansson's Schriften über technische Chemie und Hüttenwesen.* Berlin, VDI.

JOHN OF RUPESCISSA. 1549. *La vertus et propriété de la quinte essence de toutes choses.* French trans. by Antoine du Moulin Masconnois. Lyon, J. de Tournes.

JOHN OF RUPESCISSA. 1561. *De consideratione quintae essentie rerum omnium.* Basel.

JOHN OF RUPESCISSA. 1856. *The book of quinte essence*. London, Early English text society.
From BM Sloane MS 73, 15th century.

JOHNSON, ROZELLE P. 1939. *Compositiones variae*. Urbana, University of Illinois Press.

JONAS, HANS. 1963. *The Gnostic religion*. 2nd ed. Boston, Beacon Press.

JORISSEN, W. P. 1918. Iets over Glauber's Amsterdamschen Tijd. *Chemisch Weekblad*, 15: 268–71.

JORISSEN, W. P. 1919. Het eerste chemische laboratorium der Leidsche universiteit. *Chemisch Weekblad*, 16: 1054–60.

JUNCKER, JOHANNES. 1730–38. *Conspectus chemiae theoretico-practicae in forma tabularum repraesentatus*. 2 vols. Halae Magd., Orphanotrophei.

JUNG, CARL GUSTAV. 1953. *Psychology and alchemy*. New York, Pantheon.

JUNGIUS, JOACHIM. 1887. Über die Grundbestandteile (Prinzipien) der Naturkörper. *Abhandlungen aus dem Gebiete der Naturwissenschaften, Hamburg*, 10: 31–43.
Two disputations, written in 1642. Ed. by Emil Wohlwill.

JUSSIEU, ANTOINE DE. 1717. Histoire du kali d'Alicante. *ASP*, année 1717, *Mém.*: 73–8.

JUSSIEU, ANTOINE DE. 1719. Observations sur ce qui se pratique aux mines d'Almaden en Espagne pour en tirer le mercure. *ASP*, année 1719, *Mem.*: 349–60.

KEES, HERMANN. 1933. *Kulturgeschichte des Alten Orients: Ägypten*. Munich, Beck.

KENT, ANDREW and OWEN HANNAWAY. 1960. Some new considerations on Béguin and Libavius. *AS*, 16: 241–50.

KENYON, KATHLEEN. 1957. *Digging up Jericho*. New York, Praeger.

KIBRE, PEARL. 1942. Alchemical writings ascribed to Albertus Magnus. *Speculum*, 17: 499–518.

KIBRE, PEARL. 1944. An alchemical tract attributed to Albertus Magnus. *Isis*, 35: 303–16.

KIBRE, PEARL. 1949. The *Alkimia minor* ascribed to Albertus Magnus. *Isis*, 32: 267–300.

KIBRE, PEARL. 1954. The *De occultis naturae* attributed to Albertus Magnus. *Osiris*, 11: 23–39.

KIRCHVOGEL, PAUL. 1954. Der chemische Prunkofen des Landgrafen Moritz von Hessen-Kassel. *Die BASF*, 4: 3 pages (unnumbered).

KIRK, GEOFFREY S. and J. E. RAVEN. 1957. *The Presocratic philosophers*. Cambridge, Cambridge University Press.

KLAPROTH, M. H. and F. B. WOLFF. 1810. *Dictionnaire de chimie*. 4 vols. Paris, Klostermann fils.
French trans. of a work which had appeared in German in 1807–10.

KNAPP, FRIEDRICH L. 1848–9. *Chemical technology*. Ed. and English trans. by E. Ronalds and T. Richardson. 2 vols. Philadelphia, Lea and Blanchard.
The German ed. appeared in 1847.

KOCH, MANFRED. 1963. *Geschichte und Entwicklung des bergmännischen Schrifttums*. Goslar, Hermann Hübener (Schriftenreihe Bergbau-Aufbereitung, Bd. 1).

KOPP, HERMANN. 1843–47. *Geschichte der Chemie*. 4 vols. Braunschweig, F. Vieweg.

KOPP, HERMANN. 1875. *Ansichten über die Aufgabe der Chemie und über die Grundbestandtheile der Körper*, bei den bedeutenderen Chemikern von Geber bis G. E. Stahl. Braunschweig, F. Vieweg und Sohn. (Beiträge zur Geschichte der Chemie, drittes Stück Vol. 2.)

KOPP, HERMANN. 1886. *Die Alchemie in älterer und neuerer Zeit.* 2 vols. Heidelberg, Carl Winter.

KRAUS, PAUL. 1942. *Jābir ibn Hayyān.* Vol. 2. Jābir et la science Grecque. Cairo, Institut Français d'archéologie orientale.

KRAUS, PAUL. 1943. *Jābir ibn Hayyān.* Vol. 1. Le corpus des écrits Jabiriens. Cairo, Institut Français d'archéologie orientale.

KREMERS, EDWARD and GEORGE URDANG. 1940. *History of pharmacy.* Philadelphia, Lippincott.

KRISTELLER, PAUL O. 1943. *The philosophy of Marsilio Ficino.* English trans. by V. Conant. New York, Columbia University Press.

KRISTELLER, PAUL O. 1956. *Studies in Renaissance thought and letters.* Rome, Edizioni di storia e letteratura.

KRISTELLER, PAUL O. 1961. *Renaissance thought.* The classic, scholastic, and humanist strains. New York, Harper Torchbooks.

KRISTELLER, PAUL O. 1964. *Eight philosophers of the Italian Renaissance.* Stanford, Calif., Stanford University Press.

KROLL, W. 1934. Bolos und Democritus. *Hermes,* 69: 228–32.

KUGLER, FRANZ XAVIER. 1913. *Sternkunde und Sterndienst in Babel.* Münster, Aschendorff.

KUHN, THOMAS S. 1951. Newton's '31st query' and the degradation of gold. *Isis,* 42: 296–8.

KUHN, THOMAS S. 1952. Robert Boyle and structural chemistry in the seventeenth century. *Isis,* 43: 12–36.

KUHN, THOMAS S. 1957. *The Copernican revolution.* Cambridge, Mass., Harvard University Press.

LACINIUS, JANUS. 1546. *Pretiosa margarita novella* de thesauro ac pretiosissimo philosophorum lapide. Venetiis, Aldi Filios.

LACINIUS, JANUS. 1554. *Praeciosa ac nobilissima artis chymiae.* Norimbergae, G. Hayn.

LACINIUS, JANUS. 1894. *The new pearl of great price.* English trans. by A. E. Waite. London, Elliott.

LAGERCRANTZ, OTTO. 1913. *Papyrus graecus Holmiensis.* Upsala, Almquist and Wiksells.

LA ROCQUE, AURÈLE. 1957. *The admirable discourses of Bernard Palissy.* Urbana, University of Illinois Press.

LASSWITZ, KURD. 1890. *Geschichte der Atomistik* vom Mittelalter bis Newton. 2 vols. Hamberg und Leipzig, L. Voss.

LAUFER, BERTHOLD. 1919. *Sino-Iranica.* Chicago, Field Museum. Publication no. 201.

LAURIE, ARTHUR P. 1910. *The materials of the painter's craft.* London, Foulis.

LAVOISIER, ANTOINE. 1789. *Traité élémentaire de chimie.* 2 vols. (continuous pagination). Paris, Cuchet.

LAVOISIER, ANTOINE. 1862–93. *Oeuvres.* 6 vols. Paris, Imprimerie Impériale.

LAVOISIER, ANTOINE. 1865. Extrait de deux mémoires sur le gypse, lus à l'Académie Royale des Sciences, L'un le 27 février 1765, l'autre le 19 mars 1766. In Lavoisier, *Oeuvres.* Paris, Imprimerie Impériale. Vol. 3: 106–44.

The Extrait is followed by the two memoirs, the first of which was first printed in 1768. The second remained in manuscript until its publication in the *Oeuvres* (1865).

LAYARD, AUSTIN H. 1853. *Discoveries in the ruins of Nineveh and Babylon.* London, J. Murray.

LEAKE, CHAUNCEY DEPEW. 1925. Valerius Cordus and the discovery of ether. *Isis,* 7: 14–24.

LEAKE, CHAUNCEY DEPEW. 1952. *The old Egyptian medical papyri.* Lawrence, University of Kansas Press.

LE BEGUE, JEAN. 1849. Tabula de vocabulis synonymis et equivocis colorum; Experimenta de coloribus, etc. In Mary Merrifield, *Original treatises*. London, J. Murray. Vol. 1: 1–321.

From BM Latin MS 6741, dated 1431.

LE CLERC, LUCIEN. 1876. *Histoire de la médecin arabe*. 2 vols. Paris, Leroux.

LEEMANS, CONRAD. 1843–85. *Papyri graeci musei antiquarii publici Lugduni-Batavi*. 2 vols. Leyden, Brill.

First publication (text and Latin trans.) of the Leyden papyrus X.

LE FEVRE, NICOLAS. 1664. *A compleat body of chymistry*. English trans. by P. D. C. London, Th. Ratcliffe.

The 1st (French) ed. appeared in 1660.

LEIBNIZ, G. W. 1749. *Protogaea, sive de prima facie telluris et antiquissimae historiae vestigiis in ipsis naturae monumentis dissertatio*. Göettingae, I. G. Schmid.

LEMERY, LOUIS. 1705. [Experiments made on the salt drawn from Mt. Vesuvius and called natural sal ammoniac.] *ASP*, année 1705, *Hist.*: 66.

LEMERY, LOUIS. 1706. Diverses expériences et observations chymiques et physiques sur le fer et sur l'aimant. *ASP*, année 1706, *Mém.*: 119–35.

LEMERY, LOUIS. 1707. Éclaircissement sur la composition des différents espèces des vitriols. *ASP*, année 1707, *Mém.*: 538–49 (see also *Hist.*: 40–42).

LEMERY, LOUIS. 1709. Conjectures et réflexions sur la matière du feu ou de la lumière. *ASP*, année 1709, *Mém.*: 400–18.

LEMERY, LOUIS. 1717. Mémoire sur la nitre. *ASP*, année 1717, *Mém.*: 31–51, 122–46 (see also *Hist.*: 29–34).

LEMERY, LOUIS. 1728. Expériences et réflexions sur le borax. *ASP*, année 1728, *Mém.*: 273–88. année 1729, *Mém.*: 282–300.

LEMERY, LOUIS. 1735-1. Nouvel éclaircissement sur l'alun, sur les vitriols, et particulièrement sur la composition naturelle, et jusqu'à présent ignorée. *ASP*, année 1735, *Mém.*: 262–80 (see also *Hist.*: 26–34).

LEMERY, LOUIS. 1735-2. Second mémoire sur les vitriols. *ASP*, année 1735, *Mém.*: 385–402.

LEMERY, LOUIS. 1736. Supplément aux deux mémoires . . . sur l'alun et sur les vitriols. *ASP*, année 1736, *Mém.*: 263–301 (see also *Hist.*: 61–65).

LEMERY, NICOLAS. 1677. *Cours de chymie*. 2nd ed. Paris, Chez l'Auteur.

The 1st ed. appeared in 1675.

LEMERY, NICOLAS. 1686. *A course of chemistry*. English trans. (2nd English ed., from the 5th French ed.) by Walter Harris. London, L. W. Kettilby.

LEMERY, NICOLAS. 1698. *A course of chemistry*. English trans. (3rd English ed., from the 8th French ed.) by James Keil. London, L. W. Kettilby.

Keil says in the preface that he is completing a translation begun by Walter Harris.

LEMERY, NICOLAS. 1701. *Cours de chymie*. 9th ed. Paris, J-B. Delespine.

LEMERY, NICOLAS. 1759. *Dictionnaire universel des drogues simples*. Paris, L. C. D'Houry.

The 1st edition was published in 1698.

LE MORT, JACOB. 1696. *Collectanea chymica Leydensia Maetsiana & Marcgraviana*. Leyden, Boutesteyn & Haaring.

LEVEY, MARTIN. 1959. *Chemistry and chemical technology in ancient Mesopotamia*. Amsterdam, Elsevier.

Leyden papyrus X. 1889. French trans. in M. Berthelot, *Introduction à l'étude de la chimie*. Paris, Steinheil. pp. 28–50.

LIBAVIUS, ANDREAS. 1597. *D.O.M.A. Alchemia*. Frankfurt, Sautius.

LIEBIG, JUSTUS VON, et al. 1859. *Handwörterbuch der reinen und angewandten Chemie*. Vol. 7. Braunschweig, F. Vieweg.

LIPPMANN, EDMUND O. VON. 1909. Chemisches aus der Papyrus Ebers. *AGNT*, 1: 87–102.

LIPPMANN, EDMUND O. VON. 1913. *Abhandlungen und Vorträge zur Geschichte der Naturwissenschaften*. Vol. 2. Leipzig, Veit.

LIPPMANN, EDMUND O. VON. 1914. Thaddaus Florentinus (Taddeo Alderotti) über den Weingeist. *Archiv für Geschichte der Medizin*, 7: 379–89.

LIPPMANN, EDMUND O. VON. 1919. *Entstehung und Ausbreitung der Alchemie*. Berlin, Springer.

LIPPMANN, EDMUND O. VON. 1922. Das Sammelbuch des Vitalis de Furno und seine Bedeutung für die Geschichte der Chemie. *CZ*, 25.

LIPPMANN, EDMUND O. VON. 1930. *Die Geschichte des Wismuts zwischen 1400 und 1800*. Berlin, Springer.

LIPPMANN, EDMUND O. VON. 1931. *Entstehung und Ausbreitung der Alchemie*. Vol. 2. Berlin, Springer.

LIPPMANN, EDMUND O. VON. 1937. Das Natron in alten Ägypten. *Die Naturwissenschaften*, 36: 592.

LIPPMANN, EDMUND O. VON. 1938. Some remarks on Hermes and Hermetica. *Ambix*, 2: 21–25.

LIPPMANN, EDMUND O. VON. 1948. Chemical and technological references in Plutarch. *Ambix*, 3: 1–14.

LIPPMANN, EDMUND O. VON. 1954. *Entstehung und Ausbreitung der Alchemie*. Vol. 3. Weinheim/Bergstr., Verlag Chemie.

LITTLE, ANDREW G. 1911. Roger Bacon's works. Appendix to H. Rashdall, ed. *Fratris Rogeri Bacon Compendium studii theologiae*. Aberdeen, Typis academicus (British Society of Franciscan Studies, Vol. 3).

LITTLE, ANDREW G. 1912. *Part of the Opus tertium of Roger Bacon*, Aberdeen University Press (British Society of Franciscan Studies, Vol. 9).

LLOYD, SETON. 1954. Building in brick and stone. In Sir Charles Singer, ed., *A history of technology*. Oxford, Clarendon. Vol. 1: 456–90.

LÖHNEYSS, GEORG E. VON [1690?]. *Bericht vom Bergwerk* [Hamburg?].

LOWRY, H. H. 1945. *Chemistry of coal utilization*. 2 vols., continuously paginated. New York, Wiley.

LUCAS, ALFRED. 1932. The occurrence of natron in ancient Egypt. *Journal of Egyptian Archeology*, 18: 62–6.

LUCAS, ALFRED. 1848. *Ancient Egyptian materials and industries*. 3rd ed. London, Arnold.

LUCAS, ALFRED. 1962. *Ancient Egyptian materials and industries*. 4th ed., revised and enlarged by J. R. Harris. London, Arnold.

LUCRETIUS. 1924. *De la nature*. Ed. and French trans. by Alfred Ernout. 2nd ed. Paris, Les Belles Lettres (Coll. Budé).

LUCRETIUS. 1937. *De rerum natura*. Ed. and English trans. by W. H. D. Rouse. London, Heinemann (Loeb classical library).

MacCURDY, EDWARD. 1939. *The notebooks of Leonardo da Vinci*. New York, Reynal & Hitchcock.

MACQUER, PIERRE. 1764. *Elements of the theory and practice of chymistry*. 2 vols. English trans. by Andrew Reid. 2nd ed. London, A. Millar and J. Nourse. Preface dated 1758, which is supposedly the date of the 1st ed. The 1st French ed. was in 1749.

375

MACQUER, PIERRE. 1777. *A dictionary of chemistry.* Anonymous English trans. 2nd ed. London, T. Cadell and P. Elmsly.

MACQUER, PIERRE. 1778. *Dictionnaire de chymie.* 2 vols. 2nd ed. Paris, Imprimerie de Monsieur.
The 1st ed. appeared in 1766.

MADDISON, R. E. W. 1955. Boyle's operator, Ambrose Godfrey Hanckwitz, F.R.S. *Notes and Records of the Royal Society of London,* 11: 159–88 (Studies in the life of Robert Boyle, F.R.S., Pt 5).

MADKOUR, IBRAHIM. 1934. *La place d'al-Fārābī dans l'école philosophique musulmane.* Paris, Adrien-Maisonneuve.

MADSEN, EDMUND RANCKE. 1958. *The development of titrimetric analysis till 1806.* Copenhagen, G. E. C. Gad.

MAIER, ANNELIESE. 1949. *Die Vorläufer Galileis im 14. Jahrhunderts.* Rome, Edizioni di storia e letteratura.

MAIER, ANNELIESE. 1952. *An der Grenze von Scholastik und Naturwissenschaft.* 2nd ed. Rome, Edizioni di storia e letteratura.

MANGET, JEAN JACQUES. 1702. *Bibliotheca chemica curiosa.* 2 vols. Geneva, Chouet (here abbreviated Bcc).

Mappae clavicula. 1847. Ed. by Phillipps. *Archaeologia,* 32: 183–244.
From Phillipps MS 3715 (12 C.). R. P. Johnson (1939) has identified over 80 manuscripts, dating from the ninth to the seventeenth centuries.

MARCEL, RAYMOND. 1958. *Marsile Ficin.* Paris, Les Belles Lettres.

MARCUS GRAECUS. 1842–43. *Liber ignium.* In J. C. F. Hoefer, *Histoire de la chimie.* Paris, Hachette. Vol. 1: 491–97.
From BN Latin MSS 7156 (1330–1350) and 3158 (fifteenth century).

MARGGRAF, ANDREAS S. 1754. Expériences qui concern la régénération de l'alun de sa propre terre. *Histoire de l'Académie Royale des Sciences et Belles Lettres à Berlin,* année 1754 (pub. 1756): 31–40.

MARIA (alchemist). 1927. The letter of the crown and the nature of creation. In E. J. Holmyard, An alchemical tract ascribed to Mary the Copt. *Archeion,* 8: 163–67.
English trans. from an Arabic MS in the Royal Library of Cairo.

MARIETAN, JOSEPH. 1901. *Problème de la classification des sciences d'Aristote à St-Thomas.* Paris, Alcan.

MARROU, HENRI IRÉNEE. 1956. *A history of education in antiquity.* New York, Sheed and Ward.

MARTIN, GERMAIN, 1898. *La grande industrie sous la règne de Louis XIV.* Paris, A. Rousseau.

MARYON, HERBERT. 1956. Fine metal work. In Sir Charles Singer, ed., *A history of technology.* Oxford, Clarendon. Vol. 2: 449–84.

MAS'UDI (Maçoudi [Ali ibn Husain, al Mas'udi]). 1861–77. *Les prairies d'or.* Text and French trans. by C. B. de Meynard and P. de Courteille. 9 vols. Paris, Imprimerie Impériale.

MATSON, F. R. 1945. Technological development of pottery in north Syria in the chalcolithic age. *Jour. Amer. Ceramic Soc.,* 28: 20–25.

MAURACH, H. 1933. *Johann Kunckel (1630–1703).* Berlin, VDI Verlag (Deutsches Museum, Abhandlungen und Berichte 5, Heft 2).

MAYOW, JOHN. 1674. *Tractatus quinque medico–physici.* Oxford, E. Theatro Sheldoniano.

MAYOW, JOHN. 1926. *Medico–physical works.* English trans. by A. Crum Brown and L. Dobbin. Oxford, Old Ashmolean Reprints No. 5.
English trans., first published in 1907, of Mayow, 1674.

McKie, Douglas. 1952. *Antoine Lavoisier*. New York, Abelard Schuman.

Mellor, J. W. 1922–37. *A comprehensive treatise on inorganic and theoretical chemistry*. 16 vols. London, Longmans, Green.

Melsen, Andrew G. van. 1960. *From atmos to atom*. New York, Harper Torchbooks.
Reprint of 1952 ed.

Merrifield, Mary P. 1849. *Original treatises*, dating from the XII to the XVIII centuries, on the arts of painting in oil. 2 vols. London, J. Murray.

Mersenne, Marin. 1625. *La verité des sciences, contre les sceptics où Pyrrhoniens*. Paris, Toussaint du Bray.

Mersenne, Marin. 1932. *Correspondence, 1617–27*. Ed. by Cornelius de Waard. Paris, G. Beauchesne.

Mesuë, Jr. 1471. *Grabbadim medicinarum universalium et particularium*. Venice, C. Patavinus.

Mesuë, Jr. 1502. *Mesue cum expositione Mondini super canones universales*. Venice, B. Locatellus.

Mesuë, Jr. 1568. *Opera*, a Joanne Costa nunc recognata. Venice, Iuntas.

Mesuë, Jr. 1623. *Opera*. Venice, Iuntas.

Metzger, Hélène. 1923. *Les doctrines chimiques en France* du début du XVIIᵉ à la fin du XVIIIᵉ siècle. Paris, Presses Universitaires.

Metzger, Hélène. 1930. *Newton, Stahl, Boerhaave et la doctrine chimique*. Paris, Alcan.

Metzger, Hélène. 1936. La philosophie chimique de J-B van Helmont. *Annales Guébhard-Séverine*, 12: 140–55.

Meyerhof, Max. 1935. Esquisse d'histoire de la pharmacologie et botanique chez les Musulmans d'Espagne. *Al-Andalus*, 3: 1–41.

Meyerhof, Max. 1941. The philosophy of the physician, al-Razi. *Islamic Culture*, 15: 45–58.
A review of Paul Kraus' collection, (Rhazes) *Opera philosophica fragmenta quae supersunt*, Pt 1, Cairo, 1939.

Meynard, C. B. and P. de Courteille. 1861–77. *Les prairies d'or de Maçoudi*. 9 vols. Paris, Imprimerie Impériale.

Michel, Paul-Henri. 1962. *La cosmologie de Giordano Bruno*. Paris, Hermann.

Middleton, W. E. Knowles. 1964. *The history of the barometer*. Baltimore, Johns Hopkins Press.

Minderer, Raymond. 1617. *De calcantho, seu vitriolo*. Augusta Vindilicorum, S. Mangin Viduam.

Mingana, Alphonse. 1935. *Encyclopedia or book of treasures by Job of Edessa*. Cambridge, Heffer.

Mittelalterliche Hausbuch, Das. 1912. Ed. by Helmuth Bossert and W. F. Storck. Leipzig, E. A. Seemann.
From MS formerly in the possession of the family Waldburg-Wolfegg, dated *c*. 1480.

Moehsen, Johann C. W. 1783. *Leben Leonhard Thurneyssers zum Thurn*. Berlin und Leipzig, G. J. Decker (Beiträge zur Geschichte der Wissenschaften in der Mark Brandenburg, I).

Monconys, Balthasar. 1665–66. *Journal des voyages*. 3 vols. Lyon, H. Boissat & G. Remeus.

Morley, Henry. 1854. *Jerome Cardan*. 2 vol. London, Chapman and Hall.

Moxon, Joseph. 1958. *Mechanick exercises on the whole art of printing* (1683-4). Ed. by Herbert Davis and Harry Carter. London, Oxford University Press.

Mugler, Charles. 1960. *La physique de Platon*. Paris: Klincksieck.

MÜLLER, MARTIN. 1960. *Registerband zu Sudhoff's Paracelsus Gesamtausgabe.* Nova Acta Paracelsica. Supplementum.

MULTHAUF, ROBERT P. 1953. *The relationship between technology and natural philosophy, ca. 1250–1650,* as illustrated by the technology of the mineral acids. Berkeley, Calif., Doctoral dissertation (unpublished).

MULTHAUF, ROBERT P. 1954–1. John of Rupescissa and the origin of medical chemistry. *Isis,* 45: 359–67.

MULTHAUF, ROBERT P. 1954–2. Medical chemistry and 'the Paracelsians'. *BHM,* 28: 101–26.

MULTHAUF, ROBERT P. 1956. The significance of distillation in Renaissance medical chemistry. *BHM,* 30: 329–46.

MUMFORD, LEWIS. 1934. *Technics and civilization.* New York, Harcourt, Brace.

MÜNSTER, LADISLAO. 1933. Alessandro Achillini, anatomico & philosophico, professore della studio di Bologna (1463–1512). *Rivista di Storia della scienze medische e naturali,* 15: 7–22, 54–77.

MURATORI, LUDOVICO A. 1774. *Antiquitates Italicae Medii Aevi.* . . . Vol. 4. Arrettii, Michaelis Bellotti.

NAGY, ALBINO. 1897. *Die philosophischen Abhandlungen des Ja'qub ben Ishaq al-Kindi. BGPM,* 2: Heft 5.

NAIGEON, JACQUES A. 1791–an. 2 (1793/94). *Philosophie, ancienne et moderne.* 3 vols. Paris, H. Agasse. Part of the *Encyclopédie Méthodique.*

NAU, F. 1907. Une ancienne traduction latine du Belinous arabe. *Revue de l'Orient Chretienne,* 2nd ser. 12: 99–106.

NEEDHAM, JOSEPH. 1956. Iron and steel production in ancient and medieval China. *TNS,* 30: 141–4.

NEF, JOHN U. 1932. *The rise of the British coal industry.* 2 vols. London, Routledge.

NENQUIN, JACQUES. 1961. *Salt; a study in economic prehistory.* Bruges, De Tempel.

NEUGEBAUER, O. 1952. *The exact sciences in antiquity.* Princeton, Princeton University Press.

NEUMANN, BERNARD. 1904. *Die Metalle.* Halle, Wm. Knapp.

NEWTON, ISAAC. 1931. *Opticks.* London, Bell. Reprint of the 4th ed., 1730.

NEWTON, ISAAC. 1958. *Papers & letters on natural philosophy.* Ed. by I. Bernard Cohen. Cambridge, Mass., Harvard University Press. Reprints Newton's letters to Boyle, Feb. 28, 1678/9, and to Oldenburg, Jan. 25, 1675/6 (pp. 249–54) and his articles, 'De natura acidorum' and 'Some thoughts about the nature of acids' from John Harris, Lexicon technicum (pp. 255–58).

NICOLAS OF CUSA. 1944. *Der Laie über Versuche mit der Waage* (Idota de staticis experimentis). German trans. by Hildegund Menzel-Rogner. Leipzig, Felix Meiner (Schriften des Nikolaus von Cues, ed. Heidelberger Akad. d Wiss., Heft 5).

NICOLAS OF SALERNO. 1471. *Incipit antidotarium Nicolai.* Venetiis, Nic. Jenson gallicum.

NICOLAS OF SALERNO. 1896. *Antidotarium.* French trans. by Paul Dorveaux. Paris, Welter. Trans. from two versions in BN MSS 25327 (fourteenth century) and 14827 (fifteenth century).

NIERENSTEIN, M. 1934. A missing chapter in the history of organic chemistry: the link between elementary analysis by dry-distillation and combustion. *Isis,* 21: 123–30.

NIFO (NIPHUS), AUGOSTINO. 1506. *Aristoteles de generatione et corruptione liber . . . interprte et expositione.* Venice, Herred. D. Scotus.

NIFO (NIPHUS), AUGOSTINO. 1547. *In libris Aristotelis Meteorologicis commentaria.* Venice.

NORTON, THOMAS. 1893. The ordinal of alchemy. In *The Hermetic Museum.* London, Elliott. Vol. 2: 1–67.

The ordinal was written about 1477.

O'LEARY, DE LACY. 1949. *How Greek science passed to the Arabs.* London, Routledge and Kegan Paul.

ORNSTEIN, MARTHA. 1928. *The role of scientific societies in the seventeenth century.* Chicago, University of Chicago Press.

OSTWALD, WILHELM. 1912. *Outlines of general chemistry.* English trans. of the 4th German ed. by W. W. Taylor. 3rd ed. London, Macmillan.

The 1st (German) ed. was published in 1885–86.

PACHTER, HENRY M. 1951. *Magic into science.* The story of Paracelsus. New York, Abelard Schuman.

PAGEL, WALTER. 1944. The religious and philosophical aspects of van Helmont's science and medicine. *BHM,* Supp. 2.

PAGEL, WALTER. 1958. *Paracelsus.* Basel–New York, S. Karger.

PAGEL, WALTER and PYARALI RATTANSI. 1964. Vesalius and Paracelsus. *Medical History,* 8: 309–28.

PALISSY, BERNARD. 1844. *Oeuvres complètes.* Notes & notice historique par Paul A. Cap. Paris, Dubochet.

PALISSY, BERNARD. 1957. *The admirable discourses.* Ed. and English trans. by Aurèle La Rocque. Urbana, University of Illinois Press.

Translated from the 1st (French) ed., 1580.

PANSIER, P. 1903–33. *Collectio ophtalmologica.* 7 Parts. Paris, Ballière.

PARACELSUS. 1589–90. *Bücher und Schriften.* Ed. by Joh. Huser. 10 vols. Basel, K. Waldkirch.

PARACELSUS. 1893. *The hermetic and alchemical writings.* English trans. by A. E. Waite. London, J. Elliott.

Trans. from the Latin *Opera* of 1658.

PARACELSUS. 1922–33. *Sämtliche Werke,* Abteil 1. Ed. by Karl Sudhoff. 14 vols. Munich, R. Oldenbourg.

PARACELSUS. 1941. *Four treatises.* Baltimore, Johns Hopkins Press.

Translated from the original German, with intro. essays, by C. Lilian Temkin, George Rosen, Gregory Zilboorg, and Henry E. Sigerist; ed. and with a preface by Henry E. Sigerist.

1. Seven defensiones, the reply to certain calumniations of his enemies.

2. On the miners' sickness and other miners' diseases.

3. The diseases that deprive man of his reason, such as St Vitus' dance, falling sickness, melancholy and insanity, and their correct treatment.

4. A book on nymphs, sylphs, pygmies, and salamanders, and on the other spirits.

PARACELSUS. 1949. *Volumen medicinae paramirum,* English trans. and pref. by K. F. Leidecker. *BHM,* Supplement 11.

From the Latin ed. of 1589.

PARACELSUS, ?. 1656. *Paracelsus, his dispensatory and chirurgery,* faithfully Englished by W. D. London, P. Chetwind.

PARE, AMBROISE. 1952. *The apologie and treatise.* The English trans. of 1634. Ed. by Geoffrey Keynes. Chicago, University of Chicago Press.

PARKES, G. D. ed. 1939. *Mellor's modern*

inorganic chemistry. London, Longmans.

PARTINGTON, JAMES RIDDICK. 1935. *Origins and development of applied chemistry*. London, Longmans.

PARTINGTON, JAMES RIDDICK. 1936. J. B. van Helmont. *AS*, 1 359–84.

PARTINGTON, JAMES RIDDICK. 1937. Albertus Magnus on alchemy. *Ambix*, 1: 3–20.

PARTINGTON, JAMES RIDDICK. 1938–1. Trithemius and alchemy. *Ambix*, 28 53–9.

PARTINGTON, JAMES RIDDICK. 1938–2. The chemistry of Razi. *Ambix*, 1: 192–6.

PARTINGTON, JAMES RIDDICK. 1956. The life and work of John Mayow (1641–79). *Isis*, 47: 217–30, 405–17.

PARTINGTON, JAMES RIDDICK. 1960. *A history of Greek fire and gunpowder*. Cambridge (England), Heffer.

PARTINGTON, JAMES RIDDICK. 1961. *A history of chemistry*. Vol. 2. London, Macmillan.

PARTINGTON, JAMES RIDDICK. 1962. *A history of chemistry*. Vol. 3. London, Macmillan.

PATIN, GUY. 1846. *Lettres*. 3 vols. Paris, Baillière.

PATTERSON, T. S. 1931. John Mayow in contemporary setting. *Isis*, 15: 47–96, 504–46.

PATTERSON, J. S. 1937. Jean Beguin and his *Tyrocinium chymicum*. *AS*, 2: 243–98.

PAULY, AUGUST F. VON. 1894ff. *Real-encyclopädie der classischen Altertumswissenschaft, neue Bearbeitung von Georg Wissowa*. Stuttgart, Metzler (here abbreviated, PW).

PECK, E. SAVILLE. 1934. John Francis Vigani, first Professor of chemistry in the University of Cambridge (1703–12), and his materia medica cabinet in the library of Queens' College. *Proceedings of the Cambridge Antiquarian Society*, 34: 34–49.

PEPYS, SAMUEL. 1953. *Diary*. 3 vols. Ed. from Mynors Bright. London, Dent (Everyman's Library).

PETER OF SPAIN. 1497. *Summa experimentorum sive thesaurus pauperum*. Antwerp, T. Martini.

PETERSSON, R. T. 1956. *Sir Kenelm Digby*. London, Jonathan Cape.

PEYRAN, JACQUES. 1826. *Histoire de l'ancienne principauté de Sedan*. Paris, Servier.

Pharmacopoeia Augustana. 1927. Facsimile of the first edition (1564). Ed. by Theodor Husemann. Madison, Wisconsin, Wisconsin State Historical Society.

PHILLIPPS, THOMAS. 1847. Letter . . . communicating a transcript of a MS treatise on the preparation of pigments . . . entitled *Mappae clavicula*. *Archaeologia*, 32: 183–244.

PHILO. 1932. *On the confusion of tongues*. Ed. and English trans. by F. H. Colson and G. H. Whitaker. London, Heinemann (Loeb classical library). (*Works*, Vol. 4).

PHILOSTRATUS. 1927. *Life of Apollonius of Tyana*. Ed. and English trans. by F. C. Conybeare. 2 vols. London, Heinemann (Loeb classical library).

PIETSCH, ERICH. 1940. Zur Urgeschichte der chemischen Technologie. *BGTI*, 29: 15–43.

PIETSCH, ERICH. 1956. *Johann Rudolph Glauber*. München, Oldenbourg (Deutsches Museum, Abhandlungen und Berichte 24, Heft 1).

PLANIS-CAMPY, DAVID DE. 1629. *Bouquet composé des plus belles fleurs chimiques*. Paris, P. Billaine.

PLATO. 1892. *The dialogues*. Ed. and English trans. by B. Jowett. 5 vols. 3rd ed. New York, Macmillan.

PLATO. 1925. *Timée – Critias.* Ed. and French trans. by Albert Rivaud. Paris, Les Belles Lettres (Coll. Budé). (*Oeuvres complètes,* Tome 10).

PLATO. 1927. *Epinomis.* Ed. and English trans. by W. R. M. Lamb. London, Heinemann (Loeb classical library). (*Works,* Vol. 8: 426–87).

PLATO. 1937. *Timaeus.* English trans. by F. M. Cornford (as *Plato's cosmology*). London, Kegan Paul.

PLAYFAIR, JOHN. 1803. Biographical account of the late Dr. James Hutton. *Trans. of the Royal Society of Edinburgh,* 5, Pt. 3: 39–99.

PLENDERLEITH, H. J. 1950. The history of artist's pigments. *Science Progress,* 38: 247.

PLESSNER, MARTIN. 1927. Neue Materialen zur Geschichte der Tabula smaragdina. *Der Islam,* 16: 77–113.

PLINY THE ELDER. 1634. *The historie of the world:* commonly called the Natural historie. English trans. by Philemon Holland. 2 vols. London, Adam Islip.

PLINY THE ELDER. 1929–32. *Naturalis historiae.* Ed. and English trans. by K. C. Bailey (as *The elder Pliny's chapters on chemical subjects*). 2 vols. London, Arnold.

PLINY THE ELDER. 1950. *Naturalis historiae,* Bk II. Ed. and French trans. by Jean Beaujeu. Paris, Les Belles Lettres (Coll. Budé).

PLINY THE ELDER, pseudo. 1509. *Medicina Plinii.* Rome, Guillireti.

PLOTINUS. 1924. *Enneades.* Bk II. Ed. and French trans. by Emile Brehier. Paris, Les Belles Lettres. (Collection des universités de France.)

PLUTARCH. 1795–1830. *Moralia.* Ed. by Daniel Wyttenbach. 8 vols. in 15. Oxford, Clarendon.

POLYDORE VERGIL. 1868. *De rerum inventoribus.* English trans. by John Langley. New York, Agathynian Club.
Reprint of ed. of London, 1663. The 1st ed. appeared in 1499.

POMPONAZZI, PIETRO. 1563. *Dubitationes in quartum Meteorologicorum Aristotelis librum.* Venice, F. Francisci.

POPE, WALTER. 1665. Extract of a letter . . . concerning the mercury mines of Friuli. *PT,* 1: 21–6.

PORTA, GIOVANNI B. DELLA. 1569. *Magiae naturalis.* Lugduni, G. Rouillium.
This ed. in 4 books, first appeared in 1556.

PORTA, GIOVANNI B. DELLA. 1589. *Magiae naturalis.* Neapoli, H. Salvianum.
This is the 1st ed. in 20 books.

PORTA, GIOVANNI B. DELLA. 1957. *Natural magick.* New York, Basic Books.
Facsimile of the anonymous English trans. of 1658.

POTT, JOHANN H. 1743. *Vitrioli albi analysis justior quam lemeriana.* Miscellanea Berolinensis, 7: 306–17.

POTT, JOHANN H. 1752. Recherches sur le mélange d'un acide du vitriol avec le salmiac & sur les produits qui en résultent. *Histoire de l'Académie Royale des Sciences et Belles Lettres à Berlin,* année 1752 (pub. 1754): 54–82.

POUTET, M. 1828. Le traité des savons. In *Encyclopédie Méthodique. Manufactures et Arts.* Vol. 4. Paris, Agasse.

Probierbüchlien. 1949. An English trans. of the 1534 ed., in A. G. Sisco and C. S. Smith, ed., *Bergwerk- und Probierbüchlein.* New York, American Institute of Mining and Metallurgical Engineers. pp. 77–178.

PTOLEMY, CLAUDIUS. 1906. *Tetrabiblos.* Ed. and English trans. by F. E. Robbins. London, Heinemann (Loeb classical library).

PUCCINOTTI, FRANCESCO. 1850–66. *Storia della medicina*. 3 vols. Livorno, Wagner.

PUFF VON SCHRICK, MICHAEL. 1481. *Von den ausgebrannten Wassern*. [Strassburg, M. Schott].

PUHLMANN, WALTER. 1930. Die lateinische medizinische Literatur des Frühen Mittelalters. *Kyklos*, 3: 395–416.

RABANUS (RHABANUS) MAURUS. 1467. *De universo*. Strassburg, Adolf Rusch.

RASHDALL, HASTINGS, ed. 1911. *Fratris Rogeri Bacon Compendium studii theologiae*. Aberdeen, Typis academicus (British Society of Franciscan Studies, Vol. 3).

RATHGEN, BERNHARD. 1928. *Das Geschütz im Mittelalter*. Berlin, VDI.

RAUWOLF, LEONHART. 1738. *Journey into the eastern countries*. English trans. in John Ray, *Travels*. London, J. Walthoe. Vol. 2: 1–338.

RAY, JOHN. 1738. *Travels through the low countries, Germany, Italy, and France*. 2 vols. London, J. Walthoe.

READ, JOHN. 1936. *Prelude to chemistry*. London, Bell.

READ, JOHN. 1938. Michael Scot: Un pionnier Ecossais de la science. *Scientia*, 32: 96–102.

REINHARDT, KARL. 1921. *Poseidonios*. Munich, Beck.

REISCH, GREGORIUS. 1504. *Margarita philosophica*. Freiberg i. B., Joh. Schottus.
    First printed in 1503, but the dedication is dated 1495.

RESCHER, NICHOLAS. 1962. *Al-Farabi: an annotated bibliography*. Pittsburgh, University of Pittsburgh Press.

RHEES, ABRAHAM. 1819. *The Cyclopaedia, or universal dictionary of arts, sciences and literature*. 39 vols. London, Longmans, *et al.*

RICHTER, PAUL. 1913. Beiträge zur Geschichte der alkoholhältigen Getränke bei den orientalischen Völkern und des Alkohols. *AGNT*, 4: 429–52.

RICKARD, THOMAS ARTHUR. 1932. *Man and metals*. 2 vols. New York, McGraw Hill.

RIEKEL, AUGUST. 1925. *Die Philosophie der Renaissance*. Munich, E. Reinhardt.

[RIOLAN, JEAN]. 1951. *Curieuses recherches sur les éscholes en médecine, de Paris et de Montpellier*. Paris, G. Meturas.

RIPLEY, GEORGE. 1893. *Bosom book*. In *Collectanea chemica*. London, J. Elliot. pp. 121–43.
    Ripley died about 1490.

RIVAUD, ALBERT, ed. 1925. *Platon. Oeuvres complètes*. Vol. 10. *Timee-Critas*. Paris, Les Belles Lettres (Coll. Budé).

RIXNER, THADDEUS ANSELM and THADDÄ SIBER. 1820. *Bernardinus Telesius*. Sulzbach, J. E. von Seidel (Leben und Lehrmeinungen berühmter Physiker, Heft 3.)
    Biography (1–18) and summary of Telesio's *De natura rerum* (19–289).

RIXNER, THADDEUS ANSELM and THADDÄ SIBER. 1823. *Franciscus Partritius*. Sulzbach, J. E. von Seidel (Leben und Lehrmeinungen berühmter Physiker, Heft 4).
    Biography (3–20) and summary of Partizzi's *Nova de universis philosophia*.

RIXNER, THADDEUS ANSELM and THADDÄ SIBER. 1826. *Thomas Campanella*. Sulzbach, J. E. von Seidel (Leben und Lehrmeinungen berühmter Physiker, Heft 6).
    Biography (3–34) and summary of Campanella's *Physiologia*.

ROSS, WILLIAM DAVID. 1959. *Aristotle*. New York, Meridian.
    Reprint of 5th ed.

ROUELLE, G. F. 1744. Mémoire sur les sels neutres. *ASP*, année 1744, *Mém.*: 353–64.

RUSKA, JULIUS. 1913–14. Die Mineralogie in der Arabischen Literatur. *Isis*, 1: 341–50.

RUSKA, JULIUS. 1923–1. *Sal ammoniacus, Nusadir und Salmiak*. Heidelberg, C. Winter (Sitzungsberichte d. Heidelberger Akad. d. Wiss. Phil.-Hist. Klasse).

RUSKA, Julius. 1923–2. Al-Biruni als Quelle für das Leben und die Schriften al-Rāzī's. *Isis*, 5: 26–50.

RUSKA, JULIUS. 1924–1. *Arabische Alchemisten*, I. Chālid ibn Jazīd ibn Mu'āwija. Heidelberg, Winter.

RUSKA, JULIUS. 1924–2. *Arabische Alchemisten*, II. Ga'far al Sadiq. Heidelberg, Winter.

RUSKA, JULIUS. 1925. Der Urtext des Tabula Smaragdina. *Orientalische Literaturzeitschrift*, 28: 349–51.

RUSKA, JULIUS. 1926. *Tabula smaragdina*. Heidelberg, Winter.

RUSKA, JULIUS, ed. 1927–1. *Studien zur Geschichte der Chemie* (Festgabe Edmund O. v. Lippmann). Berlin, Springer.

RUSKA, JULIUS. 1927–2. Die siebzig Bücher der Gabir ibn Haijan. In J. Ruska, ed., *Studien zur Geschichte der Chemie*. Berlin, Springer, pp. 38–47.

RUSKA, JULIUS. 1928. Die Salmiak in der Geschichte der Alchemie. *Zeitschrift für angewandte Chemie*, 41: 1321–24.

RUSKA, JULIUS. 1929. Zosimos. In G. Bugge, ed., *Das Buch der grossen Chemiker*. Berlin, Verlag Chemie. Vol. 1: 1–17.

RUSKA, JULIUS. 1931. Turba philosophorum. *QS*, 1: entire volume.

RUSKA, JULIUS. 1933. Alchemie in Spanien. *Angewandte Chemie*, 46: 337–9.

RUSKA, JULIUS. 1934–1. Die Alchemie des Avicenna. *Isis*, 21: 14–51.

RUSKA, JULIUS. 1934–2. Über die Quellen des Liber Claritatis. *Archeion*, 16: 145–67.

RUSKA, JULIUS. 1935–1. Übersetzung und Bearbeitungen von al-Razi's Buch Geheimnis der Geheimnisse. *QS*, 4: 1–87.

RUSKA, JULIUS. 1935–2. *Das Buch der Alaune und Salze*. Berlin, Verlag Chemie.

RUSKA, JULIUS. 1936. Studien zu der chemischtechnischen Rezeptsammlungen des Liber Sacerdotum. *QS*, 5: 275–317.

RUSKA, JULIUS. 1937–1. History of the Jābir problem. *Islamic Culture*, 11: 303–12.

RUSKA, JULIUS. 1937–2. *Al-Rāzī's Buch Geheimnis der Geheimnisse*. QS, 6: 1–246.
Includes (pp. 83–226) a German trans. of Al-Rāzī's *Secret of Secrets*.

RUSKA, JULIUS and K. GARBERS. 1938. Vorschriften zur Herstellung von scharfen Wassern bei Geber und Razi. *Der Islam*, 25: 1–35.

RUSKA, JULIUS. 1942. Neue Beiträge zur Geschichte der Chemie. *QS*, 8: 1–131.

SALA, ANGELO. 1618. *Opiologia* . . . done into English and something enlarged by Tho. Bretnor. London, Nicholas Okes.
There was a French ed. in 1614.

SALA, ANGELO. 1647. *Opera medicochymica*. Francofurti, J. Beyeri.

SALMON, WM. 1706. *Pharmacopoeia Bateana*: or Bate's dispensatory. London, S. Smith and B. Walford.

SAMBURSKI, SAMUEL. 1959. *Physics of the Stoics*. New York, Macmillan.

SARTON, GEORGE. 1927–48. *Introduction to the history of science*. 3 vols. in 5.

Baltimore, Williams and Wilkins. (Here abbreviated as INT.)

SARTON, GEORGE. 1955. *The appreciation of ancient and medieval science during the Renaissance (1450–1600)*. Philadelphia, University of Pennsylvania Press.

SAUNDERS, (ROBERT). 1789. Observations sur l'origin du tinckal ou borax. *Annales de chimie*, 2: 299–301.

SAYRE, EDWARD V. 1963. The intentional use of antimony and manganese in ancient glasses. In F. R. Matson and G. E. Rindone, eds., *Advances in glass technology*. Pt 2. New York, Plenum Press. pp. 263–82.

SAYRE, EDWARD V. and RAY W. SMITH. 1964. Some materials of glass manufacturing in antiquity. Manuscript, presented to the American Chemical Society.

SCALIGER, J. C. 1557. *Exotericarum exercitationum . . . de Subtilitate, ad Hieronymum Cardanum*. Paris, cum privilegio regis.

SCHAFER, EDWARD H. 1963. *The golden peaches of Samarkand*. Berkeley, University of California Press.

SCHELENZ, HERMANN. 1904. *Geschichte der Pharmazie*. Berlin, Springer.

SCHRADER, OTTO. 1909. Griech. μξταλλον. In Paul Diergart, ed., *Beiträge aus der Geschichte der Chemie*. Leipzig, F. Deuticke. pp. 100–2.

SCHRÖDER, GERALD. 1957. *Die pharmazeutischchemischen Produkte deutscher Apotheken im Zeitalter der Chemiatrie*. (Veröffentlichung aus dem Pharmaziegeschichtlichen Seminar der Technischen Hochschule Braunschweig.) Bremen, Herbig.

SCOTT, SIR LINDSAY. 1954. Pottery. In Sir Charles Singer, ed., *A history of technology*. Oxford, Clarendon. pp. 376–412.

SENDIVOGIUS MICHAEL (Sandivogius). 1650. *A new light of alchymie*. English trans. by J. F. (m.d.). London, R. Cotes for T. Williams.
The 1st ed. appeared in 1614.

SENECA. 1910. *Quaestiones naturales*. English trans. by John Clarke. London, Macmillan.

SENNERT, DANIEL. 1629. *De chymicorum cum Aristotelicis et Galenicis consensu ac dissensu liber*. Wittebergae, Schüreri.
The 1st ed. appeared in 1619.

SENNERT, DANIEL. 1676. *Opera*. 6 vols. Lugdunum, J. A. Huguetan.

SENNERT, DANIEL, NICHOLAS CULPEPPER, and ABDIAH COLE. 1659. *Thirteen books of natural philosophy*. London, Peter Cole.
Books 1 through 8 are a translation of Sennert's *Epitome naturalis scientiae*, which first appeared in 1618.

SEVERINUS, PETER. 1571. *Idea medicinae philosophicae fundamenta*. Basel, Henricpetri.

SHAW, PETER. 1755. *Chemical Lectures, publickly read at London in the years 1731 and 1732*. 2nd ed. London, Longman, *et al.*

SHEPPARD, H. J. 1957. Gnosticism and alchemy. *Ambix*, 6: 86–101.

SHERRINGTON, SIR CHARLES. 1946. *The endeavour of Jean Fernel*. Cambridge, Cambridge University Press.

SIGERIST, HENRY. 1923. *Studien und Texte zur frühmittelalterlichen Rezeptliteratur*. Leipzig, Barth (Studien zur Geschichte der Medizin, Heft 3).

SIGERIST, HENRY. 1941. Laudanum in the works of Paracelsus. *BHM*, 9: 530–44.

SIGERIST, HENRY. 1951. *A history of medicine*. Vol. 1. New York, Oxford.

SILVESTRE DE SACY, A. I. 1799. La livre de la secret de creature. *Notices et extraits de manuscrits de la Bibliothèque Nationale,* 4: 107–58.

SILVESTRE DE SACY, A. I. 1810. Vie d'ebn Djoldjol, extraite de l'histoire de médicins d'ebn-abi-Osaiba. In *Relation de l'Egypte par abd-allatif.* French trans. and notes by Silvestre de Sacy. Appendix 2: 495–500.

SIMPSON, WM. 1677. *Philosophical dialogues.* London, D. Newman.

SINGER, SIR CHARLES. 1948. *The earliest chemical industry.* London, Folio Society.

SINGER, SIR CHARLES. 1957. *A short history of anatomy and physiology from the Greeks to Harvey.* New York, Dover.
    A reprint of Singer's *The evolution of Anatomy* (1925).

SINGER, SIR CHARLES, E. J. HOLMYARD, A. R. HALL, and TREVOR I. WILLIAMS, eds. 1954–58. *A history of technology.* 5 vols. Oxford, Clarendon.

SINGER, SIR CHARLES and DOROTHEA SINGER. 1917. The scientific position of Girolamo Fracastoro. *Annals of Medical History,* 1: 1–34.

SINGER, DOROTHEA WALEY. 1928. The alchemical Testament attributed to Raymond Lull. *Archeion,* 9: 43–52.

SINGER, DOROTHEA WALEY. 1928–31. *Catalogue of Latin and vernacular alchemical manuscripts in Great Britain and Ireland.* 3 vols. Brussels, Lamertin.

SINGER, DOROTHEA WALEY. 1929. Michael Scot and alchemy. *Isis,* 13: 5–15.

SINGER, DOROTHEA WALEY. 1941. The cosmology of Giordano Bruno. *Isis,* 33: 187–96.

SINGER, DOROTHEA WALEY. 1950. *Giordano Bruno.* New York, Schuman.

SISCO, ANNELIESE G. and CYRIL S. SMITH. 1949. *Bergwerk– und Probierbüchlein.* New York, American Institute of Mining and Metallurgical Engineers.

SISCO, ANNELIESE G. and CYRIL S. SMITH. 1951. *Lazarus Ercker's treatise on ores and assaying.* Chicago, University of Chicago Press.

SMEATON, W. A. 1962. *Fourcroy, chemist and revolutionary 1755–1809.* Cambridge. Printed for the author.

SMITH, CYRIL S. 1960. *A history of metallography.* Chicago, University of Chicago Press.

SMITH, CYRIL S. and MARTHA T. GNUDI. 1942. *The Pirotechnia of Vannoccio Biringuccio.* New York, American Institute of Mining and Metallurgical Engineers.

SMITH, CYRIL S. and R. J. FORBES. 1957. Metallurgy and assaying. In Sir Charles Singer, ed., *A history of technology.* Oxford, Clarendon. Vol. 3: 27–71.

SOLMSEN, FRIEDRICH. 1961. *Aristotle's system of the physical world.* Ithaca, N.Y., Cornell University Press.

SONTHEIMER, JOSEPH. 1845. *Zusammengesetzte Heilmittel der Araber,* nach den fünften Buch des Canons von Ibn Sina. Freiberg im Breisgau, Herder.

SORBIÈRE, SAMUEL. 1669. *Relation d'un voyage en Angleterre.* Cologne, P. Michel.

SPRAT, THOMAS. 1667. *The history of the Royal Society of London.* London, J. R. for J. Martyn.

SPRENGEL, KURT. 1815–20. *Histoire de la médecine.* French trans. by A. J. L. Jourdan. 9 vols. Paris, Deterville et Desoer.

STAHL, GEORG E. 1730. *Philosophical principles of universal chemistry.*

English trans. by Peter Shaw. London, J. Osborn and T. Longman.

'Principally taken' from Stahl's *Fundamenta chymiae*, Norimbergae, 1723.

STAHL, GEORG E. 1746–47. *Fundamenta chymiae dogmatico-rationalis et experimentalis*. 3 pts. Norimbergae, B. G. M. Endteri [et al.].

The 1st ed. appeared in 1723, as *Fundamenta chymiae dogmaticae & experimentalis*.

STAPLETON, H. E. 1905. Sal ammoniac, a study in primitive chemistry. *MASB*, 1: 25–41.

STAPLETON, H. E. 1953. The antiquity of alchemy. *Ambix*, 5: 1–43.

STAPLETON, H. E. and R. F. AZO. 1905. Alchemical equipment in the 11th century A.D. *MASB*, 1: 47–70.

STAPLETON, H. E. and R. F. AZO. 1910. An alchemical compilation of the thirteenth century A.D. *MASB*, 3: 57–94.

STAPLETON, H. E., R. F. AZO, and M. HIDAYAT HUSAIN. 1927. Chemistry in Iraq and Persia in the tenth century A.D. *MASB*, 8: 317–417.

STAPLETON, H. E., G. L. LEWIS and F. S. TAYLOR. 1949. The sayings of Hermes quoted in the Mā' al-waraqī of ibn Umail. *Ambix*, 3: 69–90.

STEELE, ROBERT, ed. 1909. *Opera hactenus inedita Rogeri Baconi*, fasc. 2–3. *Communia naturalium*. Oxford, Clarendon.

STEELE, ROBERT, ed. 1920. *Opera hactenus inedita Rogeri Baconi*, fasc. 5. *Secretum secretorum*. Oxford, Clarendon.

STEELE, ROBERT, ed. 1928. *Opera hactenus inedita Rogeri Baconi*, fasc. 8. *Quaestiones supra libros quatuor physicorum Aristotelis*. Oxford, Clarendon.

STEELE, ROBERT. 1929. Practical

chemistry in the twelfth century. *Isis*, 12: 10–46.

STEELE, ROBERT and D. W. SINGER. 1928. The Emerald Table. *Proceedings of the Royal Society of Medicine*, 21: 41–57.

STENO, NICOLAUS. 1958. *Canis carchariae dissectum caput*. Ed. and English trans. of the 1667 edition of Axel Garboe, under the title, *The earliest geological treatise*. London, Macmillan.

STEPHANOS [OF ALEXANDRIA]. 1937. *Lectures . . . on the great and sacred art of the making of gold*. Ed. and English trans. by F. S. Taylor. *Ambix*, 1: 120–39.

STEUER, ROBERT OTTO. 1937. *Über das wohlreichende Natron bei den alten Ägyptern*. Leyden, Brill.

STILLMAN, JOHN M. 1924. *The story of early chemistry*. New York, Appleton.

STIMSON, DOROTHY. 1940. Hartlib, Haak and Oldenburg: Intelligencers. *Isis*, 31: 309–26.

STONES, G. B. 1928. The atomic view of matter in the XVIth, and XVIIth centuries. *Isis*, 10: 445–65.

STRUNZ, FRANZ. 1907. *Johann Baptist van Helmont*. Leipzig Wien, F. Deuticke.

SUDHOFF, KARL. 1918. Daniel von Morley *Liber de naturis inferiorum et superiorum*. *AGNT*, 8: 1–40.

SUDHOFF, KARL. 1925. *The earliest printed literature on syphilis*. Adapted by Charles Singer. Florence, R. Lier.

SUDHOFF, KARL. 1926. The literary remains of Paracelsus. In *Essays in the history of medicine*. New York, Medical Life Press. pp. 275–85.

SUDHOFF, KARL, ed. 1930. *Historische Studien* (Festgabe Georg Sticker). Berlin, Springer.

SUDHOFF, KARL. 1936. *Paracelsus; ein deutsches Lebensbild aus den Tagen* der Renaissance. Leipzig, Bibliographisches Institut.

SYLVIUS, FRANÇOIS DE LA BOË. 1680. *Opera medica*. Amstelodami, D. Elsevirium et A. Wolfgang.

TACHENIUS, OTTO. 1677. *Hippocrates chymicus*. English trans. by J. W. London, N. Crouch.
The 1st (Latin) ed. appeared in 1666.

TARGIONI-TOZZETTI, GIOVANNI. 1852. *Notizie sulla storia delle scienze fisiche in Toscana*. Firenze, I. E. R. Biblioteca palatina.

TASCH, PAUL. 1948. Quantitative measurements and the Greek atomists. *Isis*, 38: 185–9.

TAYLOR, ALFRED EDWARD. 1933. *Socrates*. New York, Appleton.

TAYLOR, ALFRED EDWARD. 1956. *Plato*. 6th ed. New York, Meridian.

TAYLOR, FRANK SHERWOOD. 1930. A survey of Greek alchemy. *Journal of Hellenic Studies*, 50: 109–39.

TAYLOR, FRANK SHERWOOD. 1937. The origins of Greek alchemy. *Ambix*, 1: 30–47.

TAYLOR, FRANK SHERWOOD. 1945. The evolution of the still. *AS*, 5: 185–202.

TAYLOR, FRANK SHERWOOD. 1949-1. *The alchemists*. New York, Schuman.

TAYLOR, FRANK SHERWOOD. 1949-2. Alchemical papers of Dr. Robert Plot. *Ambix*, 4: 67–76.

TELESIO, BERNARDINO. 1586. *De rerum natura*. Naples, H. Salvianum.
The 1st ed. appeared in 1565.

TELESIO, BERNARDINO. 1910–23. *De rerum natura*. Ed. by Vincenzo Spampanato. 3 vols. Modena, Formiggini.
A reprinting of the 1586 ed. of Salvium at Naples.

THADDEUS ALDEROTTI (Tadeo de fèorentia). 1477. *De regimine sanitatis*. Bologna, D. de Lapis.

Seven leaves, following Benedetti de Noricia, *De conservatione sanitatis* (1477).

THEOPHILUS. 1961. *Schedula diversarum artium*. Ed. and English trans. (as *The various arts*) by C. R. Dodwell. London, Nelson.

THEOPHILUS. 1963. *On divers arts*. Annotated English trans. (of *Schedula diversarum artium*) by John G. Hawthorne and Cyril S. Smith. Chicago, University of Chicago Press.

THEOPHRASTUS. 1956. *On stones*. Ed. and English trans. by E. R. Caley and J. F. C. Richards. Columbus, Ohio State University Press.

[THEVENOT, MELCHISEDEC]. 1665. Of the way used in the Mogul's dominion to make saltpetre. *PT*, 1: 103–4.
Extracted from Thevenot's *Relations des divers voyages* (1663).

THOMAS AQUINAS. 1882–1930. *Opera omnia*. 15 vols. Rome, Ex typographia polyglotta.

THOMPSON, DANIEL VARNEY, Jr. 1933. *The craftsman's handbook*. New Haven, Yale University Press.
This is Vol. 2 of D. V. Thompson, ed., *Cennino Cennini, Il libro dell' arte*, and contains an English trans. of that work.

THOMPSON, DANIEL VARNEY. 1936. *The materials of medieval painting*. London, Allen and Unwin.

THOMPSON, REGINALD CAMPBELL. 1936. *A dictionary of Assyrian chemistry and geology*. Oxford, Clarendon.

THOMSON, SAMUEL HARRISON. 1939. The texts of Michael Scot's *Ars alchemie*. *Osiris*, 5: 523–59.

THOMSON, THOMAS. 1830–31. *The history of chemistry*. 2 vols. London, H. Colburn and R. Bentley.

TOCH, MAXIMILIAN. 1918. The pigments from the tomb of Perneb. *Journal of Industrial and Engineering Chemistry*, 10: 118–19.

TORNAY, STEPHEN CHAK. 1938. *Ockham*. Studies and selections. La Salle, Ill., Open Court.

TOURNEFORT, JOSEPH P. DE. 1700. Comparaison des analyses du sel ammoniac, de la soie et de la corne de cerf. *ASP*, année 1700, 2nd ed., *Mém.*: 71–4 (see also *Hist.*: 50–51).

TRICOT, J. 1941. *Aristote. Les météorologiques*. Paris, J. Vrin.

TURNBULL, G. H. 1953. Peter Stahl, the first public teacher of chemistry at Oxford. *AS*, 9: 265–70.

TYLECOTE, R. F. 1962. *Metallurgy in archaeology*. London, Arnold.

ULSTAD, PHILIP. 1550. *Le ciel des philosophes*. Paris, V. Gaultherot.
   The 1st (Latin) ed. appeared in 1525.

ULSTAD, PHILIP. 1628. *Coelum philosophorum*. Argentorati, I. Grienynger.

URDANG, GEORGE. 1943. Pharmacy in ancient Greece and Rome. *American Journal of Pharmacy*, 7: 160–73.
   English trans. of passages from Alfred Schmidt, *Drogen und Droghandel in Altertum*, Leipzig, 1924.

URDANG, GEORGE. 1948. The early chemical and pharmaceutical history of calomel. *Chymia*, 1: 93–108.

VALENTINE, BASIL. See Basil Valentine.

VERBEKE, G. 1945. *L'Evolution de la doctrine du pneuma du Stoicism à S. Augustin*. Louvain, Institut Superieur de Philosophie.

VINCENT OF BEAUVAIS (Vincentius Bellovacensis) [1481]. *Speculum naturale*. 2 vols. [Strassburg].

VITALIS OF FURNO. 1531. *Pro conservanda sanitate*. Moquntiae, I. Schoeffer.

WAITE, ARTHUR E. 1894. *The new pearl of great price*, ed. Janus Lacinius. London, Elliott.

WAITE, ARTHUR E. 1926. *The secret tradition in alchemy*. New York, Knopf.

WEDEL, GEORG W. 1675–6. Mutatio naturalis et artificialis ferri in cuprum [Academia naturae curiosorum, Leopoldinisch-Carolinische Deutsche Akademie der Naturforscher]. *Misc. curiosa med.-phys.*: 155.

WEDEL, GEORG W. 1695. *Dissertatio inauguralis chimico-medica sale ammoniaco*. Jena, Krebs.

WEDEL, GEORG W. 1715. *Compendium chimiae theoreticae et practicae methodo analytica propositae*. Jena.

WEEKS, MARY E. 1956. *Discovery of the elements*. 6th ed. Ed. by Henry M. Leicester. Easton, Pa., Journal of Chemical Education.

WELLMAN, MAX. 1928. *Die φύσικα des Bolos Demokritos und der Magier Anaxilaos aus Larissa*. Teil I. Abhandl. der Preuss. Akad. der Wiss., Phil.-Hist. Kl., Nr. 7.

WERTIME, THEODORE A. 1962. *The coming of the age of steel*. Chicago, University of Chicago Press.

WERTIME, THEODORE A. 1964. Man's first encounters with metallurgy. *Science*, 146: 1257–67.

WHITTAKER, THOMAS. 1906. *Apollonius of Tyana, and other essays*. London, Swan Sonnenschein.

WILLIS, THOMAS. 1659. *Diatribae duae medico-philosophicae*. London, T. Roycroft.

WILLIS, THOMAS. 1674–75. *Pharmaceutice rationalis*. 2 vols. Oxford, E. Theatro Sheldoniano.

WILLIS, THOMAS. 1695. *Opera omnia*. 2 vols. Genevae, S. de Tournes.

WILSDORF, HELMUT. 1956. *Georg Agricola und seine Zeit*. Berlin, VEB Deutscher Verlag der Wissenschaften (Agricola. *Ausgewählte Werke*, Bd. 1).

WILSON, CURTIS. 1953. Pomponazzi's criticism of Calculator. *Isis*, 44: 355–62.

WILSON, CURTIS. 1956. *William*

Heytesbury: Medieval logic and the rise of mathematical physics. Madison, University of Wisconsin Press.

WILSON, W. J. 1936. An alchemical manuscript by Arnaldus de Bruxella. *Osiris*, 2: 220–405.

WINDELBAND, WILHELM. 1901. *A history of philosophy*. English trans. by J. H. Tufts. 2nd ed. 2 vols. New York, Macmillan.

WINDELS, FERNAND. 1949. *The Lascaux cave paintings*. London, Faber.

WOHLWILL, EMIL. 1887. *Joachim Jungius und die Erneuerung atomistischer Lehren im 17. Jahrhundert*. Abhandlungen aus dem Gebiete der Naturwissenschaften, Hamberg 10: No. 2.

WOLFSON, HARRY A. 1947. *Philo*. 2 vols. Cambridge, Mass., Harvard University Press.

WOLFSON, HARRY A. 1956. *The philosophy of the Church Fathers*. Vol. 1. Faith, trinity, incarnation. Cambridge, Mass., Harvard University Press.

WOODWARD, JOHN. 1714. *Methodica et ad ipsam naturae norman instituta fossilium in classes distributio*. London, R. Wilkin.

Published with his *Naturalis historia*, but separately paginated.

WU LU-CHIANG and T. L. DAVIS. 1932. An ancient Chinese treatise on alchemy entitled Ts'an T'ung Ch'i. *Isis*, 18: 210–89.

WÜSTENFELD, HEINRICH FERDINAND. 1840. *Geschichte der Arabischen Aerzte und Naturforscher*. Göttingen, Vandenhoeck und Ruprecht.

ZELLER, EDUARD. 1922. *Die Philosophie der Griechen in ihrer geschichtlichen Entwicklung*. Vol. 2, Pt 1. Sokrates, Sokratiker, Platon, Alte Akademie. 5th ed. Leipzig, O. R. Reisland.

ZELLER, EDUARD. 1931. *Outlines of the history of Greek philosophy*. 13th ed., revised by Wilhelm Nestle. English trans. by L. R. Palmer. New York, Harcourt Brace.

ZELLER, EDUARD. 1962. *The Stoics, Epicurians, and Sceptics*. English trans. by O. J. Reichel. New York, Russell and Russell.
Reissue of revised ed. of 1880.

ZETZNER, LAZARUS. 1659–61. *Theatrum chemicum*. 6 vols. Argentorati, Zetzneri (here abbreviated TC).

ZIPPE, FRANZ X. M. 1857. *Geschichet der Metalle*. Wien, W. Braumueller.

Abbreviations

AAG	Berthelot, M. and C. E. Rouelle. 1887–88, *Collection des anciens alchimistes Grecs.* 3 vols. Paris, Steinhill
AGNT	*Archiv für die Geschichte der Naturwissenschaften und der Technik*
AI	*Archives internationales d'histoire des sciences*
AS	*Annals of science*
ASP	*Histoire de l'Académie Royal des Sciences* (Paris)
BCC	Manget, J. J. 1702. *Bibliotheca chemica curiosa,* 2 vols. Coloniae Allobrogum, Chouet
BGPM	*Beiträge zur Geschichte der Philosophie des Mittelalter* (Munster)
BGTI	*Beiträge zur Geschichte der Technik und Industrie* (Jahrbuch der Vereines deutscher Ingenieure)
BHM	*Bulletin of the history of medicine* (Baltimore)
BL	Hirsch, August, et al. 1962. *Biographisches Lexikon der hervorragenden Ärzte.* 5 vols. Munich-Berlin, Urban & Schwarzenberg (reprint)
CLAM	Singer, D. W., 1928–31. *Catalogue of Latin and vernacular alchemical manuscripts in Great Britain and Ireland.* Brussels, Lamertin
CMA	Berthelot, M. 1893. *La chimie du moyen age.* 3 vols. Paris, Imprimerie nationale
CZ	*Chemische Zeitschrift* (Leipzig-Berlin)
DK	Diels, Hermann. 1959–60. *Die Fragmente der Vorsokratiker.* 9th ed., ed. Walther Kranz. 3 vols. Berlin-Charlottenburg, Wiedemann
ED	Diderot, Denis, and J. d'Alembert. 1751–65. *Encyclopédie ou dictionnaire raisonné des sciences, des arts, et des mètiers.* 17 vols. Paris, various publishers
EI–1	*Encyclopedia of Islam.* 1908–38. Leyden, Brill
EI–2	*Encyclopedia of Islam.* New ed. 1960ff. Leyden and London, Brill and Luzac
GKW	*Gesamtkatalog der Wiegendrücke.* 1925ff. Leipzig
HMES	Thorndike, Lynn. 1923–58. *History of magic and experimental science.* 8 vols. New York, Columbia University Press

IHS	Sarton, George. 1927–48. *Introduction to the history of science.* 3 vols. Baltimore, William and Wilkins
JCE	*Journal of chemical education*
MASB	*Memoirs of the Asiatic Society of Bengal*
MIL	Dufresne, C., Seigneur Ducange. 1883–7. *Glossarium mediae et infimae latinitatis.* Ed. nova. 10 vols. Niort
PT	*Philosophical Transactions of the Royal Society of London*
PW	Pauly, A. F. von. 1894ff. *Real-Encyclopëdie der classischen Altertumswissenschaft,* neue Bearbeitung von Georg Wissowa. Stuttgart, Melzer
QS	*Quellen und Studien zur Geschichte der Naturwissenschaften und der Medizin*
SA	*Sudhoff's Archiv für Geschichte der Medizin und der Naturwissenschaften*
SM	Duhem, Pierre. 1914–59. *Le systeme du monde.* 10 vols. Paris, Hermann
SFV	Arnim, H. F. A. von. 1903–24. *Stoicorum veterum fragmenta.* 4 vols. Leipzig, Teubner
TC	Zetzner, Lazarus. 1659–61. *Theatrum chemicum.* 6 vols. Argentorati, Zetzneri
TNS	*Transactions of the Newcomen Society* (England)

Index

Personal names

Abd-al-Rahman III (Chalif), 160, 202

Abulcasis, 202–10

Achillini, Alexander, 237—8

Adam of Bodenstein, 223n

Agatharchides, 37

Agathodaimon, 84, 105–9, 111n, 113, 115, 125

Agricola, George, 158, 202, 257–9, 297, 315–20, 326, 332, 340, 341, 342

Agricola of Nettesheim, 315

Albertus Magnus, 146–50, 161n, 171, 175, 177–9, 183–4, 189, 191–2, 195, 202, 317; reputed alchemical works, 189, 196, 198

Alderotti, Thaddeus, 206

Alexander of Aphrodisias, 77, 80–1, 87, 238

Alexander the Great, 53, 82, 92

al-Fārābi, 120–3, 131, 161n, 165

Alfred of Orlamünde, 147n

al-Kindī, 120–1, 123, 147n

al-Nadim, *Fihrist*, 120, 124–5, 127, 130, 161n

al-Rāzī, 120–1, 123, 129–31, 136–42, 147n, 154, 159n, 160–5, 167–8, 179–80, 191–3, 195, 198, 208

al-Tabari, 217n

Anaxagoras, 42, 48–51, 69, 75, 286

Anaximander, 41, 45–6

Anaximenes, 41, 45–6, 64, 286

Apollonius of Tyana, 84, 91–2; *see also* Balinus

Aristotle, 28, 53–63, 66, 69, 76–80, 122, 146, 149, 161n, 176–8, 256, 274–5, 284, 286, 292, 299; the 'true', 78, 80–2, 123, 150, 238; commentators on, 80–1, 146, 150, 238

Aristotle (pseudo), alchemist, 163, 167–8, 187–8, 190

Arnold of Brussels, 197

Arnold of Villanova, 180–1, 193–9, 206, 210

Asclepiades, 79–80

Asfīdūs, 125

Ashmole, Elias, 267

Augustine, Saint, 145

Averroës, 124, 149–51, 238

Avicebron, *Fons vitae*, 147n, 148n

Avicenna, 120–4, 131, 149–51, 160–1, 168, 233, 237–8, 284

Avicenna (pseudo), *De anima*, 160–1, 164–8, 175, 179, 184, 188

Bacon, Francis, 245n, 247–8, 253, 270

Bacon, Roger, 147–9, 171, 175, 177–9, 183–92, 218; works of, 184–6, 188; reputed alchemical works, 190–1, 196n

Baker, George, 258n

393

Subjects

Abbasid dynasty, 120, 123, 128
Academia Caesarea Leopoldini, 270–1
Académie des Sciences (Paris), 250, 269, 272, 305–6
Academy (Platonic), 53, 55; in Florence, 244
Accademia del Cimento, 268–9
acetum, *see* vinegar
acid: primordial (or universal), 298, 322, 327; mineral, 110, 140–1, 163, 169, 172, 175, 179, 195–7, 200, 204–8, 212, 223, 225, 232, 308 (*see also* nitric, hydrochloric, sulphuric, aqua regia); recipes for mineral acids, 173, 196, 207, 225n
acidity: as a quality, 234; as a universal principle, 322–4
acid-alkali, interaction, 300, 306–7, 344; a fundamental principle, 235, 271, 332; Cartesian explanation of, 296, 301–2; Newtonian explanation of, 303; Paracelsian explanation of, 302–3
acid-alkali neutralization, 294, 306
'adhicbardic', 203n
'aereal nitre', 332
'aereal salt', 289
aerometer (specific gravity bottle), 307
affinity, 255, 295–6, 299–310
agent-patient relationship, 70–2, 74, 81, 110, 152, 241, 299
'alchalizimar', 203n, 207n
alchemy, 82–200 passim, 204, 208, 210, 213, 226, 234, 240n, 253, 261–3; esoteric, 112, 116, 181,

199–200, 242; sexual analogies, 103, 132–3; colour sequences, 104, 106, 107, 231; theoretical contrasted to practical, 178–9, 186–7, 191, 194; standardization of operations, 140–2, 162, 164; included among the sciences, 148, 167, 182–5, 187, 189; Egyptian, 92, 104, 112; Chinese, 218; western Asiatic, 113–15; Byzantine, 112; eastern Arabic, 124–42, 160, 179; western Arabic, 160–6, 179, 227; European, 166–200
alchemists, the (late references), 222–3, 226–8, 230–1, 267, 269, 274
alcohol, 110, 180, 204–6, 211, 214, 218; recipes for, 205–6
'alkahest' (Paracelsus' universal solvent), 286, 301
alkali, 33, 294–6, 300, 302, 308, 323, 345–8 (*see also* soda, potash); volatile, *see* ammonia
alloy, 21–4, 71, 98, 106, 137, 141, 158n, 187
Altdorf (Germany), 270–1
alum, 27, 28n, 31–2, 137, 161n, 162, 169, 174, 196, 198, 204, 260–1, 293, 321–5, 337–42; *see also* sodium, potassium, and ammonium alums
'alums and salts', 110, 162–3, 192
alumina, 194
aluminium sulphate, 338
alunite, 339
amalgamation process, for precious metal extraction, 314